Laws of Motion & Circular Motion

for JEE Main & Advanced
(Study Package for Physics)

Fully Solved

disha
Nurturing Ambitions

Includes Past
JEE & KVPY Questions

Useful for Class 11,
KVPY & Olympiads

- **Head Office :** B-32, Shivalik Main Road, Malviya Nagar, New Delhi-110017
- **Sales Office :** B-48, Shivalik Main Road, Malviya Nagar, New Delhi-110017
  Tel. : 011-26691021 / 26691713

Page Layout : Prakash Chandra Sahoo

Typeset by Disha DTP Team

Printed at : **Repro Knowledgecast Limited, Thane**

DISHA PUBLICATION

ALL RIGHTS RESERVED

For further information about the books from DISHA,

Log on to **www.dishapublication.com** or email to **info@dishapublication.com**

Contents

Study Package Booklet 2 - Laws of Motion and Circular Motion

Laws of Motion & Equilibrium

(203 -276)

Chapter contents

Isaac Newton

Isaac Newton (1642-1727) was one of the most brilliant of all scientists. One of his greatest achievements was to work out the laws of motion and gravity. These affect everything in the Universe from atoms and grains of sand, to the Earth, Moon, stars and galaxies in space. Newton also invented a new kind of mathematics, calculus. ....

Definitions, Explanations and Derivations

5.1 MASS

The mass of a body is the quantity of matter contained in it. Its SI unit is kg. The mass of the body which determines its inertia in translatory motion is called **its inertial mass**. This is the mass that appears in Newton's second law, which can be written as

$$F = m_i a_i \qquad \text{or} \qquad m_i = \frac{F}{a_i}.$$

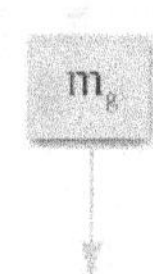

Earth surface

Figure. 5.2

The mass of a body which determines the gravitational pull due to the earth is called its **gravitational mass.**

This is the mass that appears in Newton's law of gravitation, which we can write as

$$F = \frac{GMm}{R^2} \qquad \text{or} \qquad m_g = \frac{FR^2}{GM}.$$

The principle of equivalence

Inertial and gravitational masses need not be equal to each other. Experiment shows that, to a precision of perhaps 1 part in 10^{12}, these two masses are identical. In Newtonian physics, the experimental fact that $m_i = m_g$ could be regarded as nothing but an astonishing coincidence. In Einstein theory of relativity, it enter in a natural way through the principle of equivalence; if acceleration and gravitation are equivalent, then masses measured via acceleration and gravitation must be equal.

5.2 WEIGHT

The weight of a body is the force exerted by earth on the body towards the centre of earth. If g is the gravity at any place, then the weight of body at that place, $W = mg$. As the value of gravity changes from place to place, so the weight of a body is different at different places. The SI unit of weight is newton (N).

5.3 INERTIA

Inertia is the inherent property of material body by virtue of which it resists in change of state of rest or of uniform motion. It is not a physical quantity, it is the sensation. Mass of a body is the measure of its inertia. If a body has large mass, it has more inertia. Different kinds of inertia are :

(i)   **Inertia of rest :** The tendency of a body to remain in its position of rest is called inertia of rest.
(ii) **Inertia of motion :** The tendency of a body to remain in its state of uniform motion along a straight line is called inertia of motion.
(iii) **Inertia of direction :** The inability of a body to change by itself its direction of motion is called inertia of direction.

5.4 LINEAR MOMENTUM

Momentum of a body is the amount of motion possessed by the body. Mathematically, it is equal to the product of mass and velocity of the body. Thus

$$\therefore \qquad \text{momentum} = \text{mass} \times \text{velocity}$$

$$\text{or} \qquad \vec{P} = m\vec{v}.$$

Momentum is a vector quantity, its direction is along the direction of velocity. Its SI unit is kg-m/s or N-s.

5.5 NEWTON'S LAWS OF MOTION

Sir Issac Newton (1642-1727) made systematic study of motion of objects and presented three laws of motion which are called Newton's Laws of Motion. These are :

First law : Every body remain in its state of rest or of uniform motion in a straight line unless it is compelled by some external force to change that state.

Second law : The rate of change of linear momentum of a body is directly proportional to the applied force and the change takes place in the direction of the applied force. That is

$$\frac{d\vec{P}}{dt} = \vec{F}.$$

Third law : To every action, there is always an equal and opposite reaction. Action and reaction act on two different bodies. For two bodies A and B, we can write

$$\vec{F}_{AB} = -\vec{F}_{BA} \ .$$

Newton's first law defines force : According to Newton's first law of motion a body maintains its state of rest or uniform motion unless an external force acts on it. This shows that force is an agent which changes the state of rest or uniform motion. But sometime a force applied on a body can not change its state of rest or uniform motion in a straight line. Hence first law of motion gives a qualitative definition of force.

Newton's first law defines inertia : According to Newton's first law of motion, body remains in its state of rest or uniform motion unless an external force acts on it. This shows that body by itself can not change its state. This inability of body to change its state of rest or of uniform motion in a straight line is called inertia of a body. Thus Newton's first law defines inertia and hence it is also called the law of inertia.

Newton's second law gives the measurement of force. Consider a body of mass m moving with a velocity $\vec{v}$, its momentum

$$\vec{P} = m\vec{v} \ .$$

Differentiating above equation w.r.t. time, we get

$$\frac{d\vec{P}}{dt} = \frac{d}{dt}(m\vec{v}) = m\left(\frac{d\vec{v}}{dt}\right) = m\vec{a} \ .$$

According to Newton's second law

$$\frac{d\vec{P}}{dt} = \vec{F}$$

$\therefore$

$$\boxed{\vec{F} = m\vec{a}} \ .$$

Note :

(i) The Newton's second law $\vec{F} = m\vec{a}$ is strictly applicable to a single particle. The force $\vec{F}$ in the law stands for the net external force. Any internal force in the system is not to be included in $\vec{F}$.

(ii) The second law is a local relation. It means the force $\vec{F}$ at a point in space at a certain instant of time is related to $\vec{a}$ at the same point at the same instant, where $\vec{a}$ is the acceleration produced in the body.

Absolute unit of force : In SI, the absolute unit of force is **newton** (N). Thus
$$1\,N = 1\,kg \times 1\,m/s^2 \qquad \text{or} \qquad 1\,N = 1\,kg\text{-}m/s^2$$

Gravitational unit of force : In SI , the gravitational unit of force is kilogram weight or kilogram force (kgf). Thus
$$1\,kg\text{-wt} = 1\,kg\text{-f} = 1\,kg \times 9.8\,m/s^2 = 9.8\,kg\text{-}m/s^2,$$
or $\quad 1\,kg\text{-wt} = 9.8\,N$

Newton's second law in component form :

In terms of components, the momentum can be written as $\vec{P} = P_x\hat{i} + P_y\hat{j} + P_z\hat{k}$.

Thus Newton's second law in component form, can be written as

$$\vec{F} = F_x\hat{i} + F_y\hat{j} + F_z\hat{k}$$

$$= \frac{d\vec{\mathbf{p}}}{dt}$$

$$= \frac{d}{dt}(P_x\hat{\mathbf{i}} + P_y\hat{\mathbf{j}} + P_z\hat{\mathbf{k}})$$

Equating the three components along the three coordinate axes, we get

$$F_x = \frac{dP_x}{dt} = ma_x,$$

$$F_y = \frac{dP_y}{dt} = ma_y,$$

$$F_z = \frac{dP_z}{dt} = ma_z.$$

5.6 IMPULSE

A large force acting for a short time to produce a finite change in momentum is called an impulsive force. When such a force acts for a short time, the product of the force and the time for which it acts is called *impulse of force*. Thus

Impulse = force × time duration.

Suppose a force $\vec{\mathbf{F}}$ acts for small time dt, the impulse of the force is given by,

$$d\vec{\mathbf{J}} = \vec{\mathbf{F}}\,dt.$$

For a finite interval of time, we can write

$$\vec{\mathbf{J}} = \int_{t_1}^{t_2}\vec{\mathbf{F}}\,dt.$$

For constant force $\qquad \vec{\mathbf{J}} = \vec{\mathbf{F}}(t_2 - t_1)$

or $\qquad\qquad\qquad \vec{\mathbf{J}} = \vec{\mathbf{F}}\Delta t.$

SI unit of impulse is kgm/s or N-s.

Impulse - momentum theorem

According to Newton's second law of motion, we have

$$\vec{\mathbf{F}} = \frac{d\vec{\mathbf{P}}}{dt}$$

or $\qquad\qquad\qquad \vec{\mathbf{F}}\,dt = d\vec{\mathbf{P}}$

or $\qquad\qquad\qquad \int_{t_1}^{t_2}\vec{\mathbf{F}}\,dt = \int_{t_1}^{t_2}dP$

Here $\qquad\qquad\qquad \int_{t_1}^{t_2}\vec{\mathbf{F}}\,dt = \vec{\mathbf{J}}$, is the impulse of force and

$$\int_{t_1}^{t_2}dP = \vec{\mathbf{P}_2} - \vec{\mathbf{P}} \text{ ,is the change of momentum in time from } t_1 \text{ to } t_2. \text{ Thus}$$

$$\vec{J} = \vec{P_2} - \vec{P_1}.$$

The above relation is known as **Impulse-Momentum theorem.**

Calculation of impulse by graphical method

(a) **When a constant force acts on a body :** Suppose a constant force F acts on a body from time t_1 to t_2. The magnitude of impulse

$$J = F(t_2 - t_1).$$

(b) **When a variable force acts on a body:** Suppose a varying force acts for time $t_2 - t_1 = t$.

The magnitude of impulse of force $J = \int_{t_1}^{t_2} F\,dt = $ area under the force time curve between t_1 and t_2.

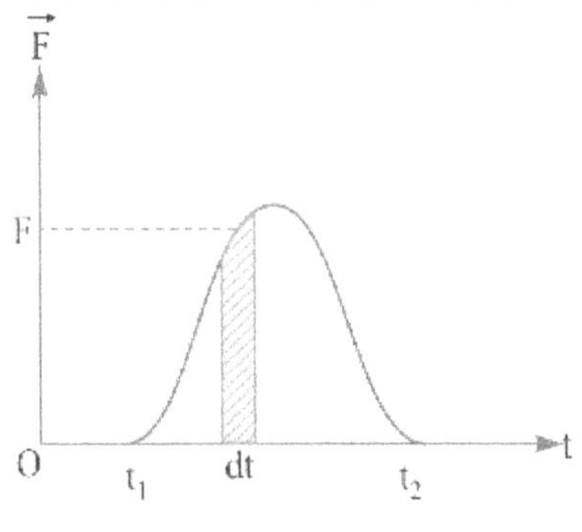

Figure. 5.3

Concept of Action and Reaction

According to Newton's third law of motion, every action is associated with an equal and opposite reaction. Thus in nature forces always occur between pairs of bodies. The two forces act simultaneously. Any one of them may be called action and the other reaction. It is clear from third law that a single force can never exist.

Following are few examples based on Newton's third law :

1. **Block is hanging from the string :** Let us consider a block is suspended by the string. Earth exerts gravitational force on the block (let action); the equal amount of force the block exerts on the earth (reaction). Similarly block does action on the support through string, the equal amount of reaction is exerted by support on the block (reaction).In this case action and reaction are equal to mg. (see fig. 5.4)

2. **The horse and the cart :** Let us consider horse starts pulling the cart from rest and gaining speed with time. The FBD of whole system is shown in the *fig.* 5.5.

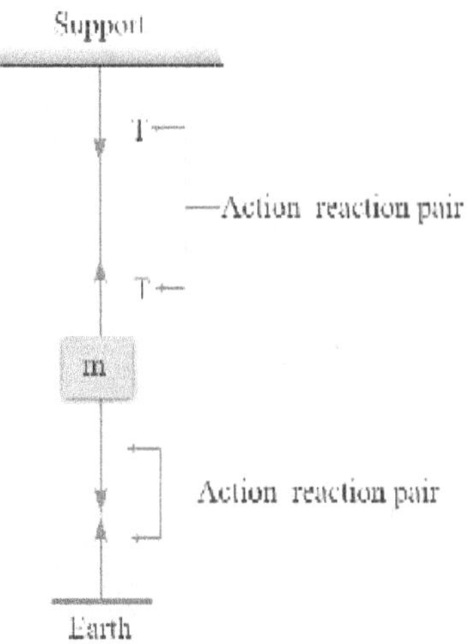

Figure. 5.4

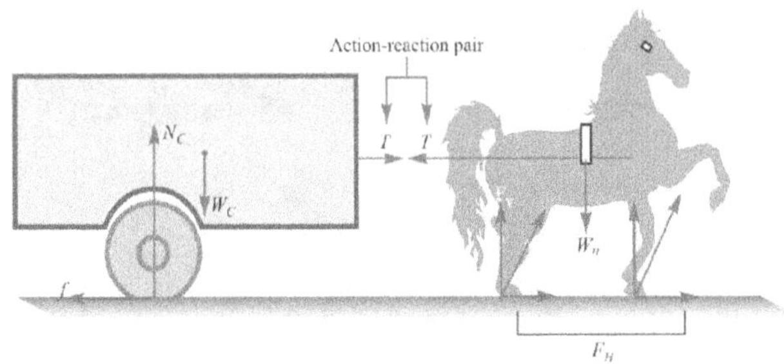

Figure. 5.5

Here ground exerts force on the horse, whose horizontal component is F_H (provided by friction). The force exerted by the horse on the cart in forward direction is T. Cart exerts a force T on the horse in backward direction. In addition to this there is frictional force on the wheels of cart in backward direction. There are three action-reaction pairs :

(i) Between horse feet and ground.

(ii) Between horse and cart.

(iii) Between wheels and ground.

The acceleration of the horse-cart is,

$$a = \frac{F_H - f}{M_H + M_C}.$$

3. **Tug-of-war:** In tug-of-war each team pulls the opposite team with equal force. But winning team exerts greater force on the ground and hence ground provides equal reaction force. This is very clear from FBD. Here force on winning team exerted by ground f_w, is greater than the force on loosing team, $f_w > f_\ell$.

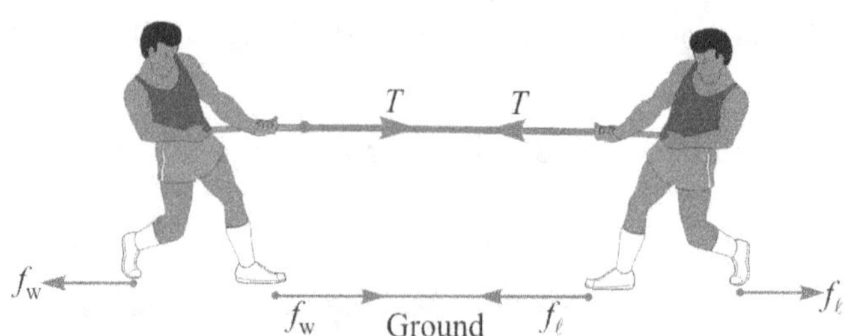

Figure. **5.6**

Normal reaction

When a body is pressed against a surface, the body experiences a force which is perpendicular to the surface at the point of contact between the body and the surface. This force is called **normal reaction** and can be denoted by N.

(i)   In case when a block is placed on a table, the normal reaction on the block by the table is, $N = mg$.

(ii) In case, when block is placed on an inclined plane the normal reaction force, $N = mg \cos \theta$ (See figure).

(i)

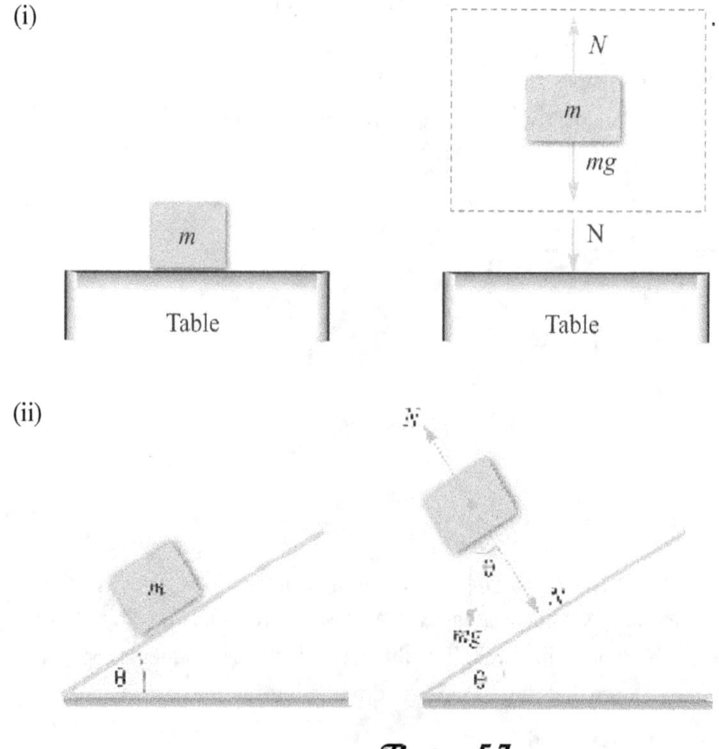

(ii)

Figure. **5.7**

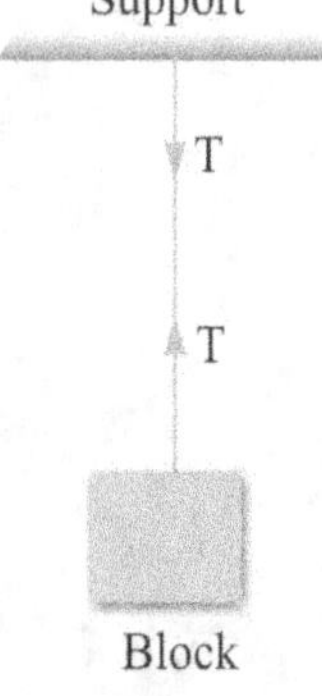

Figure. **5.8**

Tension

When a rope (string, cord etc.) is connected to a body and pulled taut, the rope is said to be under tension. It pulls the body with a force T, whose direction is away from the body and along the length of the rope. A rope is usually regarded to be massless and unstretchable. The rope exists only as a connection between two bodies. It pulls on the body at each end with the same magnitude T. Here rope pulls the block and support each with a force T as shown in *figure.* 5.8.

Free body diagram (*FBD*) or force diagram

To ensure correct use of the equations of statics or equations of dynamics, we isolate the body in a simple diagram and show all the forces from the surroundings that act on the body. Such a diagram is called **free body diagram**. Following are few examples of FBD:

1.

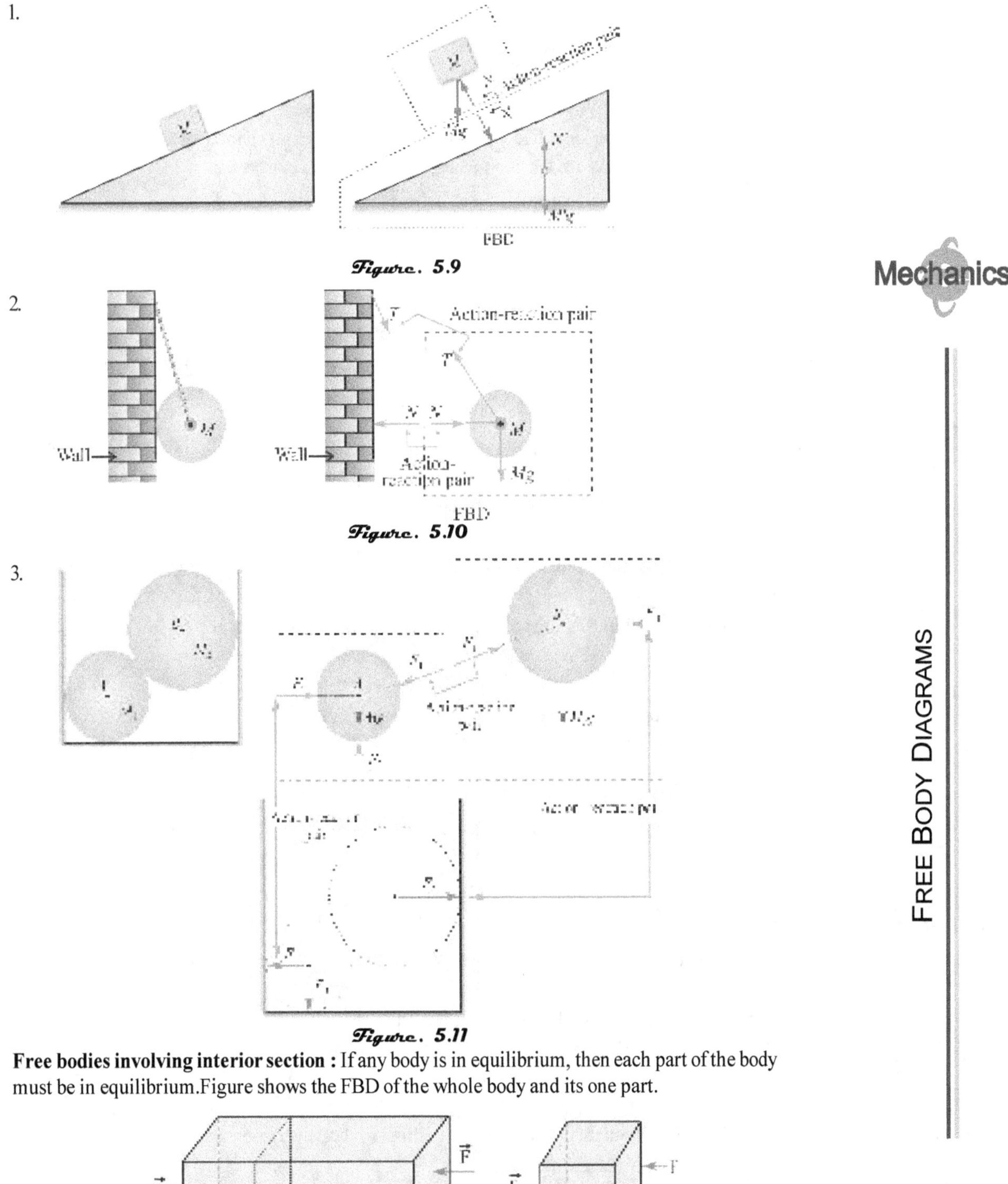

Figure. 5.9

Figure. 5.10

Figure. 5.11

2.

3.

Free bodies involving interior section : If any body is in equilibrium, then each part of the body must be in equilibrium. Figure shows the FBD of the whole body and its one part.

(a) Whole body

(b) One part of the body with interior section

Figure. 5.12

Identify the relevant concepts : In case when system is acted by forces, you have to use Newton's second law.

Identify the target variable : It usually acceleration or force.

Setup the problem using the steps

Step I : Draw a simple sketch of the problem. Identify bodies to which you will apply Newton's second law.

Step II: For each body you identified, draw a free body diagram that shows all the forces acting on the body. These forces are tension in string, weight of the objects etc.

Execute the solution as follows :

* Find net of external forces in the direction of acceleration choosen.
* Find contraint relations.
* Use Newton's second law, $\vec{F}_{ext} = m\vec{a}$, for each body of the problem, wherever need.

IMPORTANT ANALYSIS BASED ON NEWTON'S SECOND LAW

(i)   Motion in a lift /elevator

Consider a man of mass m standing on a weighing machine placed in the lift. The actual weight of the man is mg (weight of man at rest). The reading of weighing machine indicates the force experienced by it which is equal to the reaction on the man standing on it. Machine at rest with a man standing on it gives $N = mg$.

When a man is in an accelerated lift, his weight appears to change. This changed weight is known as apparent weight.

Figure. 5.13

1.   (a)   When the lift moves upward with acceleration a, we have
$$N' - mg = ma$$
or $$N' = m(g + a)$$
$\therefore$ Apparent weight, $N' = m(g + a)$.

(b)   When the lift moves upward with retardation a, we have
$$N' - mg = m(-a)$$
or $$N' = m(g - a).$$

Figure. 5.14

2.   (a)   When lift moves downward with constant acceleration a, we have $$mg - N' = ma$$
or $$N' = m(g - a).$$

(b)   When lift moves downward with constant retardation a we have, $$mg - N' = m(-a)$$
or $$N' = m(g + a)$$

3.   If the supporting cable of the lift breaks, the lift falls freely with an acceleration $a = g$. Thus we have,
$$N = m(g - g)$$
$$= 0.$$

Clearly apparent weight of man in a freely falling lift becomes zero.

Figure. 5.15

(ii)   Simple pulley or atwood machine

Consider a pulley which has negligible mass compared to the bodies connected with the cord and has negligible friction on its axle. The cord connecting the bodies is also uniform and massless. The tension at each point of cord will be same.

Consider blocks-pulley system as shown in figure. We have to find the acceleration of blocks and tension in the cord connecting the blocks.

Let magnitude of acceleration each block be a and tension in the cord be T. By Newton's second law,

For block m_1;

$$m_1 g - T = m_1 a \quad \text{...(i)}$$

For block m_2;

$$T - m_2 g = m_2 a \quad \text{...(ii)}$$

Solving equations (i) and (ii), we get

$$a = \left[\frac{m_1 - m_2}{m_1 + m_2} \right] g$$

and

$$T = \left[\frac{2 m_1 m_2 g}{m_1 + m_2} \right].$$

The force exerted by cord on the pulley

$$F = 2T = \left[\frac{4 m_1 m_2 g}{m_1 + m_2} \right].$$

Force on support from which pulley is hanging, $F = 2T$.

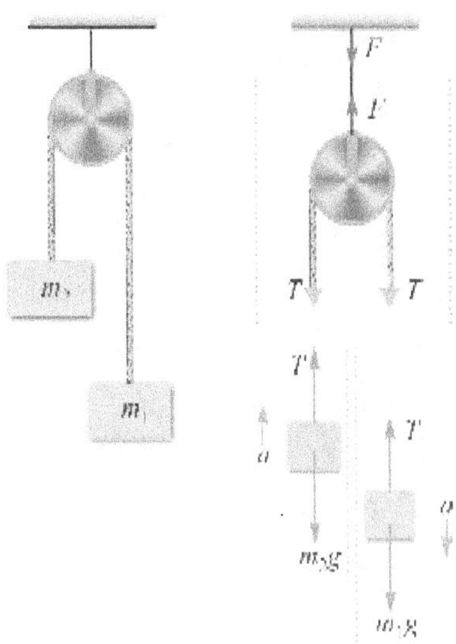

Figure. **5.16**

Short cut method : These types of problems in which all connected bodies have same acceleration magnitude, can be solved by the following method :

(i) For calculating acceleration a use $a = \dfrac{F_{net}}{M_{total}} = \dfrac{\text{Unbalanced load}}{\text{total mass}}$.

(ii) For tension in cord; use $T = m_{up}(g + a)$ or $T = m_{down}(g - a)$

For unbalanced load :

    (a) If mass moves vertically, take mg.

    (b) If mass moves horizontally, take *zero*.

    (c) If mass moves on inclined plane of inclination, take $mg \sin\theta$.

Hooke's law

When a spring is stretched by a force, the increase in its length is proportional to the applied force. If x is the extension is the spring, then applied force

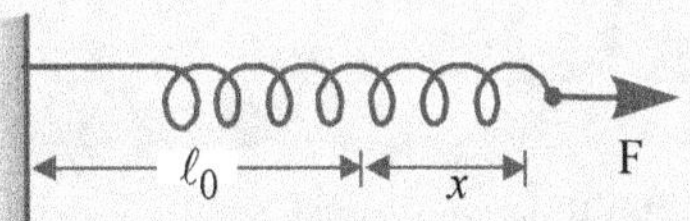

$$F = kx \qquad \text{Hooke's law}$$

Here k is known as force constant. The SI unit of force constant is N/m.

Movable pulley

Let us consider the system shown in the *figure* 5.17. It is clear from the figure that the position of m_2 is governed by the position of centre of movable pulley. Let at any instant, the block m_1 is at y_1 and centre of movable pulley is y_2 from the reference line (dotted line). The total length of the cord;

$$y_1 + 2y_2 + \ell_0 = \ell \qquad \text{...(i)}$$

ℓ_0 is the part of the cord which is over the pulleys (remains constant).

Differentiating equation (i) w.r.t. time, we get

$$\frac{dy_1}{dt} + \frac{2 dy_2}{dt} + \frac{d\ell_0}{dt} = \frac{d\ell}{dt} \qquad \text{...(ii)}$$

As ℓ_0 and ℓ are constant,

$$\therefore \qquad \frac{d\ell_0}{dt} = 0 \text{ and } \frac{d\ell}{dt} = 0$$

and

$$\frac{dy_1}{dt} = v_1 \text{ and } \frac{dy_2}{dt} = v_2.$$

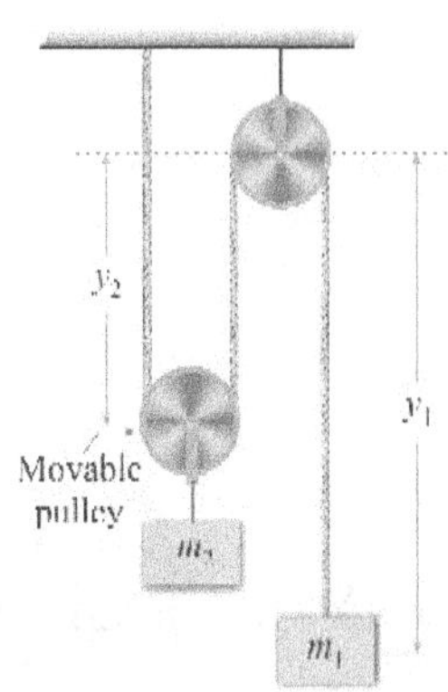

Figure. **5.17**

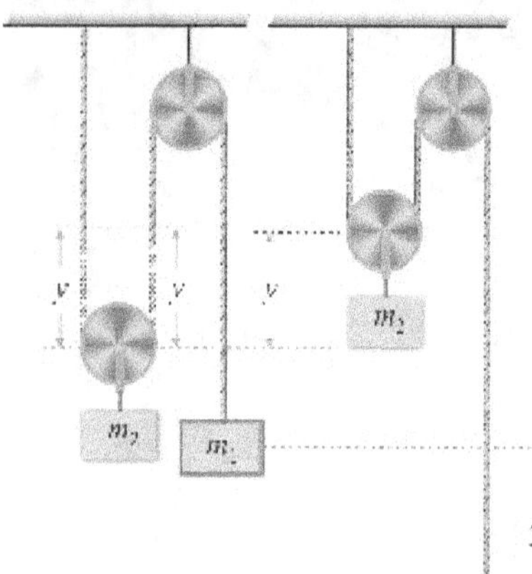

Figure. 5.18

Figure. 5.19

The equation (ii) becomes

$$v_1 + 2v_2 = 0. \qquad \ldots(iii)$$

Differentiating once more, we get

$$a_1 + 2a_2 = 0 \qquad \ldots(iv)$$

or

$$a_1 = -2a_2.$$

Negative sign indicates that y_1 is increasing while y_2 is decreasing.

If we take $a_2 = a$

then $\qquad a_1 = 2a$

The same thing can very easily be understood by displacing the centre of pulley upward by a distance y, the block m_1 will move down by $2y$. (see figure).

$$\therefore \qquad a_1 = 2a_2.$$

FBD : As both the blocks are attached with the same cord and pulleys are massless, so tension in the cord everywhere is T. Suppose acceleration of m_2 is a upward, then acceleration of m_1 will be $2a$ downward.

By Newton's second law $\qquad m_1 g - T = m_1(2a) \quad \ldots(i)$

$$2T - T' = 0 \times a \quad \ldots(ii)$$

and $\qquad T' - m_2 g = m_2 a \quad \ldots(iii)$

After solving above equations , we get

$$a = \left[\frac{2m_1 - m_2}{4m_1 + m_2} \right] g$$

and

$$T = \left[\frac{3m_1 m_2 g}{4m_1 + m_2} \right]$$

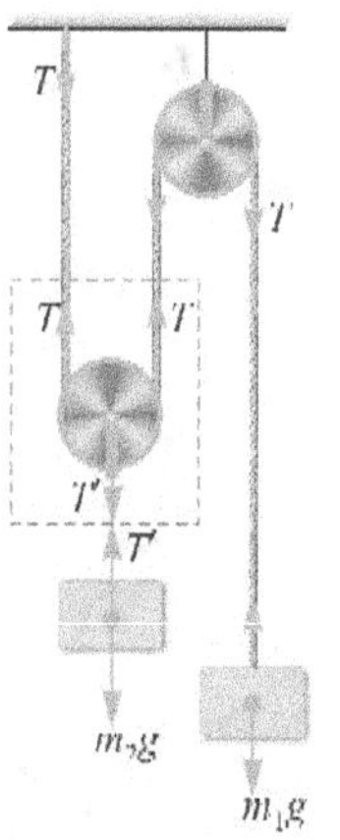

Note :

Remember that in this type of devices, block connected with movable pulley has the acceleration half the acceleration of block connected at the free end of the cord.

FORMULAE USED

1. Momentum, $\vec{P} = m\vec{v}$.

2. Impulse of force, $\vec{J} = F\Delta t$.

3. Newton's second law of motion, $\vec{F}_{ext} = \dfrac{d\vec{P}}{dt} = m\vec{a}$.

4. Impulse – Momentum theorem, $\vec{J} = \vec{P}_f - \vec{P}_i$.

5. Newton's third law of motion, $\vec{F}_{AB} = -\vec{F}_{BA}$.

6. Action and Reaction act simultaneously and two different objects.

7. Motion in a lift : The apparent weight of an observer in lift, $W' = m(g \pm a)$.

8. Hooke's law, $\vec{F}_{ext} = k\vec{x}$.

EXAMPLES BASED ON IMPULSE-MOMENTUM THEOREM AND NEWTON'S LAWS OF MOTION

Example 1. A constant retarding force of 50N is applied to a body of mass 20kg moving initially with a speed of 15 ms⁻¹. How long does the body take to stop? **[NCERT]**

Sol. Here, $F = -50$N, $m = 20$ kg, $u = 15$ ms⁻¹ and $v = 0$;

Now, $F = ma$, $a = F/m = -50/20 = -2.5$ ms⁻²

From relation, $v = u + at$, $0 = 15 - 2.6t$, $t = 15/2.5 = 6s$. *Ans.*

Example 2. The driver of a three wheeler moving with a speed of 36 km/h sees a child standing in the middle of the road and brings his vehicle to rest in 4.0s just in time to save the child. What is the average retarding force on the vehicle? The mass of the three-wheeler is 400 kg and the mass of the driver is 65 kg.

[NCERT]

Sol. Here, $u = 36$ km/h $= 10$ m/s, $t = 4s$,

$$m = 400 + 65 = 465 \text{ kg}$$

Now, retarding force, $F = ma = m\,(v - u)/t$

$$= 465\,(0 - 10)/4 = -1162.5 \text{ N}.$$

The negative sign shows that the force is a retarding force.   *Ans.*

Example 3. **A body of mass 0.40 kg moving initially with a constant speed of 10 m/s^{-1} to the north is subjected to a constant force of 8.0 N directed towards the south for 30s. Take the instant the force is applied to be $t = 0$, and the position of the body at that time to be $x = 0$, predict its position at $t = -5s, 25s, 100s$?** **[NCERT]**

Sol. Here, $m = 0.4$ kg, $u = 10$ ms^{-1} due north

$F = -8$ N, (negative sign shows the force directed opposite).

Therefore, $a = \dfrac{F}{m} = \dfrac{-8}{0.4} = -20$ ms^{-2} $(0 \le t \le 30s)$ when $t = -5s$,

$x = ut = 10(-5) = -50\ m$ (as $a = 0$)

When $t = 25s$, $x = ut + \frac{1}{2}at^2 = 10 \times 25 + \frac{1}{2}(-20)(25)^2 = -6000$ m

Upto t = 30s, motion is under acceleration, i.e.

$x = ut + \frac{1}{2}at^2 = 10 \times 30 + \frac{1}{2}(-20)(30)^2 = -8700$ m

At $t = 30s$, $v = u + at = 10 - 20 \times 30 = -590$ m/s

During $t = 30$ to $100s$, $x_2 = vt = -590 \times 70 = -41300$m

$$[\text{as the force is removed } a = 0]$$

Total distance, $x_1 + x_2 = -(8700 + 41300)$ m $= -50$ km

Example 4. **The velocity of a body of mass 2 kg as a function of t is given by** $v(t) = 2t\,\hat{i} + t^2\hat{j}$. **Find the momentum and the force acting on it, at time $t = 2s$.** **[NCERT Exemplar]**

Sol. Mass of the body $m = 2$ kg

Velocity of the body $v(t) = 2t\,\hat{i} + t^2\hat{j}$

$\therefore$ Velocity of the body $t = 2s$

$$v = 2 \times 2\hat{i} + (2)^2\,\hat{j} = \left(4\hat{i} + 4\hat{j}\right)$$

Momentum of the body, $P = mv$

$$= 2\left(4\hat{i} + 4\hat{j}\right) = \left(8\hat{i} + 8\hat{j}\right) \text{ kg-m/s}$$

Acceleration of the body, $a = \dfrac{dv}{dt}$

$$= \dfrac{d}{dt}\left(2t\hat{i} + t^2\hat{j}\right)$$

$$= \left(2\hat{i} + 2t\hat{j}\right)$$

At $t = 2s$

$$a = \left(2\hat{i} + 2 \times 2\hat{j}\right)$$

$$= \left(2\hat{i} + 4\hat{j}\right)$$

Force acting on the body, $F = ma$

$$= 2\left(2\hat{i} + 4\hat{j}\right)$$

$$= \left(4\hat{i} + 8\hat{j}\right)N .\qquad Ans.$$

Example 5. **Two masses of 5 kg and 3 kg are suspended with the help of massless inextensible strings as shown in figure.**

Calculate T_1 and T_2 when whole system is going upwards with acceleration = 2m/s^2.(use g = 9.8 m/s^2) **[NCERT Exemplar]**

Sol. Given, $m_1 = 5$ kg

$m_2 = 3$ kg

$g = 9.8$ m/s^2

and $a = 2$m/s^2 (upwards)

Tension in the upper string

$$T_1 = (m_1 + m_2)\,(g + a)$$
$$T_1 = (5 + 3)\,(9.8 + 2)$$
$$= 8 \times 11.8 \text{ N}$$
$$= 94.4 \text{ N}$$

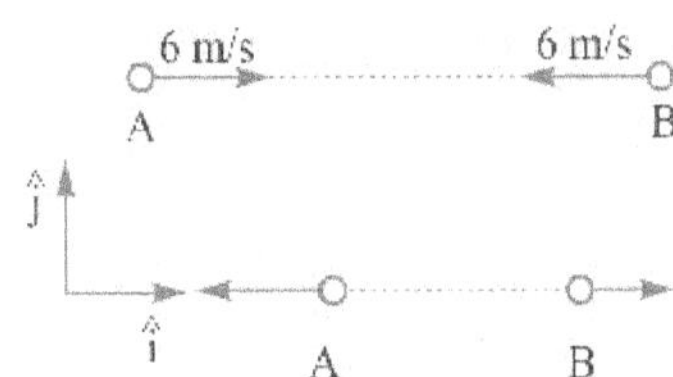

Tension in the lower string

$$T_2 = m_2(g + a)$$
$$= 3(9.8 + 2)\text{N}$$
$$= 3 \times 11.8 \text{ N}$$
$$= 35.4 \text{ N}\qquad Ans.$$

Example 6. **Two monkeys of masses 10 kg and 8 kg are moving along a vertical rope as shown in fig. 5.20. The former climbing up with an acceleration of 2 m/s^2, while the later coming down with a uniform velocity of 2 m/s. Find the tension in the rope at the fixed support.**

Figure. **5.20**

Sol. Let tension in the rope is T. By Newton's second law, we have

$$T - (10g + 8g) = 10 \times 2 + 8 \times 0$$

or $T = 18\ g + 20 = 196.4$ N   *Ans.*

Example 7. **Two billiard balls each of mass 0.05 kg moving in opposite directions with speed of 6 m/s collide and rebound with the same speed. What is the impulse imparted to each ball by the other ?** **[NCERT]**

Sol. Figure shows the motion of balls A and B.

Figure. **5.21**

For ball A :

$$\vec{P}_i = 0.05 \times 6\,\hat{i} \text{ Ns} = 0.3\,\hat{i}\text{ Ns}$$

and $$\vec{P}_f = 0.05 \times (-6)\,\hat{i} \text{ Ns} = -0.3\,\hat{i}\text{ Ns}$$

Impulse imparted to ball A due to ball B

$$\vec{J}_{AB} = \vec{P}_f - \vec{P}_i$$

$$= -0.3\,\hat{i} - 0.3\,\hat{i} = -0.6\,\hat{i}\text{ Ns}.$$

For ball B : $$\vec{P}_i = 0.05 \times (-6)\,\hat{i} = -0.3\,\hat{i}\text{ Ns}$$

and $$\vec{P}_f = 0.05 \times (6)\,\hat{i} = 0.3\,\hat{i}\text{ Ns}$$

Impulse imparted to ball B due to ball A

$$\vec{J}_{BA} = \vec{P}_f - \vec{P}_i$$

$$= 0.3\,\hat{i} - (-0.3\,\hat{i}) = 0.6\,\hat{i}\text{ Ns}.\qquad Ans.$$

Example 8. A rubber ball of mass 50 g falls from a height of 1 m and rebounds to a height of 0.5 m. Find the impulse and the average force between the ball and the ground if the time for which they are in contact was 0.1 s.

Sol.

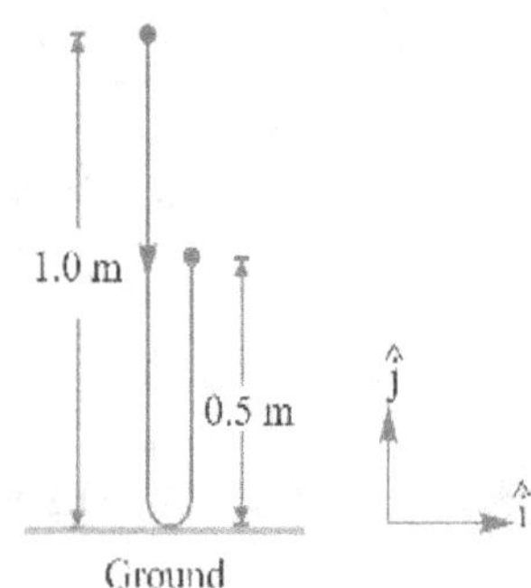

Figure. 5.22

Velocity of ball just before collision;

$$v^2 = 0 + 2gh$$

$$v = v_i = \sqrt{2gh}$$

$$= \sqrt{2 \times 9.8 \times 1} = 4.43 \text{ m/s}$$

∴   Momentum of ball before collision,

$$\vec{P}_i = m\vec{v}_i$$

$$= 0.050 \times (-4.43)\, \hat{j} \text{ Ns}$$

$$= -0.22\, \hat{j} \text{ Ns}$$

Velocity of ball just after collision, $v_f = \sqrt{2gh}$

$$= \sqrt{2 \times 9.8 \times 0.5} = 3.13 \text{ m/s}$$

∴   Momentum of ball just after collision,

$$\vec{P}_f = m\vec{v}_f$$

$$= 0.050 \times (3.13\,\hat{j}) = 0.16\,\hat{j} \text{ Ns}$$

Now impulse imparted by ground on the ball

$$\vec{J} = \Delta\vec{P} = \vec{P}_f - \vec{P}_i$$

$$= 0.16\,\hat{j} - (-0.22\,\hat{j}) = 0.38\,\hat{j} \text{ Ns}$$

The force between them

$$F = \frac{\Delta P}{\Delta t} = \frac{0.38}{0.1} = 3.8 \text{ N.} \qquad \textit{Ans.}$$

Example 9. A machine gun fires a bullet of mass m with a speed of v m/s. The person holding the gun can exert a maximum force F on it. What is the number of bullets that can be fired from the gun per second ?

Sol. The change in momentum of each bullet

$$\Delta P = m(v - u).$$

As $u = 0$,

∴ $$\Delta P = mv.$$

If n is the number of bullets fired per second, then rate of change of momentum of the gun

$$\frac{\Delta P}{\Delta t} = n\, mv.$$

Thus by Newton's second law

$$F = \frac{\Delta P}{\Delta t}$$

$$= n\, mv$$

∴ $$n = \frac{F}{mv}. \qquad \textit{Ans.}$$

Example 10. *Figure.* 5.23 shows the position time graph of a particle of mass 4 kg. What is the (i) force acting on the particle for $t < 0, t > 4, 0 < t < 4\,s$? (ii) impulse at $t = 0$ and $t = 4\,s$? Assume that the motion is one dimensional.   **[NCERT]**

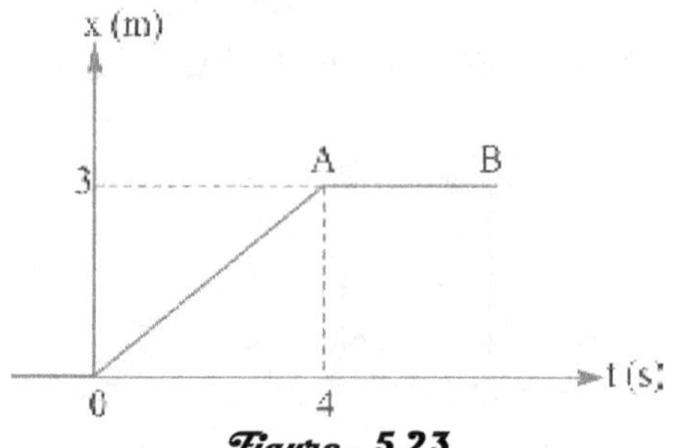

Figure. 5.23

Sol.

(i)   For $t < 0$ and $t > 4\,s$, the position of particle is not changing i.e. the particle is at rest. So the force during these intervals is zero.

For $0 < t < 4s$, the position of particle is changing. But its velocity is constant as clear from x - t graph. Thus acceleration of particle is zero. Hence no force acts on the particle during this interval also.

(ii)   Just before $t = 0$, the particle is at rest, $u = 0$.

Just after $t = 0$, the particle has constant velocity.

$$v = \frac{3}{4} \text{ m/s}$$

∴   Impulse J = Change in momentum

$$= m\,(v - u) = 4\left(\frac{3}{4} - 0\right) = 3 \text{ Ns}$$

Just before $t = 4s$, the particle has constant velocity

$$u = \frac{3}{4} \text{ m/s}$$

Just after $t = 4s$, the particle is at rest, so $v = 0$

∴   Impulse $J = m\,(v - u)$

$$= 4\left(0 - \frac{3}{4}\right) = -3 \text{ Ns} \qquad \textit{Ans.}$$

Example 11. *Figure.* 5.24 below shows the position-time graph of a particle of mass 0.04 kg. Suggest a suitable physical context for this motion. What is the time between two consecutive impulses received by the particle? What is the magnitude of each impulse ?   **[NCERT]**

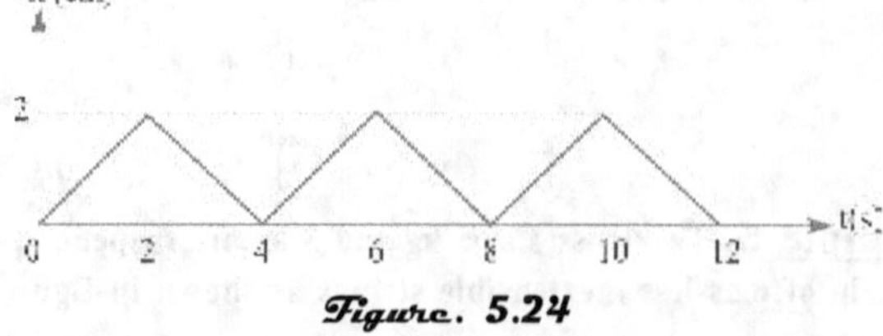

Figure. 5.24

Sol. Just before $t = 2$ s, the velocity of particle,

$$u = \frac{2-0}{2-0} = 1 \text{ cm/s} = 0.01 \text{ m/s}.$$

Just after $t = 2$ s, the velocity of particle,

$$v = \frac{0-2}{4-2} = -1 \text{ cm/s} = -0.01 \text{ m/s}.$$

The magnitude of impulse $J = |\, m\,(v - u)\,|$

$$= |\, 0.04\,(-0.01 - 0.01)\,| = 8 \times 10^{-4} \text{ Ns}.$$

The given x - t graph may represent the repeated rebounding of a particle between two elastic walls at $x = 0$ and $x = 2$ cm. The particle will get an impulse of 8×10^{-4} Ns after every 2 s.

Example 12. Two identical billiard balls strike a rigid wall with the same speed but at different angles, and get reflected without any loss of speed, as shown in *figure* 5.25. What is (i) the direction of the force on the wall due to each ball ? and (ii) the ratio of the magnitudes of the impulse imparted on the two balls by the wall ?

[NCERT]

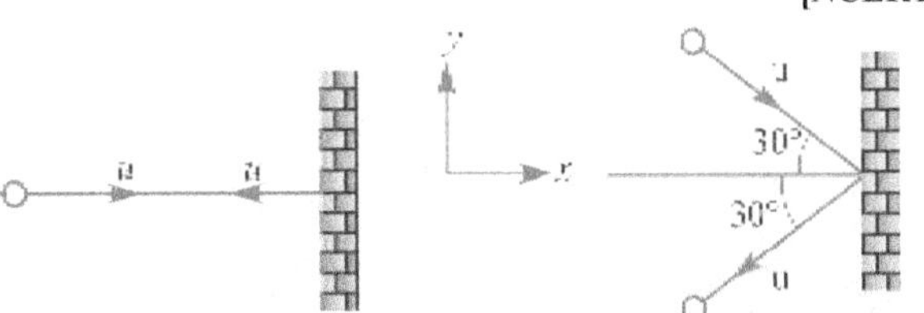

Figure. 5.25

Sol.

(i) Let ball strikes the wall with a speed of u. If its mass is m, then its momentum

$$\vec{P}_i = mu\,\hat{i}$$

and $\quad \vec{P}_f = -mu\hat{i}$

$\therefore$ Impulse $\vec{J}_x = \vec{P}_f - \vec{P}_i$

$$= -mu\,\hat{i} - mu\,\hat{i}$$

$$= -2mu\,\hat{i}.$$

As there is no motion along y-axis, the impulse along this direction will be zero;

$J_y = 0$. Thus resulting impulse is $\vec{J} = \vec{J}_x + \vec{J}_y = -2mu\,\hat{i}$.

The direction of force is along the direction of impulse. So the force exerted by wall on ball is along negative x-axis. By Newton's third law the direction of force exerted by ball on wall is along positive x-axis.

(ii) Resolve the velocity of the ball along x and y-axis, we have

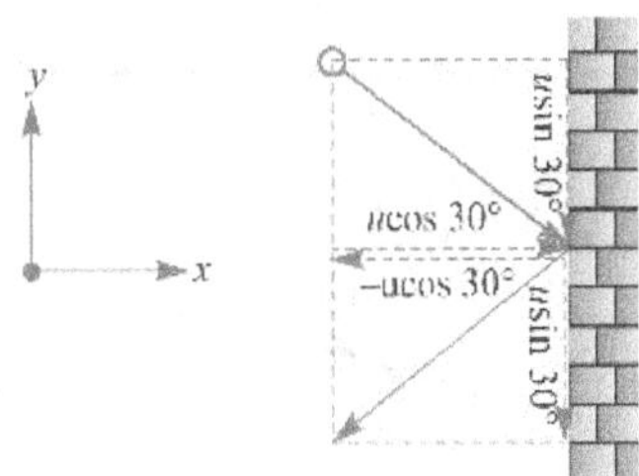

Figure. 5.26

$$\vec{u}_x = u \cos 30° \,\hat{i}\;;\; \vec{u}_y = -u \sin 30° \,\hat{j}$$

and $\quad \vec{v}_x = -u \cos 30° \,\hat{i}\;;\; \vec{v}_y = -u \sin 30° \,\hat{j}$

The impulse exerted by the wall on the ball;

$$\vec{J}_x = m\,(\vec{v}_x - \vec{u}_x) = m\,(-u \cos 30° \,\hat{i} - u \cos 30° \,\hat{i})$$

$$= -2mu \cos 30° \,\hat{i} = \sqrt{3}\, mu\,\hat{i}$$

and $\quad \vec{J}_y = m\,(\vec{v}_y - \vec{u}_y)$

$$= m\,[-u \sin 30° \,\hat{j} - (-u \sin 30° \,\hat{j})] = 0.$$

$\therefore$ Resultant impulse

$$\vec{J} = \vec{J}_x + \vec{J}_y = -\sqrt{3}\, mu\,\hat{i}.$$

The force exerted by wall on ball is along negative x-axis. By Newton's third law the direction of force on wall by ball is along positive x-axis.

The ratio of impulse imparted by the wall on balls

$$\frac{J_1}{J_2} = \frac{2mu}{\sqrt{3}mu} = \frac{2}{\sqrt{3}}. \qquad Ans.$$

Example 13. Two identical point masses, each of mass m are connected to one another by a massless string of length L. A constant force F is applied at the mid-point of the string. If ℓ be the instantaneous distance between the two masses, what will be the acceleration of each mass?

Sol. The situation is shown in *figure* 5.27.

Let T be the tension in the string. For point O, we have

$$2T \sin \theta = F$$

or $\qquad T = \dfrac{F}{2\sin\theta}.$

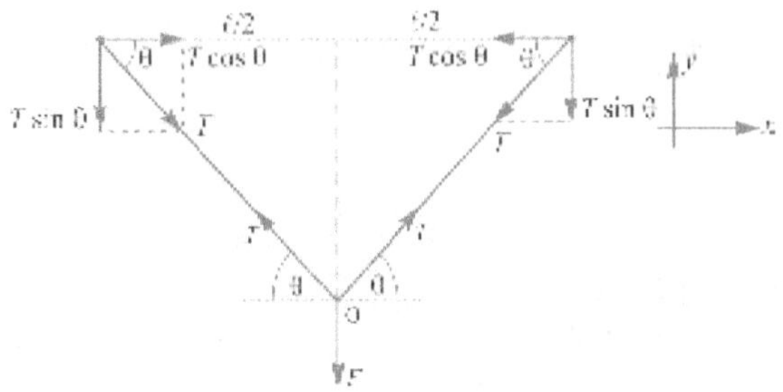

Figure. 5.27

Now acceleration of each mass;

$$a_x = F_x / m$$

or $\qquad a_x = \dfrac{T \cos\theta}{m}$

$$= \frac{(F/2\sin\theta)\cos\theta}{m}$$

$$= \frac{F \cot\theta}{2m}$$

$$= \frac{F}{2m}\frac{\ell/2}{\sqrt{(L/2)^2 - (\ell/2)^2}}$$

$$= \frac{F}{2m}\left[\frac{\ell}{\sqrt{L^2 - \ell^2}}\right] \qquad Ans.$$

Example 14. A block of mass 25kg is raised by a 50 kg man in two different ways as shown in *figure* 5.28. What is the action on the floor by the man in the two cases ? If the floor yields to a normal force of 700 N, which mode should the man adopt to lift the block without the floor yielding.   **[NCERT]**

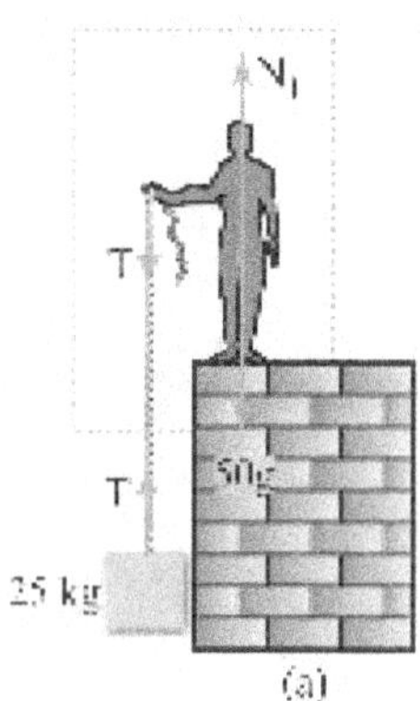

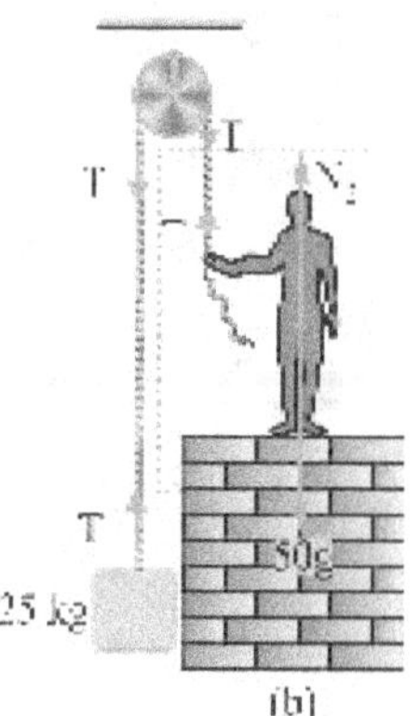

Figure. 5.28

Sol.   The *FBD* for the two cases are shown in figure.

In I case; let the force exerted by the man on the floor is N_1. Consider the forces inside the dotted box, we have

$$N_1 = T + 50\,g.$$

Block is to be raised without acceleration, so $T = 25\,g$.

$$\therefore \qquad N_1 = 25\,g + 50\,g$$
$$= 75g = 75 \times 9.8 = 735\ \text{N}$$

In II case; let the force exerted by the man on the floor is N_2. Consider the forces inside the dotted box, we have

$$N_2 = 50g - T$$
and $$T = 25\,g$$
$$\therefore \qquad N_2 = 50g - 25g$$
$$= 25\,g = 25 \times 9.8 = 245\ \text{N}.$$

As the floor yields to a downward force of 700 N, so the man should adopt mode II.

Example 15.

(*i*)   A 10 kg block is supported by a cord that runs to a spring scale, which is supported by another cord from the ceiling figure (a). What is the reading on the scale ?

(*ii*)   In figure (b) the block is supported by a cord that runs around a pulley and to a scale. The opposite end of the scale is attached by a cord to a wall. What is the reading of the scale ?

(*iii*)   In figure (c) the wall has been replaced with a second 10 kg block on the lift, and the assembly is stationary. What is the reading on the scale now ?

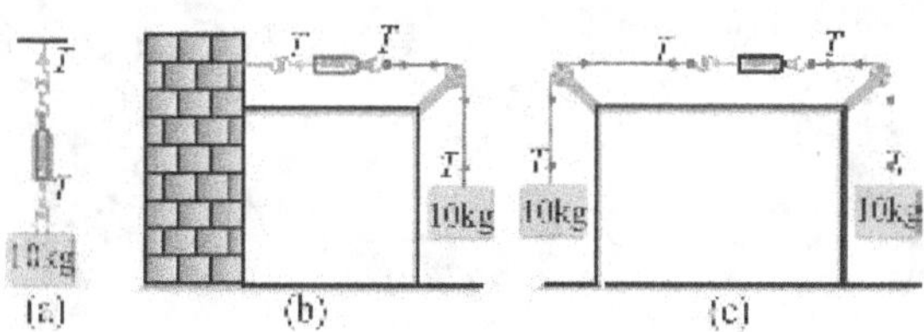

Figure. 5.29

Sol.   In all the three cases the spring balance reads 10 kg. To understand this,   let us cut a section inside the spring as shown;

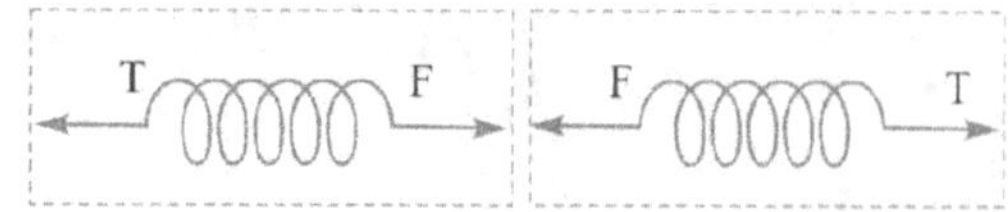

Figure. 5.30

As each part of the spring is at rest, so $F = T$. As the block is stationary, so $T = 10g = 100$ N.

Example 16. What is the reading of the spring balance in the following device ?

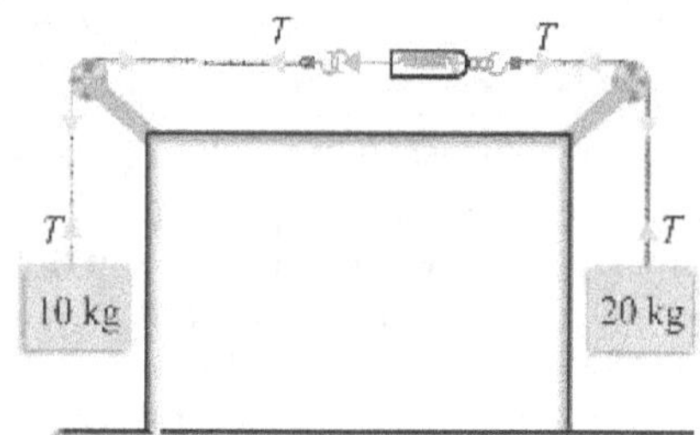

Figure. 5.31

Sol. Let T be the reading of the spring balance, then

for 20 kg block ; $\qquad 20\,g - T = 20\,a$ $\qquad$ ...(i)
for 10 kg block; $\qquad T - 10\,g = 10\,a$ $\qquad$ ...(ii)

Solving equations (i) & (ii), we get $a = \dfrac{g}{3}$ m/s^2 and $T = \dfrac{40g}{3}$ N

So the spring balance reading is $\dfrac{40}{3}$ kg .   *Ans.*

Example 17. Two blocks of masses 1 kg and 2 kg are placed in contact on a smooth horizontal surface as shown in figure. A horizontal force of 3N is applied (i) on 1 kg block (ii) on 2kg block. Find force of interaction between the blocks.

Sol.   Since both the blocks are in contact therefore they will move together with an acceleration

$$a_x = \frac{F_{net}}{M_{total}} = \frac{3}{2+1} = 1\ \text{m/s}^2.$$

Case - I

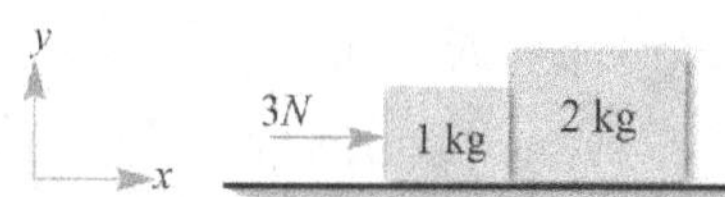

Let force of interaction between them is F_1

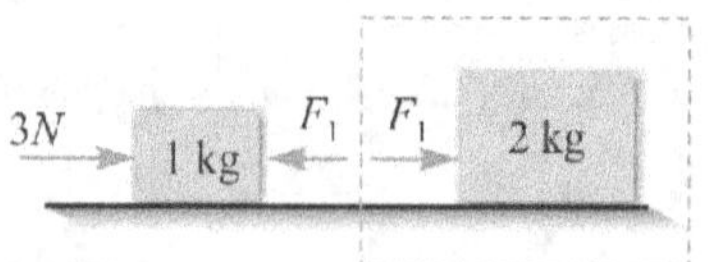

By Newton's second law for 2kg block,
we have, $\qquad\qquad F = 2a$
$$= 2 \times 1 = 2\text{N}$$

The same result can also be obtained from 1 kg block
$$3 - F_1 = 1a$$
$$= 1 \times 1$$
$$\Rightarrow \qquad F = 2\ \text{N}.$$

Case - II

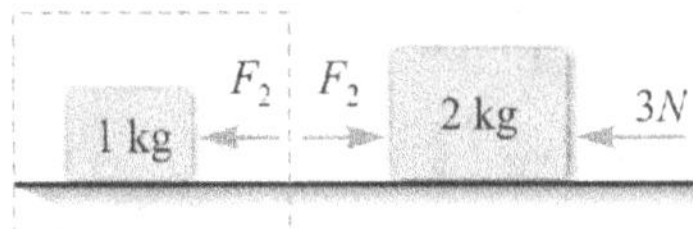

Let force of interaction between them is F_2

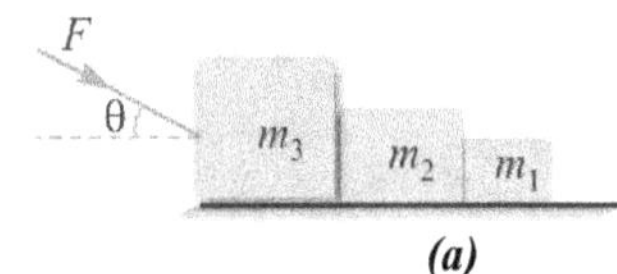

By Newton's second law for 1 kg block,
we have, $\qquad F_2 = 1a$
$\qquad\qquad\quad = 1 \times 1 = 1N.$

Example 18. Find the force of interaction between the bodies as shown in figure.

(i) **Blocks are in contact**

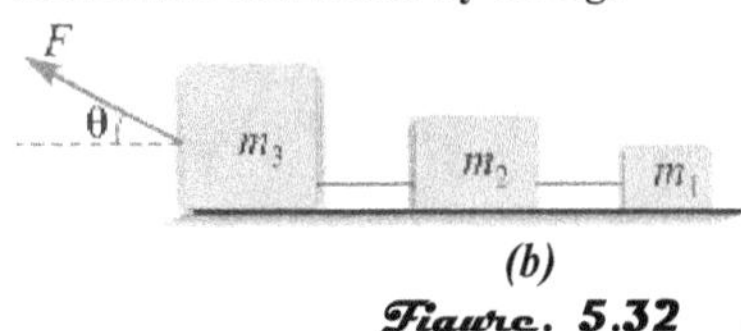

(a)

(ii) **Blocks are connected by strings**

(b)

𝓕igure. 5.32

Sol. All the bodies move together along x-axis with an acceleration

$$a_x = \frac{[F_x]_{net}}{m_{total}} = \frac{F\cos\theta}{m_1 + m_2 + m_3}$$

Case - I

By newtons second law for block m_1
$$F_1 = m_1 a$$
$$= m_1\left(\frac{F\cos\theta}{m_1 + m_2 + m_3}\right)$$

and for block m_2, we have
$$F_2 - F_1 = m_2 a$$
$$\text{or} \qquad F_2 = F_1 + m_2 a$$
$$= F_1 + m_2\left(\frac{F\cos\theta}{m_1 + m_2 + m_3}\right)$$

Here force of interaction is of compressive nature.

Case - II

By Newton's second law for block m_1
$$F_1 = m_1 a$$
$$= m_1\left(\frac{F\cos\theta}{m_1 + m_2 + m_3}\right)$$

and for block m_2, we have

$$F_2 - F_1 = m_2 a$$
$$\text{or} \qquad F_2 = F_1 + m_2 a$$
$$= F_1 + m_2\left(\frac{F\cos\theta}{m_1 + m_2 + m_3}\right).$$

Here force of interaction is of tensile nature.

Example 19. A homogeneous rod of length L and mass M is placed on smooth horizontal surface. It is acted by a force F at its one end. Find the stretching force in the cross section of a rod at a distance x from the end where the force is applied.

Sol.

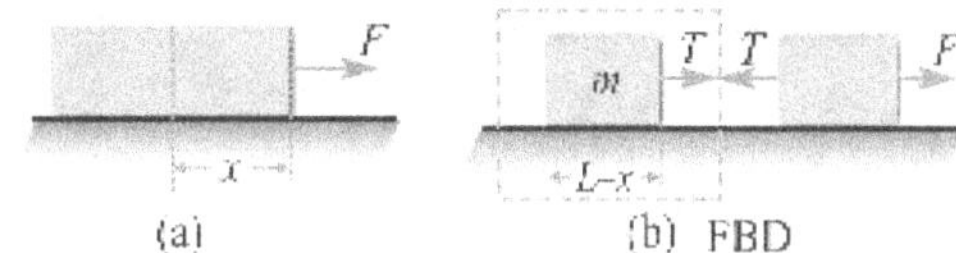

(a)   *(b)* FBD

𝓕igure. 5.33

The acceleration of the rod $a = \dfrac{F}{M}$.

Now cut the rod in two parts and connect them by hypothetical massless string as shown in figure. The mass of part of the rod of length $(L - x)$,

$m = \dfrac{M}{L}(L - x)$. By Newton's second law, for the part inside dotted box

$$T = ma$$
$$= \frac{M}{L}(L - x) \times \frac{F}{M}$$
$$\text{or} \qquad T = F\left(1 - \frac{x}{L}\right). \qquad\qquad Ans.$$

At $\quad x = 0, \qquad\quad T = F$
and $\quad x = L, \qquad\quad T = 0.$

Example 20. A chain consisting of five links, each of mass 0.100 kg is lifted vertically with a constant acceleration of 2.50 m/s², as shown in *fig. 5.34.* Find (a) the forces acting between adjacent links, (b) the force F exerted on the top link by the person lifting the chain and (c) the net force accelerating each link. (Take g = 10 m/s²)

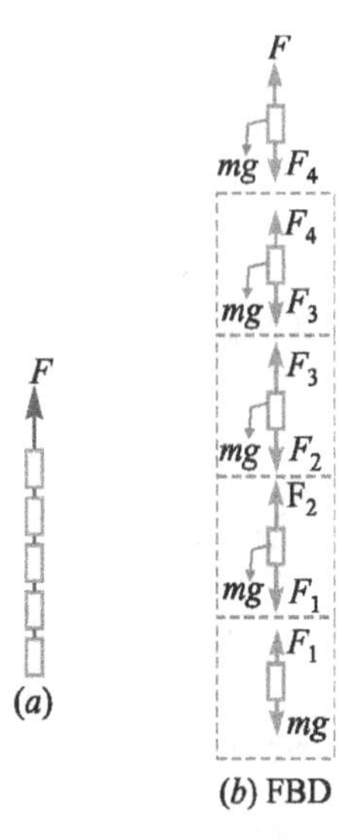

(a)   *(b)* FBD

𝓕igure. 5.34

Sol.

(a) Given, mass of each link $m = 0.100$ kg and acceleration $a = 2.50$ m/s^2. The *FBD* of each link of the chain shown in figure (b).

For link 1,
$$F_1 - mg = ma$$
or $$F_1 = m(g + a) = 0.100(10 + 2.5) = 1.25 \text{ N}.$$

For link 2,
$$F_2 - (F_1 + mg) = ma$$
or $$F_2 = F_1 + m(g + a) = 1.25 + 1.25 = 2.50 \text{ N}.$$

For link 3,
$$F_3 - (F_2 + mg) = ma$$
or $$F_3 = F_2 + m(g + a) = 2.50 + 1.25 = 3.75 \text{ N}.$$

For link 4,
$$F_4 - (F_3 + mg) = ma$$
or $$F_4 = F_3 + m(g + a) = 3.75 + 1.25 = 5.00 \text{ N}.$$

For link 5,
$$F_5 - (F_4 + mg) = ma$$
or $$F_5 = F_4 + m(g + a) = 5.00 + 1.25 = 6.25 \text{ N}.$$

(b) The force exerted by the agent on the top link $F_5 = 6.25$ N.

(c) The net force accelerating each link;

on link 1, $F_1 - mg = 1.25 - 0.100 \times 10 = 0.25$ N

on link 2, $F_2 - (F_1 + mg) = 2.50 - (1.25 + 0.100 \times 10) = 0.25$ N

on link 3, $F_3 - (F_2 + mg) = 0.25$ N

on link 4 , $F_4 - (F_3 + mg) = 0.25$ N

and on link 5, $F_5 - (F_4 + mg) = 0.25$ N.

Example 21. Consider the system shown in *figure* 5.35. The system is released from rest, find the tension in the cord connected between 1 kg and 2 kg blocks. ($g = 10$ m/s^2)

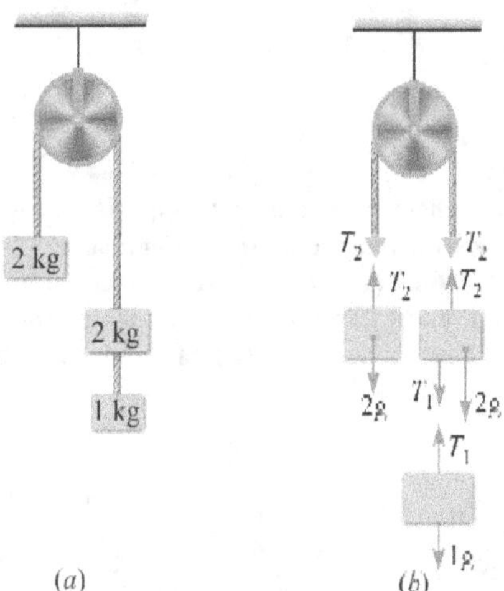

Figure. **5.35**

Sol. By Newton's second law, we have
$$1g - T_1 = 1a \qquad \text{... (i)}$$
$$(T_1 + 2g) - T_2 = 2a \qquad \text{... (ii)}$$
and $$T_2 - 2g = 2a \qquad \text{...(iii)}$$

Solving equation (i), (ii) & (iii), we get
$$a = 2 \text{ m/s}^2$$
$$T_1 = 8 \text{ N}$$
and $$T_2 = 24 \text{ N}. \qquad \textit{Ans.}$$

Force on pulley exerted by cord
$$F = 2T_2 = 48 \text{ N}. \qquad \textit{Ans.}$$

By short cut method :

$$a = \frac{\text{unbalanced load}}{\text{total mass}} = \frac{[(2+1)-2]g}{(1+2+2)} = 2 m/s^2$$

$$T_1 = m_{down}(g - a) = 1(10 - 2) = 8\text{N}$$
$$T_2 = m_{up}(g + a) = 2(10 + 2) = 24 \text{ N}.$$

Example 22. The system shown in *figure* 5.36 is released from rest. Calculate the tension in the strings and force exerted by the strings on the pulleys. Assuming pulleys and strings are massless.

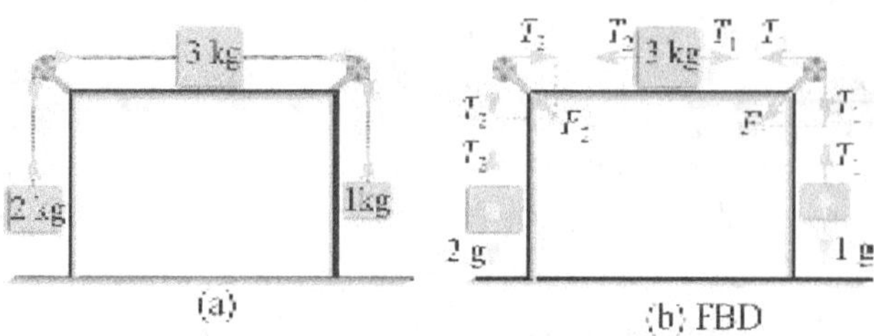

Figure. **5.36**

Sol. *Note :* As the motion of the block is on smooth horizontal surface, so no need to mark the forces along vertical direction in drawing the FBD.

By Newton's second law, we have
$$T_1 - 1g = 1a \qquad \text{...(i)}$$
$$T_2 - T_1 = 3a \qquad \text{...(ii)}$$
and $$2g - T_2 = 2a \qquad \text{...(iii)}$$

Solving above equations, we get
$$a = g/6 \text{ m/s}^2,$$
$$T_1 = \frac{7g}{6} \text{N},$$
and $$T_2 = \frac{5g}{3} \text{N}. \qquad \textit{Ans.}$$

Force on pulley P_1; $F_1 = \sqrt{T_1^2 + T_1^2}$
$$= \sqrt{2}\,T_1$$

Force on pulley P_2 ; $F_2 = \sqrt{T_2^2 + T_2^2}$
$$= \sqrt{2}\,T_2.$$

By short cut method :

$$a = \frac{\text{unbalanced load}}{\text{total mass}}$$
$$= \frac{(2-1)g}{(1+3+2)} = \frac{g}{6} m/s^2.$$

$$T_1 = m_{up}(g + a) = 1\left(g + \frac{g}{6}\right) = \frac{7g}{6}\text{N}.$$

$$T_2 = m_{down}(g - a) = 2\left(g - \frac{g}{6}\right) = \frac{5g}{3}\text{N}.$$

Example 23. Find the acceleration of the blocks in the following devices from the data shown in fig. Pulleys are massless and frictionless.

(*i*)

(*ii*)

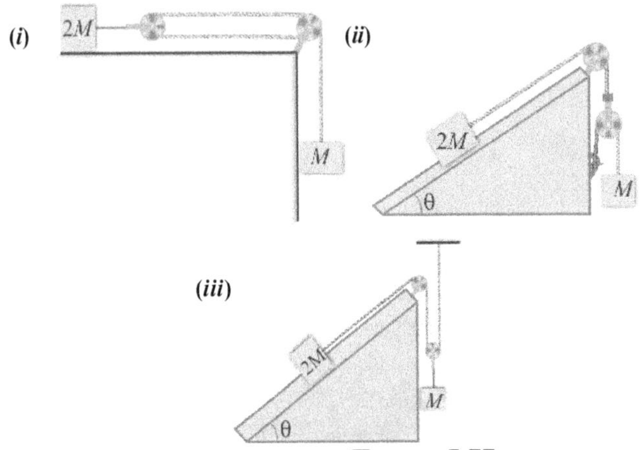

(*iii*)

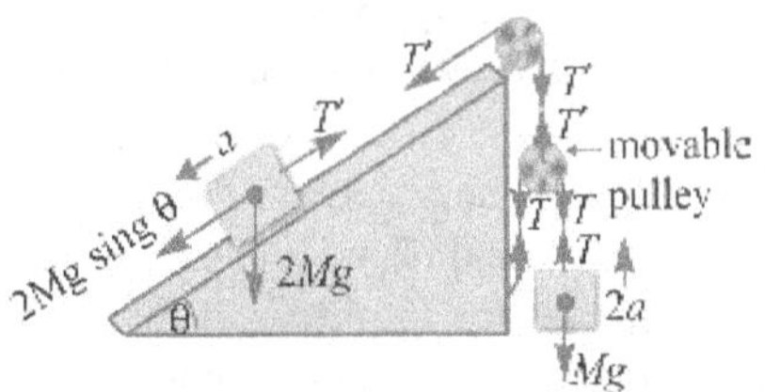

Figure. **5.37**

Sol.

(i)

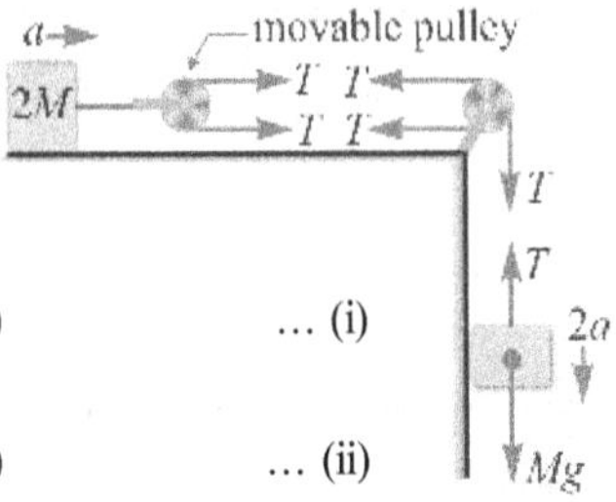

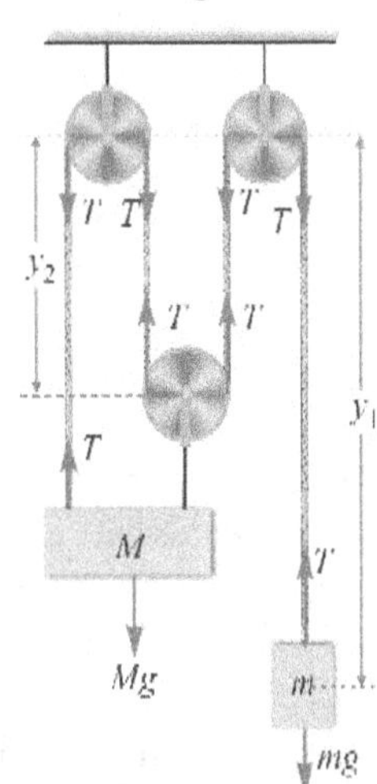

For block 2 M;
$$2T = 2M(a) \qquad \ldots \text{(i)}$$
For block M;
$$Mg - T = M(2a) \qquad \ldots \text{(ii)}$$
After solving above equations, we get
$$a = g/3 \ \text{m/s}^2.$$
Force on clamp which holds the pulley

Figure. **5.38**

$$F = \sqrt{(2T)^2 + T^2} = \sqrt{5}\,T$$

(ii)

Figure. **5.39**

For block $2M$;
$$2Mg\sin\theta - T' = 2M(a) \qquad \ldots \text{(i)}$$
For movable pulley ;
$$T' - 2T = 0 \times a \qquad \ldots \text{(ii)}$$
For block M ;
$$T - Mg = M(2a) \qquad \ldots \text{(iii)}$$
After solving above equations, we get
$$a = -g/3\,(1 - \sin\theta).$$

Note :

Here we have assumed that block 2M is moving down the plane. You may assume that it is moving up the plane. The magnitude of acceleration will remain same.

(iii)

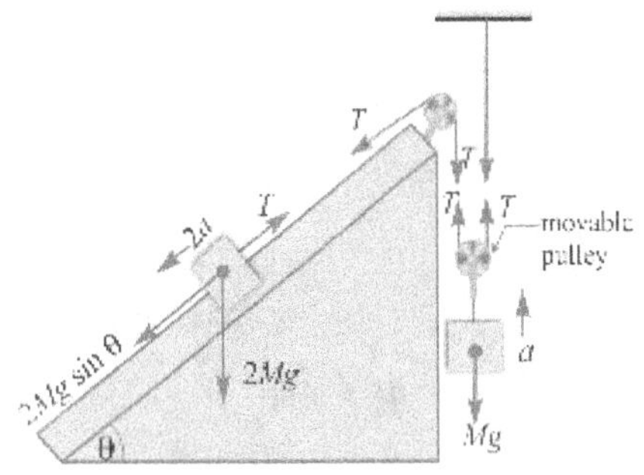

Figure. **5.40**

For block $2M$;
$$2Mg\sin\theta - T = 2M(2a) \qquad \ldots \text{(i)}$$
For block M;
$$2T - Mg = Ma \qquad \ldots \text{(ii)}$$
After solving above equation we get
$$a = \frac{g}{9}(4\sin\theta - 1)\,m/s^2.$$

Force on fixed pulley
$$F = \sqrt{T^2 + T^2 + 2TT\cos(90° - \theta)}$$

Example 24. Find the acceleration of the block in the following device from the data shown in figure.

Figure. **5.41**

Sol. Total length of the cord
$$y_1 + 3y_2 + \ell_0 = \ell \qquad \ldots \text{(i)}$$
here y_1 and y_2 changes, ℓ_0 and ℓ remain constant.
Differentiating equation (i) with respect to time, we get

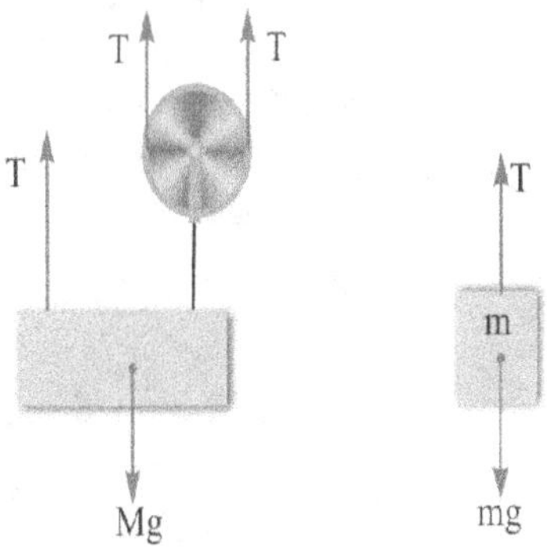

Figure. **5.42**

$$\frac{dy_1}{dt} + 3\frac{dy_2}{dt} = 0$$

or $\quad v_1 + 3v_2 = 0 \qquad\qquad$ ...(ii)

also $\quad a_1 + 3a_2 = 0$

which gives

$$a_1 = 3a_2 \qquad \text{(magnitude)}$$

If we take $\quad a_2 = a$ up

then $\qquad a_1 = 3a$ down

By Newton's second law, we have

$$mg - T = m\,(3a) \qquad ... \text{(iii)}$$
$$\text{and} \qquad 3T - Mg = Ma. \qquad ... \text{(iv)}$$

After solving equation (iii) and (iv), we get

$$a = \frac{(3m - M)g}{(9m + M)} \qquad \textit{Ans.}$$

Example 25. In the arrangement shown in *fig.* 5.43 the bodies have masses m_0, m_1 and m_2, the friction is absent, the masses of pulleys and the threads are negligible. Find the acceleration of the body m_1.

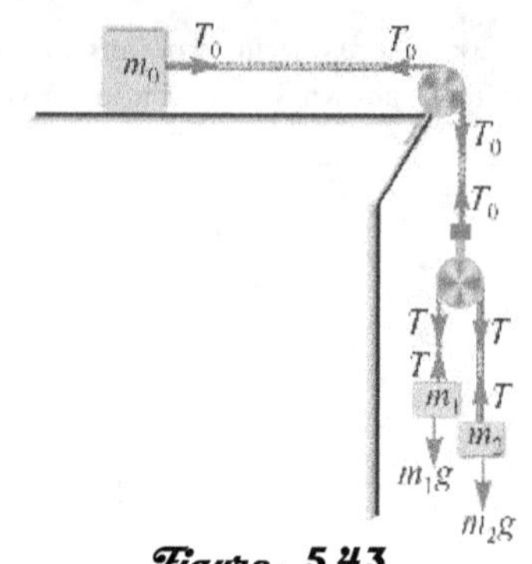

Figure. 5.43

Sol. Let the acceleration of m_0 with respect to the table is a_0 and that of m_1 and m_2 is a in magnitude with respect to the movable pulley. Suppose m_1, moves upward and m_2 moves downward, their accelerations with respect to the table will be;

$$a_1 = a - a_0 \quad \text{upward}$$
$$\text{and} \qquad a_2 = a + a_0 \quad \text{downward.}$$

By Newton's second law, we have

$$T_0 = m_0 a_0 \qquad ... \text{(i)}$$
$$T - m_1 g = m_1(a - a_0) \qquad ... \text{(ii)}$$
$$\text{and} \qquad m_2 g - T = m_2(a + a_0) \qquad ... \text{(iii)}$$

For movable pulley

$$T_0 - 2T = 0 \times a_0. \qquad ... \text{(iv)}$$

Solving above equations, we get

$$a = \frac{4m_1 m_2 + m_0(m_1 - m_2)g}{4m_1 m_2 + m_0(m_1 + m_2)}. \qquad \textit{Ans.}$$

In Chapter Exercise 5.1

1. A man of mass 70 kg stands on a weighing scale in a lift, which is moving (a) upwards with a uniform speed of 10 ms^{-1}, (b) downwards with a uniform acceleration of 5 ms^{-2}, (c) upwards with a uniform acceleration of 5 ms^{-2}. What would be the readings on the scale in each case (d) what would be the reading if the lift mechanism failed and it hurted down freely under gravity? [NCERT]

    Ans. (a) 700 N (b) 350 N (c) 1050 N (d) Zero

2. A monkey of mass 40 kg climbs on a rope (fig.) which can stand a maximum tension of 600 N. In which of the following cases will the rope break: the monkey
    (a) climbs up with an acceleration of 6 ms^{-2}
    (b) climbs down with an acceleration of 4 ms^{-2}
    (c) climbs up with a uniform speed of 5 ms^{-1}
    (d) falls down the rope nearly freely under gravity? (Ignore the mass of the rope). [NCERT]

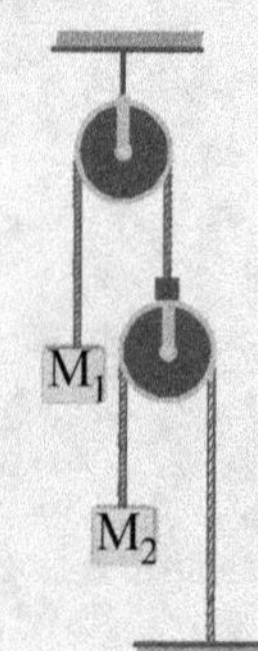

Ans. (a) T = 640 N, rope break (b) T = 240 N, rope will not break (c) T = 400 N , rope will not break (d) T = 0, rope will not break.

3. An aerostat of mass 6 kg starts coming down with a constant acceleration 2 m/s^2. Determine the ballast mass to be dumped for the aerostat to reach the upward acceleration of the same magnitude. The air drag is to be neglected. ($g = 10$ m/s^2)

    $$\textit{Ans.}\ \Delta m = \frac{2ma}{(g + a)} = 2 \text{ kg.}$$

4. Two masses $M_1 = M_2 = M$ are arranged as shown in the figure. Find the acceleration of mass M_2. The pulleys are massless and frictionless.   *Ans.* **4 m/s^2.**

5. A helicopter of mass 2000 kg rises with a vertical acceleration of 15 m/s². The total mass of the crew and passengers is 500 kg. Give the magnitude and direction of the (g = 10 m/s².)
   (a) force on the floor of the helicopter by the crew and passengers.
   (b) action of the rotor of the helicopter on the surrounding air.
   (c) force on the helicopter due to the surrounding air.

   [NCERT Exemplar]

   Ans. (a) **12500 N** (b) **62500 N↓** (c) **62500 N↑**

6. A smooth ring A of mass m can slide on a fixed horizontal rod. A string tied to the ring passes over a fixed pulley B and carries a block C of mass M as shown in figure. At an instant the string between the ring and the pulley makes an angle α with the rod. What acceleration will the ring start moving if the system is released from rest with $\alpha = \theta$?

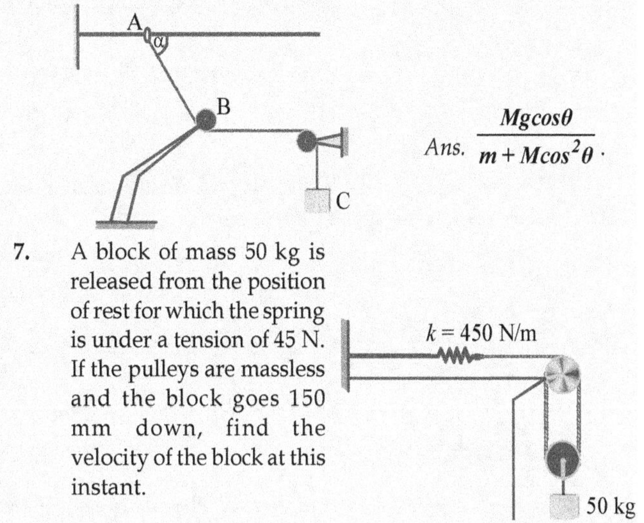

$$Ans. \ \frac{Mg\cos\theta}{m + M\cos^2\theta}.$$

7. A block of mass 50 kg is released from the position of rest for which the spring is under a tension of 45 N. If the pulleys are massless and the block goes 150 mm down, find the velocity of the block at this instant.

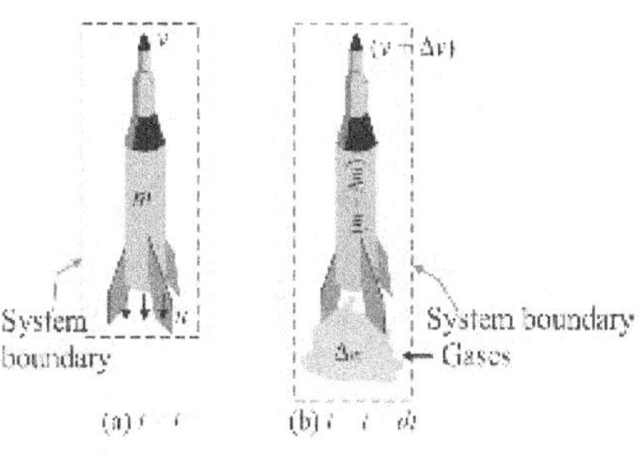

Ans. **1.28 m/s.**

5.7 CONSERVATION OF LINEAR MOMENTUM

We have, Newton's second law of motion;

$$\vec{F}_{external} = \frac{d\vec{P}}{dt}$$

If $\vec{F}_{external} = 0$ then $d\vec{P} = 0$ or $\vec{P}$ = constant

Thus if no net external force acts on the system the total momentum of the system remains constant. **This is known as principle of conservation of momentum.**

> **Note:** In many practical phenomenon like collisions, explosion in space, the gravitational force is always there. But the time of event is to small $(\Delta t \to 0)$, that any change in momentum in this duration can be neglected. And therefore we can assume that the momentum is the process remains constant in this duration.

Recoil of a gun :

Consider a system (gun + bullet) is of mass M + m. Before firing gun and bullet are at rest. If bullet is fired with velocity $\vec{v}$, then recoil velocity of gun can be obtained by conservation of momentum principle as follows :

total momentum before firing = total momentum after firing

or $\qquad 0 = m\vec{v} + M\vec{V}$

or $\qquad \vec{V} = -\frac{m}{M}\vec{v}.$

Here negative sign shows that gun moves in the direction opposite of the bullet.

5.8 VARIABLE MASS SYSTEM

Rocket propulsion: The rocket propulsion is an example of conservation of momentum. In a rocket, as the fuel starts burning, the gases emerge out forcefully through the nozzle. The large backward momentum of the emerging gases imparts an equal amount of forward momentum to the rocket. As the mass of rocket goes on decreasing, so its acceleration goes on increasing.

Suppose m_0 is the initial mass of the rocket. Let the gases be ejected at a constant rate $r = -\dfrac{dm}{dt}$. Also suppose, the gases are ejected at a constant velocity u relative to ground. At any time t, the mass of the rocket will be

$$m = \left[m_0 - \left(\frac{dm}{dt}\right)t \right].$$

Figure. 5.44

Assuming, initially that gravitational force is not there. Using principle of conservation of momentum we have,

$$\text{momentum of system at } t = \text{moment of system at } (t + \Delta t)$$

or
$$mv = (m - \Delta m)(v + \Delta v) + \Delta m(-u)$$

or
$$mv = mv - \Delta mv + m\Delta v - \Delta m\Delta v - \Delta mu$$

Since Δm and Δv are small, so their product becomes very small and therefore it can be neglected. Thus we have

$$m\Delta v = \Delta m(v + u) \qquad \ldots \text{(i)}$$

Dividing both sides of the equation by Δt, we have

$$m\frac{\Delta v}{\Delta t} = \frac{\Delta m}{\Delta t}(v + u).$$

Taking the limit $\Delta t \to 0$, we get

$$m\frac{dv}{dt} = \frac{dm}{dt}(v + u). \qquad \ldots \text{(ii)}$$

Exhaust velocity of emerging gases: It is the velocity of emerging gases with respect to the rocket at any instant. Thus we have, velocity of emerging gases

$$\vec{v}_r = \vec{v}_{\text{gases}} - \vec{v}_{\text{rocket}} = -u - v$$

or
$$v_r = -(v + u)$$

$\therefore$
$$(v + u) = -v_r$$

Substituting this value in equation (ii), we get

$$m\left(\frac{dv}{dt}\right) = -v_r\left(\frac{dm}{dt}\right). \qquad \ldots \text{(iii)}$$

Thrust force : It is the force generated when certain mass leaves or enters into the system. Its magnitude can be calculated as :

$$F_{\text{thrust}} = v_r\left(\frac{dm}{dt}\right),$$

where v_r the velocity of the leaving or entering mass relative to the body considered.

Net force on the rocket :

The net force on rocket = thrust force – gravitational force

or
$$F_{\text{net}} = v_r\left(\frac{dm}{dt}\right) - mg$$

Thus
$$a_{\text{net}} = \frac{v_r}{m}\left(\frac{dm}{dt}\right) - g \qquad \ldots \text{(iv)}$$

where g is the acceleration due to gravity (which is not constant).

Velocity of rocket : In absence of gravity, from equation (iii), we have

$$\frac{dv}{dt} = \frac{v_r}{m}\left(\frac{dm}{dt}\right)$$

or
$$dv = -v_r\left(\frac{dm}{m}\right)$$

Integrating both sides, we get

$$\int_{v_0}^{v} dv = -v_r \int_{m_0}^{m}\left(\frac{dm}{m}\right)$$

$$\left|v\right|_{v_0}^{v} = -v_r \left|\ln m\right|_{m_0}^{m}$$

or
$$v - v_0 = -v_r \ln\left(\frac{m}{m_0}\right)$$

or
$$v = v_0 + v_r \ln\frac{m_0}{m} \qquad \ldots \text{(v)}$$

Newton's second law for system of variable mass:

$$\vec{F}_{external} + \vec{F}_{thrust} = m\frac{d\vec{v}}{dt}$$

or

$$\vec{F}_{external} + \vec{v}_r\left(\frac{dm}{dt}\right) = m\frac{d\vec{v}}{dt}.$$

Here v_r is the velocity of the separated (gained) mass relative to the body considered.

Liquid jet

Rate of flow : It is the volume of liquid coming out per second from the pipe. If ΔV volume of liquid comes out from the mouth of the pipe in time Δt, then rate of flow, $Q = \dfrac{\Delta V}{\Delta t}$.

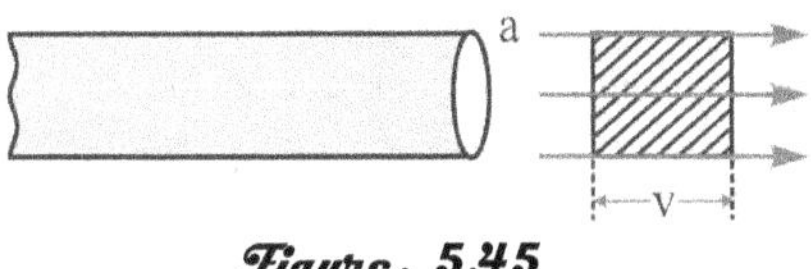

Figure. **5.45**

For $\Delta t \to 0$

$$Q = \frac{dV}{dt}.$$

If a is the area of mouth of the pipe (area of jet) and v is the velocity of jet emerging from pipe, then the rate of flow,

$$Q = \text{Volume per second}$$
$$= \text{area of jet} \times \text{distance travelled by jet in 1 second}$$

or $$Q = av \ \ \text{m}^3/\text{s}$$

Force exerted by jet on wall

1. Let us consider a jet of area 'a' strikes the stationary wall with a velocity v and splaces parallel to wall.

   Consider small element of liquid of mass Δm. The change of its momentum after strike

   $$[\Delta P_x]_{jet} = 0 - \Delta mv = -\Delta mv$$

   As $$[\Delta \vec{P}_x]_{jet} + [\Delta \vec{P}_{wall}] = 0,$$

   so transfer of momentum to wall $[\Delta P_x]_{wall} = \Delta mv$.

   If Δt is the duration of strike, then force exerted by jet on the wall

   $$F = \frac{[\Delta P_x]_{wall}}{\Delta t} = \frac{\Delta mv}{\Delta t}$$

   $$= \left(\rho\frac{\Delta V}{\Delta t}\right)v = \rho\left(\frac{\Delta V}{\Delta t}\right)v \quad (\Delta m = \rho\Delta V)$$

   or $$F = \rho Q v = \rho a v^2.$$

   If wall is moving towards jet with velocity u, then

   $$F = \rho a(v+u)^2 = \rho\left(\frac{Q}{v}\right)(v+u)^2$$

2. Now consider the jet strikes the wall at an angle θ with the normal and rebound with the same angle. The transfer of momentum to wall

   $$[\Delta P_x]_{wall} = 2\,\Delta\,mv\cos\theta$$

   and $$[\Delta P_y]_{wall} = 0.$$

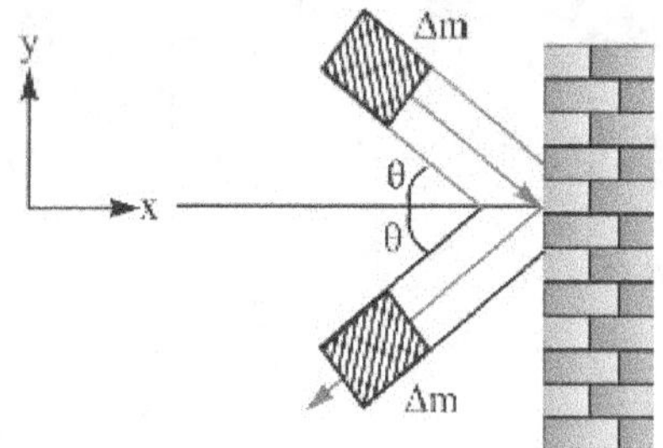

Figure. 5.47

If Δt is the duration of strike, then the force exerted by jet on wall

$$F = \frac{[\Delta P_x]_{\text{wall}}}{\Delta t}$$

$$= \frac{2\Delta mv\,\cos\theta}{\Delta t} = \left(\frac{\Delta m}{\Delta t}\right) 2v\cos\theta$$

$$= \rho\left(\frac{\Delta V}{\Delta t}\right) 2v\cos\theta$$

or $$F = 2\rho Q v\cos\theta = 2\rho v^2 a\cos\theta\ .$$

FORMULAE USED

1. Thrust force on the rocket, $F_{\text{thrust}} = v_r\left(\dfrac{dm}{dt}\right)$

2. Net force on the rocket, fired vertically, $F_{net} = v_r\left(\dfrac{dm}{dt}\right) - mg$

3. Acceleration of the rocket after time t, $a_{net} = \dfrac{v_r}{m}\left(\dfrac{dm}{dt}\right) - g$

4. Velocity of rocket after time t, in absence of gravity

$$v = v_0 + v_r \ln\frac{m_0}{m}\ .$$

   Here mass of rocket after time, $t = m_0 - \left(\dfrac{dm}{dt}\right)t$, and v_r is the exhaust velocity of gases.

5. Rate of flow, $Q = av$.

6. Force exerted jet on wall, $F = \rho Qv$

EXAMPLES BASED ON VARIABLE MASS SYSTEM

Example 26. A rocket of initial mass 6000 kg ejects mass at a constant rate of 16 kg/s with constant relative speed of 11 km/s. What is the acceleration of the rocket a minute after the blast ? Neglect gravity.

Sol. Given, initial mass of the rocket

$$m_0 = 6000\ \text{kg}\ \text{and}\ \frac{dm}{dt} = 16\ \text{kg/s}.$$

The mass of the rocket after 1 minute of the blast

$$m = m_0 - \left(\frac{dm}{dt}\right)t$$
$$= 6000 - 16 \times 60$$
$$= 5040\ \text{kg}.$$

The acceleration of the rocket is given by

$$a = \frac{v_r}{m}\left(\frac{dm}{dt}\right) - g$$
$$= \frac{11000}{5040} \times 16 - 0$$
$$= 34.92\ \text{m/s}^2. \qquad \textit{Ans.}$$

Example 27. A rocket is set for vertical firing. If the exhaust speed is 1200 m/s, how much gas must be ejected per second to supply the thrust needed (i) to overcome the weight of the rocket (ii) to give to the rocket an initial vertical upward acceleration of 29.6 m/s^2? Given mass of the rocket = 6000 kg.

Sol. (i) Thrust = weight of the rocket

or $$v_r\left(\frac{dm}{dt}\right) = mg$$

or $$\frac{dm}{dt} = \frac{mg}{v_r}$$

$$= \frac{6000 \times 9.8}{1200} = 49\ \text{kg/s} \qquad \textit{Ans.}$$

(ii) At $t = 0$, the acceleration of rocket is given by

$$a = \frac{v_r}{m}\left(\frac{dm}{dt}\right) - g$$

or $\quad 29.9 = \dfrac{1200}{6000}\left(\dfrac{dm}{dt}\right) - 9.8$

$\therefore \quad \dfrac{dm}{dt} = 197 \text{ kg/s}.$ $\qquad\qquad$ *Ans.*

Example 28. If the maximum posible exhaust velocity of a rocket be 2 kg/s, calculate the ratio m_0/m for it if it is to acquire to escape velocity of 11.2 km/s after starting from rest.

Sol. Velocity of rocket, starting from rest is given by

$$v = v_r \ell n\left(\dfrac{m_0}{m}\right)$$

$$11.2 = 2\ell n\left(\dfrac{m_0}{m}\right)$$

After simplifying, we get

$$\dfrac{m_0}{m} = 270.4 \qquad\qquad Ans.$$

<hr>

In Chapter Exercise 5.2

1. A stream of water flowing horizontally with a speed of 15ms^{-1} pushes out of tube of cross sectional area 10^{-2} m^2 and hits at a vertical wall nearby. What is the force exerted on the wall by the impact of water, assuming it does not rebound? $\qquad$ **Ans. 2200 N** $\qquad$ **[NCERT]**

2. Fuel is consumed at the rate of 50 g per second in a rocket. The exhaust gases are rejected at the rate of 5×10^5 cms^{-1}. What is the thrust experienced by the rocket? **Ans. 250 N**

3. In the first second of its flight, a rocket ejects $1/60$ of its mass with a relative velocity of 2073 ms^{-1}. What is the initial acceleration of the rocket? $\qquad$ **Ans. 24.75 ms^{-2}.**

4. A rocket motor consumes 100 kg of fuel per second, exhausting it with a speed of 6×10^3 ms^{-1}. (i) What thrust is exerted on the rocket? (ii) What will be the velocity of the rocket at the instant its mass is reduced to $(1/40)$th of its initial mass, its initial velocity being zero? Neglect gravity.

   Ans. (i) 6×10^5 N (ii) 22.13×10^3 ms^{-1}]

5. A balloon of mass m is rising up with an acceleration a. Show that the fraction of weight of the balloon that must be detached in order to double its acceleration is $[ma/(2a + g)]$, assuming the upthrust of air to remain the same.

5.9 Equilibrium

A force can change the state of motion of body in two ways. It can cause translation or it can cause translation as well as rotation.

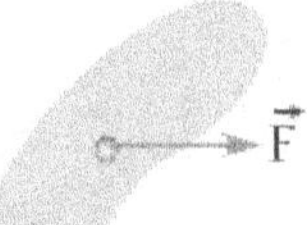

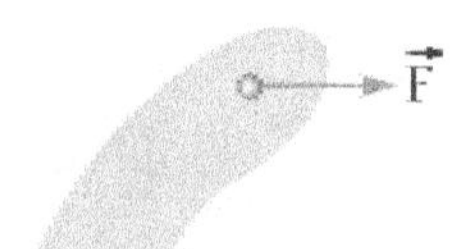

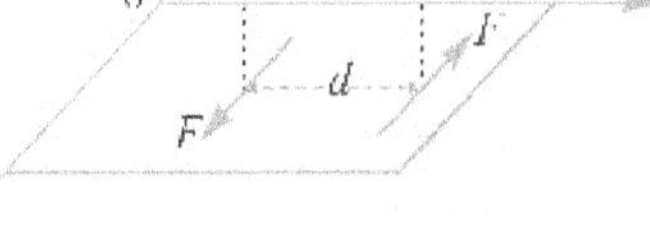

(a) Translation motion of body $\qquad$ (b) Translation and rotation

Figure. 5.49

Figure. 5.48

However when many forces act on a body simultaneously, their effects can compensate one another, with the result that there is no translation or rotational motion. When this is the case, the body is said to be in equilibrium.

Conditions of equilibrium

(1) If vector sum of forces acting on a body is zero, the body is said to be in *translational equilibrium*. Thus for translational equilibrium, $\sum \vec{F} = 0$.

(2) If vector sum of moment of forces acting on a body about any axis is zero, the body is said to be in *rotational equilibrium*. Thus for rotational equilibrium, we have $\sum \vec{\tau} = 0$.

For complete equilibrium of a body, we have

$$\sum \vec{F} = 0 \text{ and } \sum \vec{\tau} = 0$$

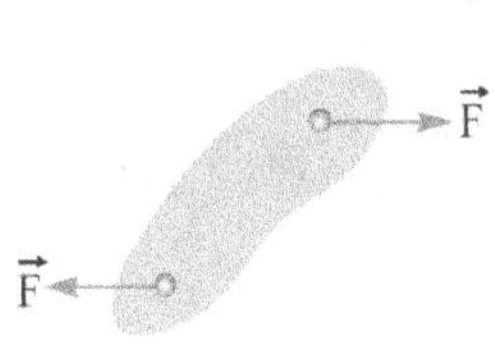

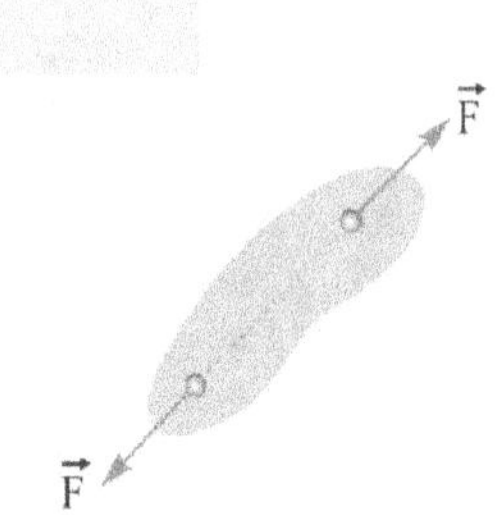

(a) Body in translational equilibrium $\qquad$ (b) Body in complete equilibrium

Figure. 5.50

Static and dynamic equilibrium

1. If $\sum \vec{F} = 0$ and body is at rest. It is known as static equilibrium.

2. If $\sum \vec{F} = 0$ and body moves with constant velocity. It is known as dynamic equilibrium.

5.10   LAMI'S THEOREM

If a body is in equilibrium under three coplanar concurrent forces, then each force is proportional to *sine* of the angle between remaining two forces. According to the theorem, we have

$$\frac{F_1}{\sin\alpha_1} = \frac{F_2}{\sin\alpha_2} = \frac{F_3}{\sin\alpha_3} = k$$

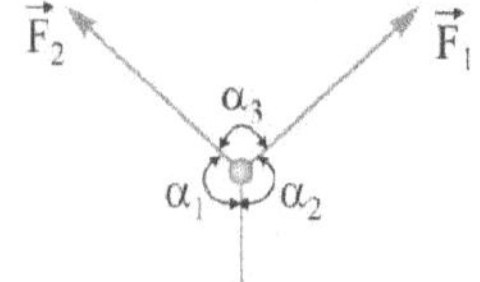

Figure. 5.51

PROBLEM-SOLVING STRATEGY IN EQUILIBRIUM

1. Make a line diagram of the given device or structure, showing all dimensions and angles.

2. Select an object (for example a knot in rope) and draw separate *FBD* of this object. If a system is composed of several bodies, it may be necessary to construct a separate *FBD* for each one.

3. Construct a system of rectangular axes and resolve all the forces acting on a body along these axes.

4. Finally use the equations of static equilibrium.

    (a) **For coplanar-concurrent forces :** (Two or more forces)

    $$\sum F_x = 0 \text{ and } \sum F_y = 0 .$$

    The number of unknown in problems should not be more than *two*.

    (b) **For coplanar non concurrent forces :** (Two or more forces)

    $$\sum F_x = 0 \text{ or } \sum F_y = 0 \text{ and } \sum \tau_z = 0 .$$

    The number of unknown in problem should not be more than *three*.

EXAMPLES BASED ON EQUILIBRIUM

Example 29. A ladder is placed on a smooth floor and held against a rough vertical wall. Is ladder remains in its position ?

Sol. It is clear from the *FBD* that there is an unbalanced force N_2 in horizontal direction. It require a force opposite and equal in magnitude of N_2 to keep the ladder in its position.

Figure. 5.52

Example 30. A smooth sphere of radius *r* and weight W hangs by a light string of length *r*. One end of the string is fastened to a point on the surface of the sphere while its other end is fixed to a point on a smooth vertical wall. Determine the reaction of the wall and the tension in the string.

Sol.

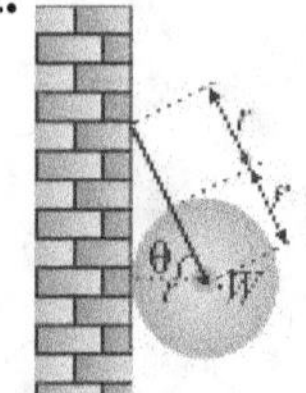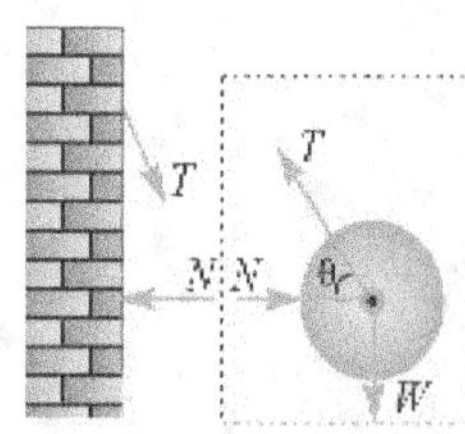

Figure. 5.53

From the geometry of the figure,

$$\cos\theta = \frac{r}{2r} = \frac{1}{2} \text{ or } \theta = 60°$$

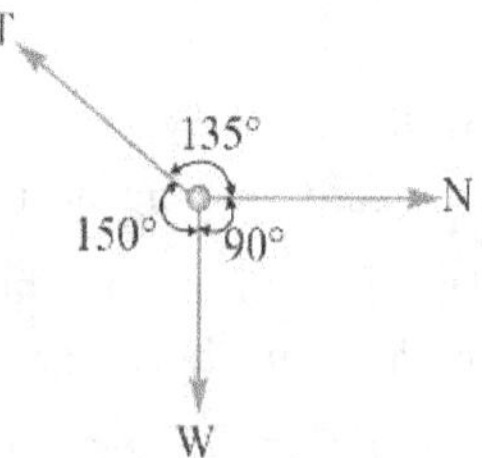

Figure. 5.54

By Lami's theorem, we have $\dfrac{T}{\sin 90°} = \dfrac{N}{\sin 150°} = \dfrac{W}{\sin 120°}$

or $T = \dfrac{W\sin 90°}{\sin 120°} = \dfrac{2W}{\sqrt{3}}$ and $N = \dfrac{W\sin 150°}{\sin 120°} = \dfrac{W}{\sqrt{3}}$

We also have, $\vec{T} + \vec{N} + \vec{W} = 0$, and $T^2 = \sqrt{N^2 + W^2}$.   *Ans.*

Example 31. Find the tension in each cord as shown in *figure* 5.55. The weight of the suspended body is 100 N.

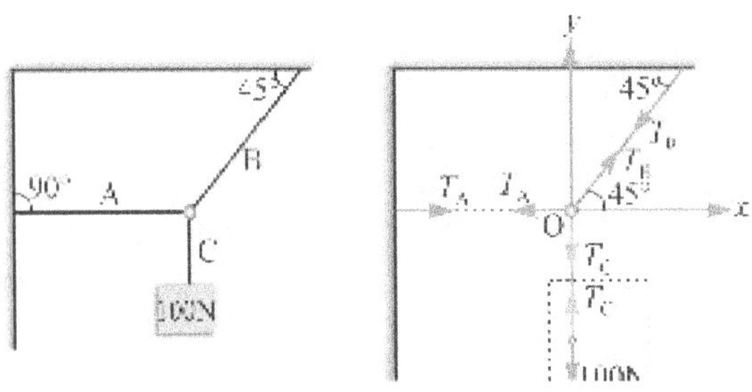

Figure. 5.55

Sol. Method - I

The whole system is in equilibrium, therefore each part of its must be in equilibrium.

From *FBD*, $T_C = 100$ N

Now consider the equilibrium of point O ;

$$\sum F_x = 0 \text{ ; or } T_B \cos 45° - T_A = 0$$

$$\therefore \quad T_A = T_B \cos 45° = \frac{T_B}{\sqrt{2}} . \qquad \text{.... (i)}$$

and $\sum F_y = 0$; or $T_B \sin 45° - T_C = 0$ .... (ii)

$$\therefore \quad T_B = \frac{T_C}{\sin 45°} = \frac{100}{1/\sqrt{2}} = 100\sqrt{2} \ N .$$

From equation (i), we get $T_A = \frac{T_B}{\sqrt{2}} = \frac{100\sqrt{2}}{\sqrt{2}} = 100 N$. **Ans.**

Method – II

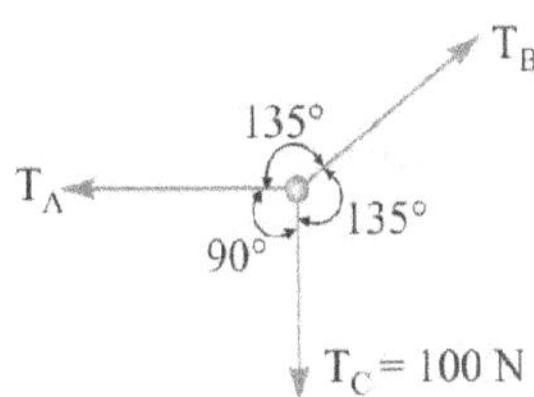

Figure. 5.56

By Lami's theorem, we have $\dfrac{T_A}{\sin 135°} = \dfrac{T_B}{\sin 90°} = \dfrac{T_C}{\sin 135°}$

which gives, $T_A = T_C = 100$ N

and $\quad T_B = \dfrac{T_C}{\sin 135°} = \dfrac{100}{1/\sqrt{2}} = 100\sqrt{2} \ N$.

<u>Example</u> 32. **A system of connected flexible cables shown in** *fig.* **5.136 is supporting two vertical forces 200 N and 250 N at points** ***B*** **and** ***D*.** **Determine the forces in various segments of the cable.**

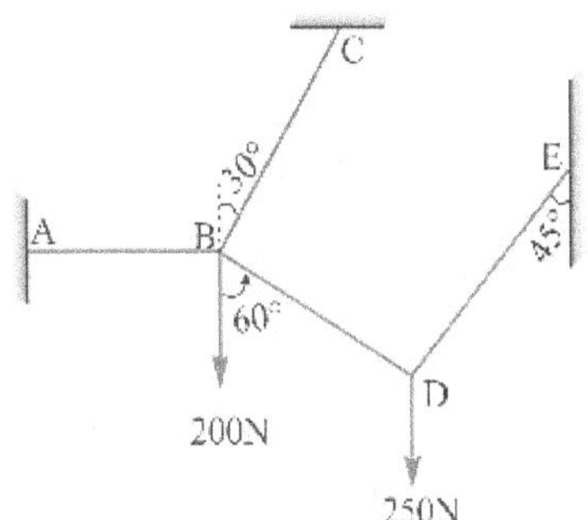

Figure. 5.57

Sol. *FBD* of whole system is shown in figure.

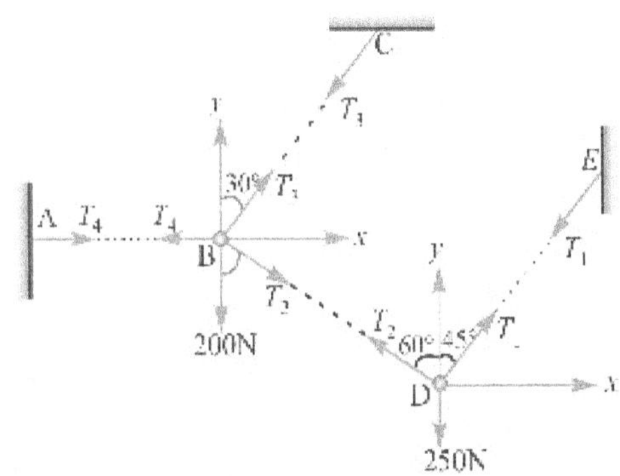

Figure. 5.58

Consider the equilibrium of point D :

$$\sum F_x = 0 \text{ , or } T_1 \sin 45° - T_2 \sin 60° = 0 \qquad \text{.... (i)}$$

and $\quad \sum F_y = 0$, or $T_1 \cos 45° + T_2 \cos 60° = 250$ .... (ii)

From (i), we have $T_2 = \dfrac{T_1 \sin 45°}{\sin 60°}$

Now from (ii), $T_1 \cos 45 + \dfrac{T_1 \sin 45°}{\sin 60°} \times \cos 60° = 250$

or $\quad \dfrac{T_1}{\sqrt{2}} + \dfrac{T_1}{\sqrt{2}} \times \dfrac{1}{\sqrt{3}} = 250$ or $T_1 = 224.4 \, N$

and $\quad T_2 = \dfrac{T_1 \sin 45°}{\sin 60°} = \dfrac{224.4 \times \left(\dfrac{1}{\sqrt{2}}\right)}{\left(\dfrac{\sqrt{3}}{2}\right)} = 183.01$ N **Ans.**

Consider the equilibrium of point B :

$$\sum F_x = 0 \text{ ; or } T_2 \sin 60° + T_3 \sin 30° - T_4 = 0 \quad \text{.... (i)}$$

and $\quad \sum F_y = 0$; or $T_3 \cos 30° - T_2 \cos 60° - 200 = 0$ .... (ii)

From (ii), $T_3 \cos 30° - 183.01 \times \dfrac{1}{2} - 200 = 0$

or $\quad T_3 = 336.60$ N

From equation (i), $T_4 = 255.81$ N . **Ans.**

In Chapter Exercise 5.3

1. Ten one rupee coins are put on top of each other on a table. Each coin has a mass m. Give the magnitude and direction of (a) the force on the 7th coin (counted from the bottom) due to all the coins on its top, (b) the force on the 7th coin by the 8th coin and (c) the reaction of the 6th coin on the 7th coin. **[NCERT]** *Ans.* **(a) 3 mg (b) 3 mg (c) –4 mg**

2. There are four forces acting at a point P produced by strings as shown in figure, which is at rest. Find the forces F_1 and F_2?

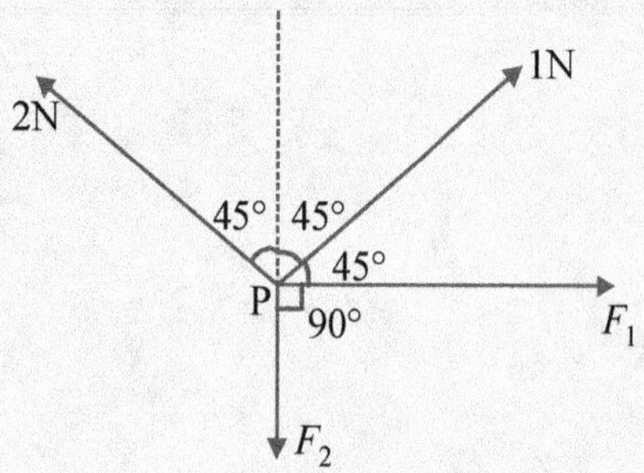

Ans. **F_1 = 0.707 N, F_2 = 2.121 N**

3. A noose is placed around a log and used to pull it with a force F. How will the tension of the ropes forming the loop depend on the magnitude of the angle α ? In what conditions will the tension of the rope in the sections *AB* and *AC* be larger than in the section *AD*?

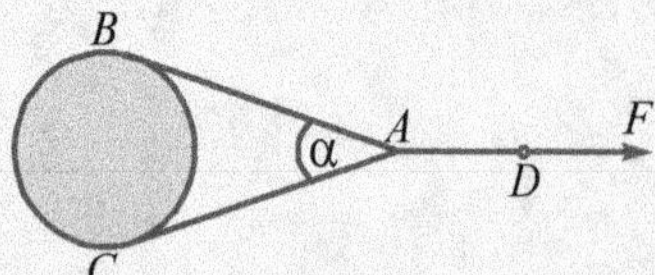

Ans. $T = \dfrac{F}{2\cos\dfrac{\alpha}{2}},\ \alpha > 120°.$

4. Two identical, uniform, frictionless spheres, each of weight W, rest in a rigid rectangular container as shown in figure, find, in terms of W, the forces acting on the spheres due to (a) the container surfaces and (b) one another, if the line of centres of the spheres makes an angle of 45° with the horizontal.

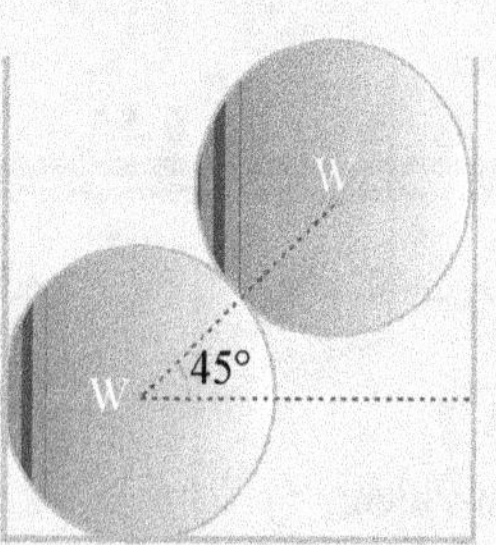

Ans. **(a) Bottom: 2W; side; W (b) $\sqrt{2}W$.**

5. Two identical rollers each of weight W = 500 N are supported by an inclined plane and a vertical wall as shown in fig. Assuming smooth surfaces find the reactions induced at the points of supports A, B and C.

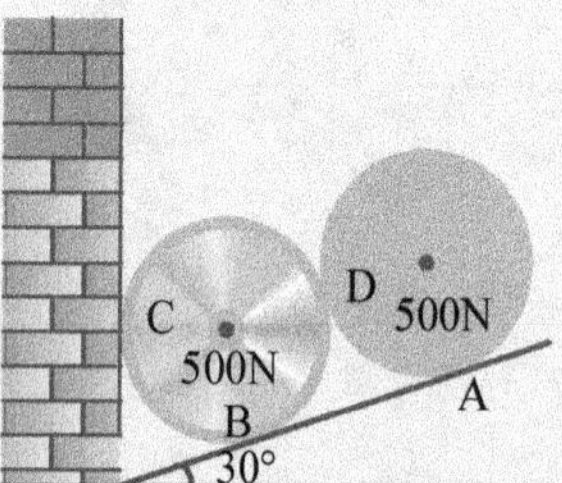

Ans. $F_A = 250\sqrt{3}\text{N}$, $F_B = \dfrac{1250}{\sqrt{3}}\text{N}$ and $F_C = \dfrac{1000}{\sqrt{3}}\text{N}$

5.11 FRICTION

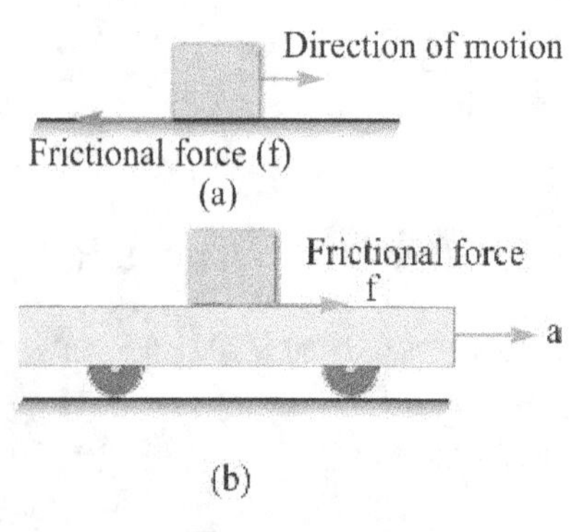

Figure. **5.59**

1. Consider a block placed on a horizontal floor and give an initial push (figure a). The block will stop after travelling some distance. According to Newton's second law, a retarding force must be acting on the block. This opposing force is called **frictional force**. The frictional force always acts along tangential direction at the point of contact and in opposite direction to the direction of relative motion of the body.

2. Now consider a block placed at rest in an accelerating cart as shown in figure (b). The block in fact accelerating along with the cart. Which force causes the acceleration of the block? It is clear that the only force in the horizontal direction is the frictional force. If there were no friction, the surface of the cart would slip and the block would remain at its initial position by inertia. Thus we can say that friction sometimes require to start the motion. Its direction may be backward or forward of the motion of the body.

Friction can be defined as a force which opposes the relative motion between surfaces in contact.

Contact Force : The resultant force at the point of contact of two bodies is called contact force.

1. Consider a block s placed on a rough surface, figure (a). The contact force on it is equal to; $R = N = Mg$.

2. Now consider the same block is acted by a horizontal force F. Let f be the frictional force on the block, then contact force

$$R = \sqrt{N^2 + f^2} = \sqrt{(Mg)^2 + f^2} \ .$$

Thus the component of the contact force R perpendicular to the contact surface is called normal force and the component parallel to the contact surface is called frictional force.

Origin of friction : The frictional force arises due to molecular interactions between the surfaces at the points of actual contact. When two bodies are placed one over the other, the actual area of contact is much smaller than the total surface area of bodies (see *fig.* 5.61). The molecular forces starts operating at the actual points of contacts of the surfaces. Molecular bonds are formed at these contact points. When one body is pulled over the other, these bonds are broken, and the material get deformed and new bonds are formed. The local deformation sends vibrations into the bodies. These vibrations ultimately damp out and the energy of vibrations appears as heat. Hence, to start or to carry-on the motion, there is need of a force.

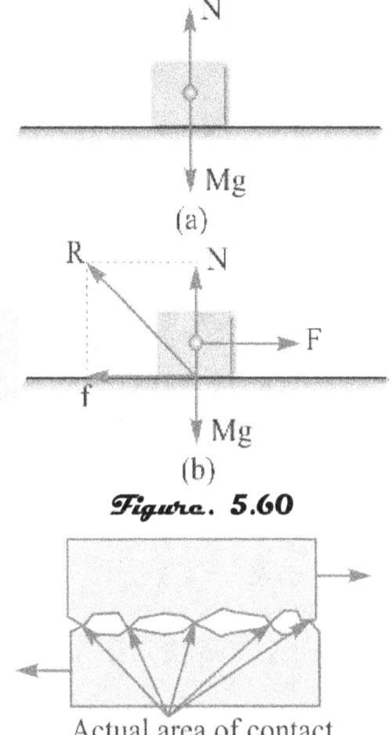
(a)

(b)

Figure. **5.60**

Actual area of contact

Figure. **5.61**

5.12 STATIC AND KINETIC FRICTION

Experiment

(i) Consider a block placed on a table, and a small force F is acted on it. The block does not move. It indicates that the frictional force f_s starts acting in opposite direction of applied force and its magnitude is equal to F figure (b). For the equilibrium of the block, we can write

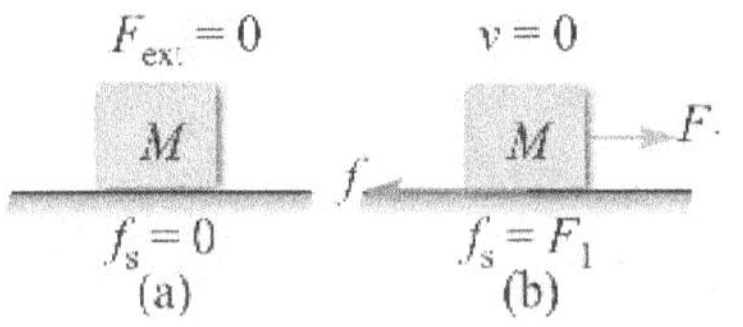

$F_{ex.} = 0$ $v = 0$

M $f_s = 0$ (a) f M — $F.$ $f_s = F_1$ (b)

$$F - f_s = 0 \quad \text{or} \quad \frac{f_s}{F} = 1$$
$$= \tan 45°$$

(ii) As the applied force increases the frictional force also increases. When the applied force is increased beyond a certain limit (f_{lim}), the block begins to move. The value of frictional force at this stage is called *limiting friction* f_{lim} (figure c).

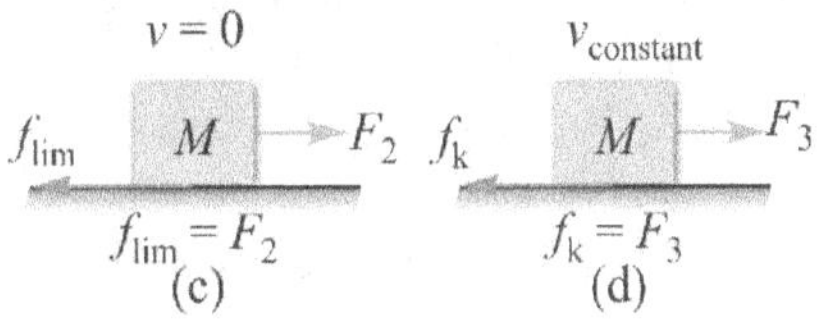

$v = 0$ $v_{constant}$

f_{lim} M — F_2 f_k M — F_3 $f_{lim} = F_2$ (c) $f_k = F_3$ (d)

Figure. **5.62**

(iii) Once the motion started, the smaller force is now necessary to keep the motion. And thus frictional force decreases. The force of friction when body is in state of motion over the surface is called *kinetic or dynamic friction* (figure d).

From the experiment it can be concluded that :

1. When a body placed on a surface attempts to slide by a force $\vec{F}$ and body does not move. Then the frictional force f_s is equal in magnitude of $\vec{F}$ and directed opposite of $\vec{F}$.

2. The maximum value of f_s is called limiting friction and is equal to

$$f_{lim} = \mu_s N \qquad \text{...(i)}$$

where μ_s is the coefficient of static friction, and N is the magnitude of the normal force.

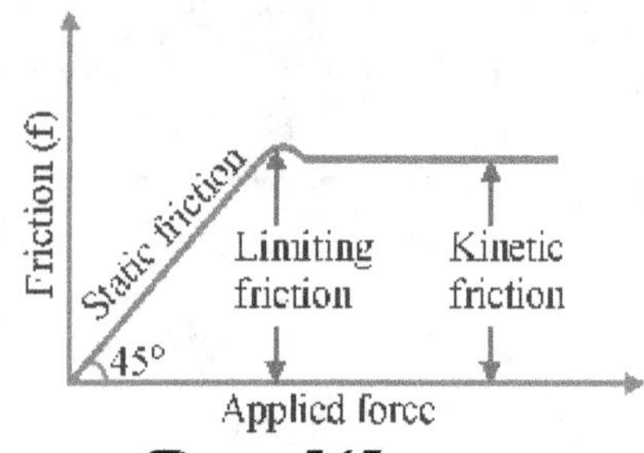

Figure. 5.63

Variation of frictional force with the applied force

3. When body begins to slide along the surface, the magnitude of the frictional force **decreases to a value** f_k which is equal to

$$f_k = \mu_k N \qquad \qquad ...(ii)$$

where μ_k is the coefficient of kinetic friction.

It is clear from above discussion that ;

$$f_k \lesseqgtr f_s \quad \text{but} \quad f_k < f_{\text{lim}}$$

More about frictional force

About static friction

(i) The limiting friction depends on the materials of the surfaces in contact and their state of polish.

(ii) The magnitude of static friction is independent of the apparent area of contact so long as the normal reaction remains the same.

(iii) The limiting friction is directly proportional to the magnitude of the normal reaction between the two surfaces. i.e., $f_{\text{lim}} = \mu_s N$

$\therefore$ We can write, $\qquad \mu_s = \dfrac{f_{\text{lim}}}{N}$

About kinetic friction

(i) The kinetic friction depends on the materials of the surface in contact.

(ii) It is also independent of apparent area of contact as long as the magnitude of normal reaction remains the same.

(iii) Kinetic friction is almost independent of the velocity, provided the velocity is not too large not too small.

(iv) The kinetic friction is directly proportional to the magnitude of the normal reaction between the surfaces. i.e., $\qquad f_k = \mu_k N$

$\therefore$ We can write, $\qquad \mu_k = \dfrac{f_k}{N}$

There are two types of kinetic friction :

(i) **Sliding friction :** The force of friction when one body slides over the surface of the another body is called sliding friction.

(ii) **Rolling friction :** When a wheel rolls without slipping over a horizontal surface, there is no relative motion of the point of contact of the wheel with respect to the plane. Theoretically for a rolling wheel the frictional force is zero. This can only possible when bodies in contact are perfectly rigid and contact of wheel with the surface is made only at a point. But in practice no material body is perfectly rigid and therefore bodies get deformed when they pressed each other. The actual area of their contact no remain a point. And thus a small amount of friction starts acting between the body and the surface. Here frictional force is called rolling friction. It is clear from above discussion that rolling friction is very much smaller than sliding friction.

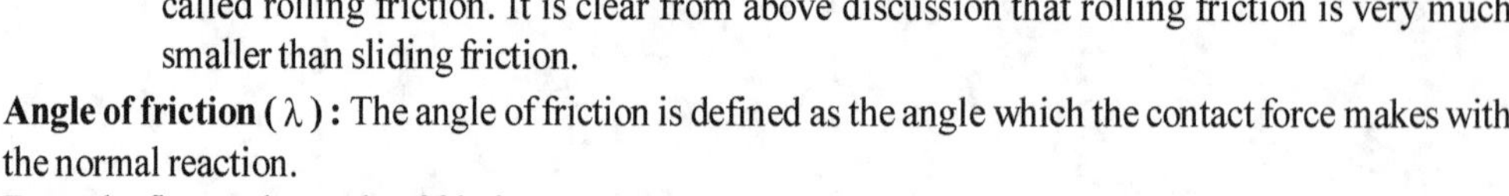

(a) Sliding of block   (b) Rolling of wheel

Figure. 5.64

Angle of friction (λ) : The angle of friction is defined as the angle which the contact force makes with the normal reaction.

From the figure, the angle of friction

$$\tan \lambda = \frac{f}{N}.$$

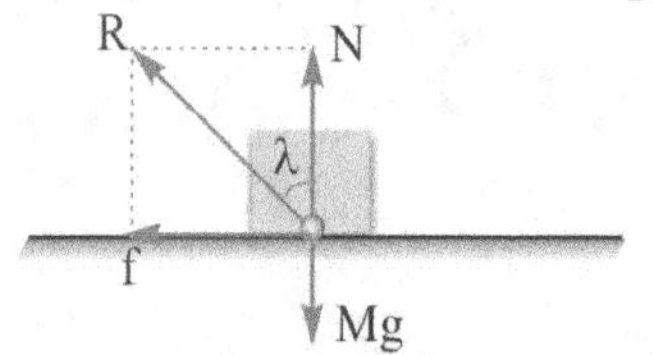

Figure. 5.65

We have

$$\mu = \frac{f}{N}$$

$$\therefore \qquad \mu = \tan \lambda$$

Contact force (R) : The value of contact force R can be ;

$$N \le R \le \sqrt{N^2 + (\mu_s N)^2}$$

or $\quad N \le R \le N\sqrt{1 + \mu_s^2}.$

About coefficient of friction :

As
$$f_k < f_{\lim} \quad \text{or} \quad \mu_k N < \mu_s N$$

$$\therefore \qquad \mu_k < \mu_s .$$

The theoretical value of μ can be 0 to infinite. But practical value; $0 < \mu \leq 1.6$.

More about rolling friction

Let us consider the situation where a wheel moves without slipping on a horizontal surface. Experiment shows that a horizontal force P is required to maintain uniform motion, so some sort of resistance must be present. We can understand this resistance by making a deformation in the surface as shown in *fig.* 5.66. In order to develope a resistance to motion, it is clear that normal force N must oriented at some angle ϕ in the direction of motion. As the wheel is moving with constant velocity, so $P = N \sin \phi$

From the figure $\sin \phi = \dfrac{a}{r}$.

$\therefore$ Rolling resistance, $f = P = N \sin \phi$

$$= N \frac{a}{r} .$$

The distance 'a' in this equation is called coefficient of rolling resistance.

Angle of repose (α) : It is the angle that an inclined plane makes with the horizontal when a body placed on it is in limiting equilibrium.

Let us consider a block is placed on a rough inclined plane of inclination α. If block is just about to slide, then we have

$$f_{\lim} = Mg \sin \alpha \qquad \text{...(i)}$$
$$\text{and} \qquad N = Mg \cos \alpha \qquad \text{...(ii)}$$

Dividing equation (i) by (ii), we get

$$\frac{f_{\lim}}{N} = \tan \alpha$$

Also we have, $\mu_s = \dfrac{f_{\lim}}{N}$

$$\therefore \mu_s = \tan \alpha$$

As $\mu_s = \tan \lambda$

$$\therefore \alpha = \lambda .$$

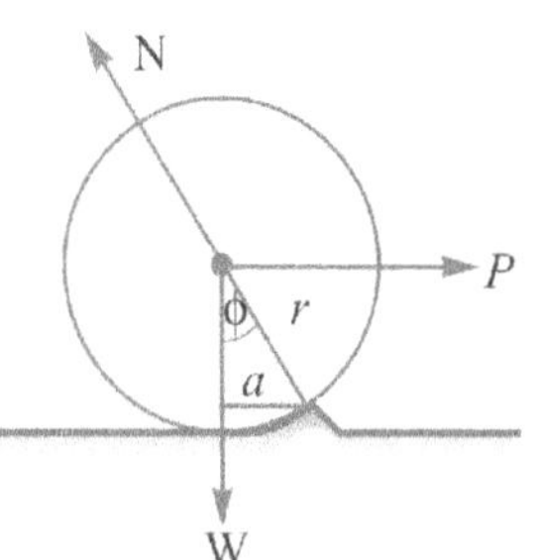

Figure. **5.66**

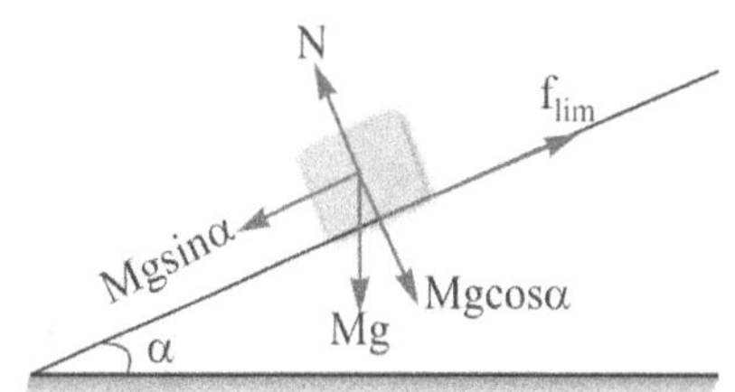

Figure. **5.67**

Pull is easier than push

Push : Consider a block of mass m placed on a rough horizontal surface. The coefficient of static friction between the block and surface is μ. Let a push force F is applied at an angle θ with the horizontal.

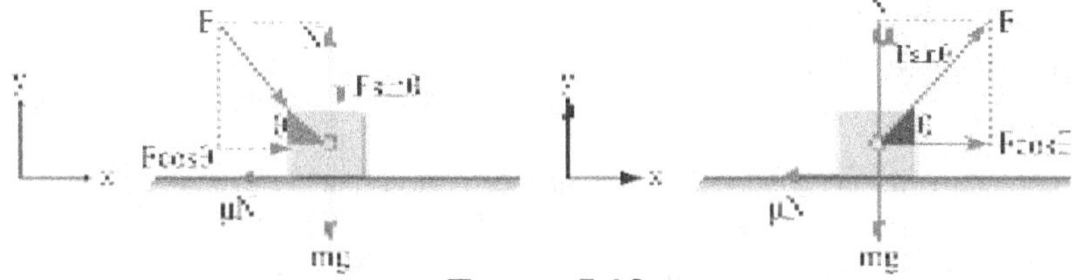

Figure. **5.68**

As the block is in equilibrium along y-axis, so we have

$$\sum F_y = 0 ;$$

or
$$N = mg + F \sin \theta .$$

To just move the block along x-axis, we have

$$F \cos \theta = \mu N = \mu (mg + F \sin \theta)$$

or
$$F = \frac{\mu mg}{\cos \theta - \mu \sin \theta} . \qquad \text{...(i)}$$

Pull : Along y-axis we have;

$$\sum F_y = 0 \ ;$$

$\therefore$ $$N = mg - F\sin\theta$$

To just move the block along x-axis, we have

$$F\cos\theta = \mu N = \mu\,(mg - F\sin\theta\,)$$

or $$F = \left(\frac{\mu mg}{\cos\theta + \mu\sin\theta}\right). \qquad ...(ii)$$

It is clear from above discussion that pull force is smaller than push force.

Minimum value of pull force :

The pull force to be minimum, $\dfrac{dF}{d\theta} = 0$

or $$\frac{d}{d\theta}\left[\frac{\mu mg}{\cos\theta + \mu\sin\theta}\right] = 0$$

or $$-\sin\theta + \mu\cos\theta = 0$$

or $$\mu = \tan\theta \quad \text{or} \quad \theta = \tan^{-1}(\mu)$$

Substituting this value in equation (ii), we get

$$F_{min} = \frac{\tan\theta\ mg}{\cos\theta + \tan\theta\sin\theta}$$

or $$F_{min} = mg\sin\theta \ .$$

FORMULAE USED

1. Limiting friction, $f_{lim} = \mu_s N$.
2. Kinetic friction, $f_k = \mu_k N$.
3. Static friction, $f_s \le f_{lim.}$
4. Kinetic friction, $f_x < f_{lim}$
5. If λ is the angle of friction, then $\mu = \tan\lambda$
6. Angle of repose, $\tan\phi = \mu_s$.
7. Angle of repose = angle of friction.

8. For body moving on rough horizontal surface retardation, $a = \dfrac{f}{m} = \dfrac{\mu mg}{m} = \mu g$.

9. For a body placed on a rough inclined plane of inclination θ,
$$N = mg\cos\theta,$$
and friction, $f = \mu mg\cos\theta$

10. When body moves down on rough inclined plane, acceleration,
$$a = (\sin\theta - \mu_k\cos\theta)g$$

11. When body moves up on rough inclined plane, retardation, $a = (\sin\theta + \mu_k\cos\theta)g$.

12. Contact force, $R = Mg\sqrt{1+\mu_s^2}$

EXAMPLES BASED ON FRICTION

Example 33. A block of mass 2 kg is placed on the floor. The coefficient of static friction is 0.4. A force of 2.5 N is applied on the block as shown in *fig.* 5.69. Calculate the force of friction between the block and the floor.

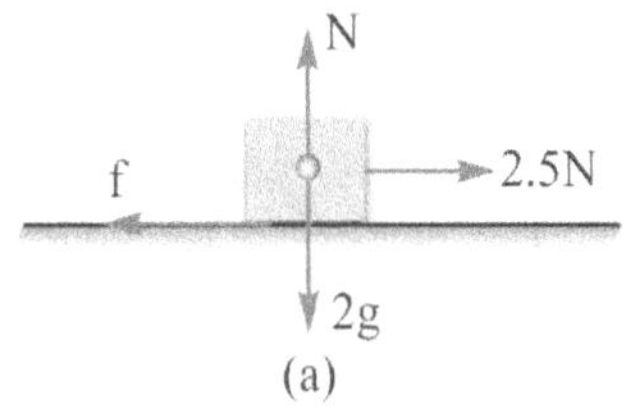

Figure. **5.69**

Sol. The value of limiting friction, $f_{\text{lim}} = \mu_s N$

$$= 0.4 \times 2\,g$$
$$= 0.4 \times 2 \times 9.8 = 7.84 \text{ N}$$

As the applied force of magnitude 2.5 N which is less than the limiting friction (7.84 N), so the block will not move. Thus, $F_{\text{net}} = 0$.

Let f is the frictional force generated between the block and the floor, then we have

$$2.5 - f = 0 \quad \text{or} \quad f = 2.5 \text{ N}. \qquad \textit{Ans.}$$

Example 34. Find the frictional force on 2 kg block in the arrangement shown in *fig.* 5.70.

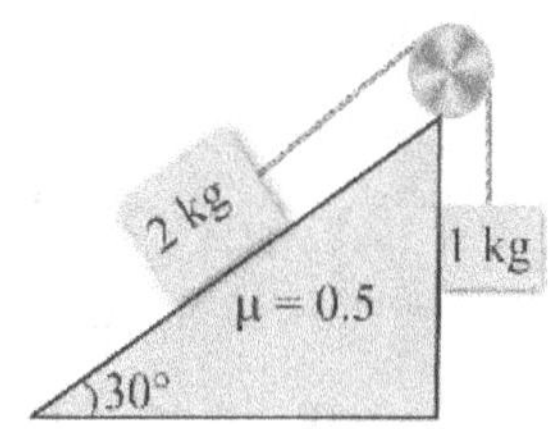

Figure. **5.70**

Sol. Suppose the inclined plane is smooth. The acceleration of 2 kg block

$$a = \frac{2g\sin 30° - 1g}{2 + 1} = 0.$$

The system of two blocks is in equilibrium on smooth inclined plane. Therefore friction will not generate.

Example 35. *Fig.* 5.71 shows a man standing stationary with respect to a horizontal conveyor belt that is accelerating with 1 m/s². What is the net force on the man ? If the coefficient of static friction between the man's shoes and the belt is 0.2, upto what acceleration of the belt can continue to be stationary relative to the belt ? Mass of the man = 65 kg. **[NCERT]**

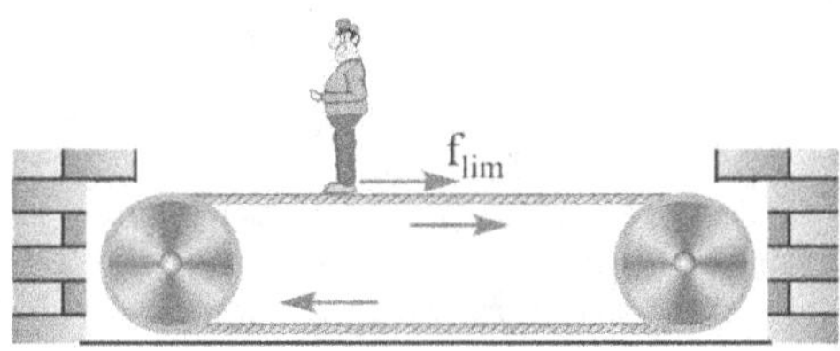

Figure. **5.71**

Sol. As the man is stationary relative to belt,

the acceleration of man = acceleration of belt
$$= 1 \text{ m/s}^2.$$

Mass of the man, $M = 65$ kg.

Net force on the man $= M a = 65 \times 1 = 65$ N.

The maximum friction available $= \mu_s N$

or $\qquad f_{\text{max}} = 0.2 \times 65\,g$

The acceleration of the man, $a = \dfrac{f_{\text{max}}}{m}$

$$= \frac{0.2 \times 65 g}{65} = 0.2 g$$
$$= 0.2 \times 9.8 = 1.96 \text{ m/s}^2$$

Example 36. A block of mass 4 kg is placed on another block of mass 5 kg, and the block *B* rests on a smooth horizontal table. For sliding the block *A* on *B*, a horizontal force 12 N is required to be applied on it. How much maximum horizontal force can be applied on *B* so that both *A* and *B* move together? Also find out the acceleration produced by this force.

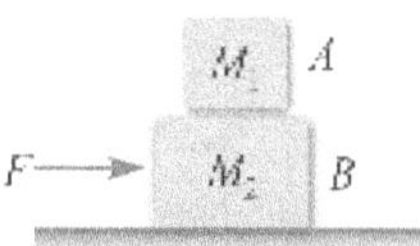

Figure. **5.72**

Sol. As 12N force is needed to slide the block A over B, so limiting friction on block A = 12 N.

The acceleration provided to block A by this frictional force,

$$a = \frac{12}{4} = 3 \text{ m/s}^2$$

Now force required to move block together with block A

$$F = (4 + 5) \times a = 9 \times 3 = 27 \text{ N}. \qquad \textit{Ans.}$$

Example 37. The rear side of a truck is open and a box of 40 kg mass is placed 5 m away from the open end as shown in *figure* 5.73. The coefficient of friction between the box and the surface is 0.15. On a straight road, the truck starts from rest and accelerates with 2 m/s². At what distance from the starting point does the box fall off the truck ? Ignore the size of the box.

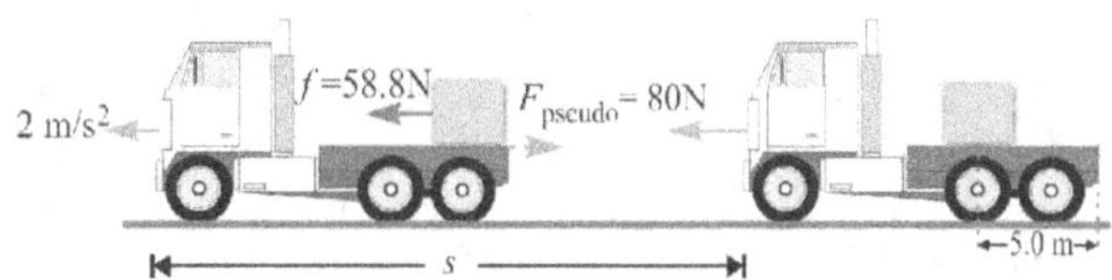

Figure. **5.73**

Sol. Because of the acceleration of the truck the pseudo force on the box $= m \times a = 40 \times 2 = 80$ N.

This force acts opposite to the acceleration of the truck.

The frictional force on the truck which acts in forward direction

$$f_k = \mu N = 0.15 \times 40\,g = 58.8 \text{ N}.$$

Since pseudo force is greater than frictional force, so block will accelerate in backward direction relative to truck with a magnitude

$$a = \frac{80 - 58.8}{40} = 0.53 \text{ m/s}^2.$$

The time taken by box to cover the distance 5 m

$$s = 0 + \frac{1}{2} at^2$$

or

$$5 = \frac{1}{2} \times 0.53 \times t^2$$

$$\therefore \qquad t = 4.34 \text{ s}.$$

The distance travelled by truck in this duration

$$s = 0 + \frac{1}{2} \times 2 \, (4.34)^2 = 18.87 \text{ m.} \textbf{\textit{Ans.}}$$

Example 38. Prism 1 and bar 2 of mass m placed on it gets a horizontal acceleration a directed towards the left. At what maximum value of this acceleration will the bar be still stationary relative to the prism, if the coefficient of friction between them $\mu < \cot \alpha$?

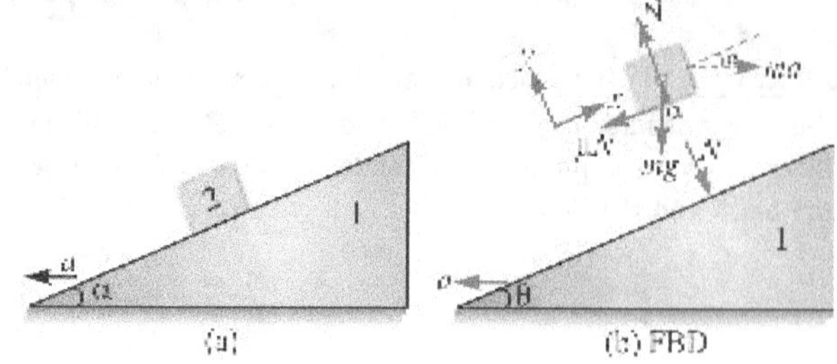

Figure. 5.74

Sol. For maximum value of acceleration of prism, the tendency of the bar is sliding up the inclined plane, and therefore frictional force on the bar acts down the inclined plane.

For the equilibrium of bar along y-axis, we have

$$\sum F_y = 0$$

or $\qquad N = mg \cos \alpha + ma \sin \alpha \qquad$ ...(i)

For the equilibrium of the bar relative to prism along x-axis, we have

$$\sum F_x = 0$$

or $\quad mg \sin \alpha + \mu N = ma \cos \alpha \qquad$ ...(ii)

Solving equations (i) and (ii), we get

$$a = \left[\frac{g(1 + \mu \cot \alpha)}{\cot \alpha - \mu} \right]. \qquad \textbf{\textit{Ans.}}$$

In Chapter Exercise 5.4

1. Block A in figure weighs 4N and block B weighs 8N. The coefficient of sliding friction between all surfaces is 0.25. Find the force P necessary to drag block B to the left at constant speed.
   (a) If A rests on B and moves with it.
   (b) If A is held at rest
   (c) If A and B are connected by a light flexible cord passing around a fixed frictionless pulley.

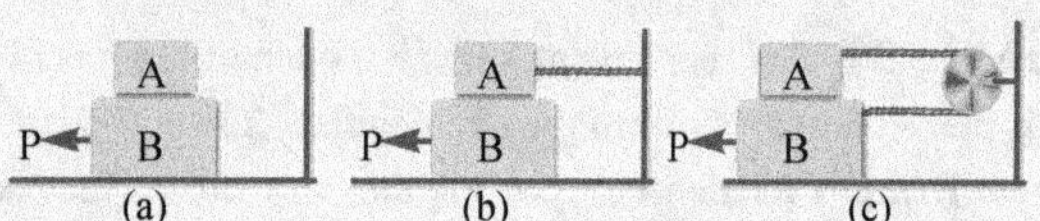

Ans. **(a) 3.00N (b) 4.00N (c) 5.00 N.**

2. In figure A is 10 kg block and B is a 5 kg block, (a) determine the minimum mass of C which must be placed on A to prevent it from sliding. If coefficient of static friction μ_s between A and the table is 0.25 (b) the block C is suddenly lifted off A, what is the acceleration of block A, if the coefficient of kinetic friction between A and the table is 0.20?

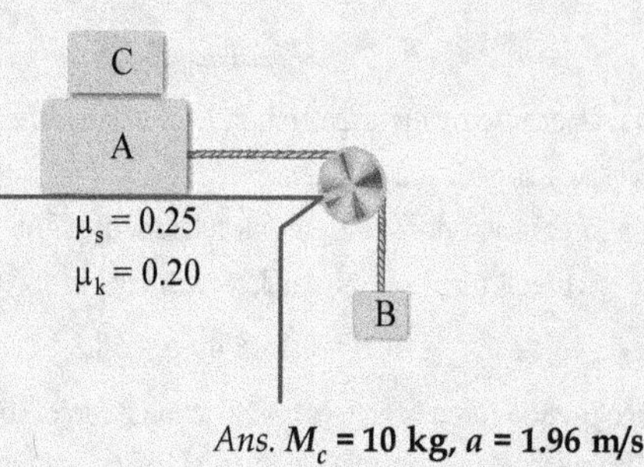

Ans. M_c = **10 kg**, a = **1.96 m/s²..**

3. A string is connected to block of mass $m = 1.2$ kg placed over rough table surface as shown in figure. Calculate minimum vertical force F (in Newton) required to move the block. Pulley string are ideal and coefficient of friction between block and table surface is $\mu = \dfrac{1}{2}$. Take g = 10 m/s².

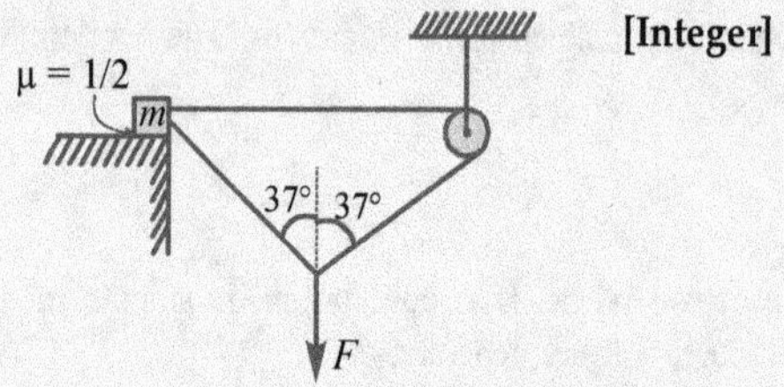

[Integer]

Ans. 8

4. Find the mass of the hanging block which will prevent the smaller block from slipping over the triangular block. All the surfaces are frictionless and the strings and the pulleys are light. **Ans. 2 kg**
   Given $m = M$ = 1kg; $\cot \theta$ = 2. **[Integer]**

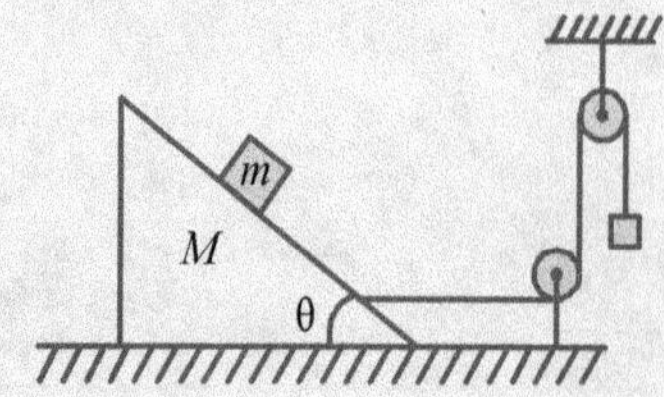

5. In the arrangement the masses of bodies are equal to m_0, m_1, and m_2, the masses of the pulley and the threads are negligible, and there is no friction in the pulley. Find the acceleration 'a' with which the body m_0 comes down, and the tension of the thread binding together the bodies m_1 and m_2, if the coefficient of friction between the bodies and the horizontal surface is equal to μ. Consider possible cases.

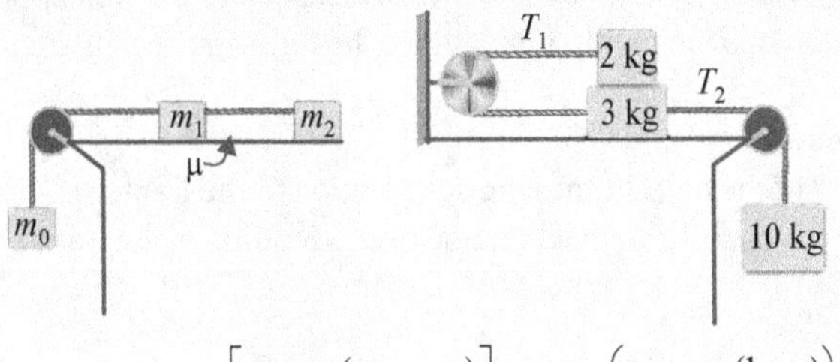

$$\text{Ans. } a = \left[\frac{m_0 - \mu(m_1 + m_2)}{m_0 + m_1 + m_2}\right] g \; ; \; T = \left(\frac{m_0 m_2 g(1+\mu)}{m_0 + m_1 + m_2}\right).$$

6. In the figure coefficient of kinetic friction between the block 3 kg and 2kg is $\mu = 0.3$. The horizontal table surface is smooth. Find
(i) the acceleration of masses
(ii) tensions in the strings
Ans. **(i) 5.75 m/s^2 (ii)** $T_1 = 17.38$ N, $T_2 = 40.5$ N

7. A heavy homogeneous sphere is suspended by a light string, one end of which is attached to a vertical wall and the other, to a point on the vertical line through the centre of sphere as shown in figure. What should be the coefficient of friction between the sphere and the wall for the sphere to remain in equilibrium ?

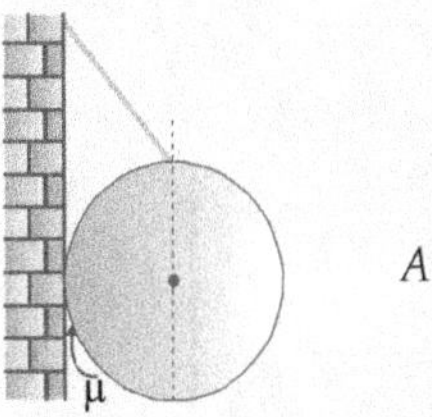

Ans. $\mu \geq 1.$

8. A short, right circular cylinder of weight W rests in a horizontal, V-shaped notch of angle 2α as shown in figure. If the coefficient of friction is μ, find the horizontal force parallel to the axis necessary for slipping to occur.

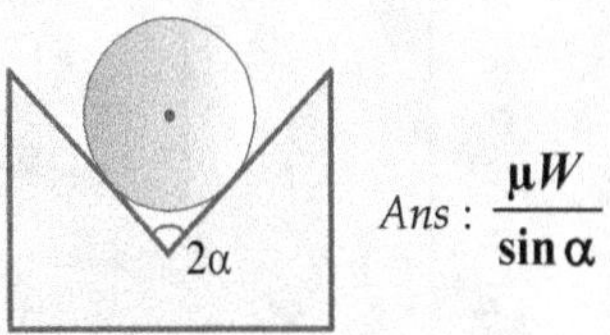

Ans : $\dfrac{\mu W}{\sin \alpha}.$

5.13   INERTIAL AND NON-INERTIAL FRAME OF REFERENCE

An inertial frame of reference is one in which Newton's first law holds good. Thus a frame, either at rest or moving with constnt velocity will be an inertial frame. All frames moving with uniform velocity relative to an inertial frame are also inertial. Frame of reference which hs acceleration or rotation with respect to an inertial frame is non-inertial.

Our frame of referenec : Because of rotation of earth about its axis and revolution revolution around sun, our frame of reference is non-inertial. But acceleration due to these two motions is negligibly small in comparison to acceleration due to gravity and therefore can be neglected. For most laboratory phenomenon, it can be assumed that our frame of reference is inertial.

Working in non-inertial frame : Pseudo force

Consider a particle, which is at rest in an inertial fram S_1. Consider another frame S_2 which is accelerating towards right with an acceleration a_0 with respect to an inertial frame.

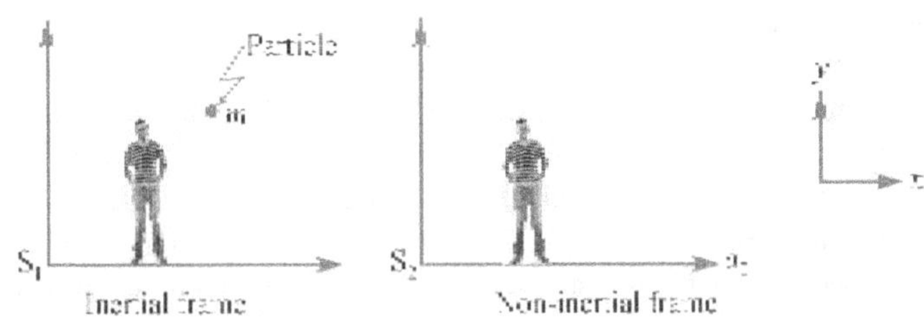

In frame S_1, the acceleration of particle is zero, so from Newton's second law, we can write

$$\vec{F} = m\vec{a} = m \times 0 = 0$$

In frame S_2, the acceleration of particle is

$$\left[\vec{a}_{particle}\right]_{S_2} = \left[\vec{a}_{particle}\right]_{S_1} - \left[\vec{a}_{frame\, s_2}\right]_{S_1}$$

$$= 0 - a_0 \hat{i}$$

$$= -a_0 \hat{i}$$

Now from Newton's second law, we can write

$$\left[\vec{\mathbf{F}}_{particle}\right]_{s_2} = m\left[\vec{\mathbf{a}}_{particle}\right]_{s_2}$$

$$= m\left(-a_0\hat{\mathbf{i}}\right)$$

$$= -ma_0\hat{\mathbf{i}}.$$

This force actually not acting on the particle, but arises due to the acceleration of the frame. So this force is called **pseudo or fictious force**. Regarding with pseudo force the following points should be noted :

(i)   It should be taken in non-inertial frame only.

(ii)   Its magnitude is equal to the mass of the object times the acceleration of the frame.

(iii)   The direction of pseudo force will be opposite to the direction of acceleration of the frame. Thus

$$\vec{\mathbf{F}}_{pseudo} = -m\vec{\mathbf{a}}_0.$$

Newton's second law in non-inertial frame

In non-inertial frame, Newton's second law may be written as follows :

$$\vec{\mathbf{F}}_{real} + \vec{\mathbf{F}}_{pseudo} = m\vec{\mathbf{a}}.$$

Here $\vec{\mathbf{a}}$ is the acceleration of the object in non-inertial frame. Above equation can also be written as :

$$\left[\vec{\mathbf{F}}_{net}\right]_{real\,and\,pseudo} = m\vec{\mathbf{a}}.$$

Working in non-inertial frame

(1)   To an object moving in non-inertial frame, apply pseudo force of magnitude ma_0 in the direction opposite of the direction of acceleration of the frame. Thereafter mark all the real forces acting on the object.

(2)   Now find net of the forces of specific direction.

Then use Newton's second law as :

$$\left[\vec{\mathbf{F}}_{net}\right]_{real\,and\,pseudo} = m\vec{\mathbf{a}}.$$

5.14 FORCES IN NATURE

At the present stage of our understanding, we know about four fundamental forces in nature. These are :

1.   **Gravitational force :** It is the force of mutual attraction between the objects by virtue of their masses. It is a universal force. The gravitational force acts over long distances and does not need any intervening medium. Compared to other fundamental forces, gravitational force is the weakest force of nature.

2.   **Electromagnetic force :** Electromagnetic force is the force between the objects due to charges on them. It may be attractive or repulsive. It acts over long distances and does not need any intervening medium. It is very much stronger than gravitational force. The forces spring, tension or compression, friction are electromagnetic in nature.

3.   **The strong nuclear force :** The strong nuclear force binds protons and neutrons in nucleus. It does not depend on charge and acts equally between a proton and a proton, a neutron and a neutron, and a proton and a neutron. Electron does not experience this force. It acts for very short distance, order of 10^{-15} m.

4.   **The weak nuclear force :** The weak nuclear force appears only in certain nuclear process such as the β-decay of a nucleus. The weak nuclear force is not as weak as gravitational force, but much weaker than strong nuclear force. The range of weak nuclear force is very small, of the order of 10^{-15} m.

Each fundamental force is thought to arise from the exchange of its characteristic particles.

(i)   The gravitational force is thought to be caused due to exchange of an undetected particles called **gravitons.**

(ii)   Electromagnetic force arises due to the exchange of **photons** between the charged particles.

(iii) The strong nuclear force arises from the exchange of **mesons** (π^-).

(iv)   Weak nuclear force arises from the exchange of **bosons** (W^-).

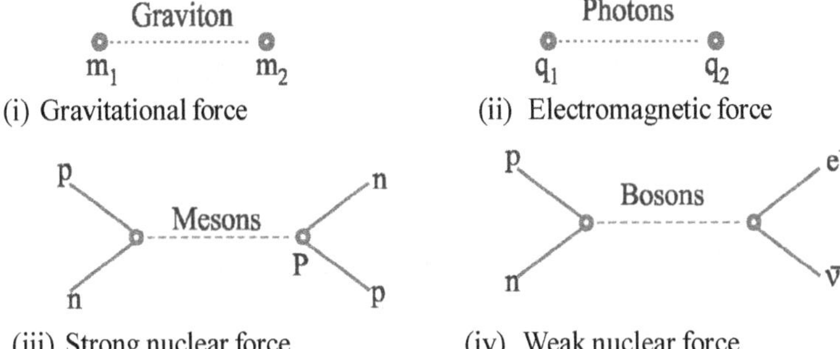

Figure. 5.75

EXAMPLES FOR JEE-(MAIN AND ADVANCED)

Example 1.   A man of mass 70 kg is running on a railroad car, which is going towards right with an acceleration of 2 m/s². The acceleration of man with respect to car is 3 m/s². Find the force acting on the man.

Sol. Solution in inertial frame :

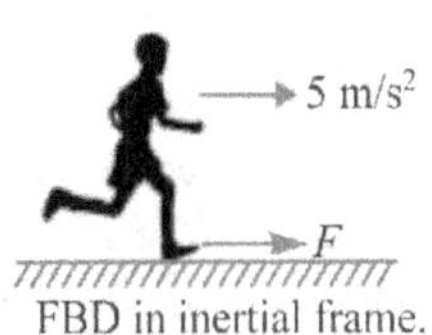

Figure. 5.76

The acceleration of the man in inertial frame is

$$\vec{a} = \left[\vec{a}_{man}\right]_{car} + \left[\vec{a}_{car}\right]_{inertial\ frame}$$

or $a = 3 + 2$
$$= 5\ \text{m/s}^2.$$

From Newton's second law

$$\vec{F} = m\vec{a}$$

or $F = 70 \times 5 = 350$ N.   *Ans.*

Solution in non-inertial frame :

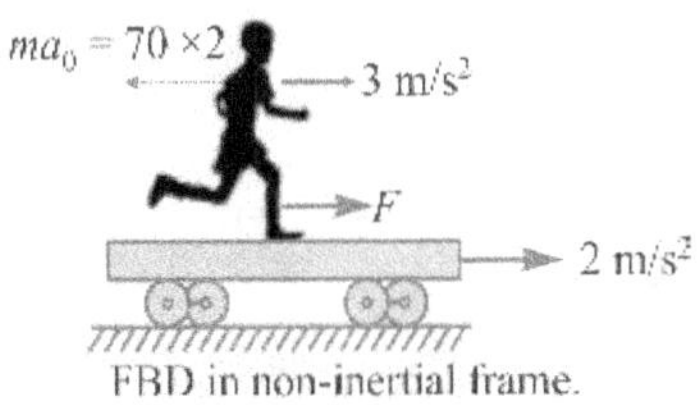

Figure. 5.77

The acceleration of the man with respect to car is 2 m/s².
Now from Newton's second law, we can write,

$$F - 70 \times 2 = 70 \times 3$$
$$\therefore \qquad F = 350\ \text{N} \qquad\qquad\qquad\qquad Ans.$$

Example 2. A block of mass m is placed on a smooth wedge of inclination θ. The whole system is accelerated horizontally so that the block does not slip on the wedge. Determine the force exerted by the wedge on the block.

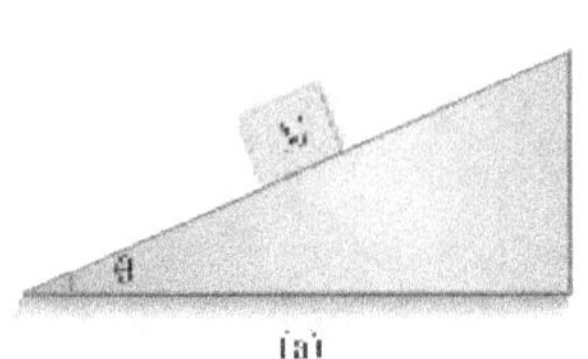

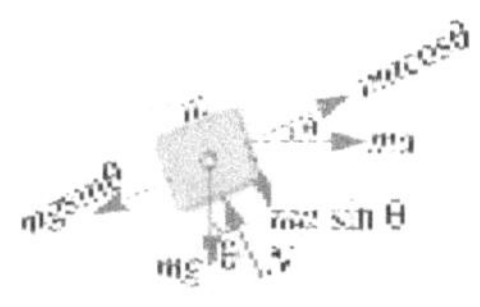

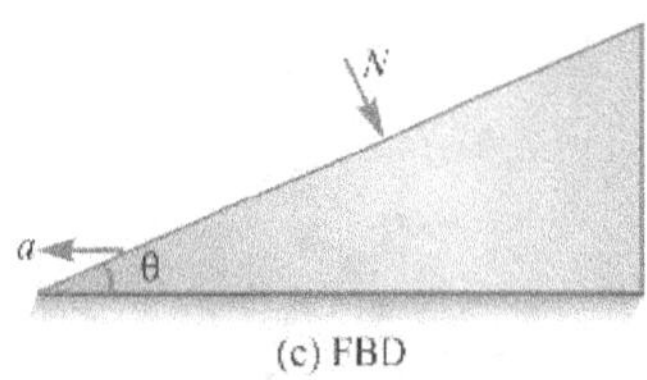

Figure. 5.78

Sol. Let the wedge is accelerated towards left with an acceleration 'a'. The *FBD* of the block in the frame from is shown in figure. The block remains at rest with respect to wedge, so along the inclined plane, we have

$$mg \sin\theta - ma \cos\theta = 0$$

or $a = g \tan\theta .$ ...(i)

Perpendicular to the inclined plane, the block is also at rest, therefore

$$N = mg \cos\theta + ma \sin\theta$$

$$= mg \cos\theta + m\,(g \tan\theta)\sin\theta = \frac{mg}{\cos\theta}.$$

Thus force exerted by the wedge on the block

$$= \frac{mg}{\cos\theta} \qquad\qquad Ans.$$

Example 3. Consider a simple pendulum is hanging in a accelerated railroad car. Pendulum makes an angle θ with the vertical. Find valeu of θ.

In inertial frame: To an observer on the ground, the forces on the bob of pendulum are;

Sol.

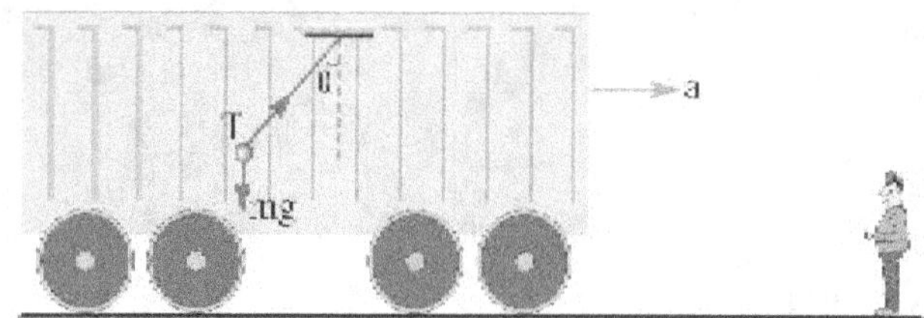

Figure. 5.79

(i)   Weight of bob, mg acts vertically downward.

(ii)   Tension in the string T.

Thus for the motion of bob relative to an observer on the ground,

$$T \sin\theta = ma, \qquad \ldots(i)$$

$$\text{and} \qquad T \cos\theta = mg. \qquad \ldots(ii)$$

Dividing equation (i) by (ii), we get

$$\tan\theta = \frac{a}{g}.$$

In non-inertial frame : To an observer inside the railroad car, the forces on the bob are;

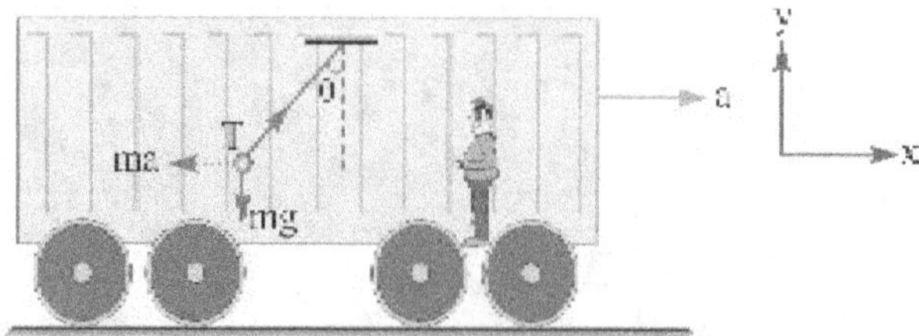

Figure. 5.80

(i)   Weight of bob, mg acts vertically downward.
(ii)   Tension in the string T and
(iii) Pseudo force ma opposite of the acceleration of car.
      As bob is stationary relative to the observer inside car, so

$$\sum F_x = 0 \; ;$$

or $T \sin\theta - ma = 0$

$\therefore \qquad T \sin\theta = ma \qquad \ldots(i)$

and $\qquad \sum F_y = 0$

or $T \cos\theta - mg = 0$

$\therefore \qquad T \cos\theta = mg. \qquad \ldots(ii)$

Dividing (i) by (ii), we get

$$\tan\theta = \frac{a}{g}.$$

Example 4. **A simple pendulum is hanging from the ceiling of a trolley which is coming down on an inclined plane. Find angle made by the string from the perpendicular of the trolley when**
(i)   it moves with constant speed,
(ii) when it moves with constant acceleration $g \sin\theta$.

Sol.   (i)

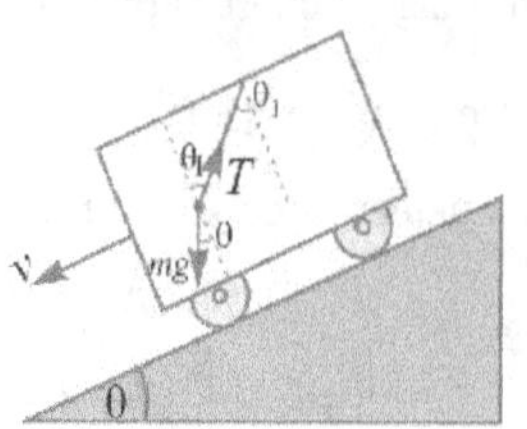

Figure. 5.81

If θ_1 is the required angle, then

$$T \cos\theta_1 = mg \cos\theta \qquad \ldots(i)$$

$$\text{and } mg \sin\theta - T \sin\theta_1 = m \times 0 \qquad \ldots(ii)$$

Solving equations (i) and (ii), we get

$$\theta_1 = \theta. \qquad\qquad \textit{Ans.}$$

(ii)

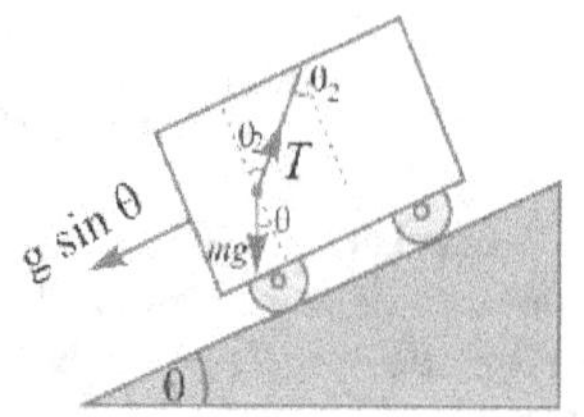

Figure. 5.82

If θ_2 is the required angle, then by Newton's second law

$$mg \sin\theta - T \sin\theta_2 = m(g \sin\theta)$$

which on solving gives, $\theta_2 = 0$.   *Ans.*

Example 5. **A block of mass m is on a wedge of mass M. Wedge M moves towards left with an acceleration a_0. If all surfaces are smooth, then find the acceleration of the block with respect to the wedge.**

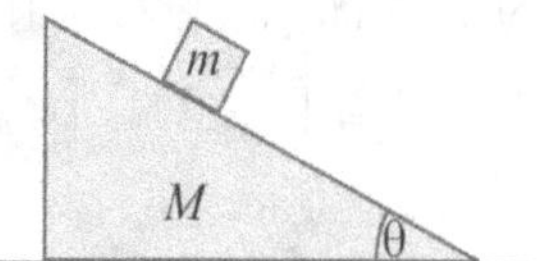

Figure. 5.83

Sol.   If a is the acceleration of the block down the plane with respect to the wedge, then acceleration of the block with respect to the ground will be $= (a\cos\theta - a_0)$ towards right. Let N be the force of interaction between block and the wedge.

For the motion of the wedge

$$N \sin\theta = Ma_0 \qquad \ldots(i)$$

For the motion of the block

$$N \sin\theta = m(a\cos\theta - a_0) \qquad \ldots(ii)$$

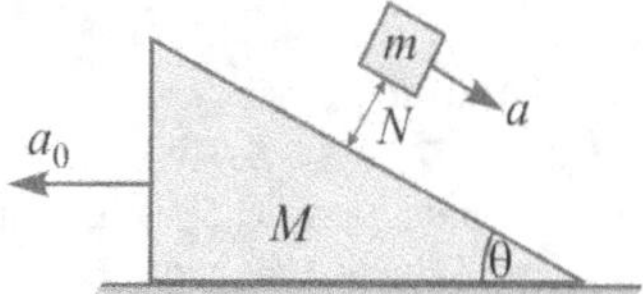

Figure. 5.84

After solving equations (i) and (ii), we get

$$a = \left[\frac{(M+m)a_0}{m\cos\theta} \right]. \qquad \textit{Ans.}$$

Example 6. A block is placed on an inclined plane moving towards right with an acceleration $a_0 = g$. The length of the inclined plane is ℓ_0. All the surfaces are smooth. Find the time taken by the block to reach from bottom to top of the inclined plane.

Sol. If m is the mass of the block, then preudo force on the block will be ma_0 towards left. Thus acceleration of the block up the plane w.r.t. the plane

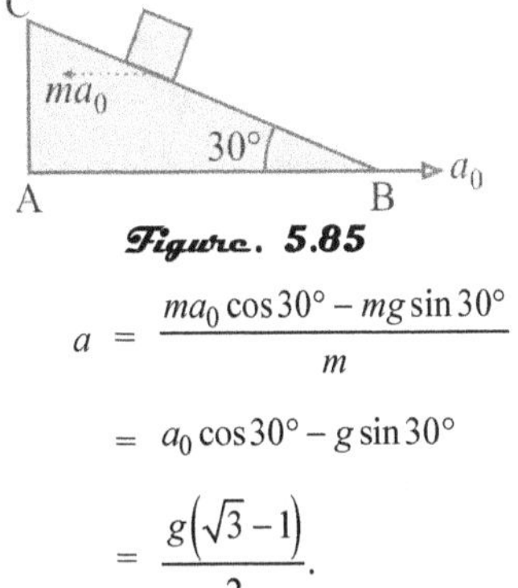

Figure. **5.85**

$$a = \frac{ma_0 \cos 30° - mg \sin 30°}{m}$$

$$= a_0 \cos 30° - g \sin 30°$$

$$= \frac{g\left(\sqrt{3} - 1\right)}{2}.$$

If t is the time taken, then

$$\ell_0 = \frac{1}{2}at^2$$

or

$$t = \sqrt{\frac{2\ell_0}{a}} = \sqrt{\frac{2\ell_0}{g\left(\sqrt{3} - 1\right)/2}}$$

$$= \sqrt{\frac{4\ell_0}{g\left(\sqrt{3} - 1\right)}}. \qquad \textit{Ans.}$$

Example 7. In the arrangement shown in *figure* 5.86, the block A is of mass m and block B is mass M. Block B is resting on a smooth horizontal surface, while friction coefficient between blocks A and B is μ. What maximum force F can be applied so that block A does not slip over the block B.

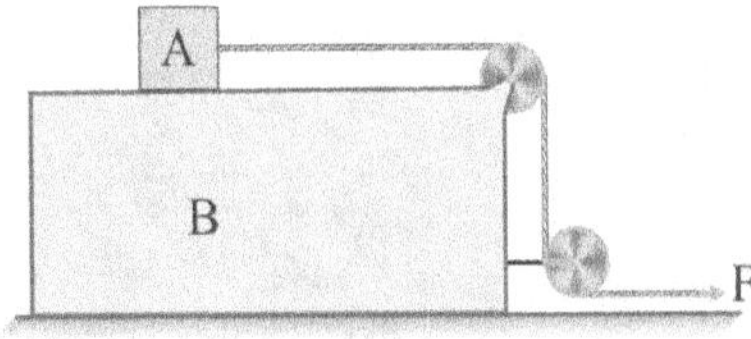

Figure. **5.86**

Sol. The maximum friction that can available for block $A = \mu mg$. If a is the maximum acceleration that this friction provides to block A, then by Newton's second law

$$\mu mg = ma$$

$$\therefore \qquad a = \mu g.$$

For both the blocks move together with acceleration a,

$$F = (M + m)a$$

$$= (M + m)\mu g. \qquad \textit{Ans.}$$

Example 8. A cart carries two blocks of masses 2 kg and 1 kg which are connected by a string passing over a pulley, as shown in *figure* 5.87. The cart is moving towards right with an acceleration of 1 m/s². Find the acceleration of blocks with respect to ground and tension in the string. (Take g = 10 m/s²)

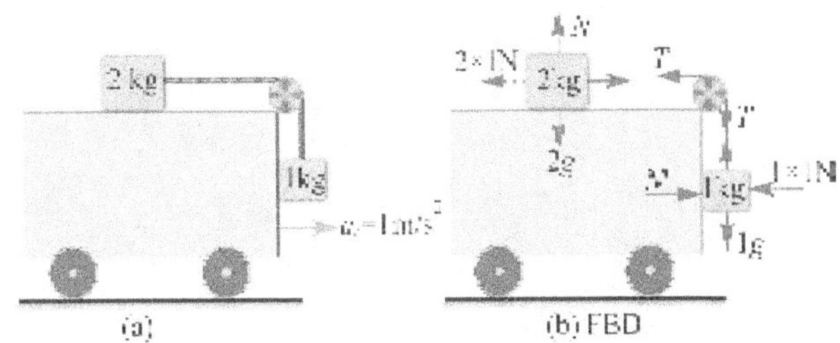

Figure. **5.87**

Sol. Let acceleration of the 2 kg block is a towards right with respect to cart. The forces on the blocks in accelerated frame are shown in figure. The forces mark by dotted arrows are pseudo forces.

For 2 kg block; $T - 2 \times 1 = 2a$ ...(i)

For 1 kg block; $1g - T = 1a$ ...(ii)

Solving equations (i) and (ii), we get

$$a = \frac{8}{3} \text{ m/s}^2 \text{ and } T = \frac{22}{3} \text{ N.}$$

Acceleration of blocks w.r.t. ground;

Acceleration of 1 kg block $= \frac{8}{3}$ m/s² along downward and 1 m/s² along horizontal

Acceleration of 2 kg block; $a = \frac{8}{3} + 1 = \frac{11}{3}$ m/s². **Ans.**

Example 9. A particle of mass m, originally at rest, is subjected to a force whose direction is constant but whose magnitude varies with the time according to the relation

$$F = F_0\left[1 - \left(\frac{t - T}{T}\right)^2\right]$$

where F_0 and T are constants. The force acts only for the time interval $2T$.

(a) Make a rough graph of F versus t.

(b) Prove that the speed v of the particle after a time $2T$ has elapsed is equal to $\dfrac{4F_0 T}{3m}$.

Sol. Given that

(a)

$$F = F_0\left[1 - \left(\frac{t - T}{T}\right)^2\right]$$

At, $t = 0$, $\quad F = F_0\left[1 - \left(\dfrac{0 - T}{T}\right)^2\right] = 0$

$t = T$, $\quad F = F_0\left[1 - \left(\dfrac{T - T}{T}\right)^2\right] = F_0$

$t = 2T$, $\quad F = F_0\left[1 - \left(\dfrac{2T - T}{T}\right)^2\right] = 0$

The graph of F versus t is shown in *fig.* 5.88.

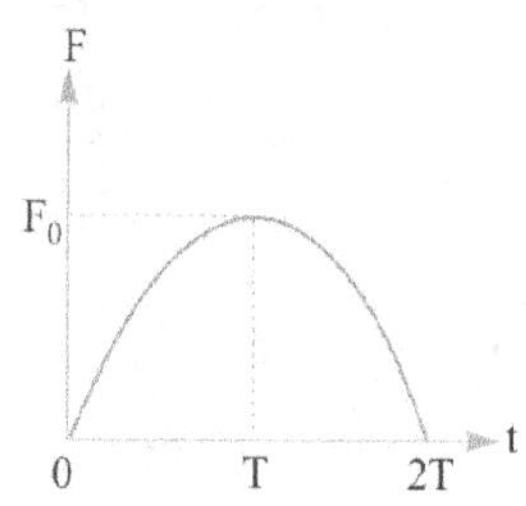

Figure. 5.88

(b) We have acceleration of the particle

$$a = \frac{F}{m} = \frac{F_0}{m}\left[1-\left(\frac{t-T}{T}\right)^2\right]$$

or

$$\frac{dv}{dt} = \frac{F_0}{m}\left[1-\left(\frac{t-T}{T}\right)^2\right]$$

or

$$v = \int_0^{2T}\frac{F_0}{m}\left[1-\left(\frac{t-T}{T}\right)^2\right]dt$$

$$= \frac{F_0}{m}\left[t-\frac{\left(\frac{t-T}{T}\right)^3 T}{3}\right]_0^{2T}$$

$$= \frac{F_0}{m}\left[\left\{2T-\frac{\left(\frac{2T-T}{T}\right)^3 T}{3}\right\}-\left\{0-\frac{\left(\frac{0-T}{T}\right)^3 T}{3}\right\}\right]$$

$$= \frac{4F_0T}{3m}.$$ **Proved**

Example 10. *A bar of mass m resting on a smooth horizontal plane starts moving due to the force $F = mg/3$ of constant magnitude. In the process of its rectilinear motion the angle α between the direction of this force and the horizontal varies as $\alpha = as$, where a is a constant, and s is the distance traversed by the bar from its initial position. Find the velocity of the bar as a function of the angle α.*

Sol. Let at any distance s, the α is the inclination of force. From Newton's second law, we have

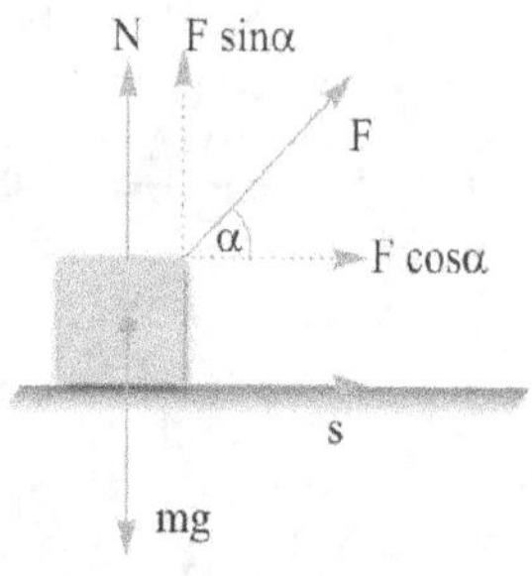

Figure. 5.89

$$F\cos\alpha = m\frac{dv}{dt}$$

or

$$\frac{mg}{3}\cos as = m\left(v\frac{dv}{ds}\right)$$

or

$$vdv = \frac{g}{3}\cos(as)ds \qquad \ldots(i)$$

Integrating equation (i), we get

$$\int_0^v vdv = \frac{g}{3}\int_0^s \cos(as)ds$$

or

$$\left|\frac{v^2}{2}\right|_0^v = \frac{g}{3a}\left|\sin as\right|_0^s$$

or

$$\left(\frac{v^2}{2}-0\right) = \frac{g}{3a}\left(\sin as - \sin 0\right)$$

$$v = \left[\frac{2g}{3a}\sin as\right]^{1/2}$$

$$= \left[\frac{2g}{3a}\sin \alpha\right]^{1/2}. \qquad \textbf{Ans.}$$

Example 11. *Figure 5.90 shows a man of mass 60 kg standing on a lift weighing machine kept in a box of mass 30 kg. The box is hanging from a pulley fixed to the ceiling through a light rope, the other end of which is held by the man himself. If the man manages to keep the box at rest, what is the weight shown by the machine ? What force should he exert on the rope to get his correct weight on the machine?*

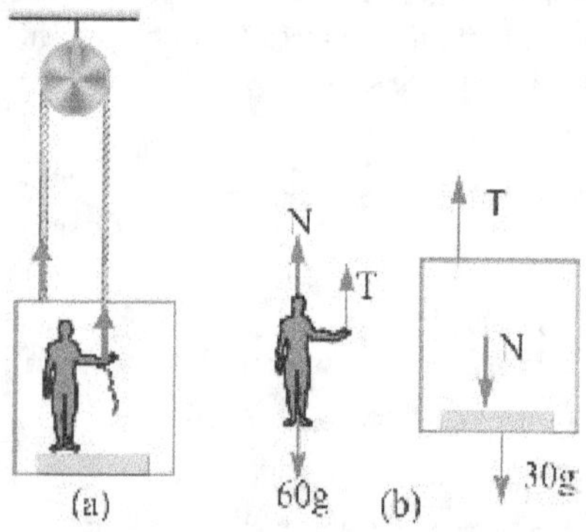

Figure. 5.90

Sol. The *FBD* is drawn in figure (b). From the *FBD* :

For man, $\qquad N + T = 60\,g$ $\qquad\qquad$ ...(i)

For box, $\qquad\quad T = N + 30\,g$ $\qquad\qquad$ ...(ii)

Solving equations (i) and (ii), we get

$$N = 15\,g = 150\,\text{N}$$

Thus, weight of man as shown by machine is 15 kg. $\qquad$ **Ans.**

To get his correct weight let the man exerts force T' on the rope. He together with the box move up with an acceleration a. Here we have $N = 60g = 600$ N.

For man, $\qquad (N + T') - 60\,g = 60\,a$

$\qquad$ or $\quad 600 + T' - 60 \times 10 = 60\,a$ $\qquad$ ... (iii)

and for box $\qquad T' - (N + 30g) = 30\,a$

$\qquad$ or $\quad T' - (600 + 30 \times 10) = 30\,a$ $\qquad$ ... (iv)

Solving equations (iii) and (iv), we get

$$a = 3 \text{ m/s}^2$$

and $\qquad T' = 1800 \text{ N}.$ ***Ans.***

Example 12. **A light vertical chain is being used to haul up an object of mass M kg attached to its lower end. The vertical pull applied has a magnitude of F newton at $t = 0$ and it decreases uniformly at a rate of f newton per meter over a distance h through the object is raised. Show that the velocity of the object after it has been raised through a small h metre is given by,**

$$v = \sqrt{\frac{2h}{M}\left(F - Mg - \frac{fh}{2}\right)}.$$

Sol. Let object be raised through a distance y in time t.

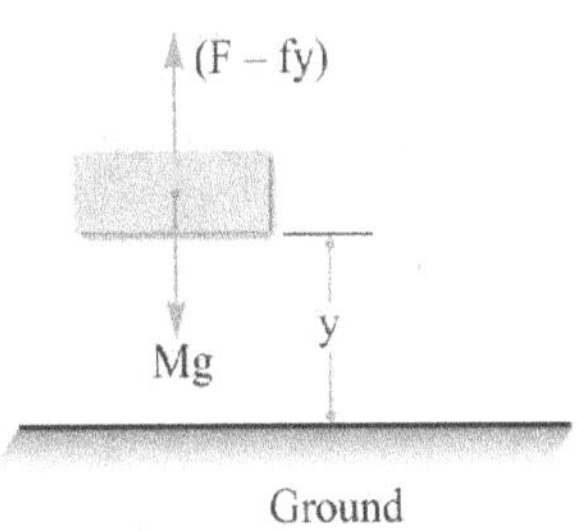

Figure. 5.91

The instantaneous pull on the object will be $(F - fy)$. By Newton's second law, we have

$$(F - fy) - Mg = Ma$$

or $\qquad a = \dfrac{dv}{dt} = \dfrac{(F - fy - Mg)}{M}$

or $\qquad v\dfrac{dv}{dy} = \dfrac{(F - fy - Mg)}{M}$ $\qquad$ ... (i)

Integrating equation (i), we have

$$\int_0^v v\,dv = \int_0^h \frac{(F - fy - Mg)}{M}\,dy$$

After solving, we get

$$v = \sqrt{\frac{2h}{M}\left(F - Mg - \frac{fh}{2}\right)}.$$ ***Ans.***

Example 13. A cylinder of mass m and radius r rests on two supports of the same height (see figure). One support is stationary, while the other slides from under the cylinder at a velocity v. Determine the force of normal pressure N exerted by the cylinder on the stationary support at the moment when the distance between the points A and B of the supports is $AB = r\sqrt{2}$, assuming that the supports were very close to each other at the initial instant. The friction between the cylinder and the supports should be neglected.

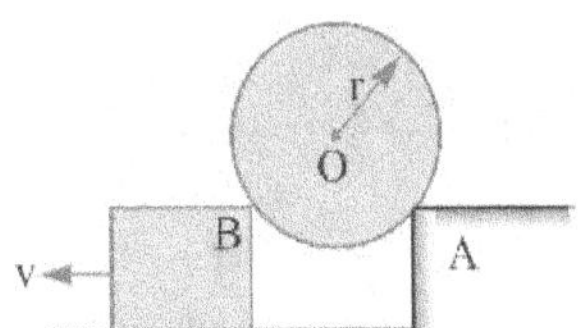

Sol. The velocity of the point B in horizontal direction is v.

The centre of the cylinder is half way between A and B, so its velocity will be

$$u = \frac{v}{2}$$

The velocity perpendicular to line AO,

$$u'\cos\theta = u = \frac{v}{2}$$

$\therefore \qquad u' = \dfrac{v}{2\cos\theta};$

$$\cos\theta = \frac{\sqrt{2}\,r/2}{r} = \frac{1}{\sqrt{2}}$$

Now $\quad mg\cos\theta - N = \dfrac{mu'^2}{r}$

$\therefore \qquad N = mg\cos\theta - \dfrac{mu'^2}{r}$

$$= mg\cos\theta - \frac{m\left(\dfrac{v}{2}\cos\theta\right)^2}{r}$$

$$= \frac{mg}{\sqrt{2}} - \frac{mv^2}{2r}$$ ***Ans.***

Example 14. **A pulley fixed to the ceiling of an elevator car carries a thread whose ends are attached to the loads m_1 and m_2 ($m_1 > m_2$). The car starts going up with an acceleration a. Assuming the masses of the pulley and the thread, as well as the friction, to be negligible find :**

(a) **the acceleration of m_1 relative to the elevator shaft and relative to car**

(b) **the force exerted by the pulley on the ceiling of the car.**

Sol.

(a) Suppose the acceleration of load m_1 with respect to car is a downward, then acceleration of m_2 will be a upward.

If their accelerations are a_1 and a_2 respectively w.r.t. an observer on the ground, then

$$a_1 = (a - a_0) \text{ downward}$$

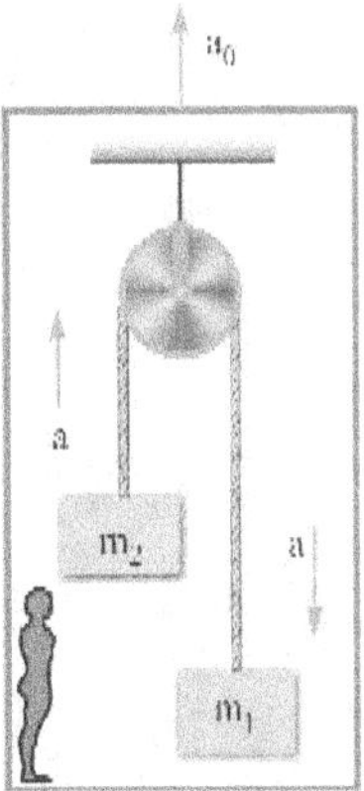

Figure. 5.92

and $\qquad a_2 = (a + a_0)$ upward

By Newton's second law, we have

$$m_1 g - T = m_1(a - a_0) \qquad ...(i)$$

and $\quad T - m_2 g = m_2(a + a_0) \qquad ...(ii)$

Solving equations (i) and (ii), we get

$$a = \frac{(m_1 - m_2)(g + a_0)}{(m_1 + m_2)} \; ; \; T = \frac{2m_1 m_2}{m_1 + m_2}(g + a_0)$$

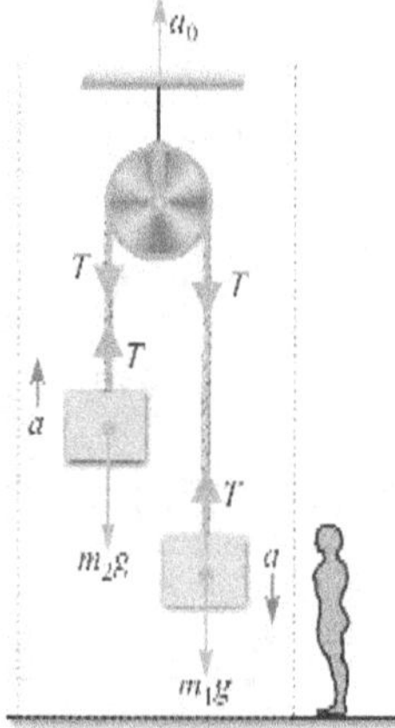

Figure. **5.93**

$$\therefore \quad a = a - a_0 = \frac{(m_1 - m_2)g - 2m_2 a_0}{(m_1 + m_2)}. \quad \textit{Ans.}$$

(b)   The force exerted by pulley on ceiling of car
$$F = 2T$$

$$= \frac{4m_1 m_2}{m_1 + m_2}(g + a_0). \quad \textit{Ans.}$$

Example 15. In the arrangement shown in *figure* 5.94 the mass of the ball 1 is $\eta = 1.8$ times as great as that of rod 2. The length of the later is $\ell = 100$ cm. The masses of the pulleys and the threads, as well as the friction are negligible. The ball is set on the same level as the lower end of the rod and then released. How soon will the ball be opposite to the other end of the rod.

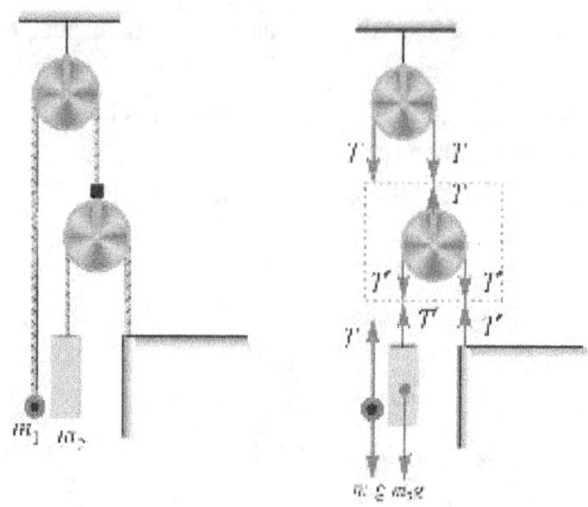

Figure. **5.94**

Sol. Let the acceleration of the mass m_1 is a upward, then the acceleration of m_2 will be $2a$ downward. From *FBD*, we have

$$\begin{aligned}
T - m_1 g &= m_1 a & \ldots \text{(i)}\\
m_2 g - T' &= m_2(2a) & \ldots \text{(ii)}
\end{aligned}$$
and
$$T = 2T' \qquad \ldots \text{(iii)}$$

Solving above equations, we get

$$a = \left[\frac{2m_2 - m_1}{m_1 + 4m_2}\right] g$$

Given
$$m_1 = 1.8 \, m_2$$

$$\therefore \qquad a = \frac{g}{29} \text{ m/s}^2$$

Acceleration of the rod relative to ball $= 2a - (-a)$
$$= 3a$$
Displacement, $\ell = 100$ cm $= 1$m.
By second equation of motion, we have

$$\ell = ut + \frac{1}{2}(3a)t^2$$

or
$$1 = 0 + \frac{1}{2} 3 \times \frac{g}{29} \times t^2$$

$$\therefore \qquad t = 1.40 \text{ s}. \qquad \textit{Ans.}$$

Example 16. In the arrangement shown in *figure* 5.95 the mass of the rod M exceeds the mass of the ball. The ball has an opening permitting it to slide along the thread with some friction. The mass of the pulley and the friction in its axle are negligible. At the initial moment the ball was located opposite to lower end of the rod. When set free both bodies began moving with constant acceleration. Find the frictional force between the ball and the thread if t seconds after the beginning of the motion the ball got opposite the upper end of the rod. The rod length equals ℓ.

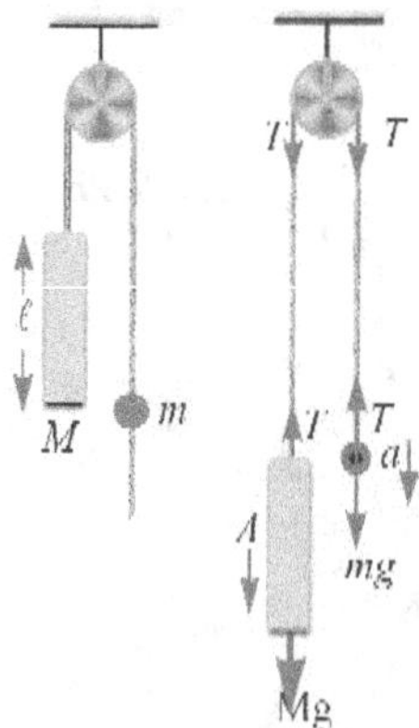

Figure. **5.95**

Sol. The situation is shown in figure.

Let T is the force in the thread due to friction between ball and thread. Suppose A and a are the accelerations of rod and the ball respectively. By Newton's second law, we have

for rod, $\qquad Mg - T = MA \qquad \ldots \text{(i)}$

for ball $\qquad mg - T = ma \qquad \ldots \text{(ii)}$

Multiplying equation (i) by m and (ii) by M and subtracting equation (ii) from (i), we get

$$T = \left(\frac{Mm}{M - m}\right)(A - a). \qquad \ldots \text{(iii)}$$

From second equation of motion, we have

$$\ell = 0 + \frac{1}{2}(A - a)t^2$$

or $\qquad (A - a) = \frac{2\ell}{t^2}. \qquad \ldots \text{(iv)}$

Now from equation (iii) and (iv), we get

$$T = \frac{2Mm\ell}{(M - m)t^2}. \qquad \textit{Ans.}$$

Example 17. In the arrangement shown in *figgure* 5.96 neglect the masses of pulleys and string and also friction. Calculate accelerations of blocks A and B.

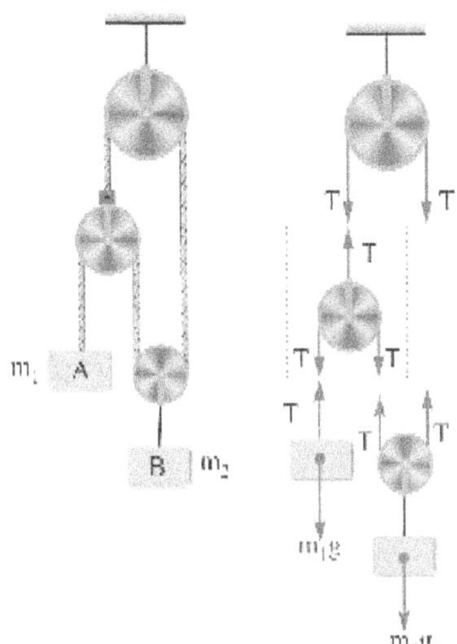

Figure. 5.96

Sol. Since string is same throughout, so the tension in it will be same everywhere. Let a_1 and a_2 are the accelerations of blocks A and B respectively and T is the tension in the string.

From *FBD*

By Newton's second law, we have

for block A, $\qquad m_1 g - T = m_1 a_1$ $\qquad$ ... (i)

for block B, $\qquad 2T - m_2 g = m_2 a_2$ $\qquad$ ... (ii)

and for pulley inside dotted box

$$2T - T = 0$$
$$\Rightarrow \qquad T = 0$$

$\therefore$ $\quad$ From equations (i) and (ii), we get

$$a_1 = g \quad \text{and} \quad a_2 = g. \qquad \qquad \textbf{\textit{Ans.}}$$

Example 18. In the pulley system shown in figure the movable pulleys A, B and C are of 1 kg each. D and E are fixed pulleys. The strings are light and inextensible. Find the accelerations of the pulleys and tension in the string.

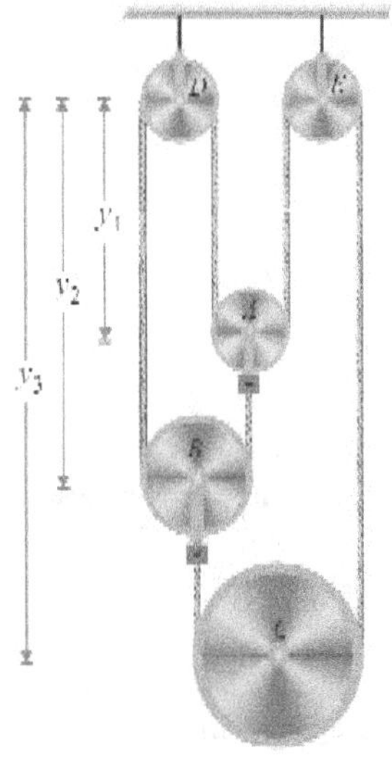

Figure. 5.97

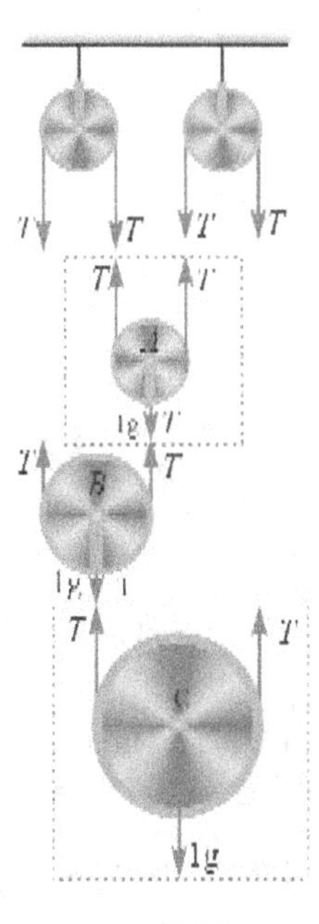

Fig. 5.98

Sol. Constraint relations;

Let y_1, y_2 and y_3 are the positions of pulleys A, B and C respectively at any instant with respect to a dotted line shown in figure. The total length of the string

$$2y_1 + y_2 + (y_2 - y_1) + y_3 + (y_3 - y_2) + \ell_0 = \ell$$
$$\text{or} \quad y_1 + y_2 + 2y_3 + \ell_0 = \ell \qquad \qquad ...(i)$$

where ℓ_0 is the length of part of string over the pulleys, which is constant. Differentiating equation (i) w.r.t. time, we get

$$\frac{dy_1}{dt} + \frac{dy_2}{dt} + 2\frac{dy_3}{dt} = 0$$

or $\qquad v_1 + v_2 + 2v_3 = 0$ $\qquad$ ... (ii)

Also $\qquad a_1 + a_2 + 2a_3 = 0$

Let $\quad a_1 = a$ upward and $a_2 = a$ upward, then

$$a_3 = \left(\frac{a_1 + a_2}{2}\right) = a \text{ downward.}$$

Since string is same throughout and uniform, the tension in it will be same every where . Thus

for pulley A;

$$2T - (T + 1g) = 1a \qquad \qquad ... (i)$$

For pulley B;

$$2T - (T + 1g) = 1a \qquad \qquad ... (ii)$$

For pulley C;

$$1g - 2T = 1a \qquad \qquad ... (iii)$$

Solving above equations, we get

$$a_1 = -\frac{g}{3}, \; a_2 = \frac{-g}{3}, \; a_3 = \frac{g}{3} \text{ and } T = \frac{2g}{3} = 6.53\text{N} . \; \textbf{\textit{Ans.}}$$

Example 19. The pulleys A and C are fixed while the pulley B is movable. A mass M_2 attached to pulley B, while the strings has masses M_1 and M_3 at the two ends. Find the acceleration of the each mass.

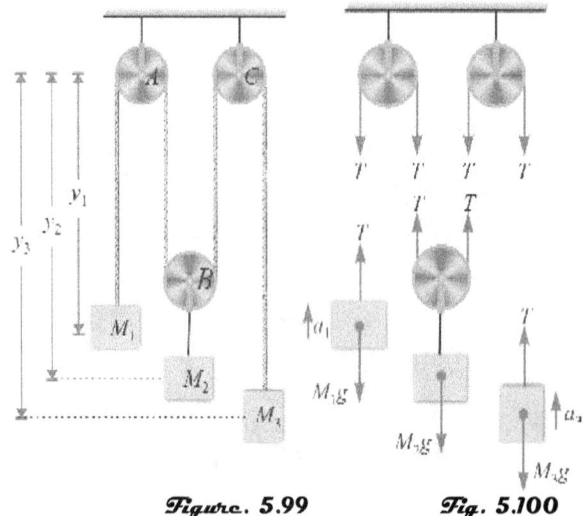

Figure. 5.99 $\qquad \qquad$ *Fig.* 5.100

Sol. Constraint relations :

Let at any instant the position of the masses are as shown in *fig.* 5.63. The total length of the string

$$y_1 + 2y_2 + y_3 + \ell_0 = \ell \qquad \qquad ... (i)$$

Differentiating w.r.t. time, we get

$$\frac{dy_1}{dt} + 2\frac{dy_2}{dt} + \frac{dy_3}{dt} = 0$$

or $\qquad v_1 + 2v_2 + v_3 = 0.$ $\qquad$ ... (ii)

Also $\qquad a_1 + 2a_2 + a_3 = 0.$ $\qquad$ ... (iii)

Suppose a_1 is upward and a_3 is upward, then

$$a_2 = \left(\frac{a_1 + a_3}{2}\right) \text{ downward.}$$

By Newton's second law, we have
for block M_1 :

$$T - M_1 g = M_1 a_1 \qquad \text{... (i)}$$

for block M_3;

$$T - M_3 g = M_3 a_3 \qquad \text{... (ii)}$$

for block M_2;

$$M_2 g - 2T = m_2 a_2 \qquad \text{... (iii)}$$

Solving above equations we get

$$a_1 = \left[\frac{-M_1 M_2 + 3M_2 M_3 - 4M_1 M_3}{M_1 M_2 + M_2 M_3 + 4M_1 M_3}\right] g \, ,$$

$$a_2 = \left[\frac{M_1 M_2 + M_2 M_3 - 4M_1 M_3}{M_1 M_2 + M_2 M_3 + 4M_1 M_3}\right] g \, ,$$

and $\quad a_3 = \left[\frac{3M_1 M_2 - M_2 M_3 - 4M_1 M_3}{M_1 M_2 + M_2 M_3 - 4M_1 M_3}\right] g \, .$ **Ans.**

Example 20. Block A of mass m is placed over a wedge of same mass m. Assuming all surfaces to be smooth, calculate the displacement of the block A in 1s.

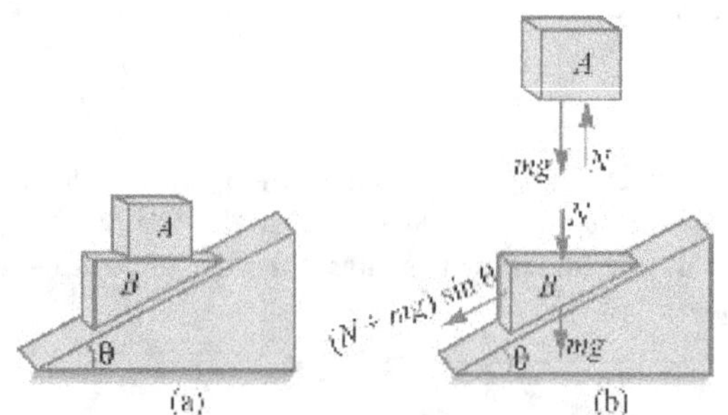

Figure. 5.101

Sol. Let acceleration of wedge be a down the plane. The acceleration of block A will be $a \sin\theta$ vertically downward
For block A; $mg - N = m(a \sin\theta)$ ... (i)
For block B; $(N + mg) \sin\theta = ma$ ... (ii)
Solving equations (i) and (ii), we get

$$a = \left[\frac{2g\sin\theta}{1 + \sin^2\theta}\right].$$

The acceleration of block A,

$$a_A = a \sin\theta$$

$$= \left[\frac{2g\sin\theta}{1 + \sin^2\theta}\right]\sin\theta = \left[\frac{2g\sin^2\theta}{1 + \sin^2\theta}\right]$$

Displacement of the block A in 1 s is

$$s = 0 + \frac{1}{2}a_A t^2$$

$$= \frac{1}{2} \times \left[\frac{2g\sin^2\theta}{1 + \sin^2\theta}\right] \times (1)^2$$

$$= \left[\frac{g\sin^2\theta}{1 + \sin^2\theta}\right] \qquad \textbf{Ans.}$$

Example 21. Find the acceleration of rod A and wedge B in the arrangement shown in *figure* 5.102. If the ratio of the mass of wedge to that of the rod equals η, and the friction between the contact surfaces are negligible.

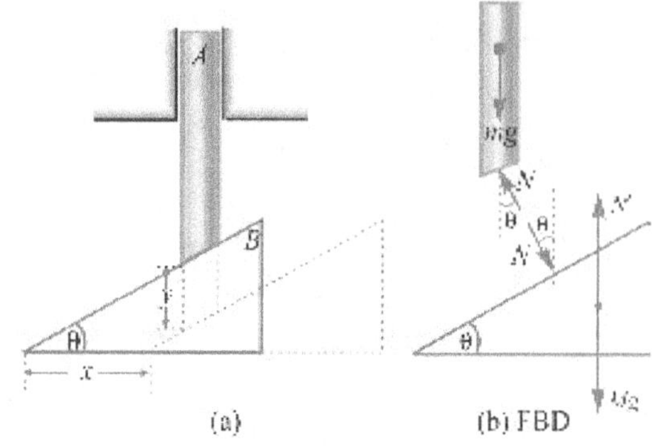

(a)   (b) FBD

Figure. 5.102

Sol. Let in any time the rod displaces down by y, the corresponding horizontal displacement of wedge will be x. From the figure, we have
$$y = x \tan\theta. \qquad \text{... (i)}$$
Differentiating both sides of equation (i), we get

$$\frac{dy}{dt} = \frac{dx}{dt}\tan\theta \, .$$

or $\qquad v_{rod} = v_{wedge} \tan\theta \qquad$ ...(ii)

Also $\qquad a_{rod} = a_{wedge} \tan\theta.$ ... (iii)
Let mass of the rod is m, then mass of wedge, $M = \eta m$.
By Newton's second law :
For vertical motion of rod;

$$mg - N\cos\theta = ma_{rod} \qquad \text{... (iv)}$$

For horizontal motion of wedge;

$$N \sin\theta = Ma_{wedge}$$

$$= M\left(\frac{a_{rod}}{\tan\theta}\right) \qquad \text{... (v)}$$

Solving equations (iv) and (v), we get

$$a_{rod} = \frac{g}{\left[1 + \dfrac{M}{m}\cot^2\theta\right]}$$

$$= \frac{g}{\left[1 + \eta\cot^2\theta\right]}$$

and $\qquad a_{wedge} = \dfrac{a_{rod}}{\tan\theta} = \dfrac{g}{[\tan\theta + \eta\cot\theta]}$

Example 22. A smooth semicircular wire of radius R is fixed in a vertical plane as shown in the *figure* 5.103. One end of a massless spring of natural length $\dfrac{3R}{4}$ is attached to the lower point O of the wire track. A small ring of mass m which can slide on the track, is attached to the lower end of the spring. The ring held stationary at point P such that the spring makes an angle 60° with the vertical. The spring constant $k = \dfrac{mg}{R}$. Consider the instant when the spring is released,

(i)   **draw free body diagram of the ring**

(ii)   **determine the tangential acceleration of the ring and the normal reaction.**

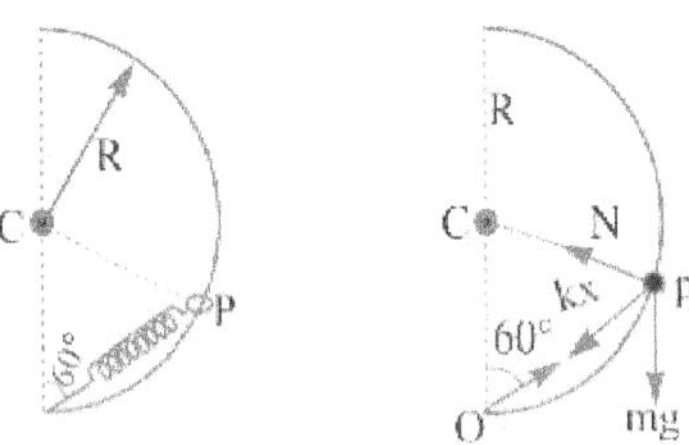

Figure. **5.103**

Sol. In the figure $\angle CPO = 60° = \angle OPC, \therefore OP = R$

The extension of spring $= R - \dfrac{3R}{4} = \dfrac{R}{4}$.

$$\therefore \qquad F = kx = \dfrac{mg}{R} \times \dfrac{R}{4} = \dfrac{mg}{4}$$

(i)   Resolving the forces along the radius of semicircle, we have

$$N + F\cos 60° = mg\cos 60°$$

or $\quad N + \dfrac{mg}{4}\cos 60° = mg\cos 60°$

$$\therefore \qquad N = \dfrac{3}{8}mg \text{ N.} \qquad\qquad \textbf{Ans.}$$

(ii)   The tangential force

$$F_t = mg\cos 30° + F\sin 30°$$

$$= mg\cos 30° + \dfrac{mg}{4}\sin 30°$$

$$= \dfrac{(4\sqrt{3}+1)mg}{8}$$

Thus tangential acceleration $a_t = \dfrac{F_t}{m} = \dfrac{(4\sqrt{3}+1)g}{8}$ m/s^2 *Ans.*

Example 23. For the system at rest shown in *figure* 5.104, determine the accelerations of all the loads immediately after the lower thread keeping the system in equilibrium has been cut. Assume that the threads are weightless, the mass of the pulley is negligible small, and there is no friction at the point of suspension.

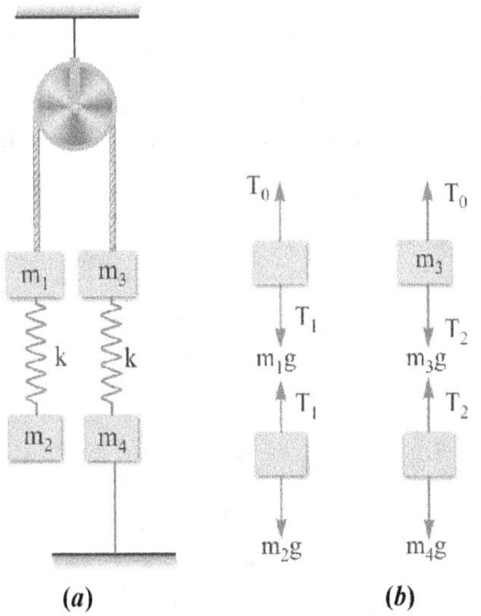

(a)   *(b)*

Figure. **5.104**

Sol. For the equilibrium of system of loads,

$$(m_1 + m_2) > (m_3 + m_4).$$

The force in the left spring, $\quad T_1 = m_2 g$.

Let T_2 is the force in the right spring then for the equilibrium of load m_3, we have

$$m_3 g + T_2 - T_0 = 0. \qquad\qquad …(i)$$

For m_1 ; $\qquad m_1 g + T_1 = T_0$

as $\qquad\qquad T_1 = m_2 g$

$\therefore \qquad m_1 g + m_2 g = \boldsymbol{T_0}$

Substituting this value in equation (i), we get

$$m_3 g + T_2 - (m_1 g + m_2 g) = 0$$

or $\qquad T_2 = (m_1 + m_2 - m_3)g \qquad …(ii)$

After cutting the lower thread, the equations of motion for the loads are;

$$m_1 g + T_1 - T_0 = m_1 a_1 \qquad …(iii)$$

$$m_2 g - T_1 = m_2 a_2 \qquad …(iv)$$

$$T_2 + m_3 g - T_0 = m_3 a_3 \qquad …(v)$$

and $\qquad T_2 - m_4 g = m_4 a_4 \qquad …(vi)$

Solving above equations, we get

$$a_1 = a_2 = a_3 = 0$$

and $\qquad a_4 = \dfrac{(m_3 + m_4 - m_1 - m_2)g}{m_4}. \qquad$ *Ans.*

Example 24. A 40 kg slab rests on frictionless floor. A 10 kg block rests on the top of the slab (see *figure* 5.105). The static coefficient of friction between the block and the slab is 0.60 while the kinetic friction is 0.40. The 10 kg block is acted upon by a horizontal force *F*. What is the resultant acceleration of the slab and the block if

(i) $F = 40$ N   (ii) $F = 100$ N ?

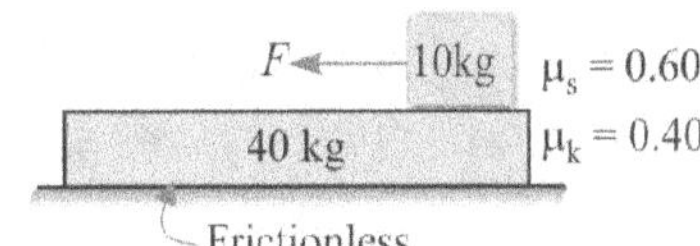

Figure. **5.105**

Sol. (i)   The limiting friction between block and slab

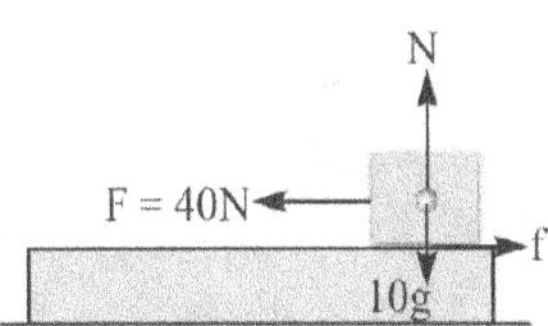

Figure. **5.106**

$$f_{\text{lim}} = \mu_s N = 0.60 \times 10 \, g = 58.8 \text{ N}$$

As applied force (40 N) is less than the limiting friction between the block and slab, so block will not slide over the slab. They will move together as one unit of mass $40 + 10 = 50$ kg by a net force of 40 N over the frictionless floor.

$$\therefore \quad a_{\text{block}} = \dfrac{40}{40+10} = 0.8 \text{ m/s}^2 = a_{\text{slab}}. \qquad \textbf{Ans.}$$

(ii)   When 100 N force is applied on the block, the block will slide over the slab (as limiting friction is 58.8 N). As motion starts, the kinetic friction starts acting. The kinetic friction between the block and the slab

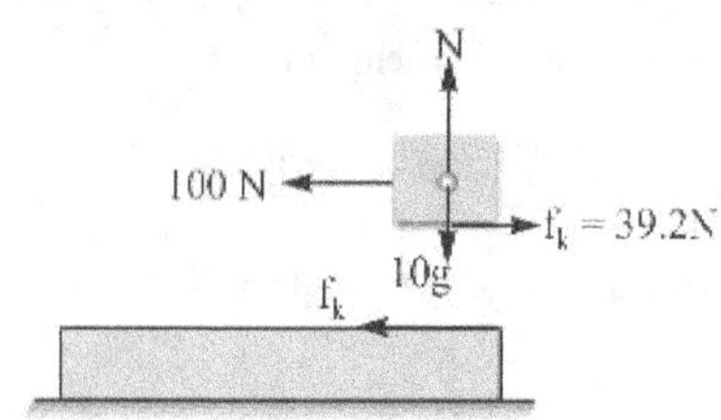

Figure. 5.107

$f_k = \mu_k N = 0.40 \times 10\,g = 39.2$ N.

Thus the acceleration of block

$$a_{block} = \frac{F_{net}}{M_{block}} = \frac{100 - 39.2}{10} = 6.08 \text{ m/s}^2$$

and $a_{slab} = \dfrac{F_{net}}{M_{slab}} = \dfrac{f_k}{M_{slab}} = \dfrac{39.2}{40} = 0.98 \text{ m/s}^2.$ *Ans.*

Example 25. **Find the acceleration** a_1, a_2, a_3 **of the three blocks shown in** *figure* **5.108, if a horizontal force of 10 N is applied on**
(a)   2 kg block   (b) 3 kg block   (c)   7 kg block. Take $g = 10 \text{ m/s}^2$

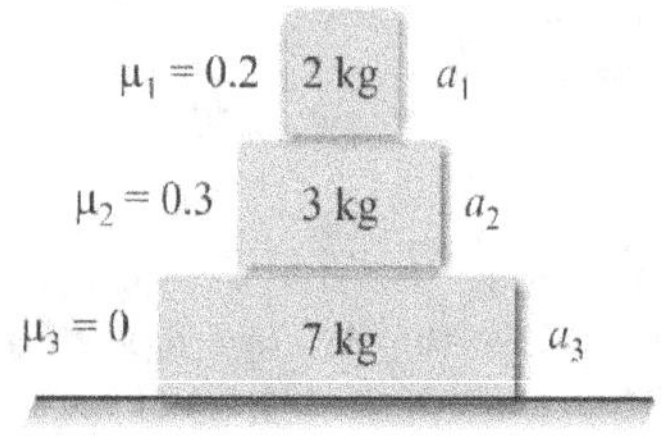

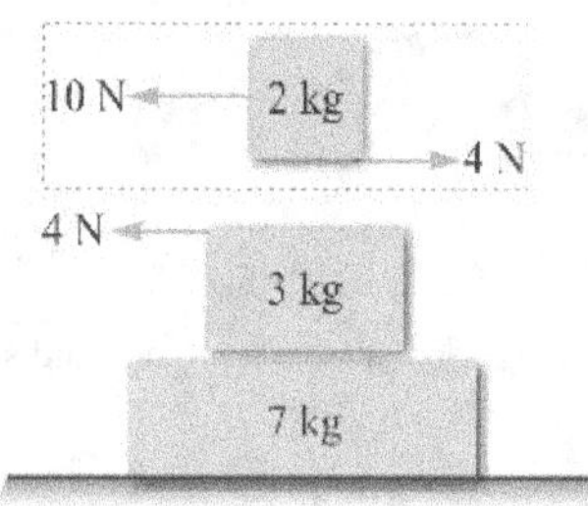

Figure. 5.108

Sol. (a)   When force of 10 N is applied on 2 kg block. The limiting frictional force between 2 kg and 3 kg blocks
$$f_1 = 0.2 \times 2g = 0.2 \times 2 \times 10 = 4 \text{ N}.$$

Figure. 5.109

The limiting frictional force between 3 kg and 7 kg blocks that can be
$$f_2 = 0.3 \times 5\,g = 0.3 \times 5 \times 10 = 15 \text{ N}$$
As applied force 10 N is greater than f_1 but less than f_2, so 2 kg block will slide over 3 kg but 3 kg will move together with 7 kg. Thus we have;

$$a_1 = \frac{10 - 4}{2} = 3 \text{ m/s}^2$$

and $a_2 = a_3 = \dfrac{4}{3 + 7} = 0.4 \text{ m/s}^2.$ *Ans.*

(b)   When force of 10 N is applied on 3 kg block : As the applied force is less than the friction between 3 kg and 7 kg blocks (that can be 15 N) so the blocks will move together as one unit with an acceleration

$$a = \frac{10}{2 + 3 + 7} = \frac{5}{6} \text{ m/s}^2.$$ *Ans.*

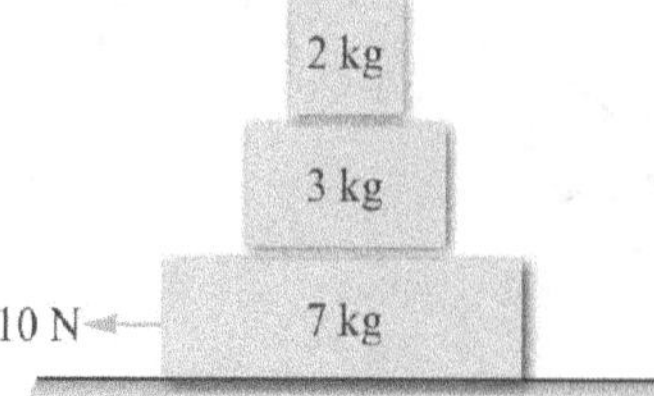

Figure. 5.110

Now find pseudo force on 2 kg block because of acceleration of 3 kg block

$$F_{pseudo} = 2 \times \frac{5}{6} = \frac{5}{3} \text{N}$$

As the F_{pseudo} is smaller than the friction between 2 kg and 3 kg (that can be 4 N), so 2 kg will move together with other blocks.

(c)   When force of 10 N is applied on 7 kg block. Supposing 3 kg and 2 kg blocks move together with 7 kg block. The acceleration of whole system , $a = \dfrac{10}{2 + 3 + 7} = \dfrac{5}{6} \text{m/s}^2.$

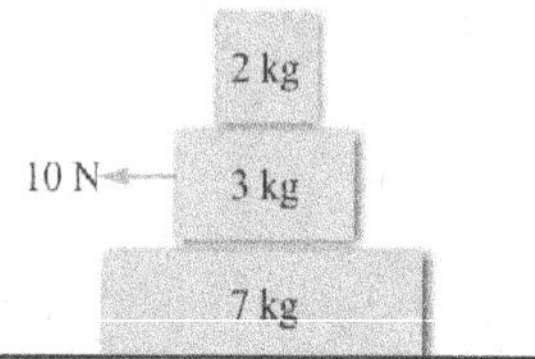

Figure. 5.111

The pseudo force on 2 kg block $= \dfrac{2 \times 5}{6} = \dfrac{5}{3}$ N which is less than the frictional force between 2 kg and 3 kg block, so they move together.

Now check whether 2 kg and 3 kg move together over 7 kg block.

The pseudo force on $(2 + 3)$ kg is $= 5 \times \dfrac{5}{6} = \dfrac{25}{6}$ N, which is also less than frictional force between 3 kg and 7 kg blocks, so all the blocks move together with a common acceleration of $\dfrac{5}{6}$ m/s^2.

Therefore $a = a_1 = a_2 = a_3 = \dfrac{10}{2 + 3 + 7} = \dfrac{5}{6}$ m/s^2.   *Ans.*

Example 26. **The friction coefficient between the board and the floor shown in** *figure* **5.112 is** μ **. Find the maximum force that the man can exert on the rope so that the board does not slip on the floor.**

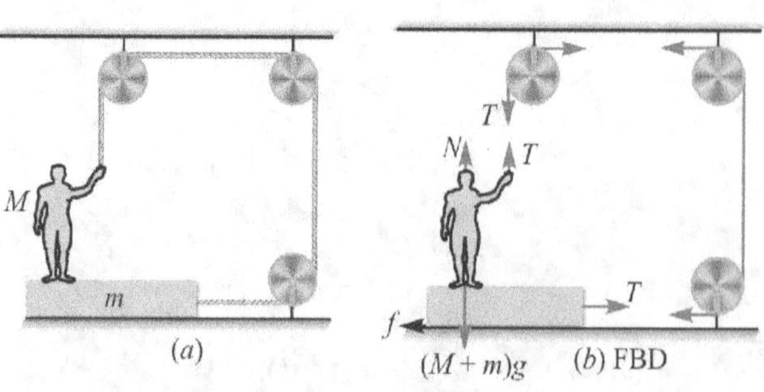

Figure. 5.112

Sol. Let T is the force exerted by the man on the rope.

Along vertical direction, $\sum F_v = 0$;

or $\quad N + T = (M + m)\, g$ or $N = (M + m)\, g - T$

The board will not slip over the floor, if

$$T \le f.$$

For maximum value of T, we have

$$T = f = \mu N$$
$$= \mu \,[(M + m)g - T]$$
$$= \mu \,(M + m)\, g - \mu\, T$$

or $\qquad T = \left[\dfrac{\mu(M + m)g}{1 + \mu}\right].$ **Ans.**

Example 27. Find the acceleration of the block of mass M in the situation of *figure* 5.113 shown. The coefficient of friction between two blocks is μ_1 and that between the bigger block and the ground is μ_2.

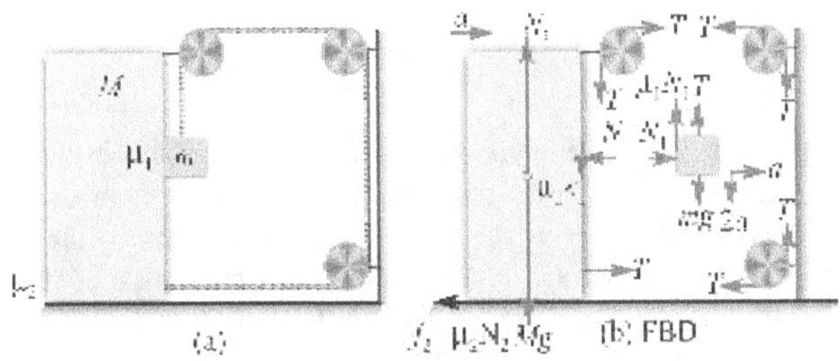

Figure. 5.113

Sol. Suppose block M moves towards right with an acceleration a. The acceleration of block m in downward direction will be $2a$ in addition to its acceleration a towards right together with block M. See the *FBD*.

For the motion of block m;

Along horizontal direction

$$N_1 = ma.$$

Along vertical direction

$$mg - (\mu_1 N_1 + T) = m\,(2a). \qquad \ldots(i)$$

After substituting value of N_1 in equation (i), we have

$$Mg - (\mu_1 ma + T) = m\,(2a). \qquad \ldots(ii)$$

For the block M;

Along vertical direction

$$\sum F_V = 0 ;$$

or $\qquad N_2 = T + \mu_1 N_1 + Mg. \qquad \ldots(iii)$

Along horizontal direction

$$2T - (N_1 + \mu_2\, N_2) = Ma. \qquad \ldots(iv)$$

From equation (i) and (iii), we have

$$2T - [N_1 + \mu_2\,(T + \mu_1 N_1 + Mg)] = Ma$$

or $\quad 2T - [ma + \mu_2 T + \mu_1 \mu_2\,(ma) + \mu_2\, Mg] = Ma \qquad \ldots(v)$

Now solving equations (ii) and (iv), we get

$$a = \frac{2m - \mu_2(M + m)g}{M + m[5 + 2(\mu_1 - \mu_2)]}. \qquad \textbf{\textit{Ans.}}$$

Example 28. *Figure* 5.114 shows a small block of mass m kept at the left end of a larger block of mass M and length ℓ. The system can slide on a horizontal road. The system is started towards right with an initial velocity v. The friction coefficient between the road and the bigger block is μ and that between the blocks is $\dfrac{\mu}{2}$.

Find the time elapsed before the smaller block separates from the bigger block.

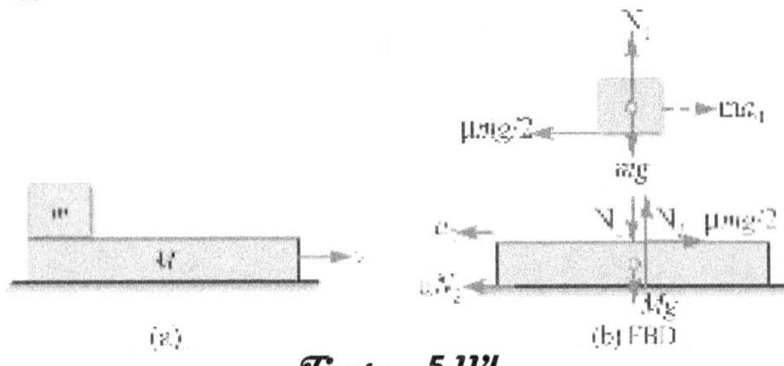

Figure. 5.114

Sol. Suppose the acceleration of the lower block is a_0 towards left $(- a_0$ toward right). The block m experiences a pseudo force of magnitude ma_0 relative to the block M. Let acceleration of the block m is 'a' relative to M. The situation is shown in figure.

For the block m;

$$N_1 = mg \qquad \ldots(i)$$

and $\quad ma_0 - \dfrac{\mu mg}{2} = ma \qquad \ldots(ii)$

For block M;

$$N_2 = Mg + N_1$$
$$= Mg + mg = (M + m)\, g$$

and $\quad \mu\, N_2 - \dfrac{\mu mg}{2} = Ma_0 \qquad \ldots(iii)$

or $\mu\,(M + m)\, g - \dfrac{\mu mg}{2} = Ma_0$

$\Rightarrow \qquad a_0 = \dfrac{\mu(2M + m)g}{2M}$

Substituting the value of a_0 in equation (ii), we get

$$a = \frac{\mu(M + m)g}{2M}.$$

Now using second equation of motion for the motion of m w.r.t. M, we have

$$\ell = 0 + \frac{1}{2}\, at^2$$

$\Rightarrow \qquad t = \sqrt{\dfrac{2\ell}{a}}$

$$= \sqrt{\dfrac{2\ell}{\left(\dfrac{\mu(M + m)g}{2M}\right)}}$$

$$= \sqrt{\dfrac{4M\ell}{(M + m)\mu g}}. \qquad \textbf{\textit{Ans.}}$$

Example 29. A flat car of mass m_0 starts moving to the right due to a constant force F shown in *figure* 5.115. Sand spills on the flatcar from a stationary hopper. The velocity of loading is constant and equal to μ kg/s. Find the time dependence of the velocity and the acceleration of the flatcar in the process of loading. The friction is negligibly small.

Sol. Method I

From newton's second law of motion

Figure. **5.115**

$$\frac{d(mv)}{dt} = F$$

or $\qquad m\,dv + v\,dm = F\,dt.$ ....(i)

Here, $m = m_0 + \mu t$ and $dm = \mu\,dt$

Substituting these values in equation (i) and simplifying, we have

$$\frac{dv}{F - \mu v} = \frac{dt}{m_0 + \mu t}.$$

Integrating above equation, we get

$$v = \frac{Ft}{(m_0 + \mu t)} + C$$

At $\quad t = 0, v = 0; \quad \therefore C = 0.$

Therefore $\qquad v = \dfrac{Ft}{m_0 + \mu t}$

and $\qquad \dfrac{dv}{dt} = \dfrac{Fm_0}{(m_0 + \mu t)^2}.$ **Ans.**

Method II : We have, $\vec{F}_{\text{external}} + v_r \dfrac{dm}{dt} = m\dfrac{dv}{dt}.$

Here, $\dfrac{dm}{dt} = \mu \; ; v_r = 0 - v = -v$

Above equation becomes $\quad F - v\mu = (m_0 + \mu t)\dfrac{dv}{dt}.$

or $\qquad \dfrac{dv}{F - \mu v} = \dfrac{dt}{m_0 + \mu t}$

Integrating above equation, we get

$$v = \frac{Ft}{m_0 + \mu t}.$$ **Ans.**

Example 30.
A chain of mass M and length l is held vertical, such that its lower end just touches the floor. It is released from rest. Find the force exerted by the chain on the table when upper end is about to hit the floor.

Sol. Force F exerted by the chain consists of two components :

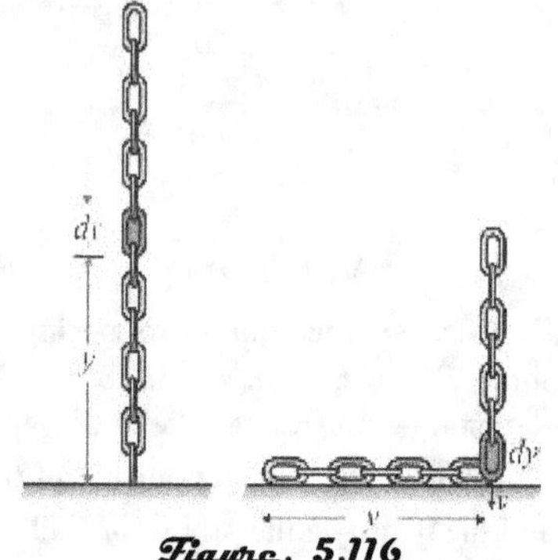

Figure. **5.116**

(i) weight of the fallen portion of the chain let F_1

(ii) thrust of the falling part of chain let F_2.

Now consider an element of chain of length dy at a height y from the floor. It will strike the floor with a velocity $v = \sqrt{2gy}$. Thus we have,

$$F_1 = \lambda yg .$$

Here λ is the mass per unit length of chain

and $\qquad F_2 = v_{\text{rel}}\dfrac{dm}{dt}$

we have $v_{\text{rel}} = v$ and $dm = \lambda dx$

$\therefore \qquad F_2 = v\dfrac{\lambda dx}{dt} = v\,\lambda\,(v) = \lambda\,v^2$

The force exerted by chain on the floor,

$$F = F_1 + F_2$$
$$= \lambda\,yg + \lambda\,v^2 = \lambda\,yg + \lambda\,(\sqrt{2gy})^2$$
$$= \lambda yg + 2\lambda g = 3\lambda yg$$

When upper end is about to hit the floor, $y = \ell$

$\therefore \qquad F = 3\lambda lg = 3\,mg.$ **Ans.**

Example 31.
The ladder shown in *figure* 5.117 has negligible mass and rests on a frictionless floor. The crossbar connects the two legs of the ladder at the middle. The angle between the two legs is 60°. The fat person sitting on the ladder has a mass of 80 kg. Find the contact force exerted by the floor on each leg and the tension in the crossbar.

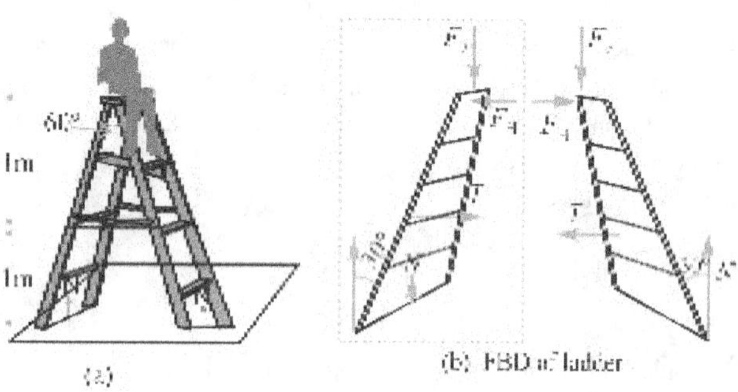

Fig. 5.117

Sol. Let tension in cross bar is T and normal reaction of floor on each bar is N. Consider the vertical equilibrium of whole system, we have

$$\sum F_V = 0 \quad \text{or} \quad 2N - 80\,g = 0$$

$$\therefore \qquad N = 40g$$
$$= 40 \times 9.8 = 392\,N$$

Equilibrium of left bar gives, $N - F_v = 0$

$$\therefore \qquad F_v = N = 392\,N.$$

Now for rotational equilibrium of the left bar (or right bar)

$\sum \tau = 0$; Taking moment of all forces acting on its about its upper end, we have

$$T \times 1 - N \times 2\tan 30° = 0$$

$$\therefore \qquad T = \frac{2N}{\sqrt{3}} = \frac{2 \times 392}{\sqrt{3}} = 450N .$$ **Ans.**

Mechanics   MCQ Type 1   Exercise 5.1

LEVEL - I (ONLY ONE OPTION CORRECT)

Laws of Motion, Spring, Constraint Relations

1. Three forces act on a particle that moves with unchanging velocity $\vec{v} = (3\hat{i} - 4\hat{j})$ m/s. Two of the forces are $\vec{F}_1 = (3\hat{i} + 2\hat{j} - 4\hat{k})$ N and $\vec{F}_2 = (-5\hat{i} + 8\hat{j} - 3\hat{k})$ N. The third force is :

   (a) $(-2\hat{i} + 10\hat{j} - 7\hat{k})$ N   (b) $(2\hat{i} - 10\hat{j} + 7\hat{k})$ N

   (c) $(7\hat{i} - 2\mathbf{k} + 10\hat{j})$ N   (d) none of these

2. There are two forces on the 2.0 kg box in the overhead view of figure but only one is shown. The figure also shows the acceleration of the box. The second force is nearly :

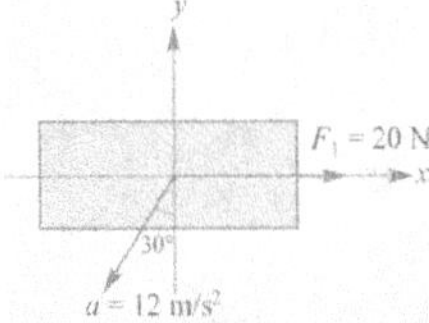

   (a) $-20\hat{j}$ N   (b) $-20\hat{i} + 20\hat{j}$ N

   (c) $-32\hat{i} - 21\hat{j}$ N   (d) $-21\hat{i} - 16\hat{j}$ N

3. The tension in the spring is :   [AMU B.Tech. 2005]

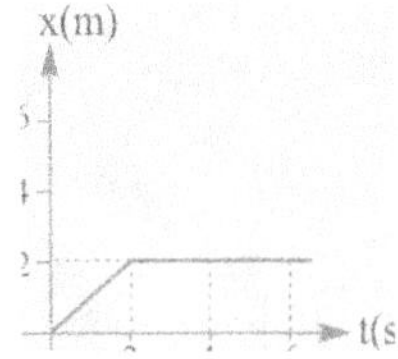

   (a) zero   (b) 2.5 N
   (c) 5 N   (d) 10 N

4. In the figure given, the position–time graph of a particle of mass 0.1 kg shown. The impulse at $t = 2\,s$ is:

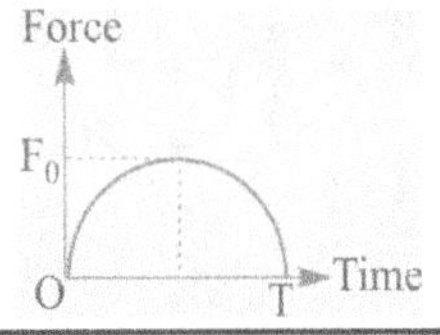

   (a) 0.2 kg m/ s   (b) – 2.0 kg m/s
   (c) –0.1 kg m/s   (d) – 0.4 kg m/s

5. A particle of mass m, initially at rest, is acted upon by a variable force F for a brief interval of time T. It begins to move with a velocity u after the force stops acting. F is shown in the graph as a function of time. The curve is a semicircle. Then;

   (a) $u = \dfrac{\pi F_0^2}{2m}$ (b) $u = \dfrac{\pi T^2}{8m}$

   (c) $u = \dfrac{\pi F_0 T}{4m}$ (d) $u = \dfrac{F_0 T}{2m}$

6. A force represented as show in figure acts on a body having a mass of 16 kg. The velocity of the body at $t = 10$ s, if the body starts from rest :

   (a) 100 m/s
   (b) 50 m/s
   (c) 49 m/s
   (d) 39 m/s

7. A particle moves in xy-plane under the influence of a force such that its linear momentum is $\vec{P}(t) = A\left[\,i\cos(kt) - \hat{j}\sin(kt)\right]$, where A and k are constants. The angle between the force and the momentum is

   (a) $0°$ (b) $30°$
   (c) $45°$ (d) $90°$

8. A 10 kg monkey climbs up a massless rope that runs over a frictionless tree limb and back down to a 15 kg package on the ground. The magnitude of the least acceleration the monkey must have if it is to lift the package off the ground is :

   (a) 4.9 m/s^2
   (b) 5.5 m/s^2
   (c) 9.8 m/s^2
   (d) none of these

9. A block of mass 10 kg is placed on smooth horizontal surface. A variable force; $F = 2t$, where t is time in second, is acting on the block at an angle $30°$ from the horizontal. The time when block will leave the contact from the surface is (g = 10 m/s^2)

   (a) 10 s   (b) 20 s
   (c) 50 s   (d) 100 s

10. Find the tension in the string which connected the blocks as shown in the following figure:

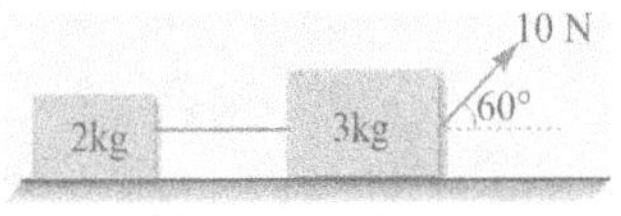

   (a) 2 N   (b) 3 N
   (c) 5 N   (d) 10 N

| Answer | 1 | (b) | 2 | (c) | 3 | (c) | 4 | (c) | 5 | (c) |
| Key | 6 | (d) | 7 | (d) | 8 | (a) | 9 | (d) | 10 | (a) |

11. A load of mass $M = 100$ kg is supported is a vertical plane by a string and pulleys. If the free end A of the string is pulled vertically downward with an acceleration $a = 2$ m /s^2, the tension in string is:

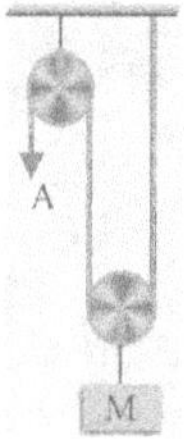

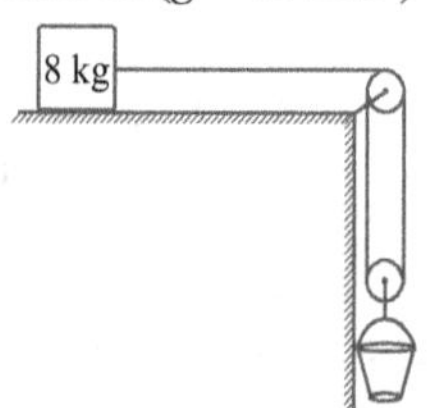

(a) 500 N

(b) 550 N

(c) 600 N

(d) 1000 N

12. A block of mass $M = 8$ kg is connected to an empty bucket of mass 1 kg by a massless cord running over an ideal pulley. The coefficients of static and kinetic friction between table top and block are 0.5 and 0.4 respectively. Sand is gradually added to the bucket until the block just being to slide. The mass of sand added is: ($g = 10$ m/s^2)

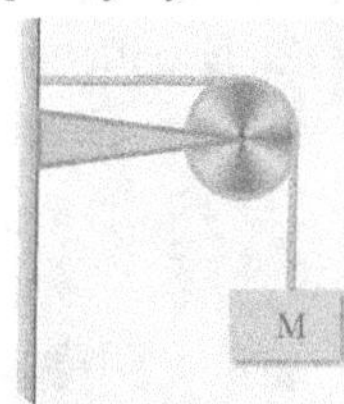

(a) 5 kg

(b) 6 kg

(c) 7 kg

(d) 10 kg

13. A string of negligible mass going over a clamped pulley of mass m supports a block of mass M as shown in the figure. The force on the pulley by the clamp is given by:

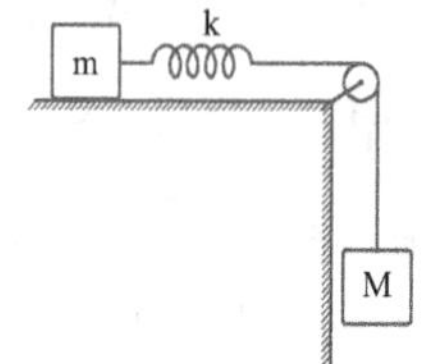

(a) $\sqrt{2}\, Mg$

(b) $\sqrt{2}\, mg$

(c) $\left(\sqrt{(M+m)^2 + m^2}\right)g$

(d) $\left(\sqrt{(M+m)^2 + M^2}\right)g$

14. Three blocks of masses 4 kg, 6 kg and 8 kg are hanging over a fixed pulley as shown. The tension in the string connecting 4 kg and 6 kg block is : ($g = 10$ m/s^2)

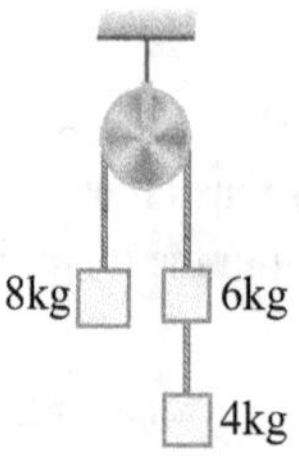

(a) 4 N

(b) 6 N

(c) $\dfrac{320}{9}$ N

(d) $\dfrac{40}{9}$ N

15. Figure shows four blocks that are being pulled along a smooth horizontal surface. The masses of the blocks and

tension in one cord are given. The pulling force F is :

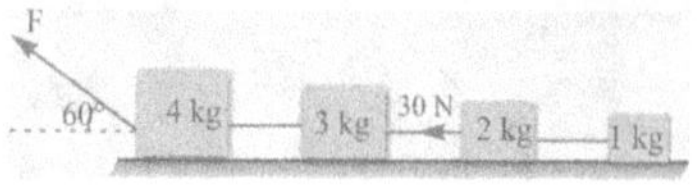

(a) 50 N

(b) 100 N

(c) 125 N

(d) 200 N

16. Two masses , M and m are connected together by a pulley two strings and a stretched spring of force constant k as shown. Assume that string, pulley and spring all are massless and surface below m is smooth. The amount by which the spring is stretched :

(a) $\dfrac{mMg}{k(m+M)}$

(b) $\dfrac{2mMg}{k(m+M)}$

(c) $\dfrac{Mg}{k}$

(d) $\dfrac{(m+M)g}{2k}$

17. An 80 kg person is parachuting and experiencing a downward acceleration of 2.5 m/s^2. The mass of the parachute is 5.0 kg. The upward force on the open parachute from the air is :

(a) 620 N

(b) 740 N

(c) 800 N

(d) 920 N

18. A block of mass M is pulled along a horizontal smooth surface by a rope of mass m. Force P is applied at one end of the rope. The force which the rope exert on the block is:

(a) $\dfrac{P}{(M-m)}$

(b) $\dfrac{PM}{(M+m)}$

(c) $\dfrac{Pm}{(M+m)}$

(d) $P\dfrac{m}{M}$

19. Two blocks, each having a mass M, rest on frictionless surface as shown in the figure. If the pulleys are light and frictionless, and M on the incline is allowed to move down, then the tension in the string will be:

(a) $2.3\, Mg \sin \theta$

(b) $\dfrac{3}{2} Mg \sin \theta$

(c) $\dfrac{Mg}{2} \sin \theta$

(d) $2\, Mg \sin \theta$

Answer	11	(b)	12	(c)	13	(d)	14	(c)	15	(d)
Key	16	(a)	17	(a)	18	(b)	19	(c)		

20. With what minimum acceleration can a fireman slide down a rope whose breaking strength is 3/4th of his weight:

(a) $\dfrac{g}{4}$ m/s^2

(b) g m/s^2

(c) $\dfrac{3}{4}g$ m/s^2

(d) zero

21. In the arrangement shown, the pulleys are fixed and ideal, the strings are light. $m_1 > m_2$ and S is a spring balance which is itself massless. The reading of S (in unit of mass) is : ($g = 10$ m/s^2)

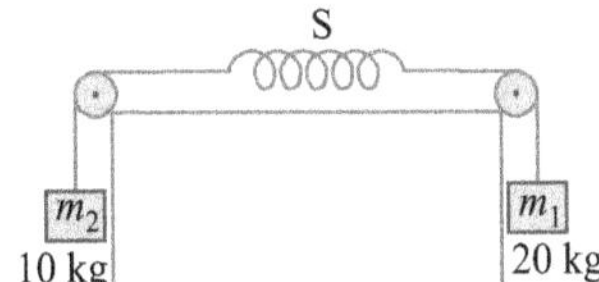

(a) 100 N

(b) 200 N

(c) $\dfrac{200}{3}$ N

(d) $\dfrac{400}{3}$ N

22. An elevator of mass M is accelerated upwards by applying a force F. A mass m is initially situated at a height of 1 m above the floor of the elevator is falling freely. It will hit the floor of the elevator after a time equal to **[NTSE -2012]**

(a) $\sqrt{\dfrac{2M}{F+mg}}$

(b) $\sqrt{\dfrac{2M}{F-mg}}$

(c) $\sqrt{\dfrac{2M}{F}}$

(d) $\sqrt{\dfrac{2M}{F+Mg}}$

23. Two weights are suspended from a string thrown over a light frictionless pulley. The mass of one weight is 2 kg. If a heavy weight is attached to its other end, the tension in the string is ($g = 10$ m/s^2)

(a) zero

(b) 20 N

(c) 40 N

(d) 50 N

Friction

24. A force $F = kt$ is applied to a block A as shown in figure, where t is time in second. The force is applied at $t = 0$, when the system was at rest. Which of the following graphs correctly gives the frictional force on block A as a function of time?

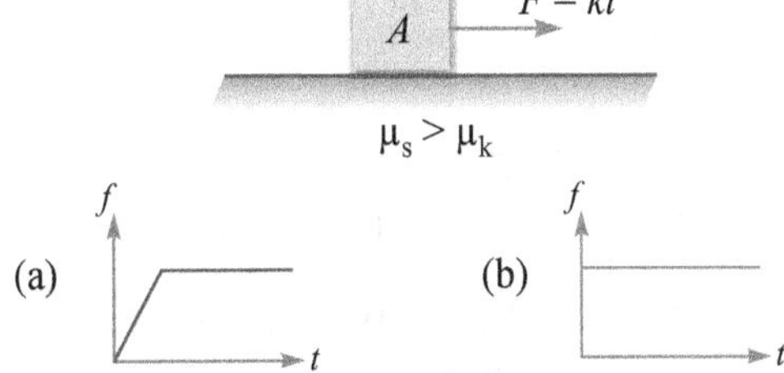

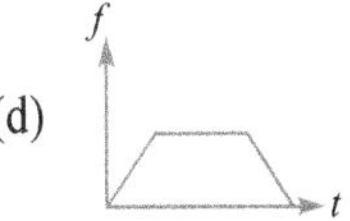

25. A block of mass 2 kg is given a push for a moment horizontally and then the block starts sliding over a figure horizontal plane. The figure shows the velocity-time graph of the motion. The coefficient of sliding friction between the plane and the block is :

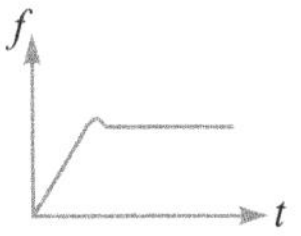

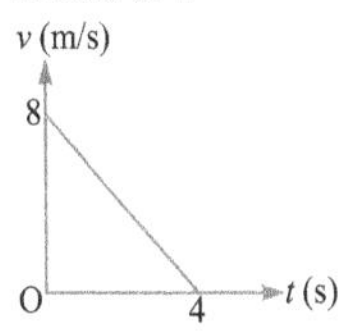

(a) 0.10

(b) 0.20

(c) 0.30

(d) 0.40

26. A 20 kg body is pushed with just enough force to start it moving across a floor and the same force continues to act afterwards. The coefficient of static and kinetic friction are 0.6 and 0.2 respectively. The acceleration of the body is : ($g = 10$ m/s^2)

(a) 1 m/s^2

(b) 2 m/s^2

(c) 3 m/s^2

(d) 4 m/s^2

27. A block of mass 10 kg is tied with the help of string rests on an rough inclined plane ($\mu = 0.5$) as shown. The frictional force on the block is: ($g = 10$ m/s^2)

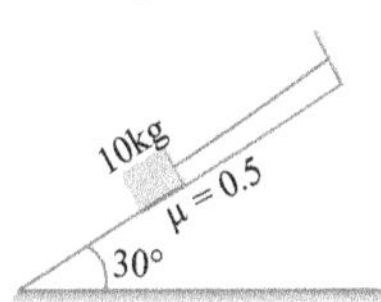

(a) 50 N

(b) $25\sqrt{3}N$

(c) 100 N

(d) zero

28. A 2.5 kg block is initially at rest on a horizontal surface. A 6.0 N horizontal force and a vertical force $\vec{P}$ are applied to the block as shown in figure. The coefficient of static friction for the block and surface is 0.4. The magnitude of friction force when $P = 9$N : ($g = 10$ m/s^2)

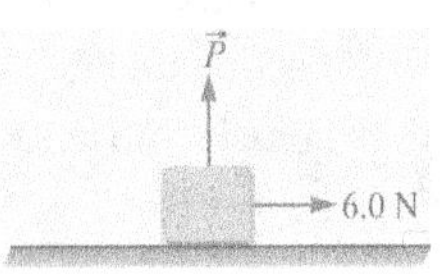

(a) 6.0 N

(b) 6.4 N

(c) 9.0 N

(d) zero.

Answer	20	(a)	21	(d)	22	(c)	23	(c)	24	(c)
Key	25	(b)	26	(d)	27	(d)	28	(a)		

29. Minimum force required to pull the lower block is (take $g = 10$ m/s^2):

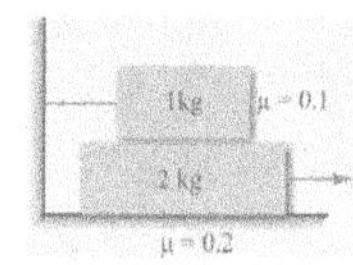

(a)   1 N   (b)   5 N

(c)   7 N   (d)   10 N

30. A 5 kg block is pushed along a horizontal floor by a force 20 N that makes an angle 30° with the horizontal (as shown in figure). The coefficient of kinetic friction between the block and floor is 0.25. The acceleration of block is: ($g = 10$ m/s^2)

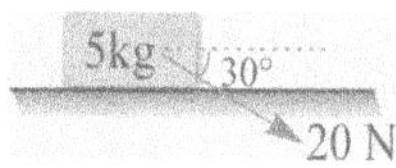

(a)   1 m/s^2 (b)   0.56 m/s^2

(c)   0.46 m/s^2 (d)   none

31. On the horizontal surface of a truck ($\mu = 0.6$), a block of mass 1 kg is placed. If the truck is accelerating at the rate of 5 m/s^2, then frictional force on the block will be:

(a)   5 N   (b)   6 N

(c)   5.88 N   (d)   8 N

32. A vehicle of mass m is moving on a rough horizontal road with momentum P. If the coefficient of friction between the tyres and the road be μ, then the stopping distance is:

(a) $\dfrac{P}{2\mu\, mg}$ (b) $\dfrac{P^2}{2\mu\, mg}$

(c) $\dfrac{P}{2\mu\, m^2 g}$ (d) $\dfrac{P^2}{2\mu\, m^2 g}$

33. A block rests on a rough inclined plane making an angle of 30° with the horizontal. The coefficient of static friction between the block and the plane is 0.8. If the frictional force on the block is 10 N, the mass of the block (in kg) is (take $g = 10$ m/s^2):

(a)   2.0   (b)   4.0

(c)   1.6   (d)   2.5

34. A block of mass 5 kg is placed on another block of mass 10 kg. A force of 60 N is acting on the 5 kg block in horizontal direction, if both the blocks move together, then frictional force on 5 kg block is ($g = 10$ m/s^2)

(a) $-10\hat{i}$ N   (b) $20i$ N

(c) $-40i$ N   (d) $60i$ N

35. A block of mass 5 kg is over 10 kg block. The coefficient of friction between the blocks is $\mu_s = 0.5$. They are moving on a smooth horizontal surface by a 60 N force acting on lower block. The frictional force on 5 kg block is : ($g = 10$ m/s^2)

(a) $-15\hat{i}N$ (b) $20\hat{i}$ N

(c) $-25i$ N   (d) $25i$ N

36. A block A of mass M_1 is connected to another block of mass M_2 by a massless string through a spring of force constant k as shown in figure. The coefficient of friction between the block A and the table is μ. The pulley is frictionless. When the block B is moving downward, the tension in the string is independent of:

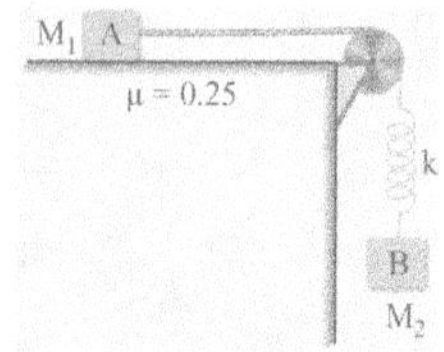

(a) M_1 (b) M_2

(c) k (d) μ

37. A block of mass m = 2 kg is resting on a rough inclined plane of inclination 30° as shown in figure. The coefficient of friction between the block and the plane is $\mu = 0.5$.

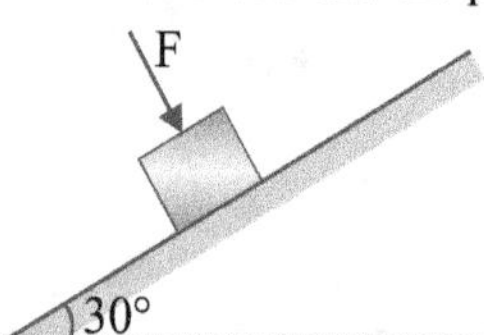

What minimum force F should be applied perpendicular to the plane on the block, so that block does not slip on the plane ($g = 10$ m/s^2)?

(a)   zero   (b)   6.24 N

(c)   2.68 N   (d)   4.34 N

38. A 40 kg slab rests on a frictionless floor A 10 kg block rests on top of the slab (as shown in figure). The coefficient of static friction μ_s between the block and slab is 0.6, where as their kinetic friction coefficient is 0.4. The 10 kg block is pulled by a horizontal force of $(100$ N$)\hat{i}$. The resulting accelerations of block and slab will be :

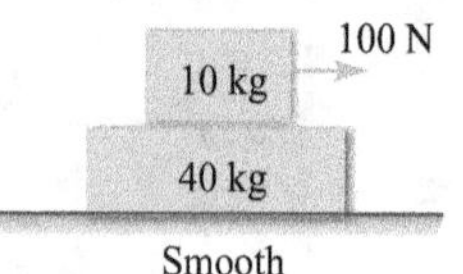

(a) $(2.0\,m/s^2)\hat{i}$, 0   (b) $(2.0\,m/s^2)\hat{i}$, $(-2.0\,m/s^2)\hat{i}$

(c) $(6.0\,m/s^2)\hat{i}$, $(1.0\,m/s^2)\hat{i}$ (d) $(4.0\,m/s^2)\hat{i}$, 0

Answer	29	(c)	30	(c)	31	(a)	32	(d)	33	(a)
Key	34	(c)	35	(b)	36	(c)	37	(c)	38	(c)

Variable Mass System

39. A block of metal weighing 2 kg is resting on a frictionless plane. If struck by a jet releasing water at a rate of 1 kg/s and at a speed of 5 m/s. The initial acceleration of the block will be:

(a) $2.5 \text{ m}/\text{s}^2$ (b) $5.0 \text{ m}/\text{s}^2$

(c) $10 \text{ m}/\text{s}^2$ (d) none of the above

Equilibrium

40. The pulleys and strings shown in the figure are smooth and of negligible mass. For the system to remain in equilibrium, the angle θ should be:

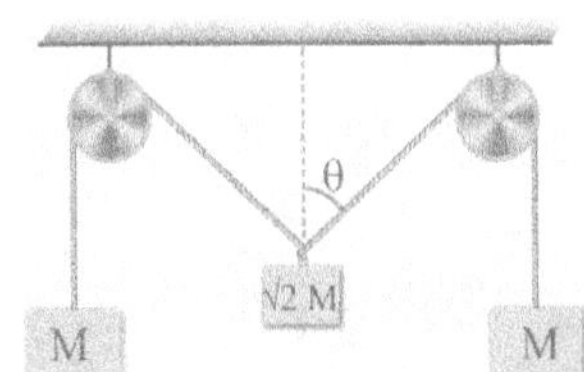

(a) $0°$ (b) $30°$

(c) $45°$ (d) $60°$

41. Two equal heavy spheres, each of radius r, are in equilibrium within a smooth cup of radius $3r$. The ratio of reaction between the cup and one sphere and that between the two sphere is

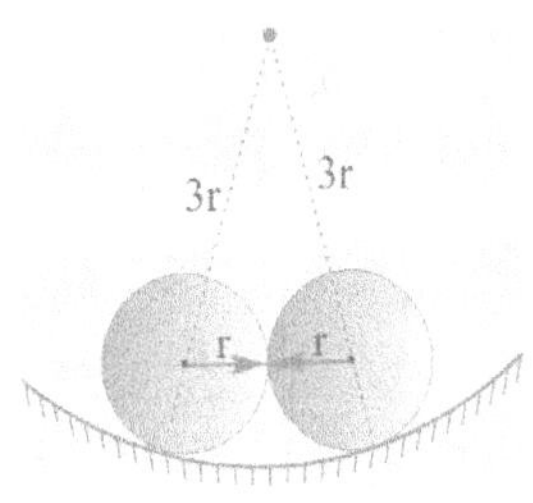

(a) 1   (b) 2

(c) 3   (d) none

Answer Key	39	(a)	40	(c)	41	(b)

LEVEL - 2 (ONLY ONE OPTION CORRECT)

Laws of Motion, Spring, Constraint Relations

1. A bullet is fired from a gun. The force on the bullet given by $F = 600 - 2 \times 10^5 \, t$ where F is in newton and t in second. The force on the bullet becomes zero as soon as it leaves the barrel. What is the average impulse imparted to the bullet

(a) 8 N-s   (b) zero

(c) 0.9 N-s   (d) 1.8 N-s

2. Find the maximum compression in the spring, if the lower block is shifted to rightwards with acceleration a. All the surfaces are smooth

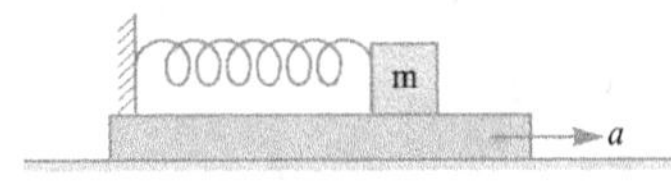

(a) $\dfrac{ma}{2k}$ (b) $\dfrac{2ma}{k}$

(c) $\dfrac{ma}{k}$ (d) $\dfrac{4ma}{k}$

3. A particle of mass m is made to move with uniform speed v along the perimeter of a regular polygon of n sides, inscribed in a circle of radius a. The magnitude of impulse applied at each corner of the polygon is :

(a) $2 \, mv \sin \dfrac{\pi}{n}$ (b) $mv \sin \dfrac{\pi}{n}$

(c) $mv \sin \dfrac{n}{\pi}$ (d) $2 \, mv \sin \dfrac{n}{\pi}$

4. A painter of mass M stands on a platform of mass m and pulls himself up by two ropes which hang over pulley as shown in figure. He pulls each rope with force F and moves upward with a uniform acceleration a. Find a neglecting the fact that no one could do this for long time :

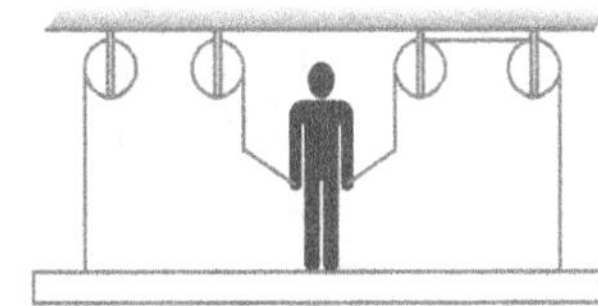

(a) $\dfrac{4F + (2M + m)g}{M + 2m}$ (b) $\dfrac{4F + (M + m)g}{M + 2m}$

(c) $\dfrac{4F - (M + m)g}{M + m}$ (d) $\dfrac{4F - (M + m)g}{2M + m}$

5. In the device the acceleration of block A is 1m/s^2. The acceleration of block B will be

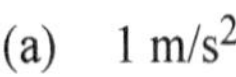

(a) 1 m/s^2

(b) 2 m/s^2

(c) 4 m/s^2

(d) 6 m/s^2

6. A block A has a velocity of 0.6 m/s to the right, determine the velocity of cylinder B.

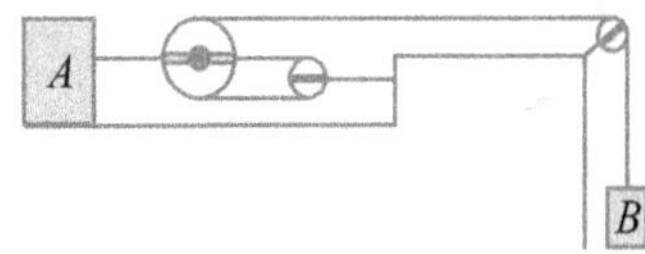

(a) 1.2 m/s   (b) 2.4 m/s

(c) 1.8 m/s   (d) 3.6 m/s

7. A bob is hanging over a pulley inside a car through a string. The second end of the string is in the hand of a person standing in the car. The car is moving with constant acceleration 'a' directed horizontally as shown. Other end of the string is pulled with constant acceleration 'a' vertically. The tension in the string is

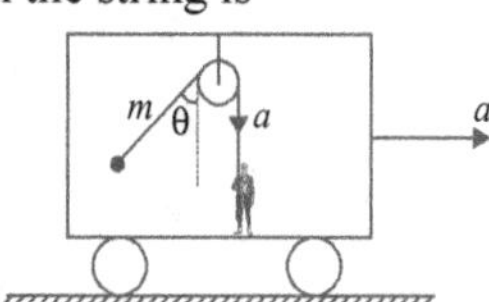

(a) $m\sqrt{g^2+a^2}$

(b) $m\sqrt{g^2+a^2}-ma$

(c) $m\sqrt{g^2+a^2}+ma$

(d) $m(g+a)$

8. In the given figure a block of mass m is tied on a wedge by an ideal string as shown in figure. String is parallel to inclined plane. All the surface involved are smooth. Wedge is spring moved towards right with a time varying velocity $v=t^2/2$ (m/s). At what time block will just leave the contact with the wedge (take $g = 10$ m/s^2)

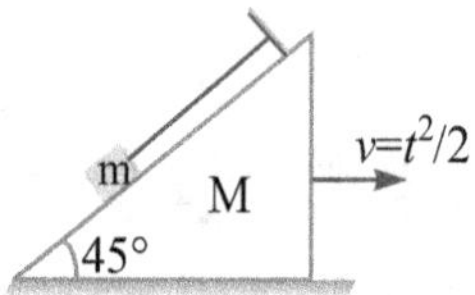

(a) 2 s

(b) 4 s

(c) 5 s

(d) 10 s

9. Two blocks each of mass m in the device are pulled by a force $F = mg/2$ as shown in figure. All the contact surfaces are smooth. The acceleration of block A is

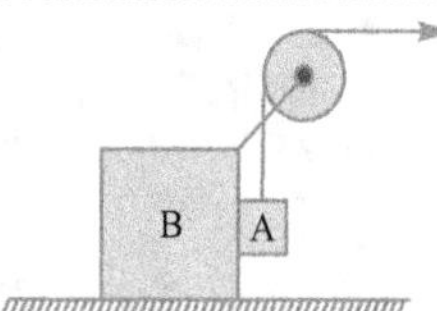

(a) $\dfrac{\sqrt{5}}{4}g$

(b) $\dfrac{\sqrt{3}}{2}g$

(c) $\dfrac{g}{2}$

(d) $\dfrac{g}{4}$

10. Three masses m_1, m_2 and m_3 are attached to a string as shown in the figure. All three masses are held at rest and then released. To keep m_3 at rest, the condition is:

(a) $1/m_3 = 1/m_1 + 1/m_2$

(b) $m_1 + m_2 = m_3$

(c) $4/m_3 = 1/m_1 + 1/m_2$

(d) $\dfrac{1}{m_1} + \dfrac{2}{m_2} = \dfrac{3}{m_3}$

11. Three block of masses $m_1 = 2.0$, $m_2 = 4.0$ and $m_3 = 6.0$ kg are connected by strings on a frictionless inclined plane

of 60°, as shown in figure. A force $F = 120$ N is applied upward along the incline to the uppermost block, causing an upward movement of the blocks. The connecting cords are light. The values of tensions T_1 and T_2 in the cords are:

(a) $T_1 = 20$ N, $T_2 = 60$ N

(b) $T_1 = 60$ N, $T_2 = 60$ N

(c) $T_1 = 30$ N, $T_2 = 50$ N

(d) $T_1 = 20$ N, $T_2 = 100$ N

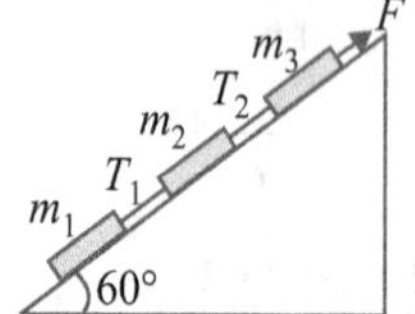

Friction

12. A block of mass 5 kg is held against wall by applying a horizontal force of 100 N. If the coefficient of friction between the block and the wall is 0.5, the frictional force acting on the block is ($g = 9.8$ m /s^2)

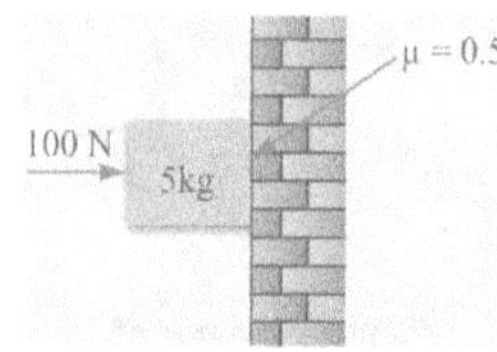

(a) 100 N

(b) 50 N

(c) 49 N

(d) 24.9 N

13. Three blocks of masses 5 kg, 3 kg and 2 kg are placed on rough surface ($\mu_k = 0.1$) as shown in figure. A horizontal force of 20 N is applied on 5 kg block. The force exerted by 3 kg block on 2 kg block is:

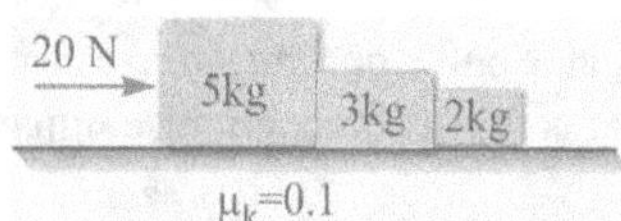

(a) 4 N

(b) 6 N

(c) 8 N

(d) 10 N

14. If μ be the coefficient of friction between the block and the cart, horizontal acceleration of the cart that is required to prevent block B from falling is: **[KVPY-2014]**

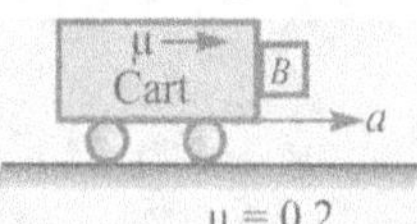

(a) μ /g

(b) g / μ

(c) g

(d) $(\mu^2 + 1) g$

15. A block is resting on a horizontal plate in the x-y plane and the coefficient of friction between the block and the plate is μ. The plate begins to move in the x-direction and its velocity is $v = bt^2$, t being time and b being a constant. At what time will the block start sliding on the plate ?

(a) $\mu b / g$

(b) $\mu gb / 2$

(c) $\mu g / b$

(d) $\mu g / 2b$

Answer	1	(c)	2	(b)	3	(a)	4	(c)	5	(b)	6	(c)	7	(c)	8	(d)
Key	9	(a)	10	(c)	11	(a)	12	(c)	13	(a)	14	(b)	15	(d)		

16. The coefficient of friction between the block A of mass m and block B of mass $2m$ is μ. There is no friction between block B & the inclined plane. If the system of blocks A and B is released from rest & there is no slipping between A & B then :

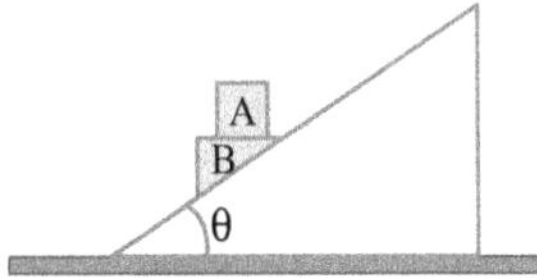

(a) $2\theta \leq \sin^{-1}(2\mu)$

(b) $\theta \leq \tan^{-1}(\mu)$

(c) $2\theta \leq \cos^{-1}(2\mu)$

(d) $2\theta \leq \tan^{-1}(\mu/2)$

17. In figure the mass of the block $M = 1$ kg, $\mu = 0.5$ and $\sin \theta = 3/5$. The acceleration of the block if $F = 10$ N:

(a) 4 m/s^2

(b) 8 m/s^2

(c) 12 m/s^2

(d) 16 m/s^2

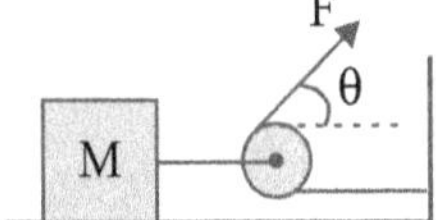

18. The blocks of masses m and M are not attached. The coefficient of static friction between the blocks is μ, but the surface beneath M is smooth. What is the maximum magnitude of the horizontal force F required to hold it against M:

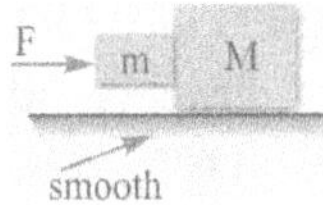

(a) $\dfrac{m(M+m)g}{M}$

(b) $\dfrac{m(M+m)g}{\mu M}$

(c) $\dfrac{M(M+m)g}{\mu M}$

(d) $m\,(M+m)g$

19. A body of mass M is kept on a rough horizontal surface (coefficient of friction μ). A person is trying to pull the body by applying a horizontal force but the body is not moving. The force by the surface on A is F where:

(a) $F = Mg$

(b) $F = \mu M g$

(c) $Mg \leq F \leq Mg\sqrt{(1+\mu^2)}$

(d) $Mg \geq F \geq Mg\sqrt{(1+\mu^2)}$

20. In the figure shown, friction force between the bead and the light string is mg/4, the time in which the bead looses contact with string after the system is released from rest

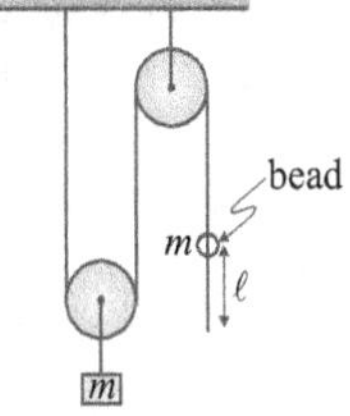

(a) $\sqrt{\dfrac{7\ell}{8g}}$

(b) $\sqrt{\dfrac{8\ell}{7g}}$

(c) $\sqrt{\dfrac{4\ell}{7g}}$

(d) $\sqrt{\dfrac{2\ell}{7g}}$

Variable Mass System

21. A plate moves normally with a speed v_1 towards a horizontal jet of water of uniform area of cross section. The jet discharges water at the rate of volume V per second at a speed of v_2. The density of water is ρ. Assume that water splashes along the surface of the plate at right angles to the original motion. The magnitude of the force acting on the plate due to the jet of water is:

(a) $\rho V v_1$

(b) $\rho V(v_1 + v_2)$

(c) $\dfrac{\rho V}{v_1 + v_2} v_1^2$

(d) $\rho\left[\dfrac{V}{v}\right](v_1 + v_2)^2$

Equilibrium

22. Find the tension T needed to hold the cart equilibrium, if there is no friction

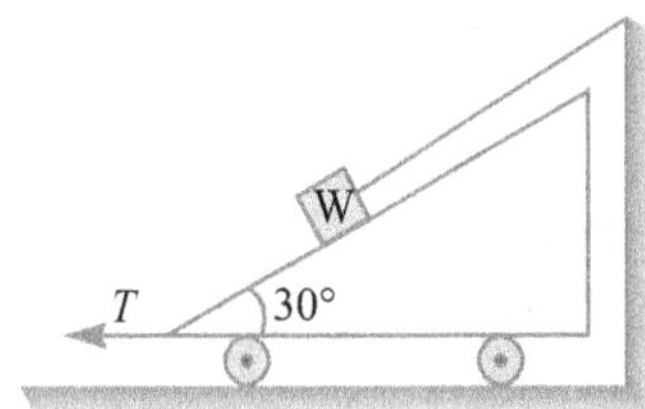

(a) $\dfrac{\sqrt{3}}{4}W$

(b) $\dfrac{\sqrt{2}}{2}W$

(c) $\dfrac{2}{\sqrt{3}}W$

(d) $\dfrac{4}{\sqrt{3}}W$

23. Two smooth cylindrical bars weighing W each lie next to each other in contact. A similar third bar is placed over the two bars as shown in figure. Neglecting friction, the minimum horizontal force on each lower bar necessary to keep them together is

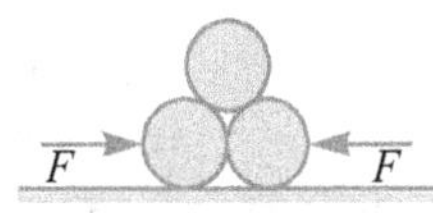

(a) $\dfrac{W}{2}$

(b) W

(c) $\dfrac{W}{\sqrt{3}}$

(d) $\dfrac{W}{2\sqrt{3}}$

Answer	16	(b)	17	(c)	18	(b)	19	(c)	20	(b)
Key	21	(d)	22	(a)	23	(d)				

24. In figure, one end of a uniform beam weighs 222 N is attached to a wall with a hinge. The other end is supported by a wire. The tension in the wire is :

(a) 111 N

(b) 192 N

(c) 222 N

(d) none of these

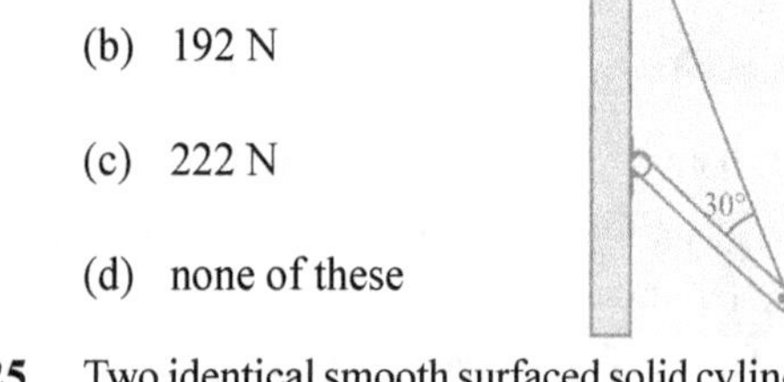

25. Two identical smooth surfaced solid cylinders of radius r are placed touching along their lengths on a horizontal surface. A third cylinder of same material but twice the radius of that

of the cylinders is placed lengthwise on them so that the system remains at rest. If all three cylinders have the same length, then minimum value of the coefficient of friction between smaller cylinders and the surface is:

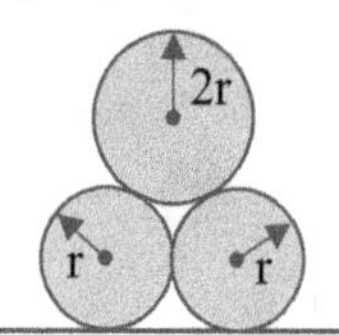

(a) $\dfrac{1}{\sqrt{2}}$

(b) $\dfrac{1}{3}$

(c) $\dfrac{1}{3\sqrt{2}}$

(d) none of these

Answer Key	23	(d)	24	(b)	25	(c)

Mechanics	MCQ Type 2	Exercise 5.2

MULTIPLE CORRECT OPTIONS

1. A body is at rest:
(a) no force acting on it
(b) body is very massive, and therefore it is at rest
(c) there may be many forces, but there net effect is zero
(d) none of these

2. A body is in translatory equilibrium:
(a) resultant force on it zero
(b) it may be at rest
(c) it has uniform speed
(d) it is accelerated

3. Which of the following systems may be adequately described by classical physics?
(a) motion of a cricket ball
(b) motion of a dust particle
(c) motion of electron is an atom
(d) a neutron inside the nucleus

4. Two protons inside a nucleus exert force on each other. The nature of force is:
(a) gravitational
(b) electromagnetic
(c) nuclear
(d) weak

5. A reference frame attached to earth
(a) is an inertial frame by definition
(b) can not be inertial frame because the earth is revolving round the sun
(c) is an inertial frame because Newton's laws are applicable in this frame
(d) can not be an inertial frame because the earth is rotating about its own axis

6. The force exerted by the lift on the foot of a person is more than his weight, the lift is:
(a) going up and slowing down
(b) going up and speeding up
(c) going down and slowing down
(d) going down and speeding up

7. The limiting friction depends on:
(a) nature of surfaces in contact
(b) the area of surfaces in contact
(c) normal reaction between surfaces
(d) foreign matter between surfaces

8. Kinetic friction is always
(a) less than rolling friction
(b) equal to rolling friction
(c) greater than rolling friction
(d) less than limiting static friction

9. Let F, F_N and f denote the magnitudes of the contact force, normal force and the friction exerted by one surface on the other kept in contact. If none of these is zero:
(a) $F > F_N$
(b) $F > f$
(c) $F_N > f$
(d) $(F_N - f) < F < (F_N + f)$

Answer	1	(a,c)	2	(a, b, c)	3	(a, b)	4	(a, b, c)	5	(b, d)	6	(b, c)
Key	7	(a, c, d)	8	(c, d)	9	(a, b, d)						

10. Two masses $M_A = 1$kg and $M_B = 2$ kg are connected by a massless spring as shown in figure. A force of 4 N acts on the 2 kg mass:

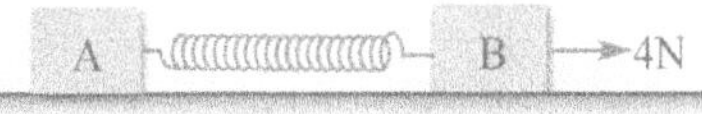

   (a) when acceleration of A is 1 m/s^2

       the acceleration of B is $\dfrac{3}{2}$ m/s^2

   (b) when acceleration of A is $\dfrac{4}{3}$ m/s^2

       the acceleration of B is $\dfrac{4}{3}$ m/s^2

   (c) the acceleration of A always be less or equal to the acceleration of B

   (d) none of the above

11. A painter is raising himself and the crate on which he stands with an acceleration of 5 m/s^2 by a massless rope–and–pulley arrangement. Mass of painter is 100 kg and that of the crate is 50 kg. If $g = 10$ m/s^2, then

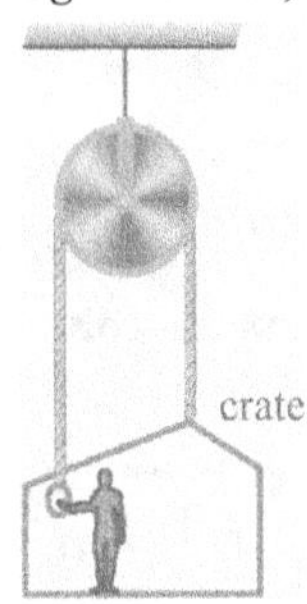

   (a) tension in the rope is 2250 N

   (b) tension in the rope is 1125 N

   (c) force of contact between painter and the floor is 750 N

   (d) force of contact between the painter and the floor is 375 N

12. A block is placed on a rough prism. The block will be stationary relative to prism if acceleration of prism a is:

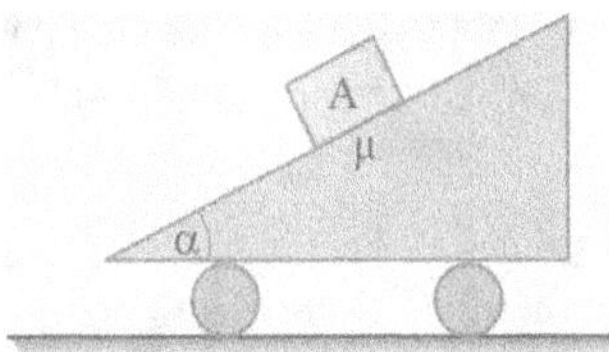

   (a) $a = g\,(1 - \mu\cot\alpha)\,/\,(\mu + \cot\alpha)$ towards left

   (b) $a = g\,(\mu + \cot\alpha)\,/\,(\mu + \tan\alpha)$ right

   (c) $a = g\,(1 + \mu\cot\alpha)\,/\,(\cot\alpha - \mu)$ towards left

   (d) none

13. Two blocks having masses m_1 and m_2 are connected by a thread and are placed on an inclined plane with thread loose as shown in figure. When the blocks are released :

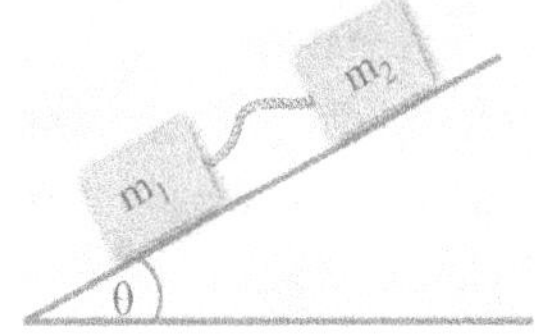

   (a) thread will remain loose if $m_1 < m_2$

   (b) thread will remain loose if plane is smooth

   (c) thread will remain loose if m_1 is smooth and m_2 is rough

   (d) thread will remain loose if m_1 is rough and m_2 is smooth

14. Small blocks A and B are simultaneously released from apex of a smooth wedge as shown in figure, select correct alternative(s):

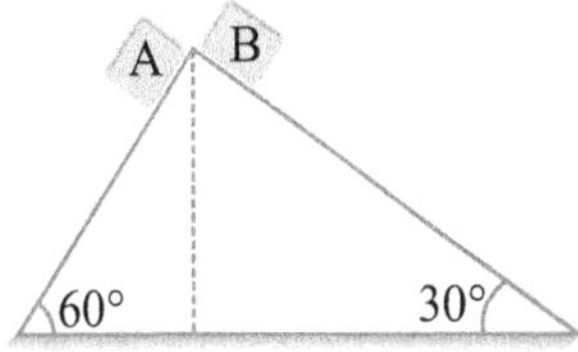

   (a) relative acceleration of block B with respect to block A is zero

   (b) magnitude of relative acceleration of block B with respect to block A is 'g' initially

   (c) speed of block A and B will be same at the bottom of inclined plane

   (d) time taken A and B to reach the bottom of inclined plane will be same.

15. Two blocks A and B of the same mass are joined by a light string and placed on a horizontal surface. An external horizontal force F acts on A. The tension in the string is T. The forces of friction acting on A and B are f_1 and f_2 respectively. The limiting value of f_1 and f_2 is f. As F is gradually increased:

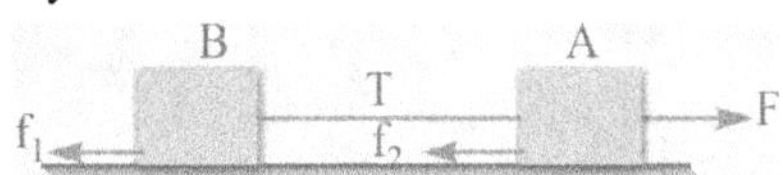

   (a) for $F < f$, $T = 0$

   (b) for $f < F < 2f$, $T = F - f$

   (c) for $F > 2f$, $T = \dfrac{F}{2}$

   (d) none of the above

16. A man tries to remain in equilibrium by pushing with his hands and feet against two parallel walls. For equilibrium:

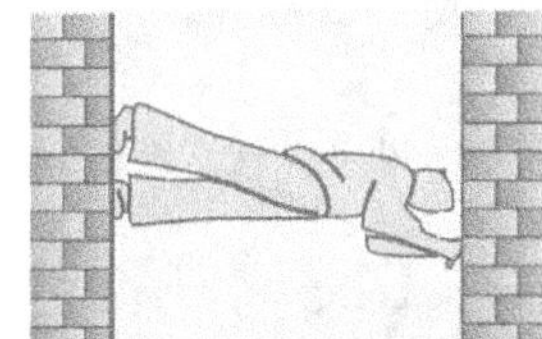

Answer	10	(a, b, c)	11	(b, d)	12	(a, c)	13	(b, d)	14	(b, c)
Key	15	(a, b, c)								

(a) he must exert equal forces on the two walls

(b) the forces of friction at the two walls must be equal

(c) friction must be present on both walls

(d) the coefficient of friction must be the same between both walls and the man

17. In the arrangement shown in figure pulley and strings are ideal. End A of string connected to pulley P_1 is moved upwards with acceleration $a_A = 2$ m/s^2 while end B of another string shown in figure is moved up with acceleration $a_B = 1$ m/s^2. Block C of mass 1 kg is moving up with acceleration 1 m/s^2. If block D to which string are connected symmetrically moves such that its orientations remains same then (assume g = 10 m/s^2)

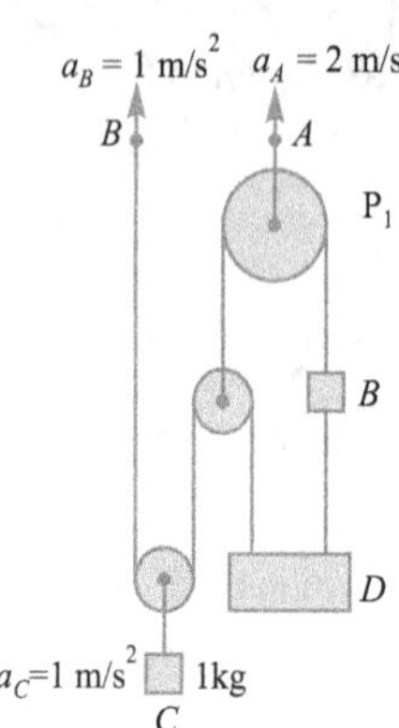

(a) acceleration of block D is 1/2 m/s^2 upwards

(b) end A is pulled with force of 22 N

(c) mass of block B is 1/2 kg

(d) acceleration of block B is 7/3 m/s^2 upwards

Answer Key	16	(a, c)	17	(b, d)

Reasoning Type Questions   Exercise 5.3

Read the two statements carefully to mark the correct option out of the options given below:

(a) **Statement - 1** is true, **Statement - 2** is true; **Statement - 2** is correct explanation for **Statement - 1**.

(b) **Statement -1** is true, **Statement - 2** is true; **Statement - 2** is not correct explanation for **Statement - 1**.

(c) **Statement - 1** is true, **Statement - 2** is false.

(d) **Statement - 1** is false, **Statement - 2** is true

1. **Statement - 1**

In writing with pen, the force between fingers and pen is electrostatics.

Statement - 2

Newtons third law applies to all types of forces, e.g., gravitational, electromagnetic etc.

2. **Statement - 1**

A body suspended with the help of three string. To find the tensions in the strings, three equations are required.

Statement - 2

$$\sum F_x = 0, \ \sum F_y = 0, \ \sum \tau_z = 0.$$

3. **Statement - 1**

Impulse of force and momentum are same physical quantities.

Statement - 2

Both quantities have same unit.

4. **Statement - 1**

A body under the action of two forces is in equilibrium.

Statement - 2

The forces must be collinear.

5. **Statement - 1**

A block placed on a table is at rest, because action force cancels the reaction force on the block.

Statement - 2

The net force on the block is zero.

6. **Statement - 1**

For the motion of electron around nucleus, Newton's second law is used.

Statement - 2

Newton's second law can be used for motion of any object.

7. **Statement - 1**

A cloth covers a table. Some dishes are kept on it. The cloth can be pulled out without dislodging the dishes from the table.

Statement - 2

For every action, there is equal and opposite reaction.

8. **Statement - 1**

It is easier to pull a heavy object than to push it on a level ground.

Statement - 2

The magnitude of frictional force depends on the nature of the two surfaces in contact.

9. **Statement - 1**

A multistage rocket is needed to launch a satellite.

Statement - 2

A single stage rocket can not produce the required velocity.

10. **Statement - 1** A man standing in a lift which is moving upward, will feel his weight to be greater than when the lift was at rest.

    Statement - 2 If the acceleration of the lift is 'a' upward, then the man of mass m shall feel his weight to be equal to normal reaction (N) exerted by the lift given by

    $N = m(g + a)$ (where g is acceleration due to gravity) Friction always opposes motion.

11. **Statement - 1** A man and a block rest on smooth horizontal surface. The man holds a rope which is connected to block. The man cannot move on the horizontal surface.

    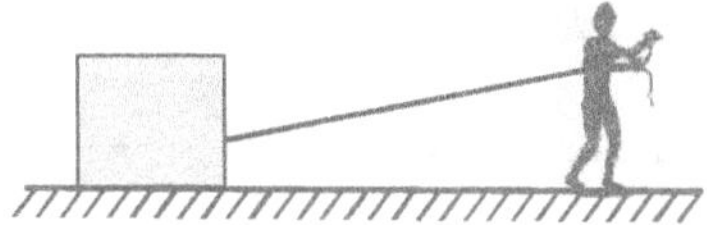

    Statement - 2 A man standing at rest on smooth horizontal surface cannot start walking due to absence of friction (The man is only in contact with floor as shown).

12. **Statement - 1**

    A cloth covers a table. Some dishes are kept on it. The cloth can be pulled out without dislodging the dishes from the table because

    Statement - 2

    For every action there is an equal and opposite reaction.

    [IIT-JEE 2007]

13. **Statement - 1** : It is easier to pull a heavy object than to push it on a level ground and

    Statement - 2 The magnitude of frictional force depends on the nature of the two surfaces in contact.

    [IIT-JEE 2008]

Answer	1	(a)	2	(b)	3	(d)	4	(a)	5	(d)	6	(c)	7	(b)
Key	8	(b)	9	(a)	10	(d)	11	(d)	12	(b)	13	(b)		

Mechanics   **Passage & Matrix**   Exercise 1.4

PASSAGES

Passage for (Questions 1 & 2)

At the moment $t = 0$ a stationary particle of mass m experiences a time dependent force $F = at(\tau - t)$, where a is a constant, τ is the time for which the force acts.

1. The momentum of the particle when the action of the force stopped:

   (a) $\dfrac{a\tau^3}{6}$ (b) $\dfrac{a\tau^3}{5}$

   (c) $\dfrac{a\tau^3}{3}$ (d) $a\tau^3$

2. The distance travelled by the particle while the force acted:

   (a) $\dfrac{a\tau^4}{m}$ (b) $\dfrac{a\tau^4}{6m}$

   (c) $\dfrac{a\tau^4}{12m}$ (d) $\dfrac{a\tau^4}{24m}$

Passage for (Questions 3 & 4)

A particle A of mass $2m$ is held on a smooth horizontal table and is attached to one end of an inelastic string which runs over a smooth light pulley at the edge of the table. At the other end of the string there hangs another particle B of mass m. The distance from A to the pulley is ℓ. The particle A is then projected towards the pulley with velocity u.

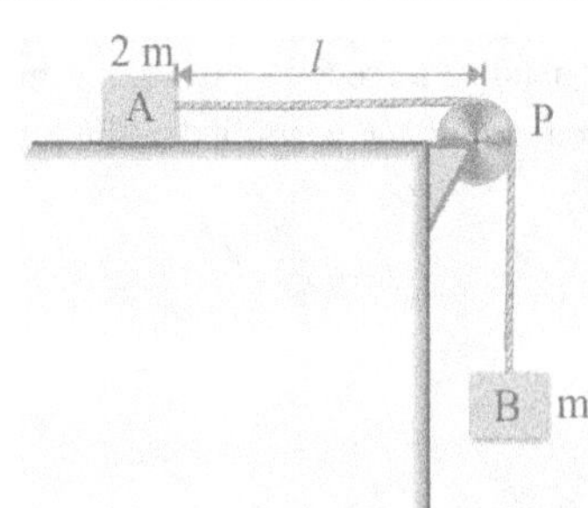

3. The speed of B, when the string becomes taut :

   (a) u (b) $\dfrac{u}{2}$

   (c) $\dfrac{3u}{4}$ (d) $\dfrac{4u}{3}$

4. The common velocity when A reaches the pulley (assume that B has not yet reached the ground)

   (a) $\dfrac{4u}{3}$ (b) $\dfrac{4u}{3}$

   (c) $\dfrac{\sqrt{4u^2 + 6gl}}{3}$ (d) $\dfrac{\sqrt{u^2 + 6gl}}{3}$

Passage for (Questions 5 to 7)

The masses of the bodies A and B in figure are 20 kg and 10 kg, respectively. They are initially at rest on the floor and are connected by a weightless string passing over a weightless and frictionless pulley. An upward force F is applied to the pulley.

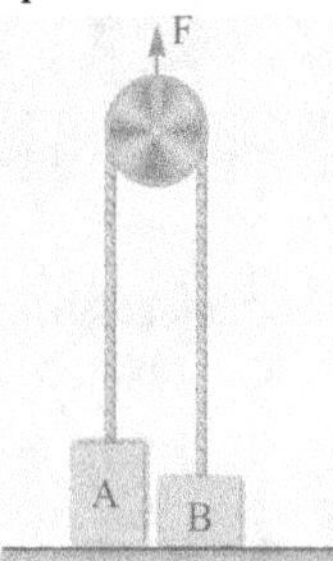

5. The acceleration a_1 of body A and a_2 of body B when F is 98 N

(a)   0, 0   (b)   3.3 m/s^2, 6.6 m/s^2

(c)   3.3 m/s^2, 3.3 m/s^2 (d)   none of these

6. Find the acceleration a_1 of body A and a_2 of body B when F is 96 N

(a)   0.05 m/s^2, 1m/s^2 (b)   0, 0

(c)   0.05 m/s^2, 0   (d)   none of these

7. Find the acceleration a_1 of body A and a_2 of body B when F is 394 N.

(a)   0.05 m/s^2, 0.05 m/s^2 (b)   9.9 m/s^2, 9.9 m/s^2

(c)   0.05 m/s^2, 9.9 m/s^2.   (d)   none of these

Passage for (Questions 8 to 10)

In figure $m_1 = 1$kg and $m_2 = 2$ kg. The pulley is movable. At $t = 0$, both masses touch the ground and the string is taut. A vertically upward, time-dependent force $F = 2t$, where t is the time in second and F is the force in newton, is applied to the pulley. Calculate

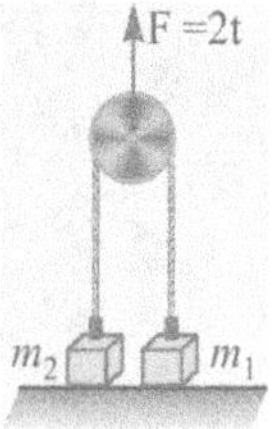

8. The time when m_1 is lifted off the ground is

(a)   9.81 s   (b)   9.89 s

(c)   8.91 s   (d)   9.91 s

9. The time when m_2 is lifted off the ground is

(a)   19.62 s   (b)   25.50 s

(c)   27.2 s   (d)   30.0 s

10. When $t = 25$ s, what is the acceleration of the masses as seen by an observer outside?

(a)   2 m/s^2, 2 m/s^2 (b)   2.69 m/s^2, 15.19 m/s^2

(c)   15.19 ms^2, 2.69 m/s^2.   (d)   none of these

Passage for (Questions 11 & 12)

In the system shown in figure, $M = 13.4$ kg, $m_1 = 1$kg, $m_2 = 2$kg and $m_3 = 3.6$ kg. The coefficient of static friction between m_1 and m_2 is 0.75 and that between m_2 and M is 0.6. All other surfaces are frictionless

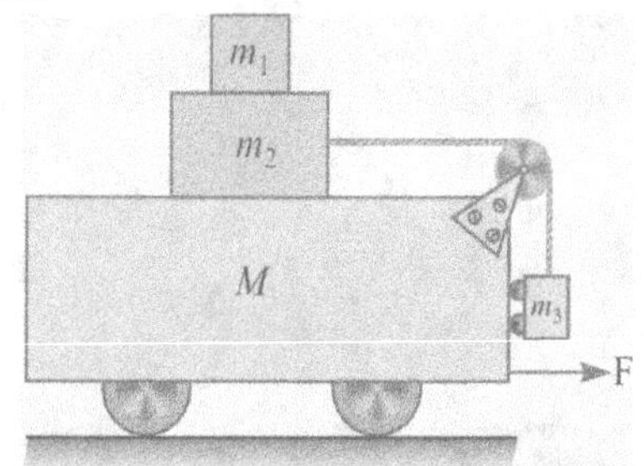

11. The minimum horizontal force F must be applied to M so that m_2 does not slip on M is

(a)   117.7 N,   (b)   120.5 N

(c)   125 N   (d)   145.5 N

12. The maximum value of F for which m_1 does not slip on m_2 is

(a)   125 N   (b)   147 N

(c)   165 N   (d)   175 N

Answer	1	(a)	2	(c)	3	(d)	4	(c)	5	(a)	6	(b)
Key	7	(c)	8	(a)	9	(a)	10	(c)	11	(a)	12	(b)

MATRIX MATCHING

13. A light string $ABCDE$ whose extremity A is fixed, has weights W_1 and W_2 attached to it at B and C. It passes round a small smooth peg at D carrying a weight of 300 N at the free end E as shown in figure. If in the equilibrium position, BC is horizontal and AB and CD make 150° and 120° with CB. *Match the columns* :

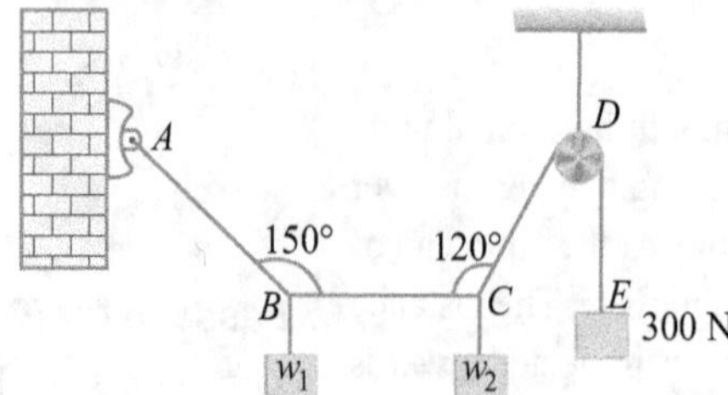

Column I		Column II	
A.	Tension in portion AB, T_{AB}	(p)	150 N
B.	Tension in portion BC, T_{BC}	(q)	173 N
C.	Weight, W_1	(r)	260 N
D.	Weight, W_2	(s)	87 N

14. In the device blocks A, B, and C are of masses 4 kg, 5 kg and 15 kg respectively. The coefficient of friction for the contact surfaces of bodies A and B is 0.4. *Match the columns* :

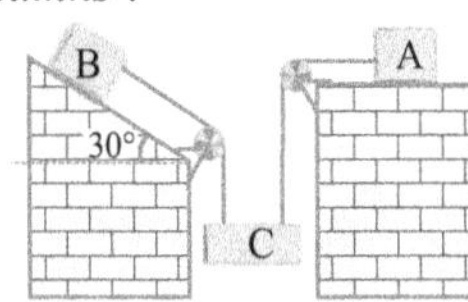

Column I		Column II	
A.	Tension in the string connected with body A, T_A	(p)	21.47 N
B.	Tension in the string connected in body B, T_B	(q)	38.88 N
C.	Acceleration of body A, a_A	(r)	5.8 m/s^2
D.	Acceleration of body B, a_B	(s)	6.4 m/s^2

Answer Key   13 | $A \rightarrow q$; $B \rightarrow p$; $C \rightarrow s$; $D \rightarrow r$ 14 | $A \rightarrow q$; $B \rightarrow p$; $C \rightarrow r$; $D \rightarrow r$

Mechanics   **Best of JEE-(Main & Advanced)**   Exercise 5.5

JEE- (Main)

[AIEE E2005]

1. When forces F_1, F_2, F_3 are acting on a particle of mass m such that F_2 and F_3 are mutually perpendicular, then the particle remains stationary. If the force F_1 is now removed then the acceleration of the particle is **[AIEEE 2002]**
   (a) F_1/m (b) F_2F_3/mF_1
   (c) $(F_2 - F_3)/m$ (d) F_2/m.

2. A spring balance is attached to the ceiling of a lift. A man hangs his bag on the spring and the spring reads 49 N, when the lift is stationary. If the lift moves downward with an acceleration of 5 m/s^2, the reading of the spring balance will be **[AIEEE 2003]**
   (a) 24 N   (b) 74 N
   (c) 15 N   (d) 49 N

3. A horizontal force of 10 N is necessary to just hold a block stationary against a wall. The coefficient of friction between the block and the wall is 0.2. The weight of the block is

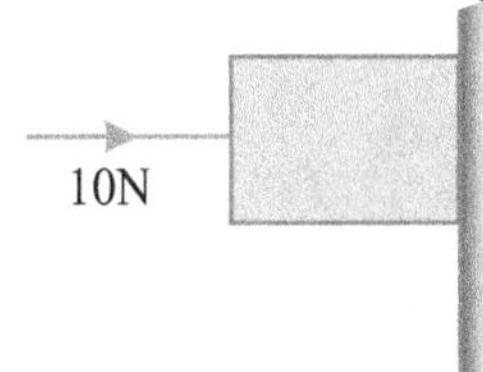

   (a) 20 N   (b) 50 N   **[AIEEE 2003]**
   (c) 100 N   (d) 2 N

4. A marble block of mass 2 kg lying on ice when given a velocity of 6 m/s is stopped by friction in 10 s. Then the coefficient of friction is **[AIEEE 2003]**
   (a) 0.02   (b) 0.03
   (c) 0.04   (d) 0.06

5. A block is kept on a frictionless inclined surface with angle of inclination 'α'. The incline is given an acceleration 'a' to keep the block stationary. Then a is equal to

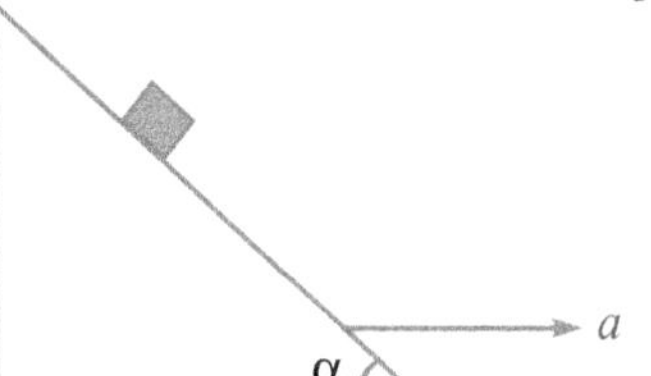

   (a) $g \, \mathrm{cosec}\,\alpha$ (b) $g / \tan \alpha$
   (c) $g \tan \alpha$ (d) g

6. A smooth block is released at rest on a 45° incline and then slides a distance 'd'. The time taken to slide is 'n' times as much to slide on rough incline than on a smooth incline. The coefficient of friction is **[AIEEE 2005]**
   (a) $\mu_k = \sqrt{1 - \dfrac{1}{n^2}}$ (b) $\mu_k = 1 - \dfrac{1}{n^2}$
   (c) $\mu_s = \sqrt{1 - \dfrac{1}{n^2}}$ (d) $\mu_s = 1 - \dfrac{1}{n^2}$

7. The upper half of an inclined plane with inclination ϕ is perfectly smooth while the lower half is rough. A body starting from rest at the top will again come to rest at the bottom, if the coefficient of friction for the lower half is : **[AIEEE 2005]**
   (a) $2 \tan \phi$ (b) $\tan \phi$
   (c) $2 \sin \phi$ (d) $2 \cos \phi$

8. Two fixed frictionless inclined planes making an angle 30° and 60° with the vertical are shown in the figure. Two blocks A and B are placed on the two planes. What is the relative vertical acceleration of A with respect to B ? **[AIEEE 2010]**

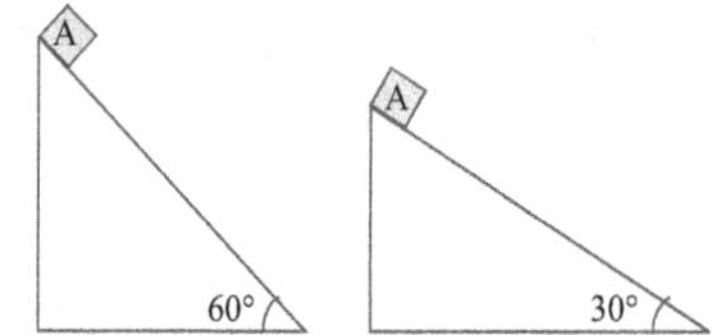

(a) $4.9\ ms^{-2}$ in horizontal direction

(b) $9.8\ ms^{-2}$ in vertical direction

(c)   Zero

(d) $4.9\ ms^{-2}$ in vertical direction

9. The minimum force required to start pushing a body up rough (frictional coefficient μ) inclined plane is F_1 while the minimum force needed to prevent it from sliding down is F_2. If the inclined plane makes an angle θ from the horizontal such that $\tan\theta = 2\mu$ then the ratio $\dfrac{F_1}{F_2}$ is **[AIEEE 2011RS]**

(a)   1   (b)   2

(c)   3   (d)   4

10. A particle of mass m is at rest at the origin at time $t = 0$. It is subjected to a force $F(t) = F_0 e^{-bt}$ in the x direction. Its speed $v(t)$ is depicted by which of the following curves? **[AIEEE 2012]**

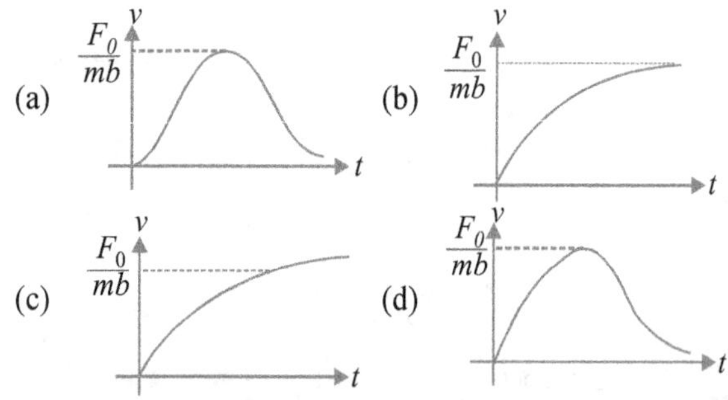

11. A block B is placed on block A. The mass of block B is less than the mass of block A. Friction exists between the blocks, where as the ground on which the block A is placed is taken to be smooth. A horizontal force F increasing linearly with time begins to act on B. The acceleration a_A and a_B of blocks A and B respectively are plotted against t. The correctly plotted graph is: **[AIEEE 2012]**

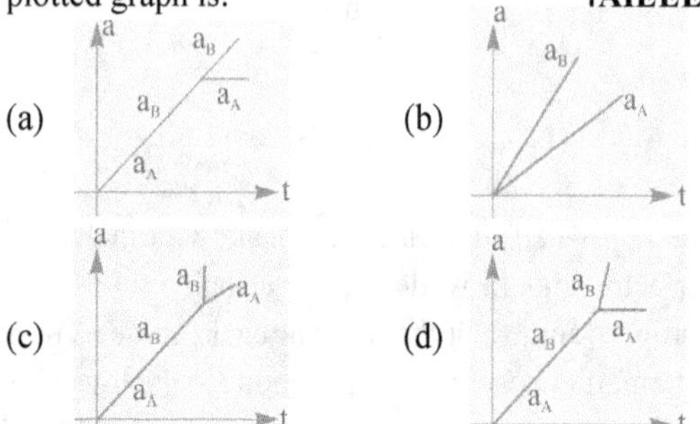

12. Given in the figure are two blocks A and B of weigh 20 N and 100 N respectively. These are being pressed against a wall by a force F as shown. If the coefficient of friction between the blocks

is 0.1 and between block B and the wall is 0.15, the frictional force applied by the wall on block B is **[JEE-(main) 2015]**

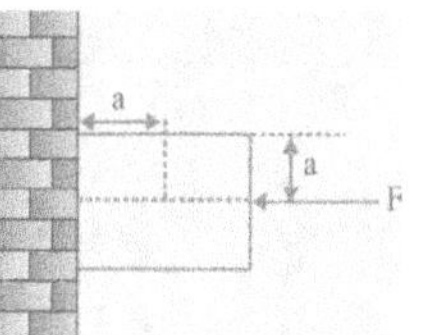

(a)   80 N

(b)   120 N

(c)   150 N

(d)   100 N

13. A particle of mass m moving in the x direction with speed $2v$ is hit by another particle of mass 2 m moving in the y direction with speed v. If the collision is perfectly inelastic, the percentage loss in the energy during the collision is close to **[JEE-(main) 2015]**

(a)   50%   (b)   56%

(c)   62%   (d)   44%

JEE- (Advanced)

14. A horizontal force F is applied such that the block remains stationary then which of the following statement is false **[IIT-JEE-2005]**

(a) $f = mg$, where f is frictional force

(b) $F = N$, where N is the normal force

(c) f does not produce any torque

(d) N does not produce any torque

15. A circular disc with a groove along its diameter is placed horizontally. A block of mass 1 kg is placed as shown. The coefficient of friction between the block and all surfaces of groove in contact is $\mu = 2/5$. The disc has an acceleration of $25\ m/s^2$. The acceleration of the block with respect to disc: **[IIT-JEE-2006]**

$$\cos\theta = \frac{4}{5}, \quad \sin\theta = \frac{3}{5}$$

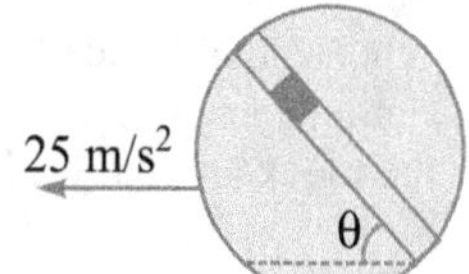

(a) $10\ m/s^2$ (b) $8\ m/s^2$

(c) $5\ m/s^2$ (d)   zero

16. Two blocks A and B of masses 2 m and m, respectively, are connected by a massless and inextensible string. The whole system is suspended by a massless spring as shown in the figure. The magnitude of acceleration of A and B, immediately after the string is cut, are respectively :

[IIT-JEE-2006]

Answer	1	(a)	2	(a)	3	(d)	4	(d)	5	(c)	6	(b)	7	(a)	8	(a)
Key	9	(c)	10	(c)	11	(d)	12	(b)	13	(b)	14	(c)	15	(a)		

(a) $g, \dfrac{g}{2}$

(b) $\dfrac{g}{2}, g$

(c) g, g

(d) $\dfrac{g}{2}, \dfrac{g}{2}$

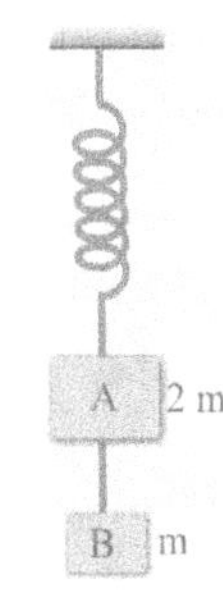

17. A satellite in force - free space sweeps stationary interplanetary dust at a rate $\dfrac{dM}{dt} = \alpha v$. The acceleration of satellite is :

(a) $\dfrac{-2\alpha v^2}{M}$

(b) $\dfrac{-\alpha v^2}{M}$

(c) $\dfrac{-\alpha v^2}{2M}$

(d) $-\alpha v^2$

18. Two particles of mass m each are tied at the ends of a light string of length $2a$. The whole system is kept on a frictionless horizontal surface with the string held tight so that each mass is at a distance 'a' from the centre P (as shown in the figure). **[IIT-JEE - 2007]**

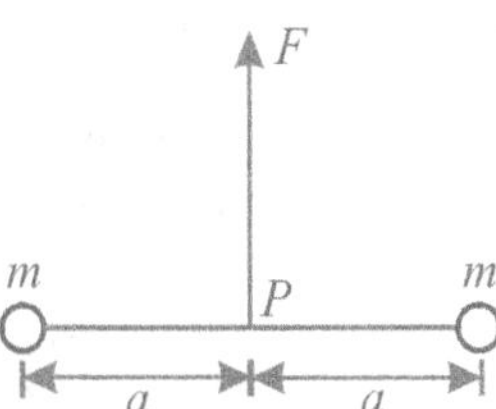

Now, the mid-point of the string is pulled vertically upwards with a small but constant force F. As a result, the particles move towards each other on the surface. The magnitude of acceleration, when the separation between them becomes $2x$, is **[IIT-JEE - 2007]**

(a) $\dfrac{F}{2m}\dfrac{a}{\sqrt{a^2 - x^2}}$

(b) $\dfrac{F}{2m}\dfrac{x}{\sqrt{a^2 - x^2}}$

(c) $\dfrac{F}{2m}\dfrac{x}{a}$

(d) $\dfrac{F}{2m}\dfrac{\sqrt{a^2 - x^2}}{x}$

19. A piece of wire is bent in the shape of a parabola $y = kx^2$ (y-axis vertical) with a bead of mass m on it. The bead can slide on the wire without friction. It stays at the lowest point of the parabola when the wire is at rest. The wire is now accelerated parallel to the x-axis with a constant acceleration a. The distance of the new equilibrium position of the bead, where the bead can stay at rest with respect to the wire, from the y-axis is **[IIT-JEE 2009]**

(a) $\dfrac{a}{gk}$

(b) $\dfrac{a}{2gk}$

(c) $\dfrac{2a}{gk}$

(d) $\dfrac{a}{4gk}$

20. A block of mass m is on an inclined plane of angle θ. The coefficient of friction between the block and the plane is μ and $\tan \theta > \mu$. The block is held stationary by applying a force P parallel to the plane. The direction of force pointing up the plane is taken to be positive. As P is varied from $P_1 = mg(\sin \theta - \mu \cos \theta)$ to $P_2 = mg(\sin \theta + \mu \cos \theta)$, the frictional force f versus P graph will look like

[IIT-JEE 2010]

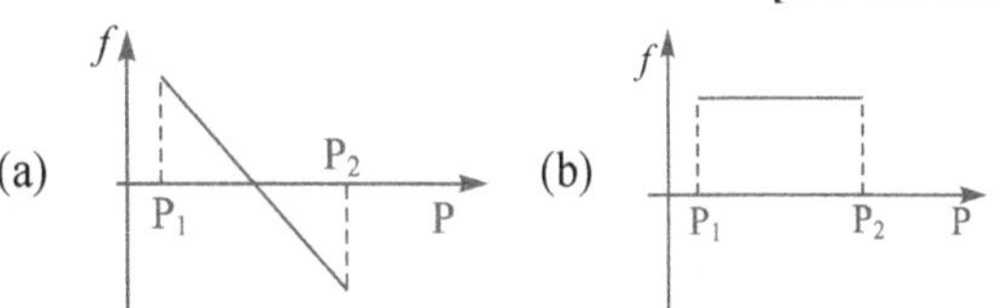

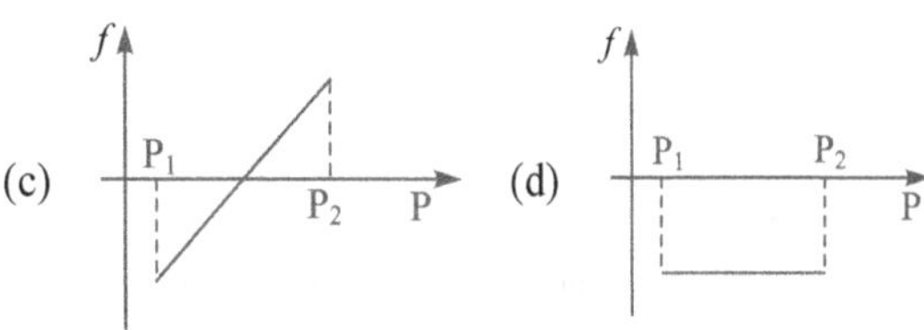

21. A small block of mass of 0.1 kg lies on a fixed inclined plane PQ which makes an angle θ with the horizontal. A horizontal force of 1 N acts on the block through its centre of mass as shown in the figure. **[IIT-JEE 2012]** The block remains stationary if (take $g = 10$ m/s^2)

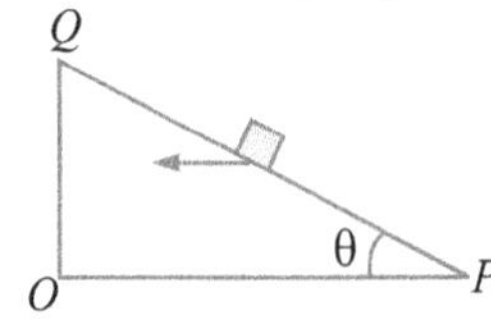

(a) $\theta = 45°$

(b) $\theta > 45°$ and a frictional force acts on the block towards P.

(c) $\theta > 45°$ and a frictional force acts on the block towards Q.

(d) $\theta < 45°$ and a frictional force acts on the block towards Q.

22 A block is moving on an inclined plane making an angle 45° with the horizontal and the coefficient of friction is m. The force required to just push it up the inclined plane is 3 times the force required to just prevent it from sliding down. If we define N = 10 m, then N is **[Integer]**

[IIT-JEE 2011]

Hints & Solutions

In Chapter Exercise -5.1

1. Given $m = 70$ kg, $a = 10$ ms^{-2}

   The weighing machine gives the reading of the reaction force, R, which is apparent weight.

   (a) When lift is moving upwards with a uniform speed, acceleration = 0,

   $\therefore R = mg = 70 \times 9.8 = 700$ N

   (b) When lift is moving downwards with acceleration $= 5$ms^{-2},

   $\therefore R = m(g - a) = 70 \times (10 - 5) = 350$ N

   (c) When lift is moving upwards with acceleration $= 5$ ms^{-2},

   $\therefore R = m(g + a) = 70 \times (10 + 5) = 1050$ N

   (d) When lift is coming down freely under gravity, acceleration, $a = g$,

   $\therefore R = m(g - g) = 0$

2. (a) When the monkey climbs up with an acceleration, then

   $T - mg = ma$

   $\therefore T = mg + ma = m (g + a)$

   or $T = 40$ kg $(10 + 6)$ ms$^{-2} = 640$ N

   But the rope can withstand a maximum tension of 600 N. So the rope will break.

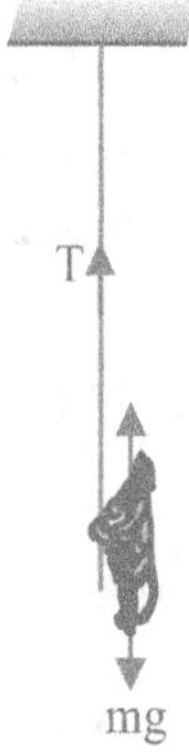

   (b) When the monkey is climbing down with an acceleration, then

   $mg - T = ma$

   $\Rightarrow \quad T = mg - ma = m (g - a)$

   or $\quad T = 40$ kg $(10 - 4)$ ms$^{-2} = 240$ N

   The rope will not break.

   (c) When the monkey climbs up with uniform speed, then

   $T = mg = 40$ kg $\times 10$ ms$^{-2} = 400$ N $[\because a = 0]$

   The rope will not break.

   (d) When the monkey is falling freely, it would be a state of weightlessness. So, tension will be zero and the rope will not break.

3. For the downward motion of the aerostat,

   $$mg - R = ma \qquad ...(i)$$

   where R is the buoyant force (assuming constant).

   If Δm is the ballast mass to be dumped from the aerostat, then

   $$R - (m - \Delta m)g = (m - \Delta m)a \qquad ...(ii)$$

After solving above equations, we get

$$\Delta m = \frac{2ma}{(g + a)}.$$

4. In the device the acceleration (magnitude) of the blocks are

   $a_1 = a$

   and $\quad a_2 = 2a$

   By Newton's second law, we have

   $$T_0 - Mg = Ma \qquad (i)$$
   $$T_0 = 2T \qquad (ii)$$

   and $\quad Mg - T = M \times 2a \qquad (iii)$

   After solving above equations, we get

   $$a = \frac{g}{5} \text{ m/s}^2$$

   $\therefore \qquad a_2 = 2a = \frac{2g}{5} \text{ m/s}^2$

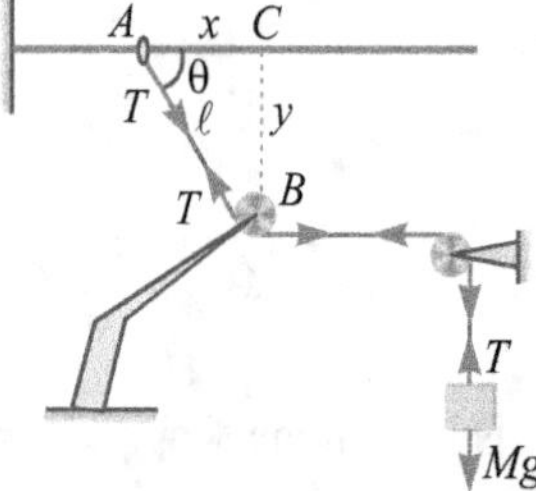

5. Given, mass of helicopter $(m_1) = 2000$ kg

   Mass of the crew and passenger $(m_2) = 500$ kg

   Acceleration in vertical direction, $a = 15$ m/s^2 $(\uparrow)$

   and $\qquad g = 10$ m/s^2 $(\downarrow)$

   (a) Force on the floor of helicopter by the crew and passengers

   $= m_2(g + a)$

   $= 500 (10 + 15)$N

   $= 12500$ N

   (b) Action of the rotor of the helicopter on the surrounding air

   $= (m_1 + m_2) (g + a)$

   $= (2000 + 500) \times (10 + 15)$

   $= 2500 \times 25$

   $= 62500$ N (downward)

   (c) Force on the helicopter due to the surrounding air

   = reaction of force applied by helicopter

   = 62500 N(upward)

6. **Kinematics of the problem :**

At any instant,

$$x^2 + y^2 = \ell^2, \qquad ...(i)$$

in which x and ℓ varies with time, while y remains constant.

Differentiating equation (i) twice with respect to time, we get

$$2x \frac{d^2 x}{dt^2} + 0 = 2\ell \frac{d^2 \ell}{dt^2}.$$

Here $\dfrac{d^2x}{dt^2}$, is the acceleration of the ring and $\dfrac{d^2l}{dt^2}$ is the acceleration of the block.

So we have

$$a_{\text{ring}} = \frac{a_{\text{block}}}{(x/l)}$$

or $$a_{\text{ring}} = \frac{a_{\text{block}}}{\cos\alpha} \qquad ...(ii)$$

Dynamics of the problem :

From the FBD, we can write;

$$Mg - T = M\,a_{\text{block}} \qquad ...(iii)$$

and $$T\cos\alpha = ma_{\text{ring}} \qquad ...(iv)$$

After solving equations (ii), (iii) and (iv) and for $\alpha = \theta$, we get

$$a_{\text{ring}} = \left[\frac{Mg\cos\theta}{m + M\cos^2\theta}\right].$$

7. The initial extension of the spring

$$x_1 = \frac{45}{450} = 0.1\,\text{m}$$

For the block to move down 0.15 m, the spring will extend by 0.3 m. The final extension of the spring

$$x_2 = 0.1 + 0.3 = 0.4\,\text{m}.$$

By conservation of mechanical energy, we can write

$$mg \times 0.15 = \frac{1}{2}mv^2 + \frac{1}{2}k\left(x_2^2 - x_1^2\right)$$

After substituting the values and solving, we get

$$v = 1.28\,\text{m/s}$$

In Chapter Exercise -5.2

1. Given, speed of water $v = 15\ \text{ms}^{-1}$; area of cross section,

$$a = 10^{-2}\,\text{m}^2 \text{ and}$$

Volume of water coming out per second $= a \times v = 10^{-2} \times 15 = 0.15\ \text{m}^3\,\text{s}^{-1}$.

$$\begin{aligned} F &= \delta Qv = 10^3 \times 0.15 \times 15 \\ &= 2250\ \text{N} \end{aligned}$$

2. $$F = v_r\left(\frac{dm}{dt}\right) = \frac{5 \times 10^5}{100} \times \frac{50}{1000} = 250\ \text{N}$$

3. Acceleration of $t = 0$ is

$$a = \frac{v_r}{m_0}\frac{dm}{dt} - g = \frac{2073}{m_0} \times \frac{1/m_0}{1} - 9.8$$

$$= 34.55 - 9.8 = 24.75\ \text{ms}^{-2}.$$

4. (i) Thrust, $F = v_r\left(\dfrac{dm}{dt}\right) = 6 \times 10^3 \times 100 = 6 \times 10^5\ N$

(ii) $v = v_0 + v_r \ln\dfrac{m_0}{m} = 0 + 6 \times 10^3 \ln 40 = 22.13 \times 10^3\ \text{m/s}.$

5. Let F be the upthrust of the air. As the balloon rises with acceleration a, so

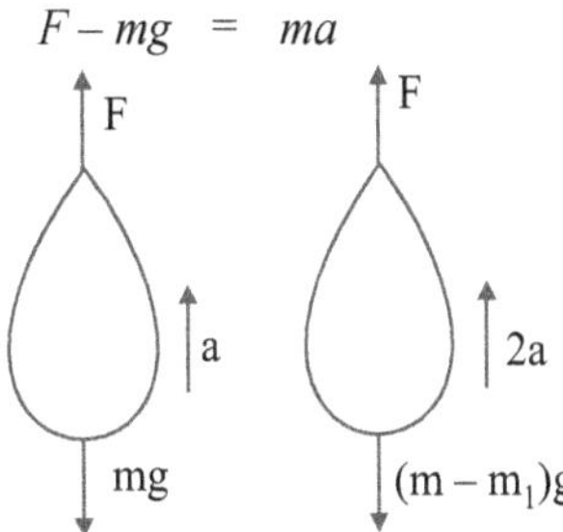

Suppose mass m_1 is removed from the balloon so that the acceleration becomes 2a. Then

$$F - (m - m_1)g = (m - m_1)2a \qquad ...(2)$$

After solving above equations, we get

$$m_1 = \frac{ma}{(g + 2a)}$$

In Chapter Exercise -5.3

1. (a) Force on the 7th coin = weight of the 3 coins lying above 7th coin, $F = 3\,mg$ N (acts vertically downwards)

(b) Eight coin is under the weight of 2 coins above it and its own weight, force on 7th coin due to 8th coin = sum of the 3 coins = $2\,mg + mg = 3\,mg$ N

(c) Sixth coin is under the weight of 4 coins above it, therefore, reaction $= -F = -4\,mg$ N (negative sign shows the reaction is vertically upwards)

2. $$F_1 + 1\cos 45° = 2 \qquad ...(i)$$

and $$F_2 = 2\cos 45° + 1\cos 45° ...(ii)$$

After solving above equations, we get

$$F_1 = 0.707\ \text{N}$$

and $$F_2 = 2.121\ \text{N}.$$

3. The FBD is shown in figure.

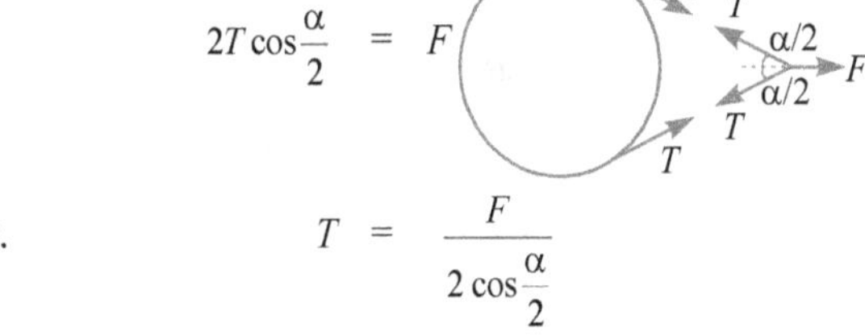

$$2T\cos\frac{\alpha}{2} = F$$

$\therefore \qquad T = \dfrac{F}{2\cos\dfrac{\alpha}{2}}$

For $\quad T > F, \cos\dfrac{\alpha}{2} < \dfrac{1}{2}$

or $\qquad \dfrac{\alpha}{2} > 60°$

$\therefore \qquad \alpha > 120° \qquad\qquad$ **Ans.**

4. The *FBD* of the system is shown in figure.

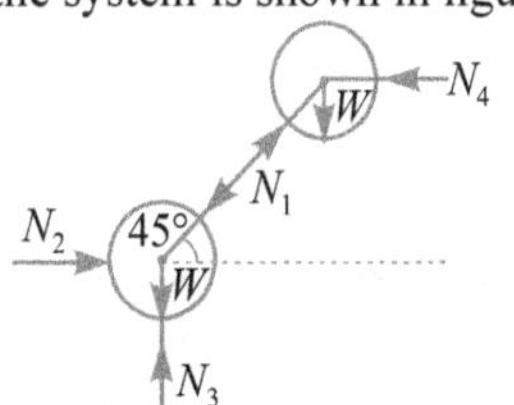

For equilibrium of upper sphere, we have

$\sum F_x = 0;$ or $N_1\cos 45° - N_4 = 0 \qquad ...(i)$

$\sum F_y = 0;$ or $N_1\sin 45° - W = 0 \qquad ...(ii)$

After solving, we get $N_1 = \sqrt{2}\,W,\ N_4 = W$

Similarly for lower sphere,

$$N_1 \cos 45° - N_2 = 0$$

$$\therefore \quad N_2 = N_1 \cos 45° = W$$

and $\quad N_1 \sin 45° + W = N_3$

or $\qquad N_3 = 2W$ **Ans.**

5.

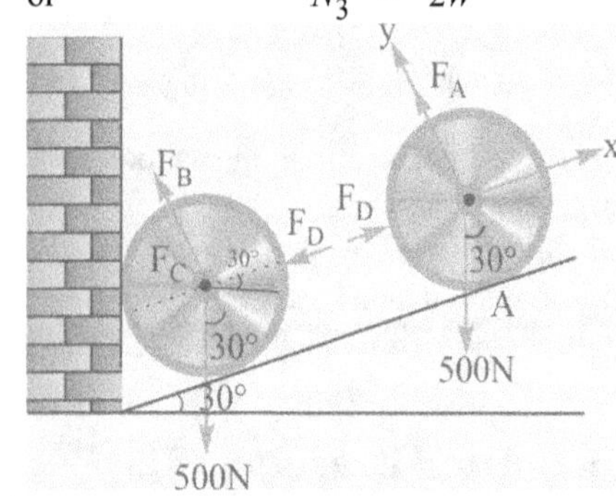

Let F_D be the force of interaction (reaction) between the rollers. Consider the equilibrium of upper roller; we have

$$\sum F_x = 0, \text{ or } F_D - 500 \sin 30° = 0$$

or $\quad F_D = 500 \sin 30° = 250$ N

and $\quad \sum F_y = 0$, or $F_A - 500 \cos 30° = 0$

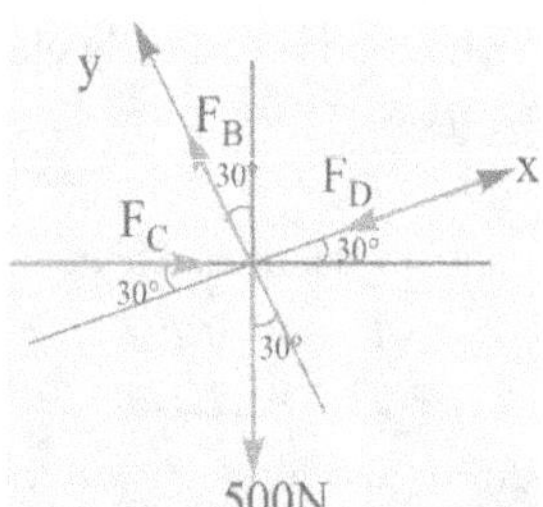

or $\quad F_A = 500 \cos 30° = \dfrac{500\sqrt{3}}{2} = 250\sqrt{3}\,N$. **Ans**

Now consider the equilibrium of lower roller ;

$$\sum F_x = 0, \text{ or } F_C \cos 30° - F_D - 500 \sin 30° = 0$$

or $\quad F_C \times \dfrac{\sqrt{3}}{2} - 250 - 500 \times \dfrac{1}{2} = 0$

or $\qquad F_C = \dfrac{1000}{\sqrt{3}}$ N

and $\sum F_y = 0$,

or $\quad F_B - F_C \sin 30° - 500 \cos 30° = 0$

or $\quad F_B - \dfrac{1000}{\sqrt{3}} \times \dfrac{1}{2} - 500 \times \dfrac{\sqrt{3}}{2} = 0$

or $\qquad F_B = \dfrac{1250}{\sqrt{3}}$ N. **Ans.**

In Chapter Exercise -5.4

1. The *FBD* of all the three cases are shown in figure.

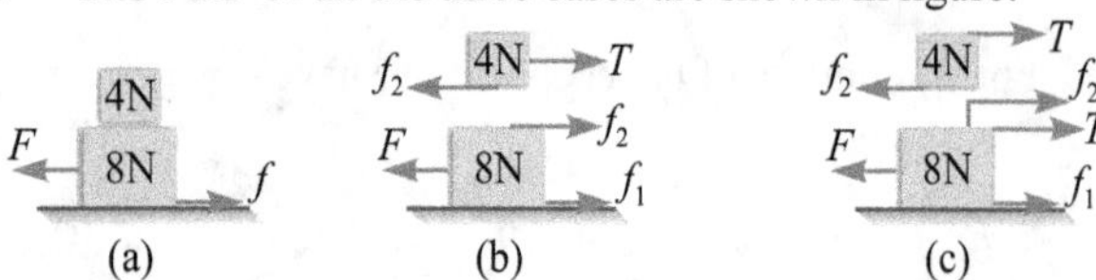

(a)

(b)

(c)

(a) $\qquad F = f = \mu N$

$\qquad\qquad = 0.25 \times (8+4) = 3N$

(b) $\qquad f_1 = 0.25 \times (8+4) = 3N,$

$\qquad\qquad f_2 = 0.25 \times 4 = 1N$

$\therefore \qquad F = f_1 + f_2 = (3+1) = 4N$

(c) $\qquad T = f_2 = 1N$

$\therefore \qquad F = f_1 + f_2 + T = 3 + 1 + 1 = 5N$

2. (a) To prevent sliding $T = 5$ g $\qquad$ ...(i)

and $\qquad T = f = \mu_s N$

$\qquad\qquad = 0.25(10 + m)g \qquad$ ...(ii)

From equations (i) and (ii), we get

$$m = 10 \text{ kg}$$

(b) When block C is lifted off, the block starts moving.

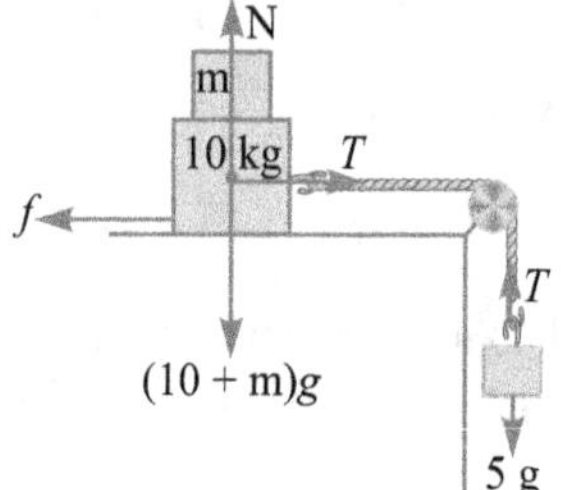

If a is acceleration, then

$$5g - T' = 5a$$
$$T' - f_k = 10a$$

where $\qquad f_k = 0.20 \times 10g$

After solving above equations, we get

$$a = 1.96 \text{ m/s}^2$$

3. $F = 8$

$$2T \cos 37° = F$$
$$T + T \sin 37° \geq \mu N$$
$$N = mg + T \cos 37°$$
$$\Rightarrow F \geq 8 \text{ N}$$

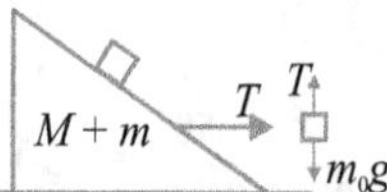

4. For m not to slide over M, acceleration of the triangular block should be $g \tan \theta$.

If m_0 is the required mass, then

$$mg - T = m_0 (g\tan\theta) \qquad ... (i)$$

and $\qquad T = (M + m)g \tan \theta$

or $\qquad T = 2g \tan \theta \qquad ... (ii)$

$$\cot \theta = 2 \qquad ... (iii)$$

After simplifying above equation, we get $m_0 = 2$ kg.

5. The *FBD* of the system is shown in figure. If a is the acceleration of the blocks, then

$$m_0 g - T_1 = m_0 a \qquad ...(i)$$
$$T_1 - (T_2 + \mu m_1 g) = m_1 a \qquad ...(ii)$$
$$T_2 - \mu m_2 g = m_2 a \qquad ...(iii)$$

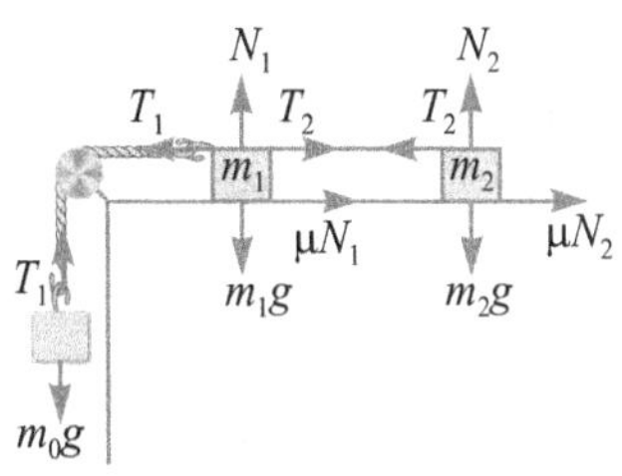

After solving above equations, we get

$$a = \left[\frac{m_0 - \mu(m_1 + m_2)}{m_0 + m_1 + m_2}\right]g, \quad T = \left[\frac{m_0 m_2 g (1+\mu)}{m_0 + m_1 + m_2}\right] \quad \textbf{\textit{Ans.}}$$

6. The *FBD* of the system shown in figure.

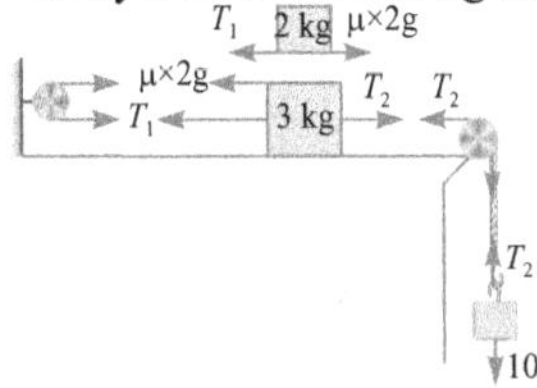

Equations of motions of the blocks are;

$$10g - T_2 = 10\,a \qquad \text{...(i)}$$

$$T_2 - [T_1 + \mu \times 2g] = 3a \qquad \text{...(ii)}$$

$$T_1 - \mu \times 2g = 2a \qquad \text{...(iii)}$$

After substituting values and solving, we get

$$a = 5.75 \text{ m/s}^2, \ T_1$$
$$= 17.38 \text{ N}, \ T_2 = 40.5 \text{ N}$$

7. The FBD is shown in figure.

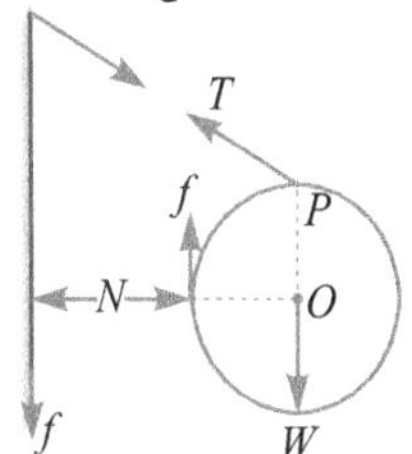

For equilibrium of the sphere, $\Sigma \vec{\tau} = 0$,

Taking moment of all the forces about P, we get

$$N \times R - f \times R = 0$$

or $$\frac{f}{N} = 1$$

or $$\mu_{\min} = 1$$

Thus for equilibrium, $\mu \geq 1$ **_Ans._**

8. For equilibrium of the cylinder in vertical direction, we have

$$2N \sin \alpha = W$$

$$\therefore \qquad N = \frac{W}{2 \sin \alpha}$$

The force needed to pull the cylinder along horizontal direction,

$$F = 2f = 2\,\mu\mathbf{N}$$
$$= 2\mu \times \frac{W}{2 \sin \alpha} = \frac{\mu W}{\sin \alpha} \quad \textbf{\textit{Ans.}}$$

1. (b) For constant velocity, $\vec{a} = 0$, or $\vec{F} = 0$.

   Thus $\vec{F}_1 + \vec{F}_2 + \vec{F}_3 = 0$

   or $$\vec{F}_3 = -(\vec{F}_1 + \vec{F}_2)$$

   $$= -\left[(3\hat{i} + 2\hat{j} - 4\hat{k}) + (-5\hat{i} + 8\hat{j} - 3\hat{k})\right]$$

   $$= -(-2\hat{i} + 10\hat{j} - 7\hat{k}) = 2\hat{i} - 10\hat{j} + 7\hat{k} \text{ N}.$$

2. (c) $$\vec{a} = -12 \sin 30° \,\hat{i} - 12 \cos 30° \hat{j}$$

   $$= -6\hat{i} - 6\sqrt{3}\hat{j}.$$

   By Newton's law, we have

   $$20\hat{i} + \vec{F} = 2 \times (-6\hat{i} - 6\sqrt{3}\hat{j})$$

   $$\therefore \qquad \vec{F} = -32\hat{i} - 21\hat{j} \text{ N}.$$

3. (c) As whole spring is at rest, and so $F = 5N$.

4. (c) Velocity of the particle just before and just after $t = 2\,s$ are

   $$v_i = 1 \ m/s \text{ and } v_f = 0,$$

   $$\therefore \qquad J = m(v_f - v_i) = 0.1\,(0 - 1)$$
   $$= 0.1 \text{ N} - \text{s}.$$

5. (c) $$J = m(u - 0)$$

   or $$\frac{\pi F_0 (T/2)}{2} = mu$$

   $$\therefore \qquad u = \frac{\pi F_0 T}{4m}$$

6. (d) $$J = m(v_f - v_i)$$
   or $$50 \times 5 + 75 \times 5 = 16(v_f - 0)$$
   $$\therefore \qquad v_f = 39 \text{ m/s}.$$

7. (d) $$\vec{F} = \frac{d\vec{P}}{dt} = \frac{d}{dt}\left[A(\hat{i} \cos kt - \hat{j} \sin kt)\right]$$

   $$= -kA(\hat{i} \sin kt + \hat{j} \cos kt)$$

   $$\vec{F}.\vec{P} = -kA(\hat{i} \sin kt + \hat{j} \cos kt)$$

   $$(A\hat{i} \cos kt - A\hat{j} \sin kt)$$

   $$= 0$$

   $\therefore$ angle between $\vec{F}$ and $\vec{P}$ is $90°$.

8. (a) $$15g = 10(g + a)$$
   $$\therefore \qquad a = 4.9 \text{ m/s}^2.$$

9. (d) $F \sin 30° + N = 10g$

   To leave the contact, $N = 0$

   or $2t \sin 30° = 10g$

   or $2t \times \dfrac{1}{2} = 10 \times 10$

   $$\therefore \qquad t = 100 \text{ s}$$

10. (a) $$a = \left[\frac{10 \cos 60°}{2 + 3}\right] = 1 \text{m/s}^2.$$

    and $$T = ma = 2 \times 1 = 2N.$$

11. (b) $$2T - 100\,g = 100 \times 1$$
    $$\therefore \qquad T = 550\,N.$$

12. (c) For 8 kg block,
$T = 0.5 \times 8g$
and for bucket, $2T = mg$
$\therefore \ m = 8$ kg
Mass of sand added = 7 kg.

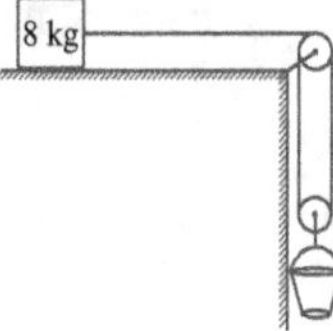

13. (d) $F = \sqrt{T^2 + (T + mg)^2}$
$= \sqrt{(Mg)^2 + (Mg + mg)^2}$.

14. (c) $a = \dfrac{(10 - 8)g}{10 + 8} = \dfrac{g}{9}$ m/s^2
Tension in the string
$T = m(g - a) = 4(g - g/9)$
$= 4 \times \dfrac{8}{9} g = \dfrac{320}{9}$ N

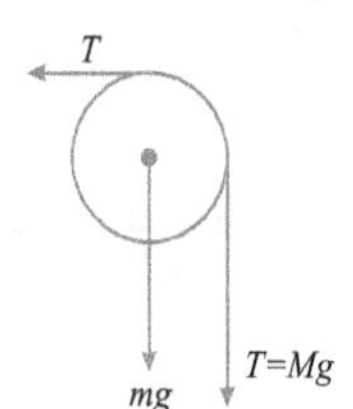

15. (d) $a_x = \dfrac{F\cos 60°}{M} = \dfrac{F}{2 \times 10} = \dfrac{F}{20}$.

Thus $\quad 30 = (2 + 1) \times \dfrac{F}{20}$

$\therefore \qquad F = 200$ N.

16. (a) Acceleration of blocks
$a = \dfrac{Mg}{m + M}$

Tension in the string /spring,

$T = ma = \dfrac{mMg}{m + M}$

$\therefore$ Extension in the string, $x = \dfrac{T}{k} = \dfrac{mMg}{k(m + M)}$

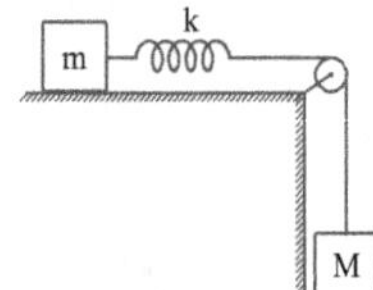

17. (a) $85g - F = 85 \times 2.5$
$\therefore \qquad F = 620$ N.

18. (b) $a = \left(\dfrac{P}{M + m}\right)$

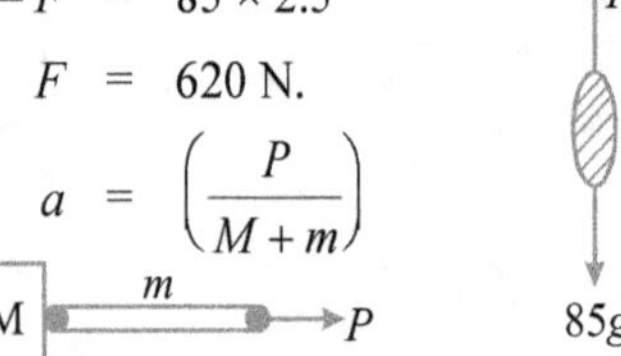

The force exerted by rope on the block
$F = Ma = \left(\dfrac{MP}{M + m}\right)$.

19. (c) $a = \dfrac{Mg\sin\theta}{(M + M)} = \dfrac{g}{2}\sin\theta$

$\therefore \qquad T = Ma = \dfrac{Mg}{2}\sin\theta$

20. (a) $mg - T = ma$
or $\quad mg - \dfrac{3mg}{4} = ma$
$\therefore \qquad a = g/4$ m/s^2.

21. (d) The reading of the spring balance will be equal to T, where
$T = \left[\dfrac{2m_1 m_2}{m_1 + m_2}\right] g = \dfrac{400}{3}$ N

22. (c)

23. (c) $T = \dfrac{2m_1 m_2 g}{m_1 + m_2} = \dfrac{2 \times 2 \times M \times 10}{2 + M}$
as $M \gg 2 \quad \therefore T = 40$ N.

24. (c)

25. (b) $a = \dfrac{0 - 8}{4 - 0} = -2$ m/s^2
$= \mu g$
$\therefore \qquad \mu = 0.20$.

26. (d) $f_s = \mu_s N$
$= 0.6 \times 20 \ g = 120$ N
Now $\quad a = \dfrac{120 - 0.2 \times 20 g}{20} = 4$ m/s^2.

27. (d)

28. (a) $f_{\lim} = \mu N = 0.4 (25 - 9) = 6.4 \ N$.
External force is 6 N and so block will not move. So frictional force = 6.0 N.

29. (c) To pull the lower block,
$F = 0.1 \times 1g + 0.2 \times 3g$
$= 7$ N.

30. (c) $N = 5g + 20\sin 30°$
$= 60N$.
Now, $20\cos 30° - f = ma$
or $\quad 20\dfrac{\sqrt{3}}{2} - 0.25 \times 60 = 5a$
$\therefore \qquad a = 0.46$ m/s^2.

31. (a) $f_{\lim} = \mu N = 0.6 \times 1g = 6$ N.
External force (pseudo force) acts on the block is
$= 1 \times 5 = 5$ N.
So, frictional force = 5 N.

32. (d) Stoping distance, $s = \dfrac{v^2}{2a} = \dfrac{(P/m)^2}{2\mu g} = \dfrac{P^2}{2m^2 \mu g}$.

33. (a) $10 = mg\sin 30°$
$\therefore \quad m = 2$kg
$f_{\lim} = \mu_s mg\cos 30° = 0.8 \times 2 \times 10 \times \dfrac{\sqrt{3}}{2} = 8\sqrt{3} \ N$

4. (c) Acceleration of blocks, $a = \dfrac{60}{15} = 4$ m/s^2

Now $60 - f = 5 \times 4$
or $\quad f = 40$ N

35. (b)

The acceleration of the blocks, $a = \dfrac{60}{15} = 4$ m/ sec^2

So frictional force on 5kg block = $ma = 5 \times 4 = 20$ N

36. (c)
$$M_2g - T = M_2a$$
and $T - \mu M_1 g = M_1 a$

On solving, we get

$$a = \left(\frac{M_2 g - \mu M_1 g}{M_1 + M_2}\right), \text{ and so}$$

T will be free from force constant of spring k.

37. (c) Since $mg \sin 30° > mg \cos 30°$

The block has a tendency to slip downwards. Let F be the minimum force applied on it, so that it does not slip. Then

$N = F + mg\cos 30°$

$$\therefore \quad mg\sin 30° = \mu N = \mu(F + mg\cos 30°)$$

or

$$F = \frac{mg \sin 30°}{\mu} - mg \cos 30° = \frac{(2)(10)(1/2)}{0.5} - (2)(10)\left(\frac{\sqrt{3}}{2}\right)$$

or $F = 20 - 17.32 = 2.68$ N

38. (c) $f_k = 0.4 \times 10\,g = 40$ N

$$a_{block} = \frac{100 - 40}{10} = 6\,\text{m/s}^2$$

and $a_{slab} = \frac{40}{10} = 4\,\text{m/s}^2$

39. (a)
$$F = \left(\frac{dm}{dt}\right)v = 1 \times 5 = 5\ N$$

$$\therefore \quad a = F/m = \frac{5}{2} = 2.5\ \text{m/s}^2.$$

40. (c) For the equilibrium of the block

$$2\,T \cos\theta = \sqrt{2}\,Mg$$

or $2(Mg)\cos\theta = \sqrt{2}\,Mg$

or $\cos\theta = 1/\sqrt{2}, \quad \therefore \ \theta = 45°.$

41. (b)
$$\sin\theta = \frac{1}{2}$$

Thus, $N_1 \sin\theta = N_2$

$$\therefore \quad \frac{N_1}{N_2} = \frac{1}{\sin\theta} = 2.$$

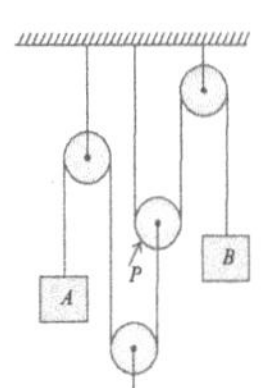

---

1. (c) The time in which force on the bullet becomes zero,

$$0 = 600 - 2 \times 10^5 t \Rightarrow t = \frac{600}{2 \times 10^5} = 3 \times 10^{-3}\ \text{s}$$

$$\text{Impulse} = \int_0^t F\,dt = \int_0^t (600 - 2 \times 10^5 t)\,dt$$

$$= \left| 600t - 2 \times 10^5 \frac{t^2}{2} \right|_0^{3 \times 10^{-3}} = 0.9\ \text{N-s.}$$

2. (b) The pseudo force on the block is, $F = ma$.

If x be the compression, then $Fx = \frac{1}{2}kx^2$

or $\quad max = \frac{1}{2}kx^2$

$$\Rightarrow \quad x = \frac{2ma}{k}.$$

3. (a) $\vec{J} = m(\vec{v}_f - \vec{v}_i)$

$$= 2\ mv \sin\theta/2 = 2mv \sin \pi/n.$$

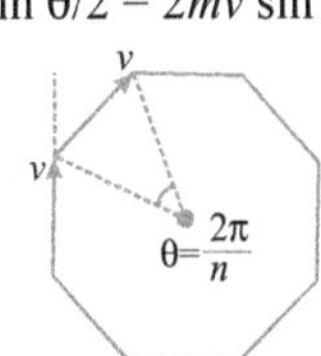

4. (c) For the painter,

$$2F - Mg = Ma$$

For platform

$$2T - mg = ma, \quad \text{here } T = F$$

Adding above equation, we get

$$a = \left[\frac{4F - (M + m)g}{M + m}\right].$$

5. (b)

Acceleration of pulley P = acc of block A
$= 1$ m/s^2

So acceleration of block B, $= 2 \times$ acc. of pulley P
$= 2 \times 1 = 2$ m/s^2

6. (c)
$$3x_A + x_B = \ell \text{ (constant)}$$

$$\therefore \quad 3v_A + v_B = 0$$

or $v_B = -3\,v_A$

$$= -3 \times 0.6 = -1.8\ \text{m/s.}$$

7. (c)

The tension in the string when it was not pulled.

$$= \sqrt{(ma)^2 + (mg)^2}$$

Now the string is pulled with constant acceleration a, so extra tension in the string, $=$ ma

Thus not tension $\sqrt{(ma)^2 + (mg)^2} + ma$

8. (d)

9. (a) For the system as a whole,

$$\frac{mg}{2} = 2\,m(a_x)$$

$\therefore \qquad a_x = g/4$

For block A, $\dfrac{mg}{2} = ma_y$

$\therefore \qquad a_y = g/2.$

Thus $\qquad a_A = \sqrt{a_x^2 + a_y^2} = \sqrt{\left(\dfrac{g}{4}\right)^2 + \left(\dfrac{g}{2}\right)^2}$

$\qquad\qquad\qquad = \dfrac{\sqrt{5}}{4}\, g$

10. (c) $\qquad T_0 = m_3 g \qquad ....(i)$

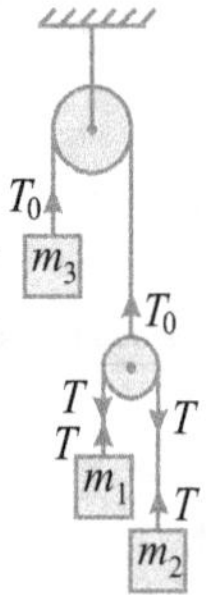

Also $\qquad T_0 = 2T \qquad ....(ii)$

$\qquad m_2 g - T = m_2 a \qquad ....(iii)$

and $\qquad T - m_1 g = m_1 a \qquad ....(iv)$

After solving, we get,

$\qquad \dfrac{4}{m_3} = \dfrac{1}{m_1} + \dfrac{1}{m_2}$

11. (a) If a is the acceleration of blocks, then

$a = \dfrac{120 - 12 g \sin 60°}{12}$

$= \dfrac{\left(120 - 120\dfrac{\sqrt{3}}{2}\right) \text{m/s}^2}{12}$

$= \left(10 - 5\sqrt{3}\right) \text{m/s}^2$

Now $T_1 = m_1 a + m_1 g \sin 60°$

$= 2 \times \left(10 - 5\sqrt{3}\right) + 2 \times 10 \times \dfrac{\sqrt{3}}{2}$

Similarly $T_2 = 60$ N

12. (c) The limiting friction (acts upwards),

$f_{\lim} = \mu N = 0.5 \times 100 = 50$N.

The external force (acts downward)

$\qquad = mg = 5 \times 9.8 = 49$ N.

Since external force is less than limiting friction,

$\therefore$ friction force $= 49$ N.

13. (a) If a is the acceleration of the blocks, then

$\qquad 20 - \mu N = 10 a$

or $20 - 0.1 \times 10 g = 10 a$

$\therefore \qquad a = 1 \text{ m/s}^2.$

Now $\qquad F_1 - f = 2 a$

or $F_1 - 0.1 \times 2 g = 2 \times 1$

$\therefore \qquad F_1 = 4$ N.

14. (b) $\qquad mg = \mu N = \mu\, ma$

$\therefore \qquad a = \dfrac{g}{\mu}.$

15. (d) frictional force = pseudo force

or $\qquad \mu mg = ma$

$\qquad\qquad = m\dfrac{dv}{dt} = m \times 2bt$

$\therefore \qquad t = \dfrac{\mu g}{2b}.$

16. (b) The acceleration of the block along the incline is $g\sin\theta$, and so its horizontal component will be $a_y = g\sin\theta\cos\theta$ also vertical component $a_y = (g\sin\theta)\sin\theta$

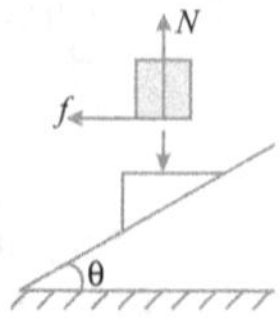

For A; $Mg - N = ma_v \qquad ....(i)$

and $\mu N \geq ma_H \qquad ....(ii)$

After simplifying, we get

$\qquad \theta = \tan^{-1}(\mu)$

17. (c) $\qquad N = Mg - f\sin\theta \qquad ...(i)$

and $\qquad f = \mu N \qquad ...(ii)$

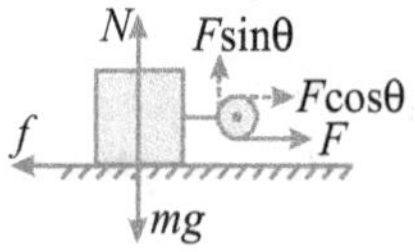

Now $(F + F\cos\theta) - f = Ma \qquad ...(iii)$

After solving above equations, we get

$\qquad a = 12 \text{ m/s}^2.$

18. (b) $\qquad F - N = ma \qquad ....(i)$

and $\qquad N = Ma$

$\therefore \qquad a = \left[\dfrac{F}{M + m}\right] \qquad ....(ii)$

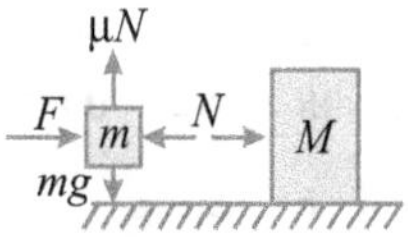

For block m remains stationary w.r.t M, then

$\qquad \mu N = mg \qquad ....(iii)$

Solving above equations, we get

$\qquad F = \left[\dfrac{m(M + m)g}{\mu M}\right].$

19. (c) Explained in theory.

20. (b) $mg - 2T = ma_1,$

$mg - T = ma_2$

Here, $T = mg/4,$

after solving above equations and

$\ell = \dfrac{1}{2}(a_1 + a_2)t^2$, we will get the answer

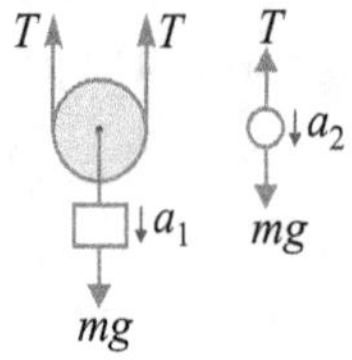

21. (d) $\qquad F = \rho A v^2 = \rho\left(\dfrac{V}{v}\right)(v_1 + v_2)^2.$

22. (a) $\qquad W\cos 30° = N,$

and $\qquad T = N\sin 30°$

$\therefore \qquad T = W\cos 30° \sin 30° = \dfrac{\sqrt{3}}{4} W.$

23. (d) $\qquad 2N\cos 30° = W,$

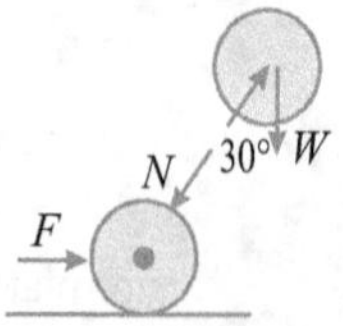

$\qquad N = \dfrac{W}{\sqrt{3}}$

and $\qquad N\sin 30° = F$

or $\qquad \dfrac{W}{\sqrt{3}} \times \dfrac{1}{2} = F,$

or $\qquad F = \dfrac{W}{2\sqrt{3}}.$

24. **(b)** About hinge, $\Sigma\tau = 0$

or $\quad 222 \times \dfrac{\ell}{2} \sin 60° = T \sin 30° \times \ell$

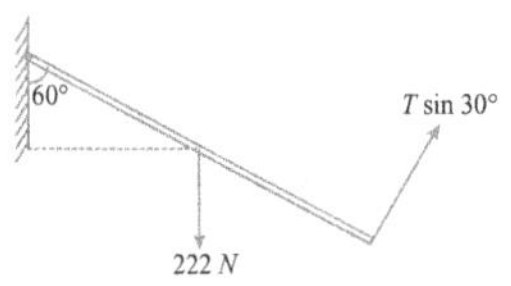

$\therefore \qquad T = \dfrac{222\sqrt{3}}{2} = 192 \text{ N.}$

25. **(c)** $\sin\theta = \dfrac{r}{3r} = \dfrac{1}{3}, \cos\theta = \sqrt{8/9}$

If mass of smaller cylinder is m, then mass of bigger one will be 4m. For the equilibrium of upper cylinder,

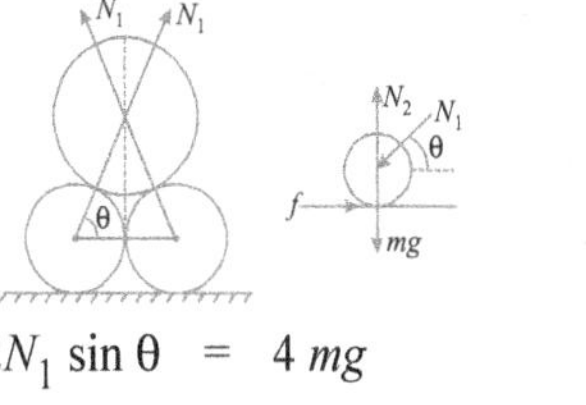

$$2N_1 \sin\theta = 4\,mg$$

$\therefore \qquad N_1 = \dfrac{2mg}{\sin\theta} \qquad ...(i)$

Now for the equilibrium of lower cylinder,

$$N_2 = N_1 \sin\theta + mg \qquad ...(ii)$$

and $\qquad f = N_1 \cos\theta$

or $\qquad \mu N_2 = N_1 \cos\theta \qquad ...(iii)$

After solving above equations, we get

$$\mu = \dfrac{1}{3\sqrt{2}}.$$

1. **(a,c)** For a body at rest, it has either no force or no net force.

2. **(a,b,c)** For translational equilibrium, $\vec{F} = 0$, or $\vec{a} = 0$, and so body is at either at rest or moves with constant velocity.

3. **(a,b)** Object of size $> 10^{-6}$ m can be described in classical physics. So (a,b) are correct.

4. **(a, b,c)** Protons, on being charged particles experience both gravitational and electromagnetic force in addition to nuclear force.

5. **(b,d)** Explained in theory.

6. **(b,c)** In case when lifting is going up with some acceleration

$$N' = m(g + a) > mg.$$

Also when lift is coming down with retardation

$$N' = m(g + a) > mg$$

7. **(a, c, d)** Explained in theory

8. **(c, d)** Kinetic friction is always less than limiting friction but greater than rolling friction (least value).

9. **(a, b, d)**

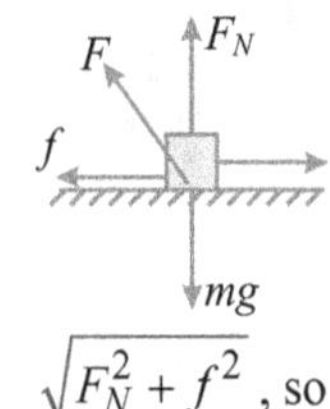

As $\qquad F = \sqrt{F_N^2 + f^2}$, so

$$F > F_N \text{ and } F > f.$$

Clearly $(F_N - f) < F < (F_N + f)$

10. **(a, b, c)** When acceleration of A is 1m/s^2, experiences a net force $1 \times 1 = 1N$. Now acceleration of block B

$$a_2 = \dfrac{4-1}{2} = \dfrac{3}{2} \text{ m/s}^2.$$

At the instant of maximum extension of the spring, both the blocks will move with same acceleration and so

$$a = \dfrac{4}{2+1} = 4/3 \text{ m/s}^2.$$

11. **(b, d)** For painter,

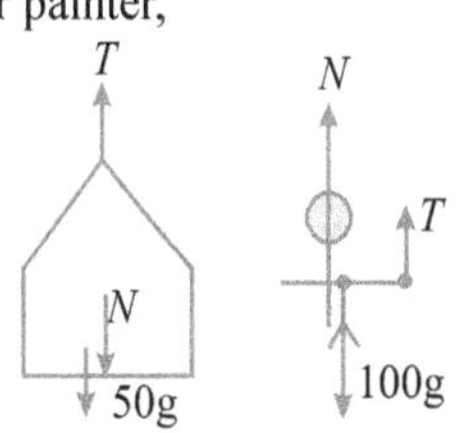

$(N + T) - 100g = 100 \times 5 \qquad ...(i)$

For crate,

$T - (N + 50\,g) = 50 \times 5 \qquad ...(ii)$

After solving above equations, we get

$$T = 1125 \text{ N}$$
$$N = 375 \text{ N.}$$

12. **(a, c)** **Minimum value of a:–** For this the sliding tendency is down the plane and friction acts up the plane:

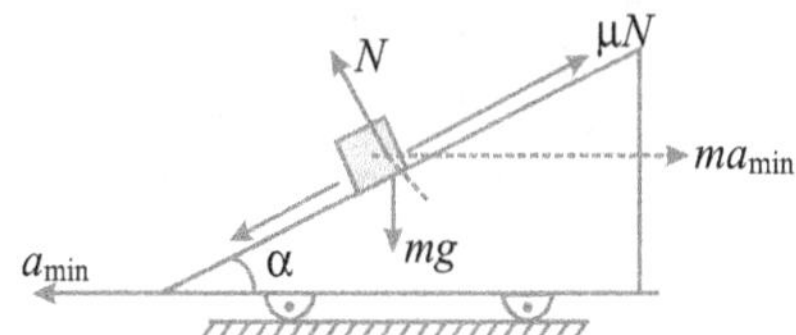

$N = mg \cos\alpha + ma_{\min} \sin\alpha \qquad ...(i)$

and $mg \sin\alpha = \mu N + ma_{\min} \cos\alpha \qquad ...(ii)$

After solving above equations, we get

$$a_{\min} = \dfrac{g(1 - \mu\cot\alpha)}{(\mu + \cot\alpha)}$$

Maximum value of a : In this case the sliding tendency of the block is up and so friction will act down the plane. After calculations, we get

$$a_{\max} = \dfrac{g(1 + \mu\cot\alpha)}{(\cot\alpha - \mu)}.$$

13. (b, d) For smooth plane, both the block will move with same acceleration, and so there is no relative motion between the blocks.

14. (b, c) The speed of block of smooth inclined plane is
$v = \sqrt{2gh}$, and so $v_A = v_B$
Acceleration on smooth inclined is given by, $a = g \sin\theta$.

$a_A = g \sin 60° = \dfrac{\sqrt{3}g}{2}$, and $a_B = g \sin 30° = \dfrac{g}{2}$

$a_R = \sqrt{(\sqrt{3}g/2)^2 + (g/2)^2} = g$.

15. (a, b, c) For $F < f$, the block A will not move and so $T = 0$.
For $f < F > 2f$, the block A has tendency of motion, and so string becomes tight, then
$$F = T + f \Rightarrow T = F - f.$$
For $F > 2f$, both the blocks start moving with constant acceleration,
$$a = \dfrac{F - 2f}{2m}$$

Now $\qquad T - f = ma$

or $\qquad T - f = m\left[\dfrac{F - 2f}{2m}\right]$

$\therefore \qquad T = F/2.$

16. (a, c) For the equilibrium, the situation is shown in *FBD*.
For horizontal equilibrium
$$\Sigma F_x = 0,$$
or $\qquad N_1 = N_2 = N.$
Also $\qquad f_1 = f_2.$

17. (b, d) By constraint
$$a_B + 4a_A = 2a_C + 3a_D$$
$$\Rightarrow \qquad a_D = \dfrac{7}{3}\,\text{m/s}^2$$
$$2T - 10 = 1 \Rightarrow T = 11/2 \text{ N}$$

---

1. (a) When we press the pen with the finger, the force between fingers and pen is frictional force, which is electromagnetic in nature.

2. (b) To get tensions in the strings, we need three force equations.

3. (d) Impulse and momentum are different quantities, but both has same unit (N–s).

4. (a) For the body to be in equilibrium under two forces, we have
$$\vec{F_1} + \vec{F_2} = 0,$$
$$\vec{F_1} = -\vec{F_2}$$

5. (d) The net force on the block is zero, but action cannot cancel the reaction because these two act on different bodies.

6. (c) Newton's second law can not be used for any object.

7. (b) Due to inertia the dishes remain at their position and fall on to the table.

8. (b) Explained in theory.

9. (a) A single stage rocket can give nearly 4 km/s, which is not enough for practical purpose.

10. (d) If the lift is retarding while it moves upward, the man shall feel lesser weight as compared to when lift was at rest. Hence statement 1 is false and statement-2 is true.

11. (d) The man can exert force on block by pulling the rope. The tension in rope will make the man move. Hence statement-1 is false.

12. (b) **Statement 1 :** Cloth can be pulled out without dislodging the dishes from the table because of inertia. Therefore, statement – 1 is true.
Statement 2 : This is Newton's third law and hence true. But statement 2 is not a correct explanation of statement 1.

13. (b) It is easier to pull a heavy object than to push it on a level ground. Statement-1 is true. This is because the normal reaction in the case of pulling is less as compared by pushing. ($f = \mu N$). Therefore the frictional force is small in case of pulling.
statement-2 is true but is not the correct explanation of statement-1.

Passage for (Questions 1 &2)

1. (a) For F to be zero,
$$0 = at(\tau - t),$$
$$\therefore \qquad t = \tau$$
$$P_f - P_i = J$$
or $\qquad P_f - 0 = \displaystyle\int_0^\tau F\, dt$
or $\qquad P_f = \displaystyle\int_0^\tau at(\tau - t)\, dt$

$$= \left|\dfrac{at^2\tau}{2} - \dfrac{at^3}{3}\right|_0^\tau$$

$$= \dfrac{a\tau^3}{6}.$$

2. (c) Acceleration, $a = \dfrac{F}{m} = \dfrac{at(\tau - t)}{m}$

$$\frac{dv}{dt} = \frac{at\tau - at^2}{m}$$

or

$$\int_0^v dv = \int_0^t \left(\frac{at\tau - at^2}{m}\right) dt$$

or

$$v = \frac{\left(\dfrac{at^2}{2}\tau - \dfrac{at^3}{3}\right)}{m}$$

Now

$$\frac{dx}{dt} = \frac{\left(\dfrac{at^2}{2} - \dfrac{m\,at^3}{3}\right)}{m}$$

or

$$\int_0^x (dx) = \int_0^\tau \left[\frac{\dfrac{at^2}{m} - \dfrac{at^3}{3}}{m}\right] dt$$

$$\therefore \qquad x = \frac{a\tau^4}{12m}$$

Passage (Questions 3 & 4)

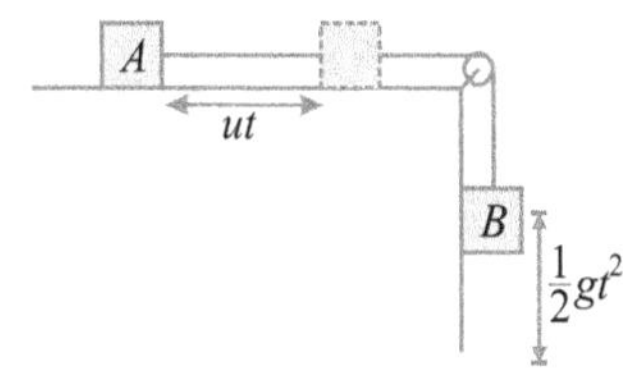

3. (d) In time t, $\quad ut = \dfrac{1}{2}gt^2$

or

$$t = \frac{2u}{g}.$$

Velocity of block B in this duration

$$v_i = 0 + gt = g \times \frac{2u}{g} = 2u.$$

When string gets taut, then
For block A,
$$2m(v_f - u) = J$$
and for block B,
$$m(v_f - 2u) = -J$$

$$\therefore \quad 2m(v_f - u) = -m(v_f - 2u)$$

or

$$v_f = \frac{4u}{3}.$$

4. (c) When string becomes taut, both the blocks will move

with constant acceleration

$$a = \frac{mg}{m + 2m} = g/3.$$

Now

$$v^2 = v_f^2 + 2a \times (\ell - ut)$$

$$= \left(\frac{4u}{3}\right)^2 + 2\frac{g}{3}(\ell - u \times \frac{2u}{g})$$

$$= \frac{16}{9}u^2 + \frac{2g\ell}{3} - \frac{4u^2}{3}$$

$$= \frac{4u^2}{9} + \frac{6g\ell}{9}$$

or

$$v = \frac{\sqrt{4u^2 + 6g\ell}}{3}.$$

Passage for (Questions 5 to 7)
5. (a) 6. (b) 7. (c)

The downward load $= (20 + 10)g$
$$= 294 \text{ N}.$$
The pulley system can be lifted only when $F > 294$ N.
Thus in case (a) and (b) the accelerations of the blocks
will be zero.
For $F = 394$ N : If a_0 is the acceleration of the system
as a whole, then
$$394 - 2T = 0 \times a_0$$
$$\therefore \qquad T = 197 \text{ N}$$
If a is the acceleration of each block with respect to
pulley, then with respect to ground their accelerations
are
$$a_1 = (a_0 - a)\downarrow$$
and $\qquad a_2 = (a_0 + a)\uparrow$

$$20g - T = 20(a_0 - a) \quad ...(i)$$
and $\qquad T - 10g = 10(a_0 + a) \quad ...(ii)$

After solving above equations, we get
$a_0 = 4.925$ m/s^2, $a = 4.97$ m/s^2
$\therefore \quad a_1 = 0.05$ m/s^2, $a_2 = 9.9$ m/s^2

Passage for (Questions 8 to 10)
8. (a) For m_1 to be lifted off $T = m_1 g$
and $\qquad F = 2T$
or $\qquad 2t = 2m_1 g$
$$\therefore \qquad t = m_1 g = 1 \times 9.81$$
$$= 9.81 \text{ s}$$
9. (a) For m_2 to be lifted off
$$T = m_2 g$$
and $\qquad F = 2T$
or $\qquad 2t = 2 \times m_2 g$
$$\therefore \qquad t = m_2 g = 2 \times 9.81 = 19.62 \text{ s}$$
10. (c) At $\qquad t = 25$ s, $F = 2 \times 25 = 50$ N
For the pulley,
$$2T - 50 = 0 \times a_0,$$
where a_0 is the acceleration of the pulley.
$$\therefore \qquad T = 25 \text{ N}$$
If a is the acceleration of the block w.r.t. pulley, then
$$a_1 = (a + a_0)\uparrow$$
and $\qquad a_2 = (a - a_0)\downarrow$
By Newton's second law, we have
$$T - 1g = 1(a + a_0) \qquad ...(i)$$
and $\qquad 2g - T = 2(a - a_0) \qquad ...(ii)$
Substituting $T = 25$ N and solving equations (i) and
(ii), we get
$$a = 6.25 \text{ m/s}^2$$
and $\qquad a_0 = 8.94 \text{ m/s}^2$
$$\therefore \qquad a_1 = 6.25 + 8.94 = 15.19 \text{ m/s}^2$$

$$a_2 = 8.94 - 6.25 = 2.69 \text{ m/s}^2$$

Passage for (Questions 11 & 12)

Suppose a_0 is the acceleration of the system corresponding to force F. The FBD of the system shown in figure.

Given $\quad M = 13.4$ kg, $m_1 = 1$kg, $m_2 = 2$ kg, $m_3 = 3.6$ kg

$\qquad \mu_1 = 0.75$ and $m_2 = 0.6$

11. (a) For no slipping between m_2 and M, we have

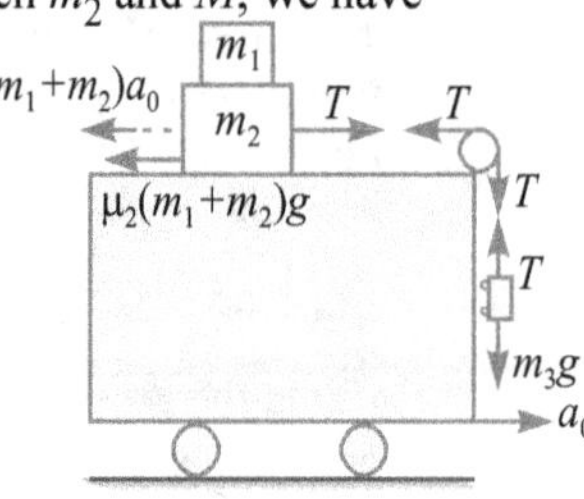

$$T - \left[\mu_2(m_1 + m_2)g + (m_1 + m_2)a_0\right] = 0$$

or $\quad T - \left[0.6(1+2) \times 9.8 + (1+2)a_0\right] = 0$

or $\qquad\qquad T = 17.64 + 3a_0 \qquad ...(i)$

For block m_3 :

$$T - m_3 g = 0$$

or $\qquad\qquad T = m_3 g = 3.6 \times 9.8$

$$= 35.28 \qquad ...(ii)$$

From equations (i) and (ii), we get

$$a_0 = 5.88 \text{ m/s}^2$$

Thus $\qquad F = (M + m_1 + m_2 + m_3)a_0$

$$= (13.4 + 1 + 2 + 3.6) \times 5.88$$

$$= 117.7 \text{ N}$$

12 (b) For no slipping, between m_1 and m_2, we have

$$m_1 a_0 = \mu_1 m_1 g$$

$\therefore \qquad\qquad a_0' = \mu_1 g = 0.75 \times 9.8 = 7.35 \text{ m/s}^2.$

This acceleration is greater than a_0, so the block m_2 together with m_1 will move backward relative to M.

Thus $\qquad F = (M + m_1 + m_2 + m_3)a_0'$

$$= (13.4 + 1 + 2 + 3.6) \times 7.35$$

$$= 147 \text{ N}$$

13. **A $\to$ q ; B $\to$ p ; C $\to$ s ; D $\to$ r**

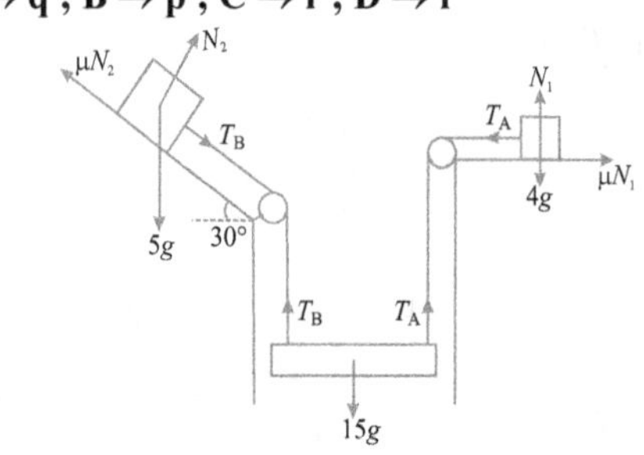

Applying Lami's equation, we have

$$\frac{T_{BC}}{\sin 150°} = \frac{W_2}{\sin 120°} = \frac{300}{\sin 90°}$$

and $\quad \dfrac{T_{AB}}{\sin 90°} = \dfrac{W_1}{\sin 150°} = \dfrac{T_{BC}}{\sin 120°}$

After simplifying, we get

$T_{AB} = 173$ N, $T_{BC} = 150$ N, $W_1 = 87$ N, $W_2 = 260$ N.

14. **A $\to$ q ; B $\to$ p ; C $\to$ r ; D $\to$ r**

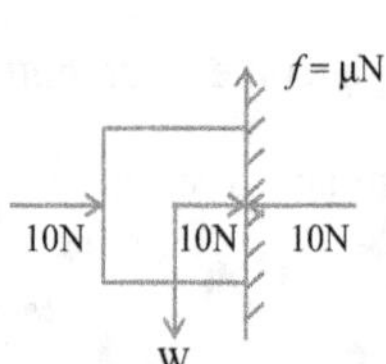

$$a_A = a_B = a_C$$
$$N_1 = 4g, N_2 = 5g \cos 30°$$
$$T_A - \mu N_1 = 4a_A,$$
$$T_B + 5g \sin 30° - \mu N_2 = 5a_B$$

and $\quad 15g - (T_A + T_B) = 15a_C$

After solving above equations, we get

$$a_A = a_B = 5.8 \text{ m/s}^2.$$
$$T_A = 38.88 \; N,$$
$$T_B = 21.47 \; N.$$

1. (a) When F_1, F_2 and F_3 are acting on a particle then the particle remains stationary. This means that the resultant of F_1 F_2 and F_3 is zero. When F_1 is removed, F_2 and F_3 will remain. But the resultant of F_2 and F_3 should be equal and opposite to F_1.

   i.e. $|\vec{F_2} + \vec{F_3}| = |\vec{F_1}|$

   $\therefore \quad a = \dfrac{|\vec{F_2} + \vec{F_3}|}{m} \Rightarrow a = \dfrac{F_1}{m}$

2. (a) For the bag accelerating down

   $$mg - T = ma$$

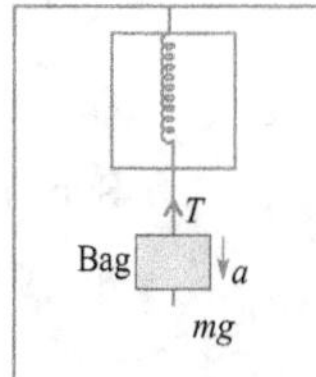

   $\therefore \; T = m(g-a) = \dfrac{49}{10}(10-5) = 24.5 \text{ N}$

3. (d) For the block to remain stationary with the wall

   $$f = W$$

   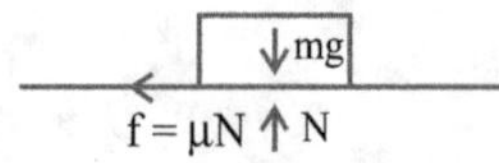

   $$\mu N = W \quad 0.2 \times 10 = W \Rightarrow W = 2N$$

4. (d) $u = 6$ m/s, $v = 0$, $t = 10s$, $a = ?$

   $$v = u + at \Rightarrow 0 = 6 + a \times 10$$

   $$\Rightarrow \quad a = \frac{-6}{10} = -0.6 \text{m} / \text{s}^2$$

   The retardation is due to the frictional force

$\therefore f = ma \Rightarrow \mu N = ma \Rightarrow \mu mg = ma$

$\Rightarrow \mu = \dfrac{a}{g} = \dfrac{0.6}{10} = 0.06$

5. (c) From diagram,

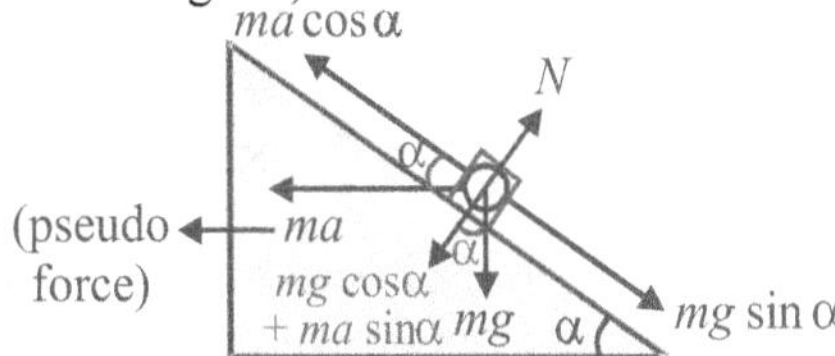

For block to remain stationary,

$mg \sin \alpha = ma \cos \alpha \Rightarrow a = g \tan \alpha$

6. (b)

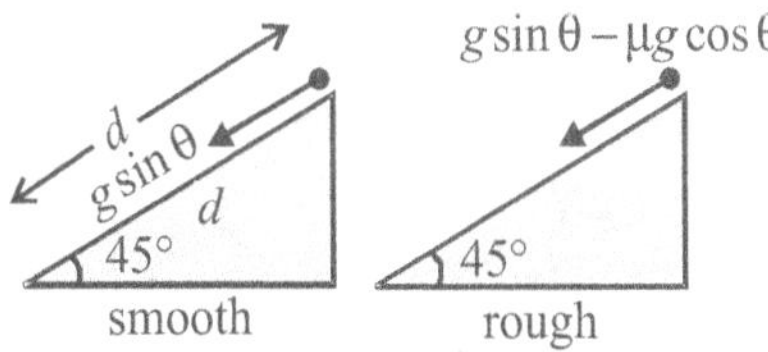

When surface is smooth | When surface is rough

$d = \dfrac{1}{2}(g \sin \theta)t_1^2$, $\quad d = \dfrac{1}{2}(g \sin \theta - \mu g \cos \theta)t_2^2$

$t_1 = \sqrt{\dfrac{2d}{g \sin \theta}}$, $\quad t_2 = \sqrt{\dfrac{2d}{g \sin \theta - \mu g \cos \theta}}$

According to question, $t_2 = nt_1$

$n\sqrt{\dfrac{2d}{g \sin \theta}} = \sqrt{\dfrac{2d}{g \sin \theta - \mu g \cos \theta}}$

μ, as applicable here, is coefficient of kinetic friction as the block moves over the inclined plane.

$n = \dfrac{1}{\sqrt{1-\mu_k}} \qquad \left(\because \cos 45° = \sin 45° = \dfrac{1}{\sqrt{2}}\right)$

$n^2 = \dfrac{1}{1-\mu_k}$ or $1-\mu_k = \dfrac{1}{n^2}$ or $\mu_k = 1-\dfrac{1}{n^2}$

7. (a) If v is the speed of the block after moving a distance ℓ on smooth inclined

$v^2 = 0 + 2(g \sin \phi)\ell$

The retardation on the rough inclined

$a' = (\mu g \cos \phi - g \sin \phi)$

Thus $\quad 0 = v^2 - 2a' \times \ell$

or $\quad 0 = 2g\ell \sin \phi - 2(\mu g \cos \phi - g \sin \phi)$

$\therefore \quad \mu = 2 \tan \phi.$

8. (a) $mg \sin \theta = ma$

$\therefore a = g \sin \theta$

where a is along the inclined plane

$\therefore$ vertical component of acceleration is $g \sin^2 \theta$

$\therefore$ relative vertical acceleration of A with respect to B is

$g(\sin^2 60 - \sin^2 30] = \dfrac{g}{2} = 4.9$ m/s^2 in vertical direction

9. (c)

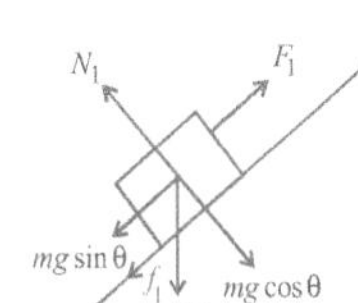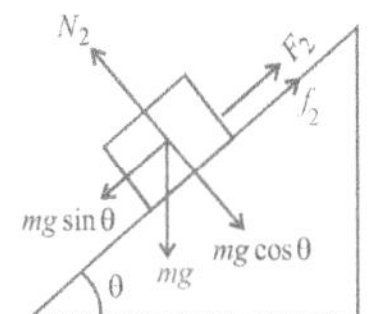

For the upward motion of the body

$mg \sin \theta + f_1 = F_1$

or, $\quad F_1 = mg \sin \theta + \mu mg \cos \theta$

For the downward motion of the body,

$mg \sin \theta - f_2 = F_2$

or $F_2 = mg \sin \theta - \mu mg \cos \theta$

$\therefore \quad \dfrac{F_1}{F_2} = \dfrac{\sin \theta + \mu \cos \theta}{\sin \theta - \mu \cos \theta}$

$\Rightarrow \quad \dfrac{\tan \theta + \mu}{\tan \theta - \mu} = \dfrac{2\mu + \mu}{2\mu - \mu} = \dfrac{3\mu}{\mu} =$

10. (c) Given that $F(t) = F_0 e^{-bt}$

$\Rightarrow \quad m\dfrac{dv}{dt} = F_0 e^{-bt}$

$\dfrac{dv}{dt} = \dfrac{F_0}{m} e^{-bt}$

$\int_0^v dv = \dfrac{F_0}{m} \int_0^t e^{-bt} dt$

$v = \dfrac{F_0}{m}\left[\dfrac{e^{-bt}}{-b}\right]_0^t = \dfrac{F_0}{mb}\left[-\left(e^{-bt} - e^{-0}\right)\right]$

$\Rightarrow \quad v = \dfrac{F_0}{mb}\left[1 - e^{-bt}\right]$

11. (d) The acceleration of blocks:

Till $F \le f_{\text{lim}}$, $\quad a = \left[\dfrac{F}{m_A + m_B}\right]$

For $F > f_{\text{lim}}$, $\quad a_A = \dfrac{f}{m_A}$ (constant)

and $\quad a_B = \left[\dfrac{kt - f}{m_B}\right]$,

which increases with time.

12. (b) Normal forces on block A due to B and between B and wall will be F. Friction on A due to $B = 20$ N

$\therefore$ Friction on B due to wall $= 100 + 20 = 120$

13. (b) $E_{initial} = \dfrac{1}{2}m(2v)^2 + \dfrac{1}{2}2m(2v)^2 = 3mv^2$

$E_{final} = \dfrac{1}{2}3m\left(\dfrac{4}{9}v^2 + \dfrac{4}{9}v^2\right) = \dfrac{4}{3}mv^2$

$\therefore$ Fractional loss $= \dfrac{3 - \dfrac{4}{3}}{3} = \dfrac{5}{9} = 56\%$

14. (c) For the rotational equilibrium, torque produced by f and torque produced by N must be equal.

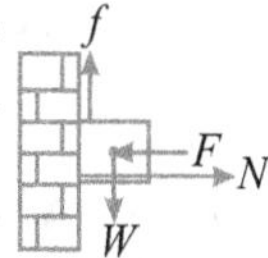

15. **(a)**
$$N_1 = 25 \sin\theta,$$
$$\therefore \quad f_1 = \mu N_1 = \frac{2}{5} \times 25 \times \frac{3}{5} = 6N.$$
$$f_2 = \mu N_2 = \frac{2}{5} mg = \frac{2}{5} \times 1 \times 10$$
$$= 4N.$$

Now from Newton's second law
$$25 \cos\theta - (f_1 + f_2) = ma$$
or $25 \times \dfrac{4}{5} - (6+4) = 1\,a$

$$\therefore \quad a = 10 \text{ m/s}^2.$$

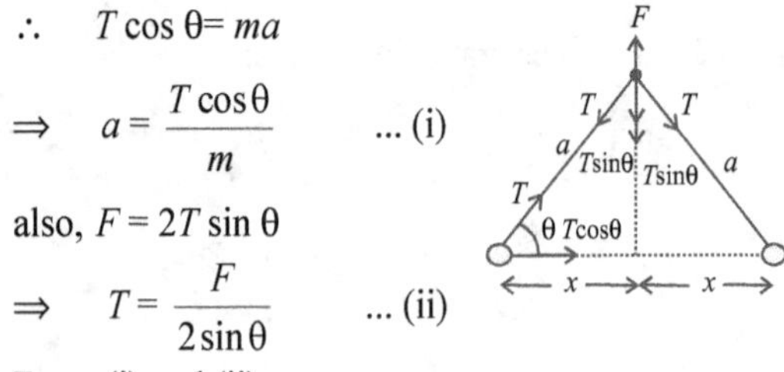

16. **(b)** Before the string is cut the situation is shown in figure.
$$T = mg$$
When string is cut, the unbalanced force on A is T.

$\therefore$ Acceleration of block $A = \dfrac{T}{2m} = \dfrac{mg}{2m} = \dfrac{g}{2}$

The acceleration of $B = \dfrac{mg}{m} = g$

17. **(b)** In force free space, momentum of satellite remains constant, and so
$$mv = k \qquad \text{or} \frac{d(mv)}{dt} = 0$$
or $\quad m\dfrac{dv}{dt} + v\dfrac{dm}{dt} = 0$ or $M\dfrac{dv}{dt} + v \times (\alpha v) = 0$

$$\therefore \quad \frac{dv}{dt} = -\frac{\alpha v^2}{M}$$

18. **(b)** The acceleration of mass m is due to the force $T\cos\theta$

$\therefore \quad T\cos\theta = ma$

$\Rightarrow \quad a = \dfrac{T\cos\theta}{m}$ ... (i)

also, $F = 2T\sin\theta$

$\Rightarrow \quad T = \dfrac{F}{2\sin\theta}$ ... (ii)

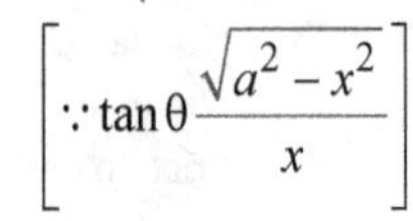

From (i) and (ii)
$$a = \left(\frac{F}{2\sin\theta}\right)\frac{\cos\theta}{m} = \frac{F}{2m\tan\theta} = \frac{F}{2m}\frac{x}{\sqrt{a^2 - x^2}}$$
$$\left[\because \tan\theta = \frac{\sqrt{a^2 - x^2}}{x} \right]$$

19. **(b)** The forces acting on the bead as seen by the observer in the accelerated frame are : (a) N ; (b) mg ; (c) ma (pseudo force). Let θ is the angle which the tangent at P makes with the X- axis. As the bead is in equilibrium with respect to the wire, therefore

$N\sin\theta = ma$ and $N\cos\theta = mg$

$$\therefore \quad \tan\theta = \frac{a}{g} \qquad \text{... (i)}$$

But $y = k\,x^2$. Therefore,
$$\frac{dy}{dx} = 2kx = \tan\theta \qquad \text{... (ii)}$$

From (i) & (ii) $2kx = \dfrac{a}{g} \Rightarrow x = \dfrac{a}{2kg}$

20. **(a)** As $\tan\theta > \mu$, the block has a tendency to move down the incline. Therefore a force P is applied upwards along the incline. Here, at equilibrium $P + f = mg\sin\theta$
$$\Rightarrow f = mg\sin\theta - P$$

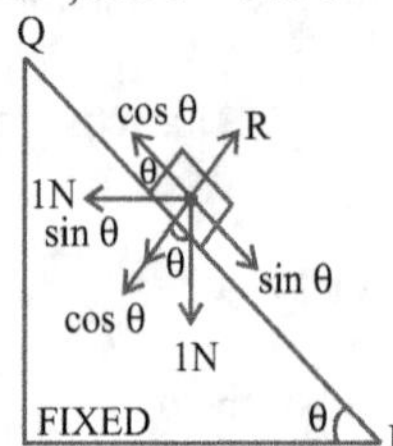

Now as P increases, f decreases linearly with respect to P.

When $P = mg\sin\theta, f = 0$.

When P is increased further, the block has a tendency to move upwards along the incline.

Therefore the frictional force acts downwards along the incline.

Here, at equilibrium $P = f + mg\sin\theta$

$\therefore \quad f = P - mg\sin\theta$

Now as P increases, f increases linearly w.r.t P. This is represented by graph (a) .

21. **(a, c)** The forces are resolved as shown in the figure.
When $\theta = 45°$, $\sin\theta = \cos\theta$

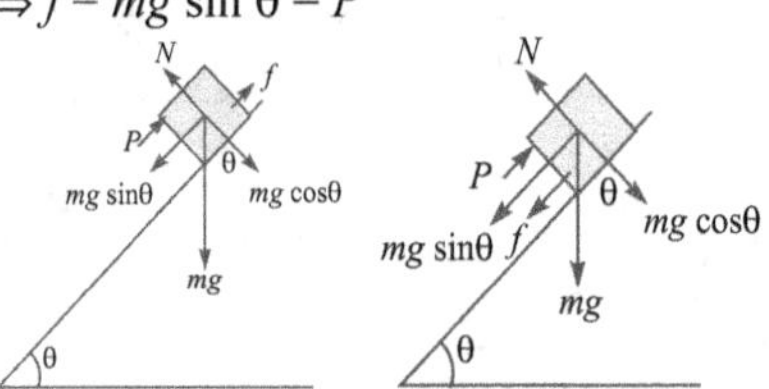

The block will remain stationary and the frictional force is zero. When $\theta > 45°$, $\sin\theta > \cos\theta$

Therefore a frictional force acts towards Q.

22. **5**

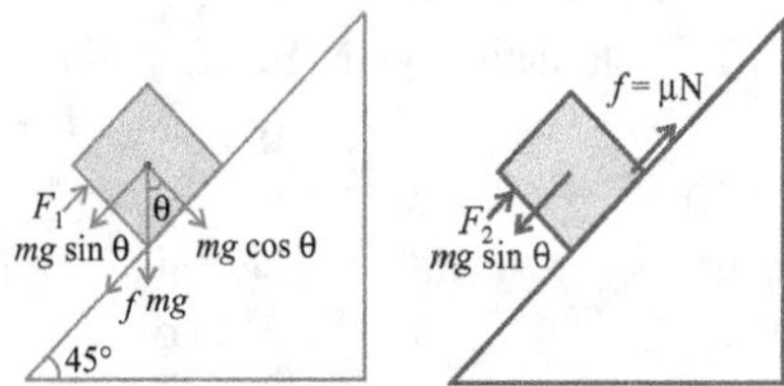

The pushing force $F_1 = mg\sin\theta + f$

$\because F_1 = mg\sin\theta + \mu\, mg\cos\theta = mg(\sin\theta + \mu\cos\theta)$

The force required to just prevent it from sliding down
$$F_2 = mg\sin\theta - \mu N = mg(\sin\theta - \mu\cos\theta)$$

Given , $F_1 = 3F_2$

$\therefore \quad \sin\theta + \mu\cos\theta = 3(\sin\theta - \mu\cos\theta)$

$\therefore \quad 1 + \mu = 3(1-\mu)\,[\because \sin\theta = \cos\theta]$

$\therefore \quad 4\mu = 2 \therefore \ \mu = 0.5 \qquad \therefore \text{ N} = 10\,\mu = 5$

Chapter 6

Circular Motion

(277 - 318)

Chapter contents

Henry Becquerel

Henry Becquerel's (1852-1908) work was concern with the plane polarization of light, with the phenomenon of phosphorescence and with the absorption of light by crystals (his doctorate thesis). He also worked on the subject of terrestrial magnetism. In 1896, his previous work was overshadowed by his discovery of the phenomenon of natural radioactivity. ....

Definitions, Explanations and Derivations

6.1 ANGULAR VELOCITY

Consider a particle moving along a circle. Let it undergoes an angular displacement $\Delta\vec{\theta}$ in time Δt. We can define the average angular velocity of the particle as

$$\vec{\omega} = \frac{\Delta\vec{\theta}}{\Delta t}.$$

The instantaneous angular velocity

$$\vec{\omega} = \lim_{\Delta t \to 0} \frac{\Delta\vec{\theta}}{\Delta t} \quad \text{or} \quad \vec{\omega} = \frac{d\vec{\theta}}{dt}.$$

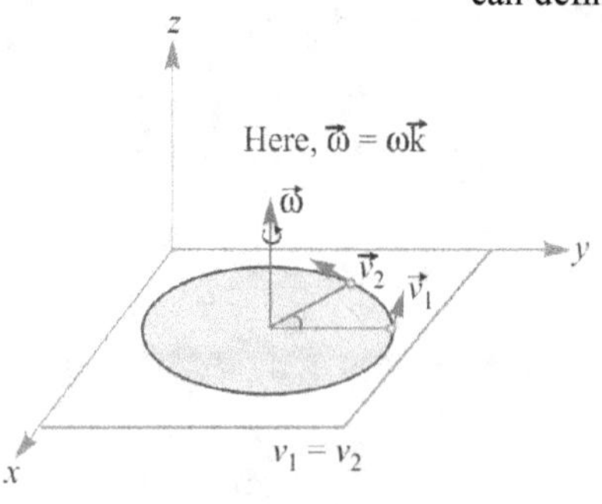

Figure. 6.1

Angular velocity is a vector quantity whose direction is along the axis of rotation and given by right hand screw rule. Its SI unit is rad/s. If particle makes n cycles or revolutions in one second, then

$$\omega = n \times 2\pi \quad \text{or} \quad \omega = 2\pi n.$$

Since $n = \dfrac{1}{T}$, where T is the time to complete one revolution

$$\therefore \quad \omega = \frac{2\pi}{T}.$$

6.2 ANGULAR ACCELERATION

If the angular velocity of a rotating particle is not constant, then the body has an angular acceleration. Let ω_1 and ω_2 be the angular velocity at time t_1 and t_2 respectively. The average angular acceleration

$$\vec{\alpha} = \frac{\vec{\omega}_2 - \vec{\omega}_1}{t_2 - t_1} = \frac{\Delta\vec{\omega}}{\Delta t}.$$

The instantaneous angular acceleration

$$\vec{\alpha} = \lim_{\Delta t \to 0} \frac{\Delta\vec{\omega}}{\Delta t} = \frac{d\vec{\omega}}{dt}.$$

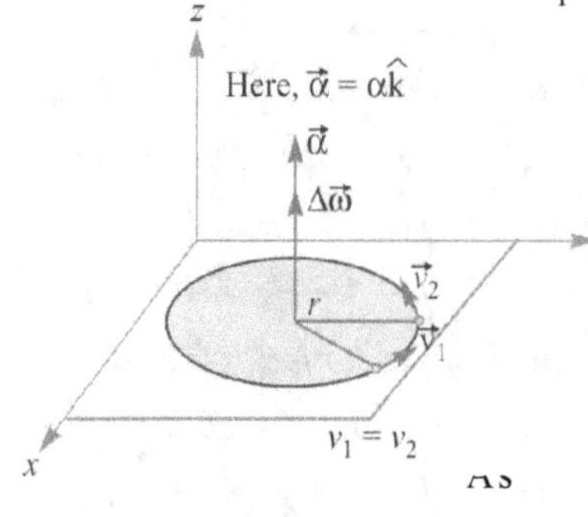

Figure. 6.2

$$\omega = \frac{d\theta}{dt};$$

$$\therefore \quad \alpha = \frac{d^2\theta}{dt^2}.$$

Angular acceleration is a vector quantity, its direction is along the axis of rotation. Its SI unit is rad/s^2.

6.3 RELATIONSHIP BETWEEN ANGULAR AND LINEAR PARAMETERS

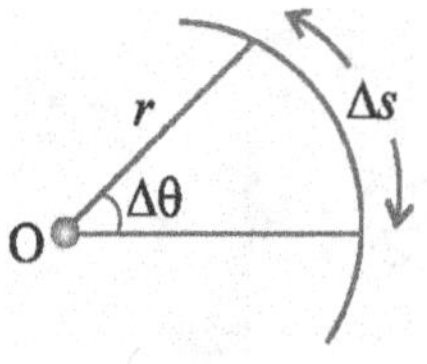

Let in time Δt the arc distance travelled by particle is Δs, then we have

$$\Delta s = r\,\Delta\theta$$

or

$$\frac{\Delta s}{\Delta t} = r\frac{\Delta\theta}{\Delta t}$$

or

$$v = r\omega$$

Differentiating above equation with respect to time, we get tangential acceleration

$$a_t = \frac{dv}{dt} = r\frac{d\omega}{dt}$$

or

$$a_t = r\alpha.$$

Figure. 6.3

In the uniform circular motion, speed of the particle remains constant hence $a_t = 0$.

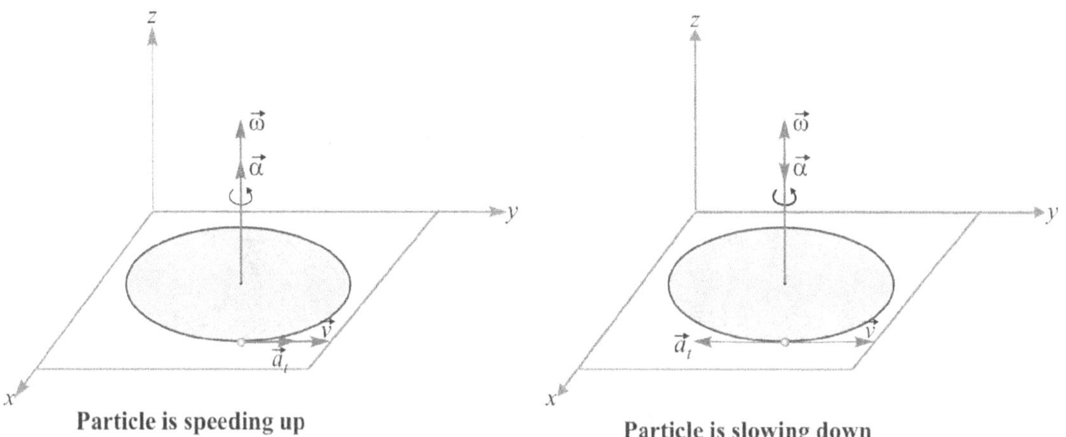

Particle is speeding up   Particle is slowing down

Figure. 6.4

Vector angular velocity $\vec{\omega}$

Consider a particle P revolving around an axis with an angular velocity $\vec{\omega}$. Let $\vec{r}$ be the position vector of the particle with respect to any point O on the axis. Since the particle describes a circle of radius $(r \sin\theta)$ lying in the plane perpendicular to the axis of rotation, the magnitude of linear velocity

$$v = \omega r \sin\theta$$

and its direction is perpendicular to the plane containing $\vec{r}$ and $\vec{\omega}$.
By right hand screw rule, we can write

$$\vec{v} = \vec{\omega} \times \vec{r}.$$

Change in position (linear displacement)

If particle changes its position from P to Q in time t, then displacement

$$\overrightarrow{PQ} = \Delta\vec{r} = \vec{r_2} - \vec{r_1}$$

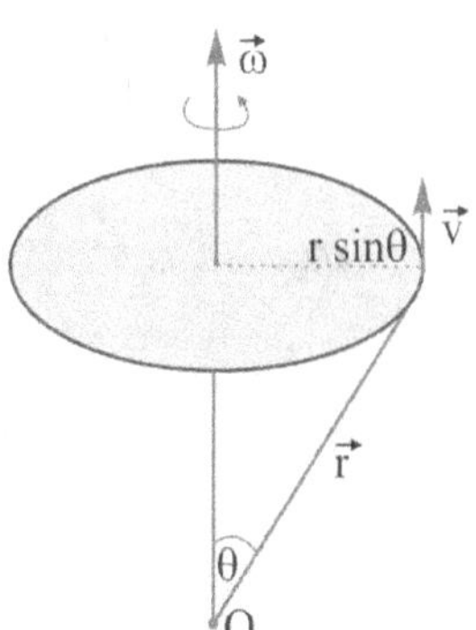

Figure. 6.5

or $\qquad \Delta r = |\vec{r_2} - \vec{r_1}| = \sqrt{r_1^2 + r_2^2 - 2r_1 r_2 \cos\theta}$

For $\qquad r_1 = r_2 = r$

$$\Delta r = \sqrt{r^2 + r^2 - 2r^2 \cos\theta} = \sqrt{2r^2(1 - \cos\theta)}$$

$$\Delta r = 2r\sin\frac{\theta}{2}$$

Change in velocity

Change in velocity after traversing angle θ

$$\Delta\vec{v} = \vec{v_2} - \vec{v_1}$$

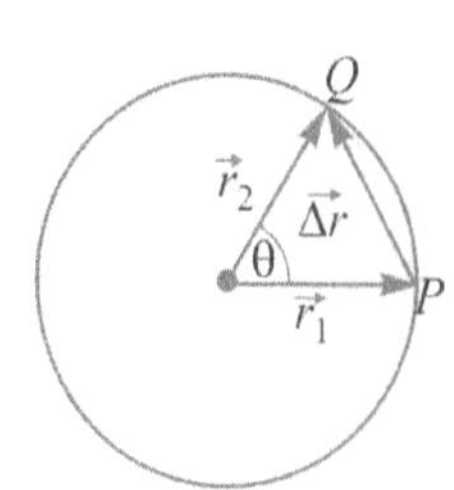

Figure. 6.6

or $\qquad \Delta v = |\vec{v_2} - \vec{v_1}| = \sqrt{v_1^2 + v_2^2 - 2v_1 v_2 \cos\theta}$

For uniform speed $\qquad v_1 = v_2 = v = \omega r$

$$\Delta v = \sqrt{v^2 + v^2 - 2v^2 \cos\theta}$$

$$= \sqrt{2v^2(1 - \cos\theta)} \qquad [1 - \cos\theta = 2\sin^2\frac{\theta}{2}]$$

or $\qquad \Delta v = 2v\sin\frac{\theta}{2}.$

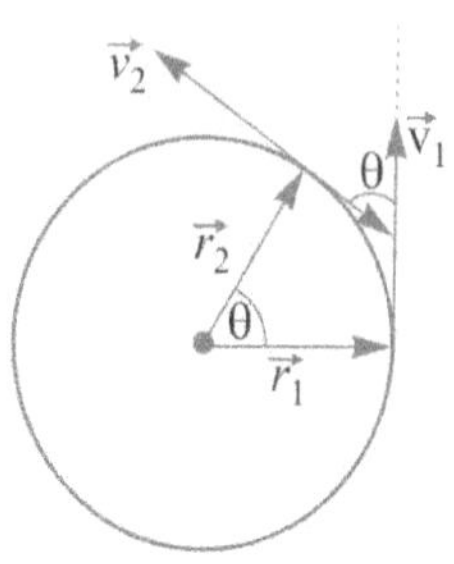

Figure. 6.7

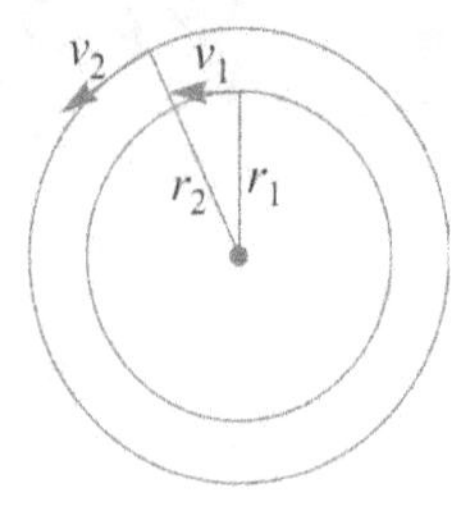

Figure. 6.8

If two particles are moving on same circle or different circles in same plane with different angular velocities ω_1 and ω_2 respectively, the angular velocity of 2 relative to 1 will be

$$\vec{\omega}_{21} = \vec{\omega}_2 - \vec{\omega}_1$$

or

$$\omega_{21} = \omega_2 - \omega_1.$$

Time taken by 2 to complete one revolution w.r.t. particle 1 is given by

$$T = \frac{2\pi}{\omega_{21}} = \frac{2\pi}{\omega_2 - \omega_1} = \frac{2\pi}{\dfrac{2\pi}{T_1} - \dfrac{2\pi}{T_2}}.$$

$$\therefore \qquad T = \frac{T_1 T_2}{T_2 - T_1}.$$

6.4 ANGULAR VELOCITY IN GENERAL

Consider the situation, in which particle is not on a circular path. Suppose the particle P at any instant going along the tangent of the curve. Let its speed be v and its direction of motion makes an angle θ with the radius vector $\vec{r}$ relative to P (see *fig.* 6.9).

The angular velocity of particle P is defined as;

$$\omega = \frac{\text{The velocity component perpendicular to } OP}{OP}$$

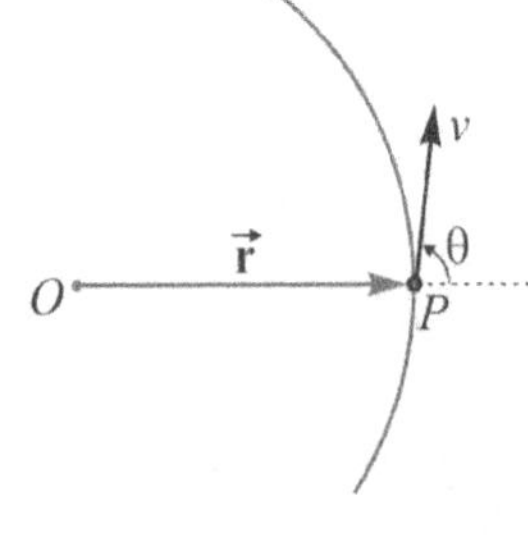

Figure. 6.9

or

$$\omega = \frac{v_\perp}{r} \qquad \text{........(1)}$$

Here,

$$v_\perp = v\sin\theta$$

$$\therefore \qquad \omega = \frac{v\sin\theta}{r} = \frac{rv\sin\theta}{r^2}$$

or

$$\omega = \frac{|\vec{r} \times \vec{v}|}{r^2} \qquad \text{........(2)}$$

6.5 ACCELERATION IN CIRCULAR MOTION

Uniform circular motion

The motion of a particle moving along a circular path with constant speed is called **uniform circular motion** (UCM). In motion along circular path, the velocity of particle always changes due to change in direction of motion. Due to which there is an acceleration, which is called **normal or centripetal acceleration**. Its magnitude is found to be $\dfrac{v^2}{r}$.

Non-uniform circular motion

If a particle is moving along a circular path with variable speed, its velocity changes due to change in direction of motion and also by change in magnitude of the velocity. In such a case there are two perpendicular accelerations :

(i) Normal or centripetal acceleration (a_c) :

This acceleration is due to change in direction of motion and is given by,

$$a_c = \frac{v^2}{r}.$$

(ii) Tangential acceleration (a_t) :

This acceleration is due to change in magnitude of velocity and is given by,

$$a_t = \frac{dv}{dt} = \alpha r.$$

Thus resultant acceleration

$$\vec{a} = \vec{a}_c + \vec{a}_t$$

or

$$\vec{a} = -\left(\frac{v^2}{r}\right)\hat{r} + \left(\frac{dv}{dt}\right)\hat{\theta}.$$

and

$$a = \sqrt{a_c^2 + a_t^2}.$$

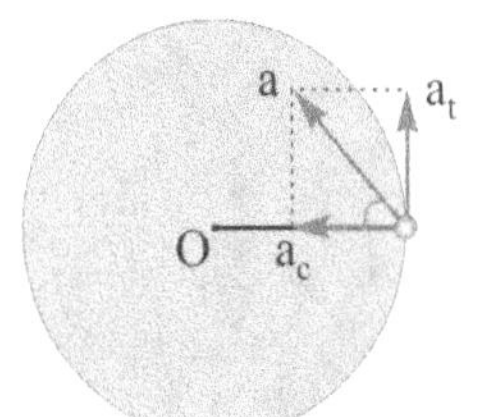

Figure. 6.10

Unit vector along the radius and the tangent

Let us draw a unit vector $\overrightarrow{OP} = \hat{r}$ along the outward radius and a unit vector $\overrightarrow{PQ} = \hat{\theta}$ along the tangent in direction of increasing θ. We call $\hat{r}$ radial unit vector and $\hat{\theta}$ the tangential unit vector. Thus

$$\overrightarrow{OP} = OP\cos\theta\,\hat{i} + OP\sin\theta\,\hat{j} \quad (\text{as } OP = 1)$$

$$\therefore \quad \hat{r} = \cos\theta\hat{i} + \sin\theta\hat{j}$$

Similarly,

$$\overrightarrow{PQ} = -PQ\sin\theta\,\hat{i} + PQ\cos\theta\,\hat{j} \quad (\text{as } PQ = 1)$$

$$\therefore \quad \hat{\theta} = -\sin\theta\hat{i} + \cos\theta\hat{j}$$

As $\hat{r}$ and $\hat{\theta}$ are mutually perpendicular,

So

$$\hat{r}.\hat{\theta} = 0.$$

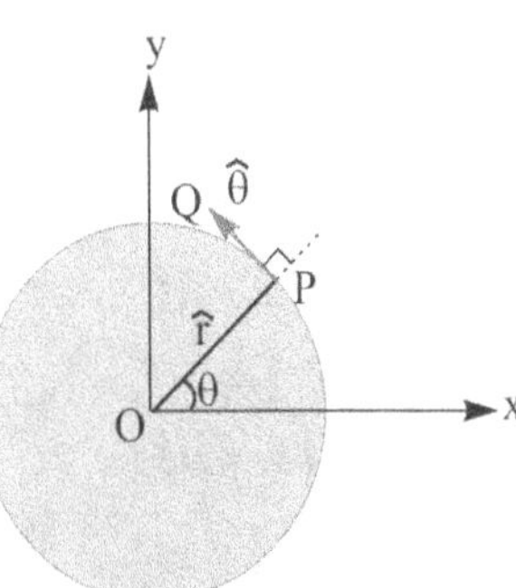

Figure. 6.11

6.6 CENTRIPETAL ACCELERATION (DERIVATION)

Method - I : Let us consider a particle moving along a circular path of radius r with constant angular speed ω. Its position vector at any time t is given by

$$\vec{r} = \overrightarrow{OP}$$
$$= OP\,\hat{r}$$

Here $\hat{r}$ is the unit vector along radius, and $\hat{r} = (\cos\theta\,\hat{i} + \sin\theta\,\hat{j})$

$$\therefore \quad \vec{r} = r(\cos\theta\,\hat{i} + \sin\theta\,\hat{j}) \quad\quad ....(i)$$

Differentiating equation (i) with respect to time, we get velocity

$$\vec{v} = \frac{d\vec{r}}{dt} = r\left(-\sin\theta\,\frac{d\theta}{dt}\,\hat{i} + \cos\theta\,\frac{d\theta}{dt}\,\hat{j}\right)$$

$$= r\left(\frac{d\theta}{dt}\right)(-\sin\theta\,\hat{i} + \cos\theta\,\hat{j})$$

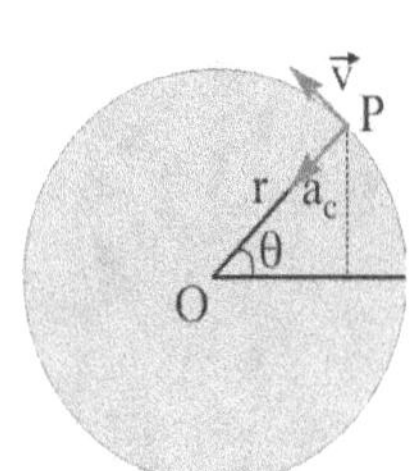

Figure. 6.12

or

$$\vec{v} = r\omega(-\sin\theta\,\hat{i} + \cos\theta\,\hat{j}) \quad\quad ....(ii)$$

We know that,

$$\frac{d\theta}{dt} = \omega \text{ and } (-\sin\theta\,\hat{i} + \cos\theta\,\hat{j}) = \hat{\theta}$$

$$\therefore \quad \vec{v} = r\omega\hat{\theta} \text{ and } |\vec{v}| = \omega r.$$

The acceleration can be obtained by differenting equation (ii). Thus

$$\vec{a}_c = \frac{d\vec{v}}{dt} = \frac{d}{dt}[r\omega(-\sin\theta\,\hat{i} + \cos\theta\,\hat{j})]$$

$$= r\omega\left[-\cos\theta\,\frac{d\theta}{dt}\,\hat{i} - \sin\theta\,\frac{d\theta}{dt}\,\hat{j}\right]$$

$$= -r\omega\left(\frac{d\theta}{dt}\right)[\cos\theta\,\hat{i} + \sin\theta\,\hat{j}]$$

$$= -r\omega^2\,\hat{r} \quad\quad \left[\frac{d\theta}{dt} = \omega\right]$$

or

$$\vec{a}_c = -\omega^2\vec{r} \text{ and } a_c = \omega^2 r = \frac{v^2}{r}.$$

Here $\vec{a}_c$ is called **normal acceleration** and its direction is towards the centre of circular path. Because of centre seeking it is also called **centripetal acceleration.**

Method - II : Let us consider a particle which traverses angle $\Delta\theta$ in time Δt, with reference to the coordinate axes shown in figure given below, we have

$$v_{Px} = v\sin\frac{\Delta\theta}{2} \text{ and } v_{Py} = v\cos\frac{\Delta\theta}{2}$$

and

$$V_{Qx} = -v\sin\frac{\Delta\theta}{2}, \quad V_{Qy} = v\cos\frac{\Delta\theta}{2}$$

$\therefore$

$$\Delta v_y = v_{Qy} - v_{Py}$$

$$= -v\cos\frac{\Delta\theta}{2} - v\cos\frac{\Delta\theta}{2} = 0$$

and

$$\Delta v_x = v_{Qx} - v_{Px}$$

$$= -v\sin\frac{\Delta\theta}{2} - v\sin\frac{\Delta\theta}{2} = -2v\sin\frac{\Delta\theta}{2}.$$

As $\Delta\theta$ is small, so

$$\sin\frac{\Delta\theta}{2} \approx \frac{\Delta\theta}{2}$$

$\therefore$

$$\Delta v_x = -2v\frac{\Delta\theta}{2} = -v\Delta\theta \qquad \text{...(i)}$$

Dividing equation (i) by Δt, we get centripetal acceleration

$$a_c = \frac{\Delta v_x}{\Delta t} = -v\frac{\Delta\theta}{\Delta t}$$

As $\dfrac{\Delta\theta}{\Delta t} = \omega$

$\therefore$

$$a_c = -v\omega = -(\omega r)\omega = -\omega^2 r.$$

The minus sign tells us that the acceleration is towards the origin (centre of circle).

6.7 CENTRIPETAL FORCE

For a particle moving in a circular path, it has an acceleration towards the centre of path. According to Newton's second law the particle must experience a net force towards the centre of path. This force is called centripetal force. If a_c be the centripetal acceleration, then centripetal force is given by

$$\vec{F}_c = m\vec{a}_c$$

or

$$F_c = \frac{mv^2}{r}.$$

Centripetal force is not a new kind of force, it may be gravitational force, tension, frictional or Coulomb's force.

For example : A body is rotating in a circle with the help of string. Here tension in the string is the centripetal force.

For example : Motion of earth around sun. Here gravitational force is the centripetal force.

6.8 CENTRIFUGAL FORCE

Consider a block of mass m placed on a table at a distance r from its centre. Suppose the table rotates with constant angular velocity ω and block remains at rest with respect to table. Let us first analyse the motion of the block relative to an observer on the ground (inertial frame). In this frame the block is moving in a circle of radius r. It, therefore, has an acceleration $\dfrac{v^2}{r}$ towards the centre. The resultant force on the block must be towards the centre and its magnitude is $\dfrac{mv^2}{r}$. In this frame the forces on the block are :

(i)   weight, mg

(ii)   normal reaction, N

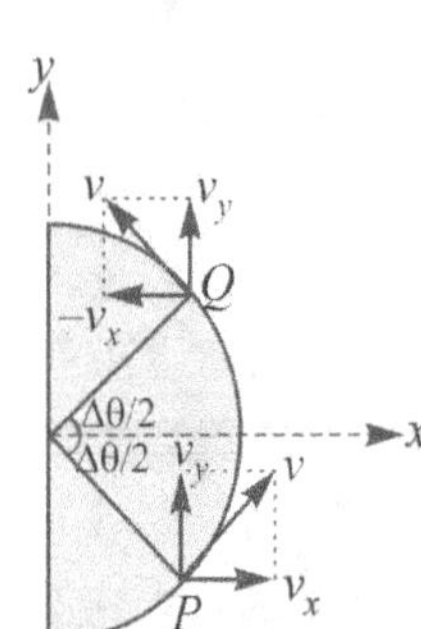

Figure. 6.13

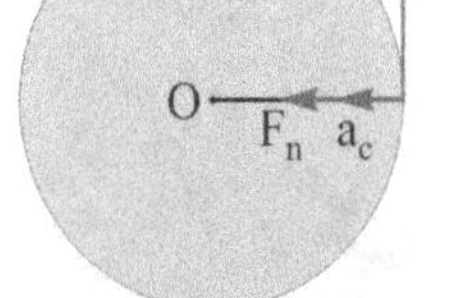

Figure. 6.14

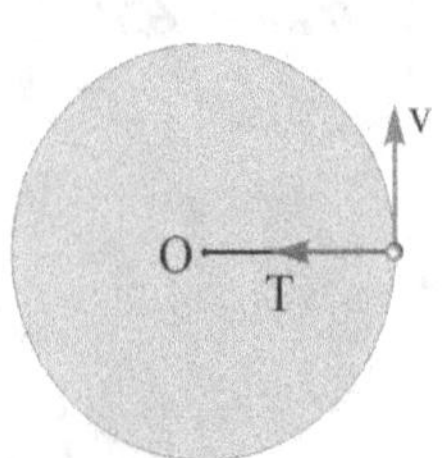

Figure. 6.15

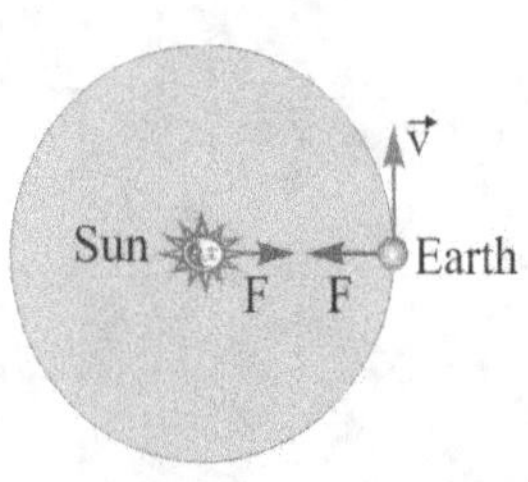

Figure. 6.16

(iii)   frictional force, f by the table.

Thus we have, $N = mg$ ....(i)

and by Newton's Second law of motion

$$f = \frac{mv^2}{r}.$$ ....(ii)

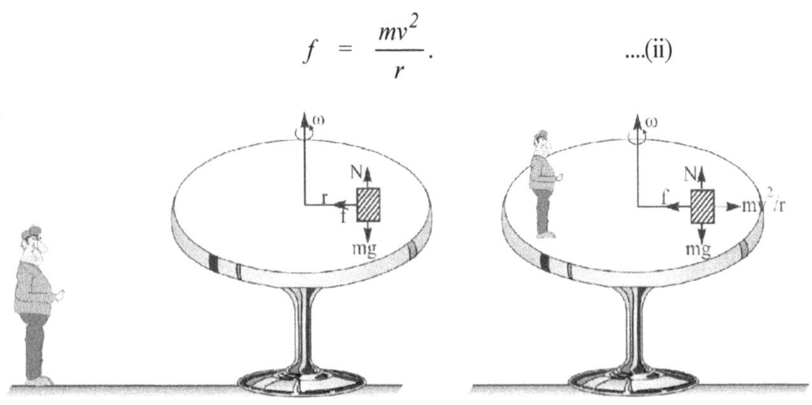

(a) FBD of the block in inertial frame   (b) FBD of the block in non-inertial frame

Figure. 6.17

Now observe the same block in a frame attached with the rotating table. The observer here finds that the block is at rest. Thus the net force on the block in this frame must be zero. The weight and normal reaction balance each other but frictional force, f acts on the block towards the centre of the table. To make the resultant zero, a pseudo force must be assumed which acts on the block away radially

outwards and has a magnitude $\dfrac{mv^2}{r}$. This pseudo force is called **centrifugal force.** In this frame the

forces on the block are:

(i)   weight, mg

(ii)   normal reaction, N

(iii)   frictional force, f

(iv)   centrifugal force, $\dfrac{mv^2}{r}$

Thus we have, $\qquad \sum F_{\text{vertical}} = 0$

or $\qquad\qquad\qquad N - mg = 0,\ \text{or}\ N = mg$ ....(i)

and $\qquad\qquad\qquad \sum F_{\text{radius}} = 0$

or $\qquad\qquad\qquad f - \dfrac{mv^2}{r} = 0$

or $\qquad\qquad\qquad f = \dfrac{mv^2}{r}$ ....(ii)

Note :

We have got the same result in non-inertial frame as in inertial frame. It should be remembered that the centrifugal force is taken into account only in rotating frame (non-inertial frame).

6.9 ANALYSIS OF CONICAL PENDULUM

Consider a conical pendulum of length ℓ. It is made to rotate about a vertical axis. Suppose string of the pendulum makes an angle θ with the axis. Its motion can be studied in two frames. These are : inertial frame and rotating frame.

(a)   **In inertial frame of reference :** we have

$$T \sin\theta = m\omega^2 r$$ ....(i)

and $\qquad\qquad T \cos\theta = mg.$ ....(ii)

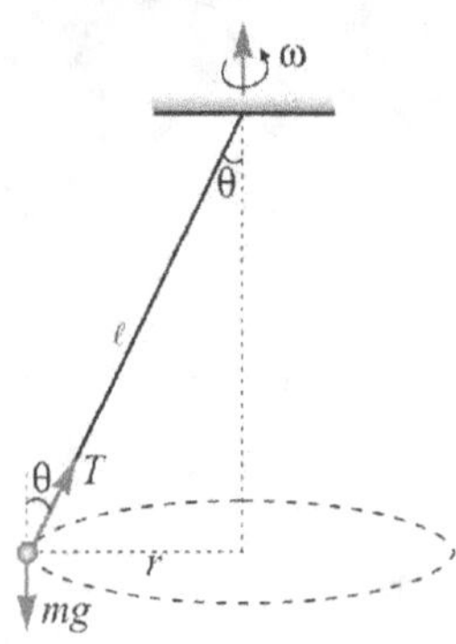

Figure. 6.18 (a)

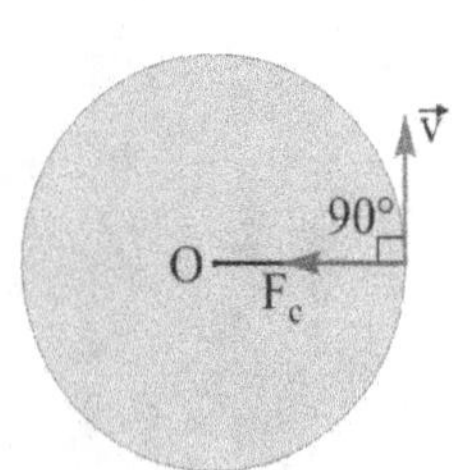

Figure. 6.18 (b)

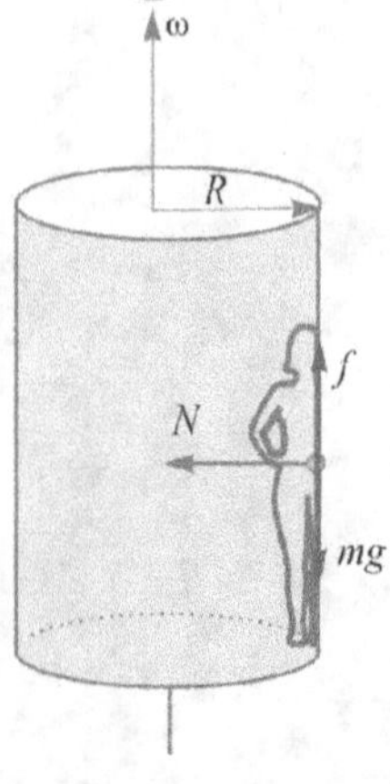

Figure. 6.19

From above equations, we get

$$\tan\theta = \frac{\omega^2 r}{g}$$

or $$\tan\theta = \frac{\omega^2 \ell \sin\theta}{g}$$

From above equations, we get

$$\therefore \quad \omega = \sqrt{\frac{g}{\ell\cos\theta}}.$$

(b) **In non-inertial frame:**

$$\sum F_{radius} = 0$$

or $$T\sin\theta - m\omega^2 r = 0 \qquad ....(i)$$

and $$\sum F_{vertical} = 0$$

or $$T\cos\theta - mg = 0. \qquad ....(ii)$$

After solving these equations, we get

$$\tan\theta = \frac{\omega^2 r}{g} = \frac{\omega^2 \ell \sin\theta}{g}$$

or $$\omega = \sqrt{\frac{g}{\ell\cos\theta}}.$$

Work done in circular motion

(i) In uniform circular motion, the only force is centripetal force, which acts perpendicular to the velocity. So the rate of doing work or power

$$P = \frac{dW}{dt} = \vec{F}_n \cdot \vec{v} = F_c\, v\cos 90° = 0.$$

(ii) In non uniform circular motion, there are normal and tangential forces. The rate of doing work

$$P = \frac{dW}{dt} = (\vec{F}_c + \vec{F}_t)\cdot\vec{v}$$

$$= \vec{F}_c \cdot \vec{v} + \vec{F}_t \cdot \vec{v}$$

$$= F_c\, v\cos 90° + F_t\, v\cos 0°$$

or $$P = F_t v,$$

where F_t is the tangential force which comes into play due to tangential acceleration in non-uniform circular motion and given by $F_t = ma_t$.

Rotor

Consider a rotor, a hollow vertical cylindrical device which rotates about its axis and a person rests against the inner wall. As the person is at rest w.r.t. rotor, so

$$N = m\omega^2 R. \qquad ....(i)$$

and frictional force

$$f = mg. \qquad ....(ii)$$

Minimum speed of rotation of rotor : At the minimum speed, the friction is limiting one, that is

$$f = \mu_s N.$$

or $$mg = \mu_s(m\omega^2 R)$$

$$\therefore \quad \omega = \omega_{min} = \sqrt{\frac{g}{\mu_s R}}.$$

Figure. 6.20

6.10 MOTION OF CYCLIST ON CIRCULAR ROAD

When a cyclist goes round a circular road, a centripetal force is required. The frictional force between the tyres and ground provides the necessary centripetal force. To get rotational equilibrium he leans from vertical. Let θ be the angle, the contact force on tyres makes with vertical. Then to prevent skidding, we have

$$ma_c \leq f_{\lim}$$

or

$$\frac{mv^2}{r} \leq \mu_s N$$

$$\leq \mu_s (mg)$$

$$\Rightarrow \quad v \leq \sqrt{\mu_s r g}.$$

Again we have

$$f_{\lim} = \frac{mv^2}{r} \qquad ....(i)$$

and

$$N = mg \qquad ....(ii)$$

Dividing equation (i) by (ii), we get

$$\frac{f_{\lim}}{N} = \frac{v^2}{r g}$$

As

$$\frac{f_{\lim}}{N} = \tan \theta$$

$$\therefore \quad \tan \theta = \frac{v^2}{rg}.$$

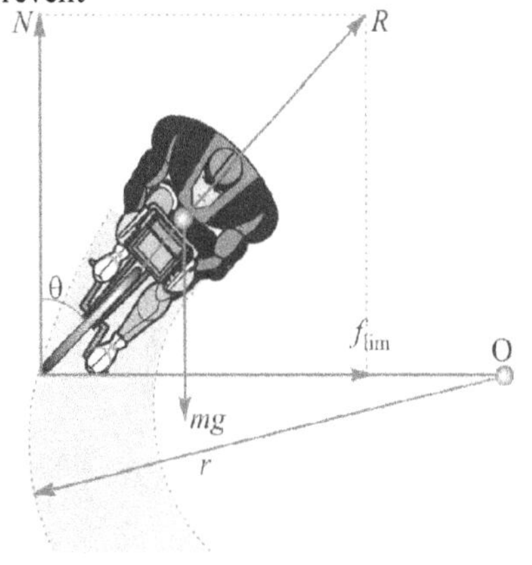

Figure. **6.21**

6.11 BANKING OF ROAD

On circular path, if frictional force is not enough to provide required centripetal force, then outer edge of the road is raised with respect to inner edge of the road. This is called **banking of road**.

Consider a car of mass m going on a circular path of radius r with a speed v. The outer edge of road is raised by h with respect to inner edge. Geometrically banking of road (also known as superelevation) is defined as

$$\tan \theta = \frac{h}{b}$$

for small θ,

$$\tan \theta \simeq \frac{h}{W},$$

where W is the width of the road.

Now let tendency of car is to slip up (this corresponds to maximum speed), then friction will act down the elevation.

Along vertical direction, we have

$$\sum F_v = 0$$

or

$$N \cos \theta = mg + \mu_s N \sin \theta$$

or

$$N \cos \theta - \mu_s N \sin \theta = mg. \qquad ....(i)$$

And along horizontal direction by Newton's second law

$$N \sin \theta + \mu_s N \cos \theta = \frac{mv^2}{r}. \qquad ....(ii)$$

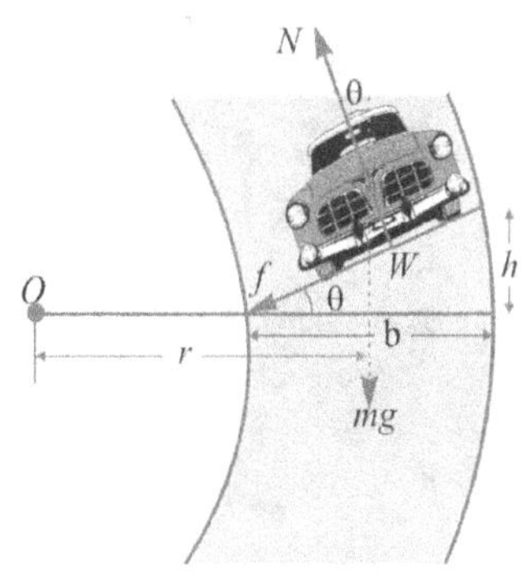

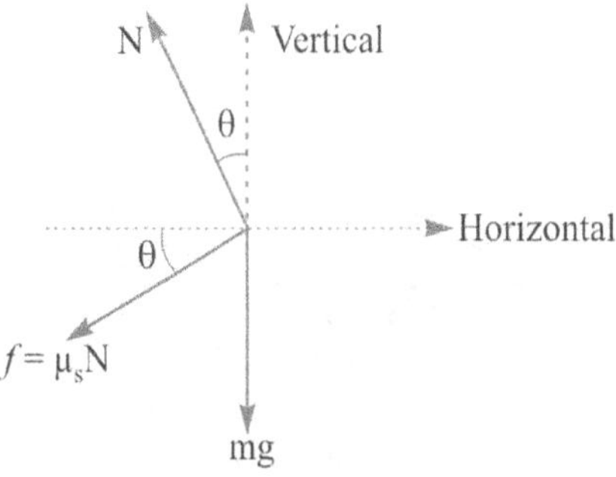

Simplified *FBD* assuming car as a point object
Figure. **6.22**

Dividing equation (ii) by (i), we have

$$\frac{\sin\theta + \mu_s\cos\theta}{\cos\theta - \mu_s\sin\theta} = \frac{v^2}{r\,g}.$$

Again dividing numerator and denominator each by $\cos\theta$, we get

$$\left[\frac{\mu_s + \tan\theta}{1 - \mu_s\tan\theta}\right] = \frac{v_{max}^2}{r\,g}. \qquad\qquad ...(1)$$

If tendency of car is to slip down the plane, it corresponds to minimum speed of the car, then

$$\left[\frac{-\mu_s + \tan\theta}{1 + \mu_s\tan\theta}\right] = \frac{v_{min}^2}{r\,g}. \qquad\qquad ...(2)$$

Special case : when there is no friction between the tyres and road, $\mu_s = 0$, then we have

$$\tan\theta = \frac{v^2}{r\,g}. \qquad\qquad ...(3)$$

6.12 MOTION ON A PLANE CIRCULAR PATH

Consider a car whose centre of gravity is at a height h from the road and separation between the wheels is $2a$. Car is going with a constant speed v on a circular path of radius r.

For the vertical equilibrium of the car

$$N_1 + N_2 = mg. \qquad\qquad ...(i)$$

The maximum value of centripetal force that can be available is

$$f = f_1 + f_2 = \mu_s N_1 + \mu_s N_2$$
$$= \mu_s (N_1 + N_2) = \mu_s\, mg.$$

Skidding : To prevent skidding, we have

$$\frac{mv^2}{r} \leq f$$
$$\leq \mu_s\, mg$$

or
$$v \leq \sqrt{\mu_s r\, g} \qquad\qquad ...(ii)$$

$$\therefore \qquad v_{max.} = \sqrt{\mu_s r\, g}.$$

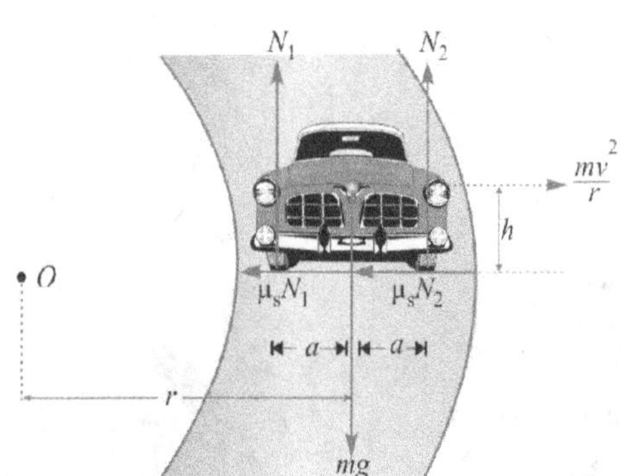

Figure. 6.23

Now taking moment of all the forces acting on the car about centre of gravity (or any other point) we have

$$\mu_s (N_1 + N_2) \times h + N_1 \times a - N_2 \times a = 0 \qquad\qquad ....(iii)$$

From equation (i), $N_2 = mg - N_1$ and from equation (ii) we have $\mu_s = \dfrac{v^2}{rg}$. Substituting these values in equation (iii) and after simplification, we get

$$N_1 = \frac{mg}{2}\left(1 - \frac{v^2 h}{r\,g\,a}\right), \qquad\qquad ....(iv)$$

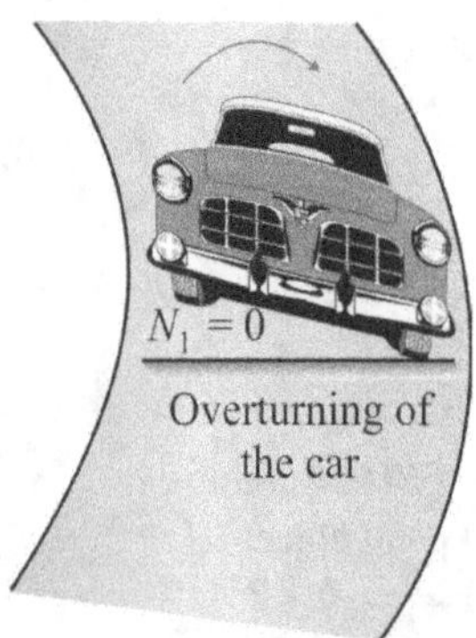

and

$$N_2 = \frac{mg}{2}\left(1 + \frac{v^2 h}{r\,g\,a}\right). \qquad\qquad ....(v)$$

Figure. 6.24

Overturning

With the increase in speed of the car normal reaction N_2 increases while N_1 decreases. For a particular value of speed $v = v_{max}$, N_1 becomes zero, and car is then about to overturn. Thus to prevent overturning,

$$N_1 \geq 0$$

or

$$\frac{mg}{2}\left(1 - \frac{v^2 h}{r g a}\right) \geq 0$$

or

$$v \leq \sqrt{\frac{r g a}{h}}.$$

FORMULAE USED

1. Angular displacement, $\theta = \dfrac{s}{r}$

2. Angular velocity, $\omega = \dfrac{\theta}{t}$

3. If T is the time period of rotation, angular velocity $\omega = \dfrac{2\pi}{T} = 2\pi f$

4. Linear velocity, $\vec{v} = \vec{\omega} \times \vec{r}$ or $v = \omega r$

5. Tangential acceleration, $\vec{a}_t = \vec{\alpha} \times \vec{r}$ or $a_t = \alpha r$

6. Centripetal acceleration, $a_c = \dfrac{v^2}{r} = \omega^2 r$

7. Centripetal force, $F_c = \dfrac{mv^2}{r} = m\omega^2 r$

8. Total acceleration (in non-uniform circular motion), $a = \sqrt{a_n^2 + a_t^2}$

9. Centrifugal force is taken into account in rotating frame and its magnitude is equal to that of centripetal force and act away from the centre of the path.

10. Bending of cyclist : In order to take a circular turn of radius r with speed v the cyclist should

    bend himself from vertical at an angle, $\tan\theta = \dfrac{v^2}{rg}$

11. Banking of roads : The banking angle of the road (in absence of friction) is given by, $\tan\theta = \dfrac{v^2}{rg}$

12. If μ_s the coefficient of static friction, then banking angle is given by,

    $$\frac{\mu_s + \tan\theta}{1 - \mu_s \tan\theta} = \frac{v_{max}^2}{rg}$$

    and

    $$\frac{-\mu_s + \tan\theta}{1 + \mu_s \tan\theta} = \frac{v_{min}^2}{rg}$$

13. Motion of vehicle on plane circular road :

    To prevent skidding of the vehicle, the speed $v \leq \sqrt{\mu_s rg}$

    To prevent overturning, $v \leq \sqrt{\dfrac{rga}{h}}$,

    where $(2a)$ is the separation between wheels and h is the height of centre of gravity.

EXAMPLES BASED ON MOTION IN HORIZONTAL CIRCLE

Example 1. A cyclist starts from the centre O of a circular park of radius 1 km, reaches the edge P of the park, then cycles along the circumference, and returns to the centre along QO as shwon in Fig. If the round trip takes 10 min, what is the (a) net displacement, (b) average velocity, and (c) average speed of the cyclist ? [NCERT]

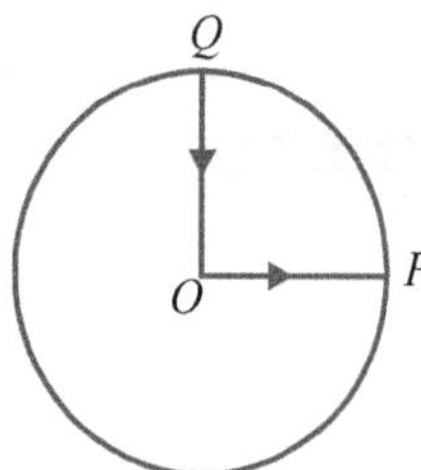

Sol. (a) Since both the initial and final positions are the same therefore the net displacement is zero.

(b) Average velocity is the ratio of net displacement and total time taken. Since the net displacement is zero therefore the average velocity is also zero.

(c) Average speed $= \dfrac{\text{distance covered}}{\text{time taken}}$

$$= \dfrac{OP + \text{actual distance } PQ + QO}{10\,\text{minute}}$$

$$= \dfrac{1\,\text{km} + \dfrac{1}{4} \times 2\pi \times 1\,\text{km} + 1\,\text{km}}{\dfrac{10}{60h}}$$

$$= 6\left(2 + \dfrac{22}{14}\right)\,\text{km h}^{-1} = 6 \times \dfrac{50}{14}\,\text{km h}^{-1}$$

$$= 21.43\ \text{km h}^{-1}.$$

Example 2. An aircraft executes a horizontal loop of radius 1.00 km with a steady speed of 900 km/h. Compare its centripetal acceleration with the acceleration due to gravity. [NCERT]

Sol. Here $r = 1$ km $= 10^3$ m,

$$v = 900\ \text{km } h^{-1} = 900 \times \dfrac{5}{18} = 250\ \text{ms}^{-1}$$

$$\text{Centripetal acceleration} = a_c = \dfrac{v^2}{r} = \dfrac{(250)^2}{10^3}$$

$$= 62.5\ \text{ms}^{-2}$$

Now, $\dfrac{a_c}{g} = \dfrac{62.5}{9.8} = 6.38.$

Example 3. Read each statement below carefully and state, with reasons, if it is true or false : [NCERT]

(a) The net acceleration of a particle in circular motion is always along the radius of the circle towards the centre.

(b) The velocity vector of a particle at a point is always along the tangent to the path of the particle at that point.

(c) The acceleration vector of a particle in uniform circular motion averaged over one cycle is a null vector.

Sol. (a) False, the net acceleration of a particle in circular motion is along the radius of the circle towards the centre only in uniform circular motion.

(b) True, because while leaving the circular path, the particle moves tangentially to the circular path.

(c) True, the direction of acceleration vector in a uniform circular motion is directed towards the centre of circular path. It is constantly changing with time. The resultant of all these vectors will be a zero vector.

Example 4. A particle starts from the origin at $t = 0$ s with a velocity of $10.0\ \hat{j}$ m/s and moves in the x-y plane with a constant acceleration of $8.0\hat{i} + 2.0\hat{j}$ m/s^{-2}. (a) At what time is the x-coordinate of the particle 16 m? What is the y-coordinate of the particle at that time? (b) What is the speed of the particle at that time? [NCERT]

Sol. (a) Using, $\vec{v} = \vec{u} + \vec{a}t$, we have

$$\vec{v} = \vec{u} + (8.0\hat{i} + 2.0\hat{j})t \qquad \text{... (i)}$$

$$= 10\hat{j} + (8.0\hat{i} + 2.0\hat{j})t$$

$$x = u_x + \dfrac{1}{2}a_x t^2$$

$$16 = 0 + \dfrac{1}{2} \times 8 \times t^2$$

or $\qquad t = 2s$

(b) Velocity of the particle at time t is $v = 10\hat{j} + 8t\hat{i} + 2t\hat{j}$, when, $t = 2$ s, then,

$$v = 10\hat{j} + 8 \times 2t\hat{i} + 2 \times 2t\hat{j} = 16\hat{i} + 14\hat{j}$$

$$\text{Speed} = |\vec{v}| = \sqrt{16^2 + 14^2} = 21.26\ \text{ms}^{-1}$$

Example 5. A rigid body is spinning with an angular velocity of 4 rad/s about an axis parallel to $3\hat{j}-\hat{k}$ passing through the point $\hat{i}+3\hat{j}-\hat{k}$. Find the velocity of the particle at the point $4\hat{i}-2\hat{j}+\hat{k}$.

Sol. Let $\hat{n}$ be the unit vector in the direction of $3\hat{j}-\hat{k}$ then,

$$\hat{n} = \frac{3\hat{j}-\hat{k}}{\sqrt{3^2+(-1)^2}} = \frac{(3\hat{j}-\hat{k})}{\sqrt{10}}$$

$\therefore$ angular velocity of the particle

$$\vec{\omega} = \omega\,\hat{n}$$

$$= \frac{4}{\sqrt{10}}\,(3\hat{j}-\hat{k})\ \text{rad/s}.$$

The position vector of the point with reference to point $(\hat{i}+3\hat{j}-\hat{k})$

$$\vec{r} = (4\hat{i}-2\hat{j}+\hat{k})-(\hat{i}+3\hat{j}-\hat{k})$$

$$= 3\hat{i}-5\hat{j}+2\hat{k}\ \text{m}.$$

Hence linear velocity

$$\vec{v} = \vec{\omega} \times \vec{r}$$

$$= \frac{4}{\sqrt{10}}\,(3\hat{j}-\hat{k}) \times (3\hat{i}-5\hat{j}+2\hat{k})$$

$$= \frac{-4}{\sqrt{10}}\,(\hat{i}+3\hat{j}+9\hat{k})\ \text{m/s}. \qquad \textit{Ans.}$$

Example 6. A particle is going parallel to x-axis with constant speed v at a distance a from the axis. Find its angular velocity about an axis passing through the origin O, at the instant when radial vector of the particle makes angle θ with the x-axis.

Sol. The velocity of the particle perpendicular to the radial vector $\vec{r}$ is $v\sin\theta$. Also $r\sin\theta = a$. Thus by the definition

$$\omega = \frac{v_\perp}{r}$$

$$= \frac{v\sin\theta}{(a/\sin\theta)} = \frac{v}{a}\sin^2\theta. \qquad \textit{Ans.}$$

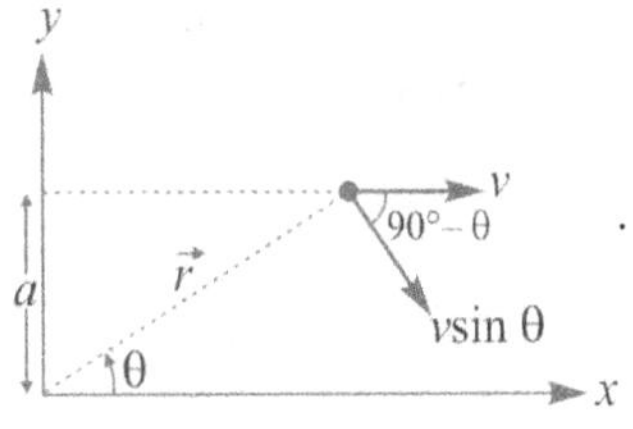

Figure. **6.25**

Example 7. A cyclist is riding with a speed of 27 km/h. As he approaches a circular turn on the road of radius 80 m, he applies brakes and reduces his speed at the constant rate 0.5 m/s². What is the magnitude and direction of the net acceleration of the cyclist on the circular turn ?

Sol. This is an example of non-uniform circular motion, and therefore it has two accelerations :

Centripetal acceleration

$$a_c = \frac{v^2}{r} = \frac{(27 \times 5/18)^2}{80}$$

$$= 0.70\ \text{m/s}^2$$

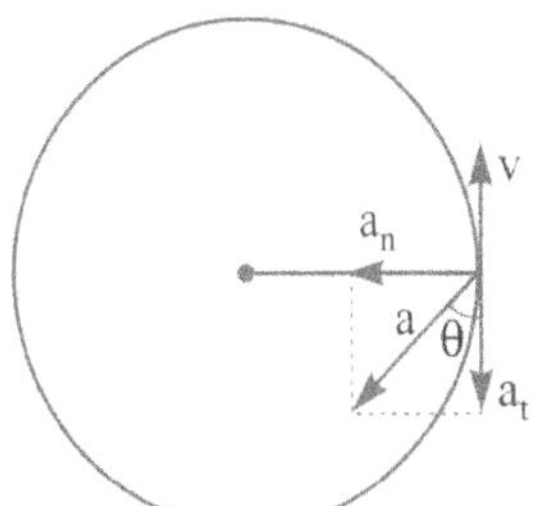

Figure. **6.26**

and tangential acceleration

$$a_t = 0.5\ \text{m/s}^2.$$

$\therefore$ Total acceleration

$$a = \sqrt{a_c^2 + a_t^2}$$

$$= \sqrt{0.70^2 + 0.5^2} = 0.86\ \text{m/s}^2.$$

If θ is the angle between the total acceleration and the velocity of the cyclist, then

$$\tan\theta = \frac{a_n}{a_t} = \frac{0.7}{0.5}$$

or $$\theta = \tan^{-1}(1.4). \qquad \textit{Ans.}$$

Example 8. A particle moves in a circle of radius 4.0 cm clockwise at constant speed of 2 cm/s. If $\hat{x}$ and $\hat{y}$ are unit acceleration vectors along x-axis and y-axis respectively, find the acceleration of the particle at the instant half way between P and Q. Refer to *figure 6.27*.

Figure. **6.27**

Sol. The centripetal acceleration

$$a = \frac{v^2}{r}$$

$$= \frac{2^2}{4} = 1\ \text{cm/s}^2$$

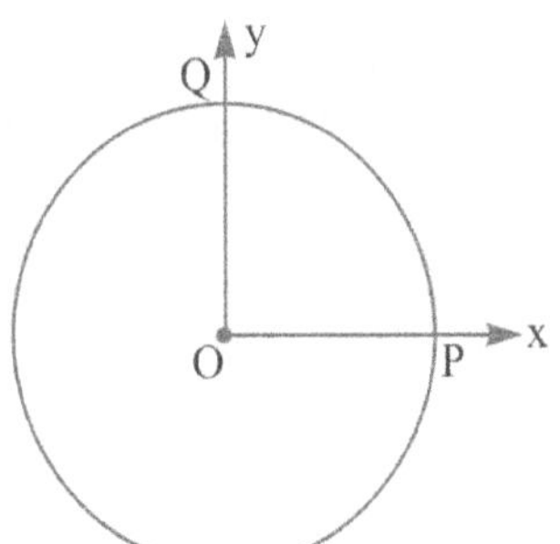

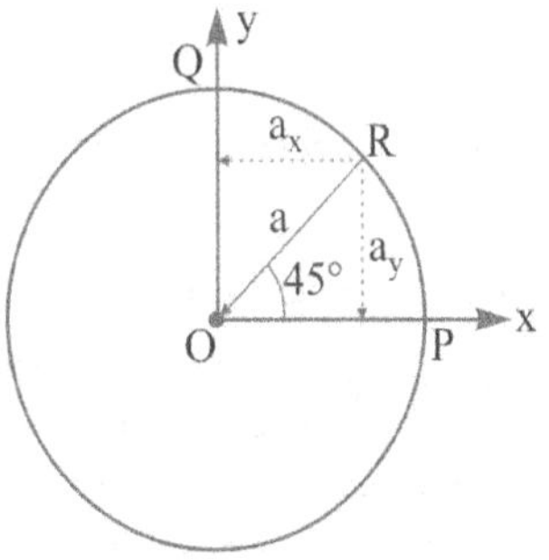

Figure. **6.28**

If R be the midpoint of the arc PQ, then $\angle POR = 45°$.

Thus, if a_x and a_y are the components of the acceleration along x and y-axis respectively, then

$$\vec{a}_x = a \cos 45° \left(-\hat{x}\right) = -\frac{1}{\sqrt{2}}\hat{x}$$

and

$$\vec{a}_y = a \sin 45° \left(-\hat{y}\right) = -\frac{1}{\sqrt{2}}\hat{y}.$$

Hence

$$\vec{a} = \vec{a}_x + \vec{a}_y$$

$$= -\frac{1}{\sqrt{2}}\left(\hat{x} + \hat{y}\right). \qquad \text{Ans.}$$

Example 9. One often comes across the following type of statement concerning circular motion : "A particle moving uniformly along a circle experiences a force directed towards the centre (centripetal force) and an equal and opposite force directed away from the centre (centrifugal force). Thus two forces together keep the particle in equilibrium". Explain what is wrong with this statement.

Sol. The given statement is wrong relative to an inertial frame. The statement is correct relative to the frame attached to the particle (non-inertial frame).

Example 10. A particle of mass m is moving in a circular path of constant radius r such that, its centripetal acceleration a_c is varying with time t as $a_c = k^2 r\, t^2$, where k is a constant. What is the power delivered to the particle by the forces acting on it ?

Sol. Given that, $\quad a_c = k^2 r\, t^2$

or $\qquad \dfrac{v^2}{r} = k^2 r\, t^2$

$\therefore \qquad\qquad v = k\, r\, t \qquad\qquad ...(i)$

Tangential acceleration,

$$a_t = \frac{dv}{dt} = \frac{d(krt)}{dt} = kr$$

and $\qquad F_t = ma_t = m\, k\, r$

Power delivered, $\qquad P = F_t\, v \cos\theta = mkr \times krt \cos 0°$

$$= mk^2 r^2 t. \qquad \text{Ans.}$$

Example 11. An aircraft executes a horizontal loop at a speed of 720 km/h with its wings banked at 15°. What is the radius of the loop?   [NCERT]

Sol. Given,

$\quad \alpha = 15°, v = 720$ km/h $= 200$ m/s, $g = 10$ ms^{-2}.

$\quad \therefore \ \tan\alpha = v^2/rg,$

$\qquad r = v^2/g \tan\alpha = (200)^2/ (10 \times \tan 15°) = 15.23$ m

Example 12. A train runs along an unbanked circular track of radius 30m at a speed of 54 km/h. The mass of the train is 10^6 kg. What provides the centripetal force required for this purpose, the engine or the rails? What is the angle of banking required to prevent wearing out the rails?   [NCERT]

Sol. Here, lateral thrust exerted by the rails to wheel is providing the necessary centripetal force and the train would exert an equal and opposite thrust (by Newton's 3rd law) on the rails

$\quad \therefore \ \tan\alpha = v^2/rg,$

Given, $r = 30$ m, $v = 54$ km/h $= 15$ m/s, $g = 10$ ms^{-2}.

$\quad \alpha = \tan^{-1} v^2/rg \ \tan^{-1} (15)^2/ (30 \times 10) \approx 37°$

Example 13. A disc revolves with a speed of $33\dfrac{1}{3}$ rev/min and has a radius of 15 cm. Two coins are placed at 4 cm and 14cm away from the center of the record. If the coefficient of friction between the coins and the record is 0.15, which of the coins will revolve with the record?   [NCERT]

Sol. When the frictional force is sufficient to provide the centripetal force the coin revolves with the disc. Coin would slip the record, if this force is not sufficient.

The coin will rotate together with record

if $\qquad\qquad m\omega^2 r \ \leq \ \mu mg$

or $\qquad\qquad r \ \leq \ \dfrac{\mu g}{\omega^2}$

$$\leq \dfrac{0.15 \times 9.8}{\left\{2\pi \times \left(\dfrac{100}{180}\right)\right\}^2}$$

$$\leq 12 \text{ cm}$$

Thus coin at a distance 4 cm rotates together with record while coin at 15 cm will move radially away.

Example 14. A 70 kg man stands in contact against the inner wall of a hollow cylindrical drum of radius 3 m rotating about its vertical axis with 200 rev/min. The coefficient of friction between the wall and his clothing is 0.15. What is the minimum rotational speed of the cylinder to enable the man to remain stuck to the wall (without falling) when the floor is suddenly removed?   [NCERT]

Sol. Given, $m = 70$ kg, $r = 3$ m, $n = 200$ rpm $= 200/60$ rps, and $\mu = 0.15$

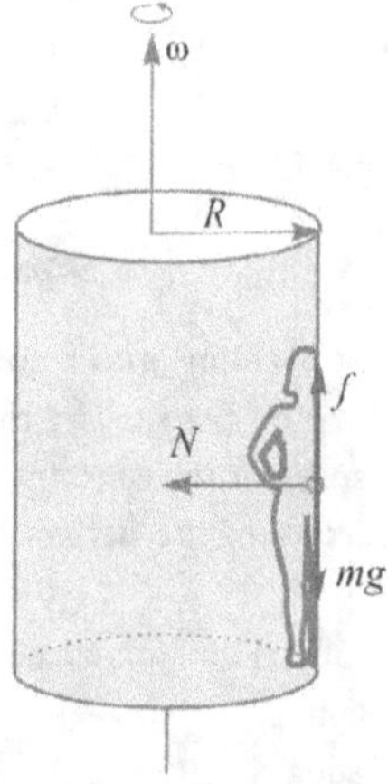

Horizontal force provided by the wall on the man N = centripetal force $= m\, r\, \omega^2$. Frictional force, acting vertically upwards, opposes the weight of the man.

For minimum speed

$$\mu N = mg$$

or $$\mu (m\omega^2 r) = mg$$

$$\therefore \quad \omega = \sqrt{\frac{g}{\mu r}} = \sqrt{\frac{10}{0.15 \times 3}} = 4.7 \text{ rad/s}$$

Example 15. A sleeve A can slide freely along a smooth rod bent in the shape of a half circle of radius R. The system is set in rotation with a constant angular velocity ω about a vertical axis OO'. Find the angle θ corresponding to the steady position of the sleeve.

Sol. If θ is the angle corresponding to steady position, then

$$N \sin\theta = m\omega^2 r = m\omega^2 (R \sin\theta)$$

or $$N = m\omega^2 R \qquad ....(i)$$

and $$N \cos\theta = mg \qquad ....(ii)$$

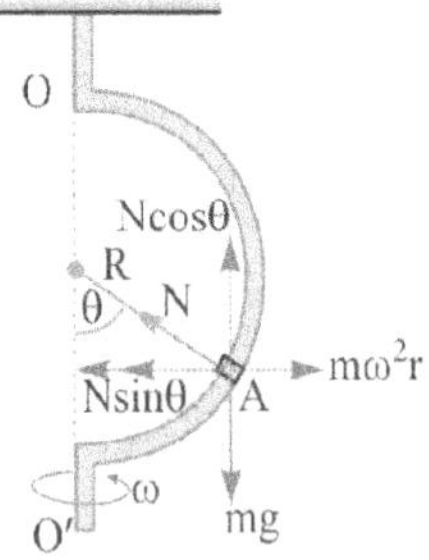

FBD of sleeve in rotating frame

***Figure.* 6.29**

Solving equations (i) and (ii), we get

$$\cos\theta = \frac{g}{\omega^2 R}. \qquad (\text{for } g < \omega^2 R)$$

If $g > \omega^2 R$, then steady position will correspond to $\theta = 0$.

In Chapter Exercise 6.1

1. The radius of the earth's orbit around the sun is 1.5×10^{11} m. Through how much angle does the earth revolve in 2 days ?

   Ans. $\omega = 1.99 \times 10^{-7}$ **rad/s**, $v = \omega r = 2.99$ **m/s**, $\theta = 0.0344$ **rad.**

2. The angular velocity of a particle moving along a circle of radius 50 cm is increased in 5 minutes from 100 revolutions per minute to 400 revolutions per minute. Find
   (i) angular acceleration and
   (ii) linear acceleration *Ans.* (i) $\dfrac{\pi}{30}$ **rad/s^2** (ii) $\dfrac{5\pi}{3}$ **cm/s^2.**

3. Calculate the linear acceleration of a particle moving in a circle of radius 0.4 m at the instant when its angular velocity is 2 rad/s and its angular acceleration is 5 rad/s^2.
   Ans. **2.6 m/s^2, 38°40′ with** a_T.

4. Two balls of mass $M = 9$ g and $m = 3$ g are attached by threads AD and OB whose combined length is $\ell = 1$m to a vertical axis O (figure) and are set in rotational motion in a horizontal plane about this axis with a constant angular velocity ω. Determine the ratio of the lengths AO and OB for which the tensions in the threads will be the same. Disregard the weight of the threads.

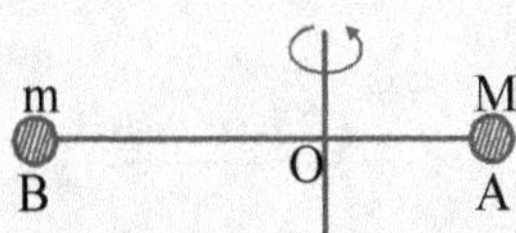

   Ans. **OA = 25 cm, OB = 75 cm.**

5. A particle describes a horizontal circle on the smooth inner

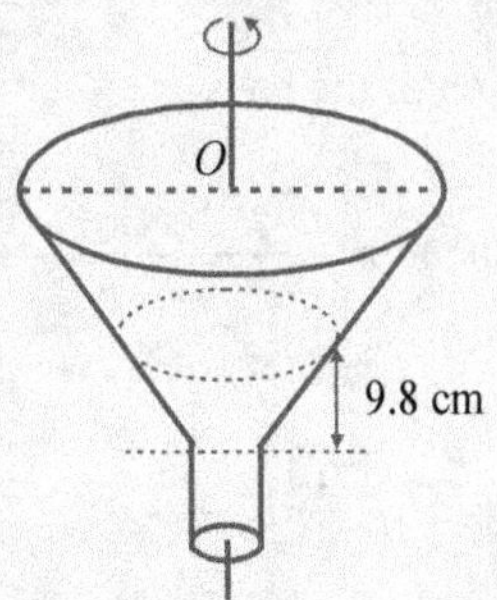

surface of a conical funnel as shown in fig. If the height of plane of the circle above the vertex is 9.8 cm, find the speed of the particle. *Ans.* $v = $ **0.98 m/s**

6. A man is running with constant speed of $v = 10\sqrt{5}$ m/s on a horizontal track of radius $R = 20$ m as shown in figure. At position A man launches a stone in space (without changing his own speed) so that he can catch stone at B (diametrically opposite to A). The speed of launch will be approximately 4 K m/sec. Then find the value of K. (take $\pi^2 = 10$ and $g = 10$ m/s^2) **[Intiger]**

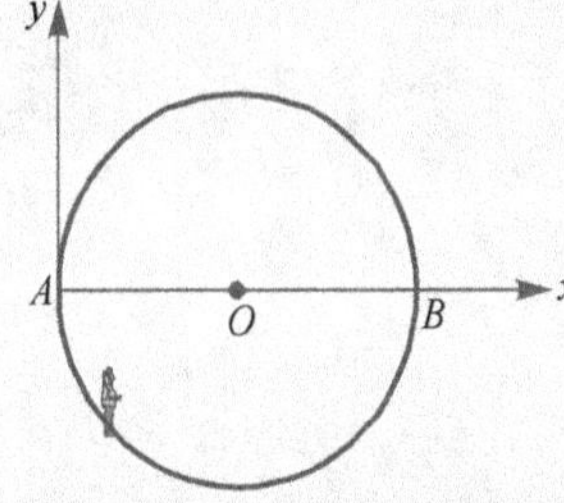

   Ans. **5**

7. A wheel rotates around a stationary axis so that the rotation angle $\phi = at^2$, where $a = 0.20$ rad/s^2. Find the total acceleration a of the point A at the rim at the moment $t = 2.5$ s if the linear velocity of the point A at this moment $v = 0.65$ m/s. *Ans.* $a = $ **0.7 m/s^2**

8. A tube of length L is filled completely with an incompressible liquid of

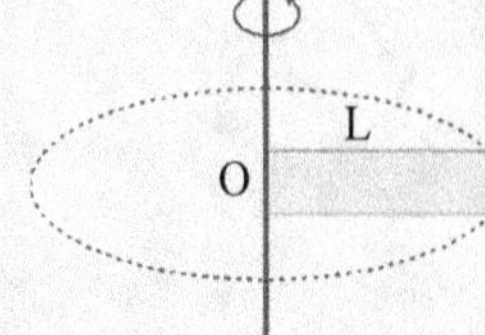

mass M and closed at both ends. The tube is then rotated in a horizontal plane about one of its end with a uniform angular velocity ω. Find the force exerted by the liquid at the other end.

   Ans. $\dfrac{1}{2} M\omega^2 L$

9. Two bodies A and B separated by a distance of $2R$ are moving counter clockwise along a circular path of radius R, each with a uniform speed v. If at time $t = 0$, A is given a constant tangential deceleration $a_\theta = \left(\dfrac{72}{25}\right)\left(\dfrac{v^2}{R\pi}\right)$, determine the time when B collides with A.

Ans. $\dfrac{5\pi R}{6v}$

10. A large mass M and a small mass m hangs at the two ends of

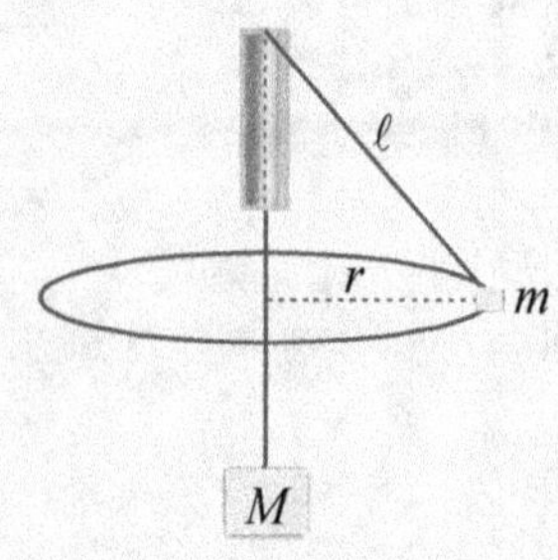

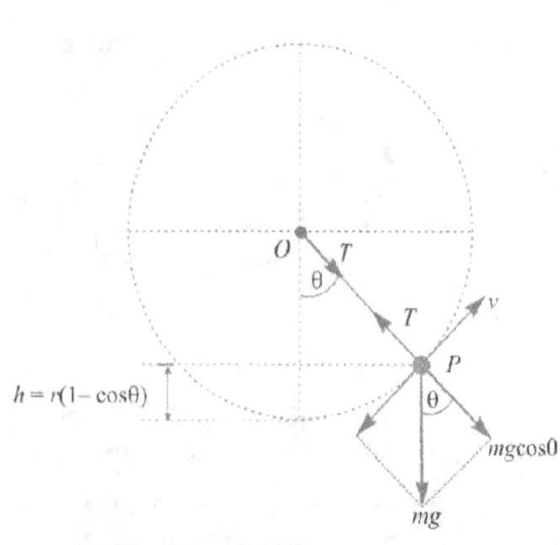

the string that passes through a smooth tube as shown in the figure. The mass m moves round in a circular path which lies in the horizontal plane. The length of the string from the mass m to the top of the tube is ℓ, and θ is the angle this length makes with the vertical. What should be the frequency of rotation of the mass m so that the mass M remain stationary.

Ans. $\omega = \sqrt{\dfrac{Mg}{ml}}$

11. A vehicle whose wheel track is 1.7 m wide and whose centre of gravity is 1m above the road and central between the wheels, takes a curve whose radius is 50 m, on a level road. Find the speed at which the inner wheel would leave the road. Show that if centre of gravity were displaced 0.5 m towards the inner wheels, the overturning speed would be increased by 25%.

Ans. 20.4 m/s

6.13 MOTION IN A VERTICAL CIRCLE

Consider a body of mass m tied to the one end of the string and made to rotate in a vertical circle of radius r as shown in *figure* 6.30. Let u be the velocity of the body at its lowest position. Its velocity for any angular position θ is v. Height of the body, $h = r - r\cos\theta = r(1 - \cos\theta)$.

By third equation of motion

$$v^2 = u^2 - 2gh$$
$$= u^2 - 2gr(1 - \cos\theta)$$

or

$$v = \sqrt{u^2 - 2gr(1 - \cos\theta)}. \qquad \text{...(i)}$$

Tension in the string;

By Newton's second law

$$T - mg\cos\theta = \frac{mv^2}{r}$$

$$\therefore \qquad T = mg\cos\theta + \frac{mv^2}{r}$$

Figure. 6.30

or

$$T = mg\cos\theta + m\frac{u^2 - 2gr(1 - \cos\theta)}{r} \qquad \text{...(ii)}$$

(i) For $\theta = 0°$ and $180°$:

At the highest position of the body, $\theta = 180°$.

Thus the tension in the string at the highest position of the body

$$T_H = mg\cos 180° + m\left[\frac{u^2 - 2gr(1 - \cos 180°)}{r}\right]$$

or

$$T_H = -mg + m\left[\frac{u^2 - 4gr}{r}\right]$$

To complete the circle $\qquad T_H \geq 0$

or $\qquad -mg + m\left[\dfrac{u^2 - 4gr}{r}\right] \geq 0$

$\therefore \qquad u \geq \sqrt{5gr}.$

Thus the minimum velocity required at lowest position of the body to complete the

circle is $\sqrt{5gr}$. The corresponding tension in the string; from equation (ii),

$$T_L = 6mg$$

The velocity at the highest position of the body corresponds to $u = \sqrt{5gr}$;

From equation (i), we get $\qquad v = \sqrt{5gr - 2gr(1 - \cos 180°)}$

or $\qquad v = \sqrt{gr}$

The most critical position at which body can leave the circle is its highest position.

Thus the critical velocity will be $v_c = \sqrt{gr}$.

(ii) **For $\theta = 90°$:**

From equation (i), we get $\qquad v = \sqrt{5gr - 2gr(1 - \cos 90°)}$

$$= \sqrt{3gr},$$

and $\qquad T = mg \cos 90 + \dfrac{m(\sqrt{3gr})^2}{r} = 3\,mg.$

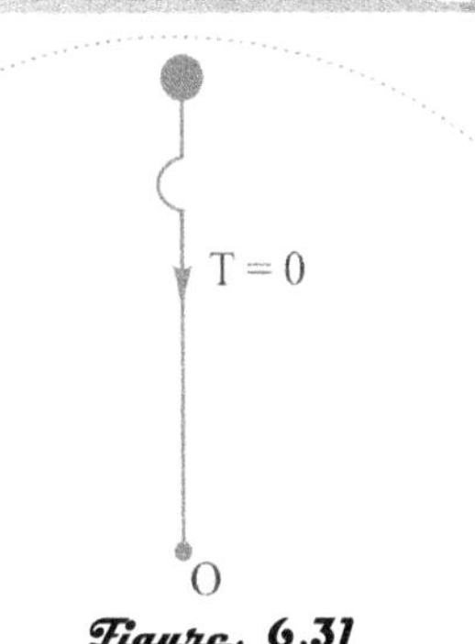

Figure. 6.31

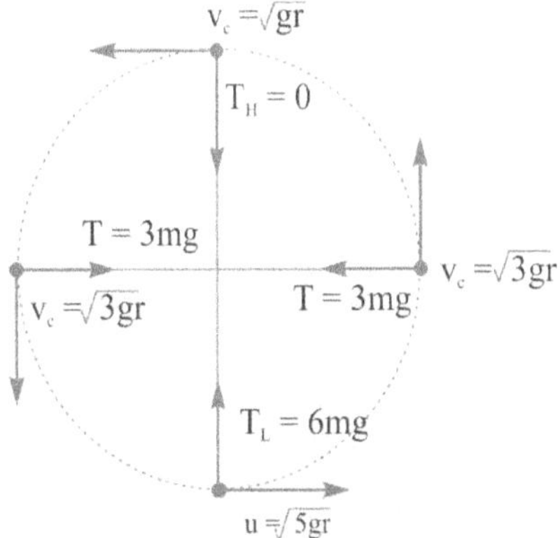

Critical circle Figure. 6.32

It can be shown that, $T_L - T_H = 6\,mg.$

Condition for oscillations or to leave the circle

(i) **For $u \leq \sqrt{2gr}$:**

Let us consider a body attached to a string of length r. It is projected from its lowest position

with a velocity $\qquad u = \sqrt{2gr}$.

The body will go to a height;

$$v^2 = u^2 - 2gh$$

or $\qquad 0 = (\sqrt{2gr})^2 - 2gh$

$\Rightarrow \qquad h = r.$

For $\qquad u < \sqrt{2gr}, \quad h < r.$

Thus for velocity $u \leq \sqrt{2gr}$, the body can not cross the position P and there after return back

towards initial position and due to inertia cross the mean position (L), and will oscillate about L.

(ii) **For $\sqrt{2gr} < u < \sqrt{5gr}$:**

As the velocity $u > \sqrt{2gr}$, the body will cross the position P but can not go upto H, because (u

$< \sqrt{5gr}$). So body will leave the circle somewhere between P and H and will follow parabolic

path.

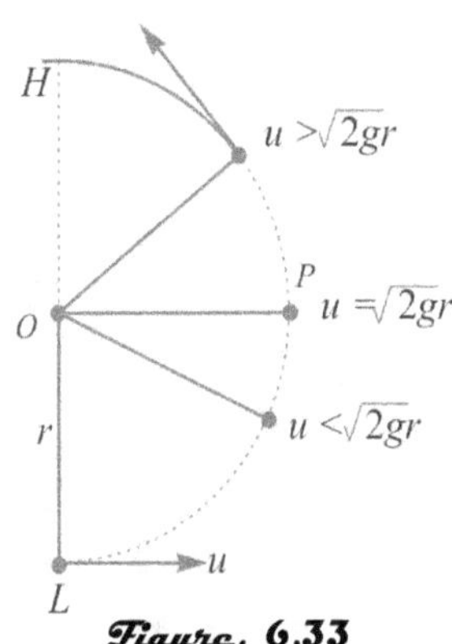

Figure. 6.33

FORMULAE USED

1. If u is the velocity at lowest point of the circle, then at a height h, velocity

$$v = \sqrt{u^2 - 2gh}$$

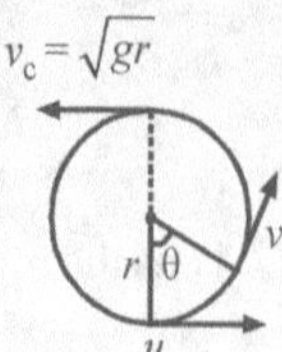

2. Tension at any angle θ, $T = mg\cos\theta + \dfrac{mv^2}{r}$

3. The minimum velocity to complete the circle (at highest point), $v_c = \sqrt{gr}$,

and at lowest point of the circle $= \sqrt{5gr}$.

4. The tension in the string at the lowest point corresponding to critical velocity, $T_L = 6$ mg

5. Also, $T_L - T_H = 6$ mg.

6. For, $u \le \sqrt{2gr}$, the body will oscillate about lowest point.

7. For, $\sqrt{2gr} < u < \sqrt{5gr}$, the body will leave the circle.

EXAMPLES BASED ON MOTION IN VERTICAL CIRCLE

Example 16. A ball suspended by a thread swing in a vertical plane so that its acceleration values in the extreme and the lowest position are equal. Find the thread deflection angle in the extreme position.

Sol. Suppose θ is the required angle. At extreme position the velocity of the ball is zero, thus normal acceleration $a_c = \dfrac{v^2}{\ell} = 0$, and tangential acceleration $a_t = g\sin\theta$. At mean position the velocity of the ball

$$v = \sqrt{2g(\ell - \ell\cos\theta)}.$$

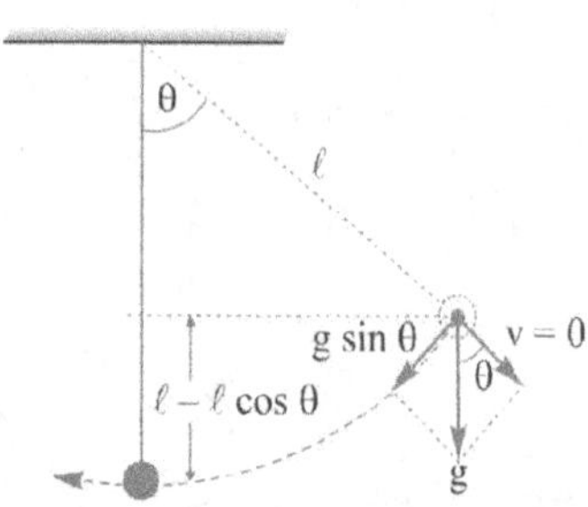

Figure. 6.34

The normal acceleration at this position

$$a_c = \frac{v^2}{\ell}$$

$$= \frac{2g(\ell - \ell\cos\theta)}{\ell} = 2g\,(1 - \cos\theta)$$

and tangential acceleration

$$a_t = g\sin\theta = 0.$$

Thus total acceleration at mean position

$$a = 2g\,(1 - \cos\theta)$$

According to given condition, we have

$$g\sin\theta = 2g\,(1 - \cos\theta)$$

After solving, we get $\theta = 53°$.   ***Ans.***

Example 17. A simple pendulum is oscillating with angular displacement 90°. For what angle with vertical the acceleration of bob directed horizontally ?

Sol. Let θ be the required angle. The velocity of the body at angular position θ is;

$$v^2 = 0 + 2g\,(\ell\cos\theta) \qquad \ldots(i)$$

Figure. 6.35

The normal acceleration of the bob,

$$a_c = \frac{v^2}{\ell}$$

$$= \frac{2g\ell\cos\theta}{\ell} = 2\,g\cos\theta ,$$

and tangential acceleration of the bob, $a_t = g\sin\theta$.

As the resultant acceleration directed horizontally, so

$$\tan\theta = \frac{a_c}{a_t}$$

or $$\frac{\sin\theta}{\cos\theta} = \frac{2g\cos\theta}{g\sin\theta}$$

or $$2\cos^2\theta = \sin^2\theta = (1 - \cos^2\theta)$$

$$\Rightarrow \quad \cos^2\theta = \frac{1}{3} \text{ and } \theta = \cos^{-1}\left(\frac{1}{\sqrt{3}}\right). \qquad ***Ans.***$$

Example 18. A nail is located certain distance vertically below the point of suspension of a simple pendulum. The pendulum bob is released from the position where the string makes the angle 60° from the vertical. Calculate the distance of the nail from the point of suspension such that the bob will just perform revolutions with the nail as the centre. Assume the length of the pendulum to be 1m.

Sol. The velocity of the bob at its lowest position; by third equation of motion

$$v^2 = 0 + 2g\,(\ell - \ell\cos 60°) = 2g \times \frac{\ell}{2}$$

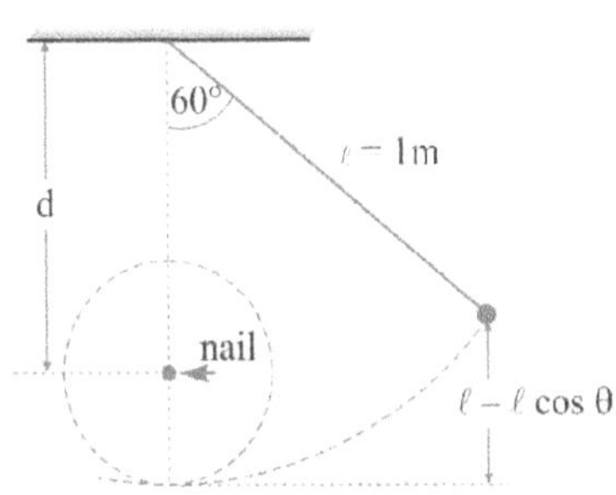

Figure. 6.36

or $\quad v = \sqrt{g\ell} = \sqrt{g \times 1}$ $\qquad$ ...(i)

$$= \sqrt{g}.$$

Let d be the distance of nail from the point of suspension. The bob will have to complete the circle of radius $r = 1 - d$.

For the bob to just perform the revolutions about nail, the minimum speed at the lowest position must be

$$\sqrt{5gr} = \sqrt{5g(1-d)}. \qquad ...\text{(ii)}$$

Equating equations (i) and (ii), we get

$$\sqrt{g} = \sqrt{5g(1-d)}$$

After solving, $\quad d = \dfrac{4}{5} = 0.80$ m. $\qquad$ **Ans.**

Example 19. A particle of mass m slides from the top of the surface of a sphere of radius R. It looses contact and strikes the ground. At what depth below the top the particle will loose contact with the surface? At what horizontal distance from the initial position the body strikes the ground ?

Sol. Let the particle loose the contact at point P. At point P normal reaction by the contact surface becomes zero. If v is the velocity of the particle at P, then we have

$$v^2 = 0 + 2gh$$

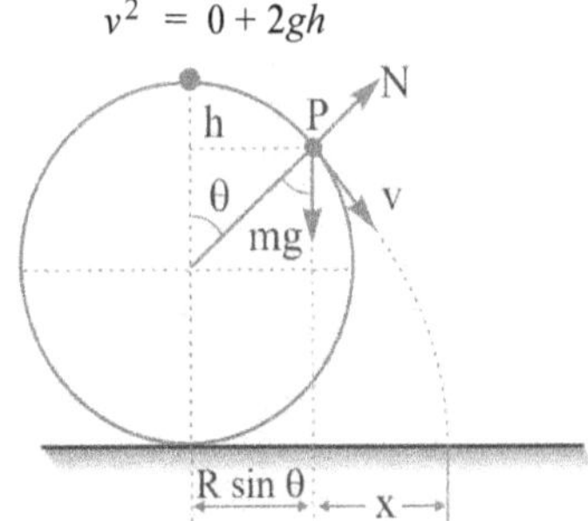

Figure. 6.37

or $\quad v = \sqrt{2gh}.$ $\qquad$ ....(i)

By Newton's second law, we have

$$mg\cos\theta - N = \frac{mv^2}{R}$$

At point P, $\qquad N = 0,$

$$\therefore \qquad mg\cos\theta = \frac{mv^2}{R} = \frac{m(2gh)}{R}$$

$$\Rightarrow \qquad \cos\theta = \frac{2h}{R}. \qquad ....\text{(ii)}$$

But from the geometry,

$$\cos\theta = \frac{R-h}{R}.$$

Therefore $\qquad \dfrac{2h}{R} = \dfrac{R-h}{R}$

or $\qquad h = \dfrac{R}{3}$

and $\qquad \cos\theta = \dfrac{R-h}{h} = \dfrac{2}{3}.$

and $\qquad \sin\theta = \dfrac{\sqrt{5}}{3}$

Velocity at point P becomes

$$v = \sqrt{2gh} = \sqrt{\frac{2gR}{3}}.$$

Vertical component of velocity at $P = v\sin\theta$ and horizontal component of velocity is $v\cos\theta$. Height of P from ground

$$= 2R - h = 2R - \frac{R}{3} = \frac{5R}{3}.$$

If t is the time taken by the particle to reach the ground from P, then by second equation of motion

$$\frac{5R}{3} = v\sin\theta\, t + \frac{1}{2}\,gt^2 \qquad ....\text{(iii)}$$

and $\qquad x = v\cos\theta\, t.$ $\qquad$ ....(iv)

Solving equations (iii) and (iv), we get

$$x = 0.71\,R$$

Thus horizontal distance from A at which the particle strikes is

$$= R\sin\theta + x = R \times \frac{\sqrt{5}}{3} + 0.71$$

$$R = 1.5\,R. \qquad\qquad \textbf{Ans.}$$

Example 20. A small heavy block is attached to the lower end of a light rod of length l which can be rotated about its clamped end. What minimum horizontal velocity should the block be given so that it moves in a complete circle ?

Sol. As rod is a rigid member, so it can take compression $(T < 0)$. The velocity of the block at its highest position can be zero to just cross this position.

Let block be given a velocity v at its lowest position, then by third equation of motion, we have

$$v_H^{\,2} = v_L^{\,2} - 2gh$$

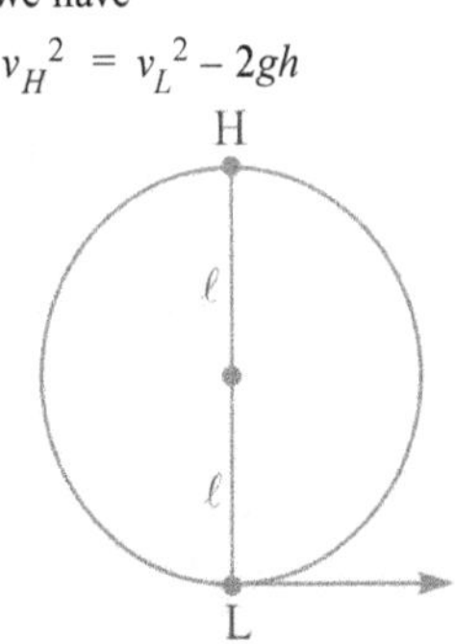

Figure. 6.38

or $\qquad 0 = v^2 - 2g \times 2\ell$

$\Rightarrow \qquad v = 2\sqrt{g\ell}.$ $\qquad\qquad$ **Ans.**

Example 21. You may have seen in a circus a motorcyclist driving in vertical loops inside a 'death well' (a hollow spherical chamber with holes, so the spectators can watch from outside). Explain clearly why the motorcyclist does not drop down when he is at the uppermost point, with no support from below. What is the minimum speed required at the uppermost position to perform a vertical loop if the radius of the chamber is 25 m?   [NCERT]

Sol. If N is the normal reaction from ceiling then,

$$N + mg = \frac{mv^2}{r}$$

or

$$N = \frac{mv^2}{r} - mg$$

The complete loop,

$$N \geq 0 \quad \text{or} \quad \frac{mv^2}{r} - mg \geq 0$$

$$v \geq \sqrt{gr}$$

$$v_{min} = \sqrt{gr} = \sqrt{9.8 \times 25} = 15.65 \text{ m/s}$$

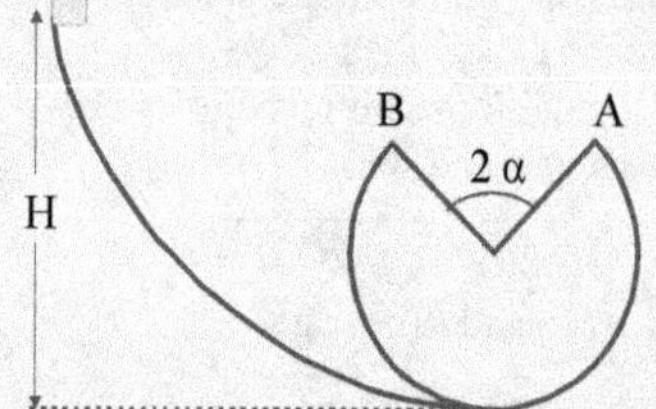

In Chapter Exercise 6.2

1. A weightless rod of length ℓ carries first a mass $2m$ at its end and then two equal masses m, one secured at the end and other in the middle of the rod (figure). The rod can revolve in a vertical plane around the point A. What horizontal velocity must be imparted to the end of the rod C in the first and second cases to deflect it to the horizontal position ?

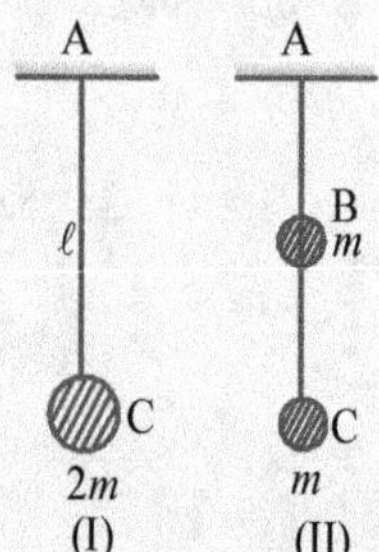

$$Ans. \ v_1 = \sqrt{2gl}, v_2 = \sqrt{\frac{12gl}{5}}$$

2. A mass m is released from the top of a vertical circular track of radius r with a horizontal speed v_0. Calculate the angle θ with respect to the vertical where it leaves contact with the track.

$$Ans. \ \theta = \cos^{-1}\left[\frac{v_0^2}{3rg} + \frac{2}{3}\right]$$

3. A small object slides without friction from the height $H = 50$ cm

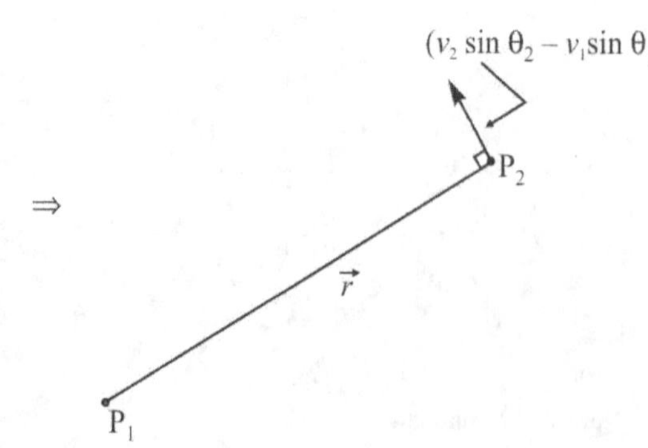

and then loops, the vertical loop of radius $R = 20$ cm from which a symmetrical section of angle 2α has been removed. Find angle α such that after loosing at A flying through the air, the object will reach point B.

$$Ans. \ \alpha = 60°.$$

6.14 RELATIVE ANGULAR VELOCITY

1. Suppose two particles P_1 and P_2 are moving with speeds v_1 and v_2 as shown in *figure* 6.39.

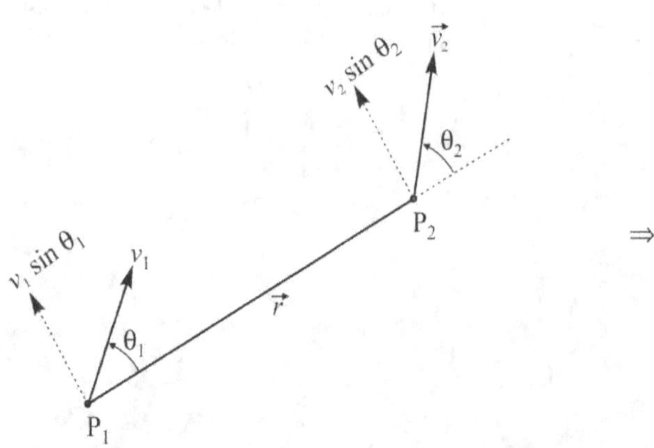

Figure. **6.39**

We wish to find angular velocity of particle 2 with respect to 1. It is ;

$$\vec{\omega}_{21} = \vec{\omega}_2 - \vec{\omega}_1$$

or

$$\omega_{21} = \frac{v_{\perp 2} - v_{\perp 1}}{r}$$

or

$$\omega_{21} = \left[\frac{v_2 \sin\theta_2 - v_1 \sin\theta_1}{r}\right] \quad \text{.......(1)}$$

2. Consider two particles P_1 and P_2 which are moving with velocities $\vec{v}_1$ and $\vec{v}_2$. At an instant their position vectors are $\vec{r}_1$ and $\vec{r}_2$ relative to the origin. Let θ be the angle between their position vectors, then angular velocity $\vec{\omega}$ of P_2 with respect to P_1 is given by

$$\vec{v}_2 - \vec{v}_1 = \vec{\omega} \times (\vec{r}_2 - \vec{r}_1)$$

or

$$(\vec{r}_2 - \vec{r}_1) \times (\vec{v}_2 - \vec{v}_1) = (\vec{r}_2 - \vec{r}_1) \times \{\vec{\omega} \times (\vec{r}_2 - \vec{r}_1)\}$$

By using vector triple product, we can write

$$(\vec{r}_2 - \vec{r}_1) \times (\vec{v}_2 - \vec{v}_1) = \{(\vec{r}_2 - \vec{r}_1).(\vec{r}_2 - \vec{r}_1)\}$$
$$\vec{\omega} - \{(\vec{r}_2 - \vec{r}_1).\vec{\omega}\}(\vec{r}_2 - \vec{r}_1) \quad \text{.......(1)}$$

As $\vec{\omega}$ is perpendicular to the plane of $\vec{r}_2 - \vec{r}_1$,

$$\therefore \quad \{(\vec{r}_2 - \vec{r}_1).\vec{\omega}\} = 0$$

and

$$\{(\vec{r}_2 - \vec{r}_1).(\vec{r}_2 - \vec{r}_1)\} = |(\vec{r}_2 - \vec{r}_1)|^2$$

Now equation (1) becomes

$$\vec{\omega} = \frac{(\vec{r}_2 - \vec{r}_1) \times (\vec{v}_2 - \vec{v}_1)}{|\vec{r}_2 - \vec{r}_1|^2}. \quad \text{......(2)}$$

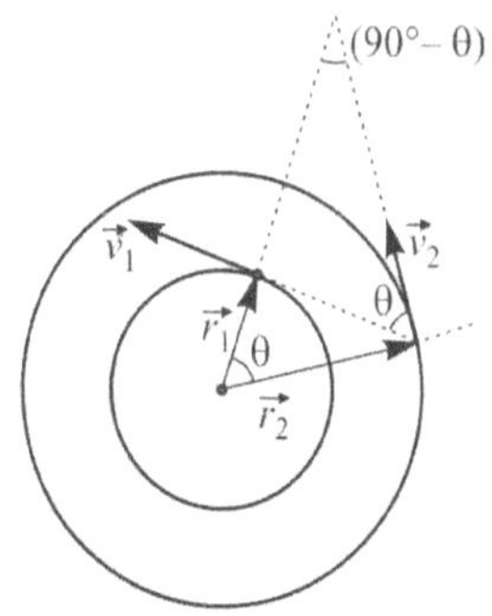

Figure. 6.40

If $\hat{\eta}$ is the unit vector perpendicular to the plane of the motion, then

$$\vec{\omega} = \frac{\vec{r}_2 \times \vec{v}_2 + \vec{r}_1 \times \vec{v}_1 - \vec{r}_2 \times \vec{v}_1 - \vec{r}_1 \times \vec{v}_2}{|\vec{r}_2 - \vec{r}_1|^2} \quad \text{....(3)}$$

For particles on circular paths,

$$\vec{r}_2 \times \vec{v}_2 = r_2 v_2 \sin 90° \hat{\eta} = r_2 v_2 \hat{\eta}$$

and

$$\vec{r}_1 \times \vec{v}_1 = r_1 v_1 \sin 90° \hat{\eta} = r_1 v_1 \hat{\eta}.$$

$$\vec{r}_2 \times \vec{v}_1 = r_2 v_1 \sin(90° + \theta)\hat{\eta} = r_2 v_1 \cos\theta \hat{\eta}$$

and

$$\vec{r}_1 \times \vec{v}_2 = r_1 v_2 \sin(90° - \theta)\hat{\eta} = r_1 v_2 \cos\theta \hat{\eta}$$

$$\therefore \quad \omega = \left[\frac{r_2 v_2 + r_1 v_1 - (r_2 v_1 + r_1 v_2)\cos\theta}{r_1^2 + r_2^2 - 2 r_1 r_2 \cos\theta}\right]\hat{\eta}. \quad \text{...(4)}$$

Special cases

1. When P_2 is nearest to P_1, $\theta = 0°$ and eq(4) reduces to,

$$\omega = \frac{v_2 - v_1}{r_2 - r_1}.$$

2. When P_2 is farthest to P_1, $\theta = 180°$ and $\cos\theta = -1$

$$\therefore \quad \omega = \frac{v_2 + v_1}{r_2 + r_1}.$$

3. For ω to be zero,

$$\cos\theta = \left[\frac{v_2 r_2 + v_1 r_1}{v_1 r_2 + v_2 r_1}\right].$$

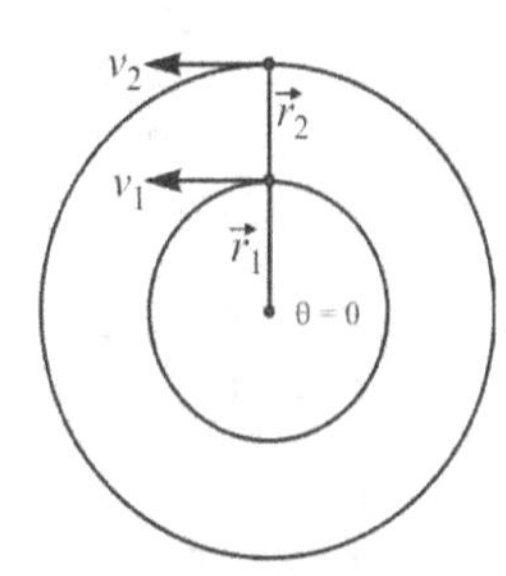

Figure. 6.41

EXAMPLES FOR JEE-(MAIN AND ADVANCE)

Example 1. Two particles A and B are moving as shown in *figure* 6.42. At this moment of time, find the angular speed of A relative to B.

Sol. We know that

$$[v_{AB}]_y = v_{Ay} - v_{By}$$
$$= v_A \sin \theta_A - v_B \sin \theta_B$$

and

$$\omega = \frac{[v_{AB}]_y}{AB}$$

$$= \left[\frac{v_A \sin \theta_A - v_B \sin \theta_B}{r}\right]$$

in clockwise direction.

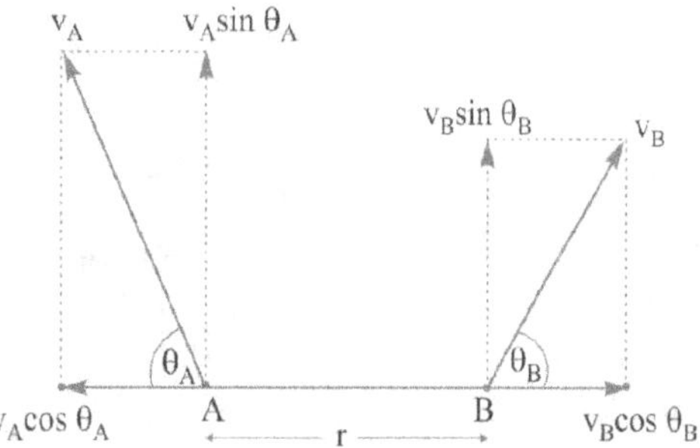

Figure. 6.42

As there is no separation between the velocity component along x-axis, thus there is no specific rotation due to $(v_{AB})_x = v_A \cos \theta_A - v_B \cos \theta_B$.

Example 2. A horizontal disc rotates with a constant angular velocity $\omega = 6.0$ rad/s about a vertical axis passing through its centre. A small body of mass $m = 0.50$ kg moves along a diameter of the disc with a velocity $v = 50$ cm/s which is constant relative to the disc. Find the force that the disc exerts on the body at the moment when it is located at the distance $r = 30$ cm from the rotation axis.

Sol. The body will experience three mutually perpendicular forces in the rotating table.

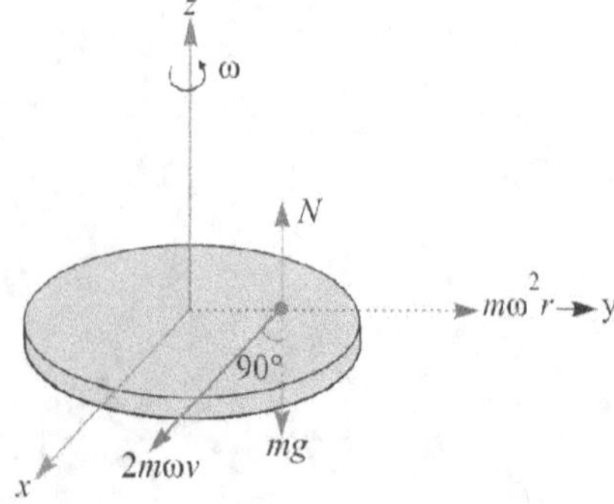

Figure. 6.43

(a) Centrifugal force $m \omega^2 r$.
(b) Normal reaction $N = mg$.
(c) Coriolis force $2m \omega v$.

The resultant force $= \sqrt{(m\omega^2 r)^2 + (mg)^2 + (2m\omega v)^2}$

$$= 8N \qquad \qquad Ans.$$

Example 3. A table with smooth horizontal surface is turning at an angular speed ω about its axis. A groove is made on the surface along a radius and a particle is gently placed inside the groove at a distance a from the centre. Find the speed of the particle with respect to the table as its distance from the center becomes b.

Sol. In a turning table the force along the radius of the table is the centrifugal force. Thus the acceleration of a particle when it is at a distance x from the centre is

$$a = \omega^2 x$$

or

$$v \frac{dv}{dx} = \omega^2 x$$

or

$$v \, dv = \omega^2 x \, dx$$

Integrating above equation, we get

$$\int_0^v v \, dv = \int_a^b \omega^2 x \, dx$$

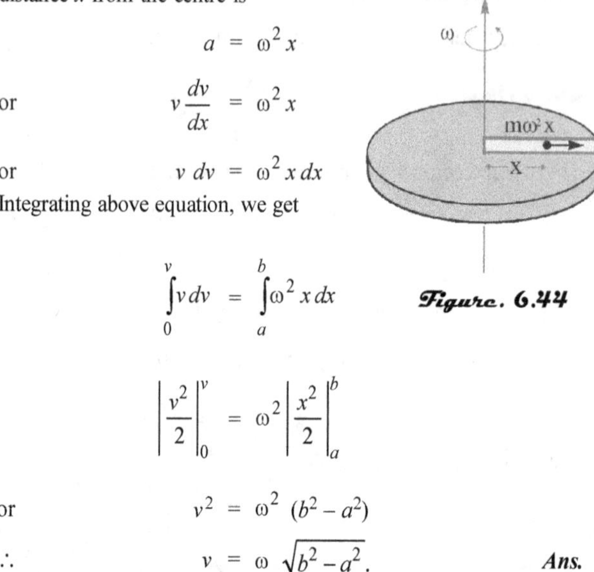

Figure. 6.44

$$\left|\frac{v^2}{2}\right|_0^v = \omega^2 \left|\frac{x^2}{2}\right|_a^b$$

or

$$v^2 = \omega^2 (b^2 - a^2)$$

$$\therefore \quad v = \omega \sqrt{b^2 - a^2}. \qquad Ans.$$

Example 4. A metal ring of mass m and radius R is placed on a smooth horizontal table and is set rotating about its own axis in such a way that each part of the ring moves with a speed v. Find the tension in the ring

Sol.

Take a small part of the ring which subtends an angle $\Delta \theta$ at the centre of the ring. Let T be the tension in the ring. The forces act on this part in the plane of rotation are shown in *figure* 6.45 The mass of the small part of ring

$$\Delta m = \frac{m}{2\pi} \Delta \theta.$$

The centripetal force on this part is $2T \sin \dfrac{\Delta \theta}{2}$.

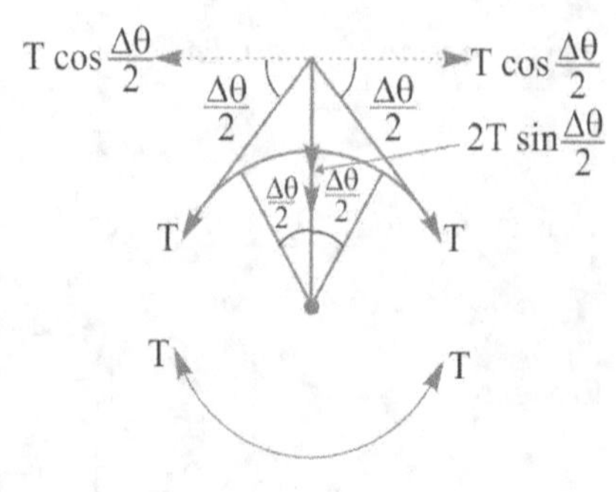

Figure. 6.45

By Newton's second law, we have

$$2T \sin \frac{\Delta\theta}{2} = \frac{\Delta m v^2}{R}.$$

As $\Delta\theta$ is small,

$$\therefore \quad \sin \frac{\Delta\theta}{2} \simeq \frac{\Delta\theta}{2}.$$

The above equation reduces to,

$$2T \left(\frac{\Delta\theta}{2}\right) = \left(\frac{m}{2\pi}.\Delta\theta\right) \frac{v^2}{R}$$

or

$$T = \frac{mv^2}{2\pi R}. \qquad \textbf{\textit{Ans.}}$$

Example 5. A thin uniform rod of length ℓ and mass m rotates uniformly with an angular velocity ω in a horizontal plane about a vertical axis passing through one of its ends. Determine the tension in the rod as a function of the distance x from the rotation axis.

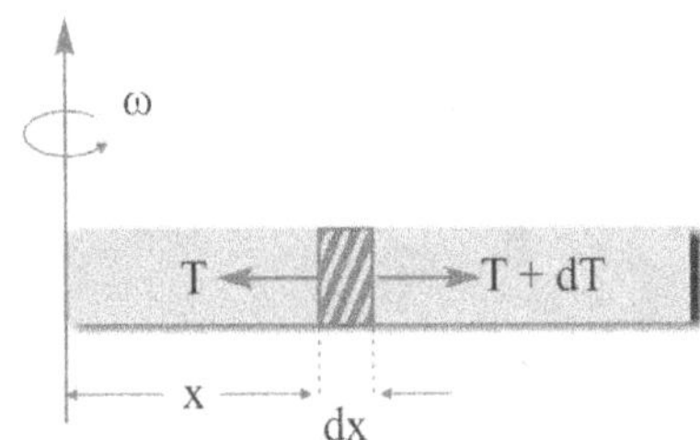

Figure. 6.46

Sol. Choose a small element of width dx at a distance x from one end of the rod. The mass of the element $dm = \dfrac{m}{\ell} dx$. Let T be the tension in the rod at a distance x. By Newton's second law for the motion of element of mass dm, we have

$$T - (T + dT) = (dm)\,\omega^2 x$$

or

$$-dT = \left(\frac{m}{\ell} dx\right)\omega^2 x$$

Integrating above equation, we get

$$-\int_{T}^{0} dT = \frac{m\omega^2}{\ell} \int_{x}^{\ell} x\, dx$$

or

$$-|T|_{T}^{0} = \frac{m\omega^2}{2\ell} |x^2|_{x}^{\ell}$$

or

$$-(0 - T) = \frac{m\omega^2}{2\ell}(\ell^2 - x^2)$$

or

$$T = \frac{m\omega^2}{2\ell}(\ell^2 - x^2) \qquad \textbf{\textit{Ans.}}$$

At $\quad x = 0, \quad T = T_{\max} = \dfrac{m\omega^2 \ell}{2}.$

At $\quad x = \dfrac{\ell}{2}, \quad T = \dfrac{3m\omega^2\ell}{8}.$

Example 6. A conical pendulum, a thin uniform rod of length ℓ and mass m, rotates uniformly about a vertical axis with angular velocity ω (the upper end of the rod is hinged). Find the angle θ between rod and the vertical.

Sol. Choose an element of the rod of width dx at a distance x from the hinge.

Mass of the element, $dm = \dfrac{m}{\ell} dx$. The centrifugal force on this element

$$dF = (dm)\,\omega^2\,(x \sin\theta).$$

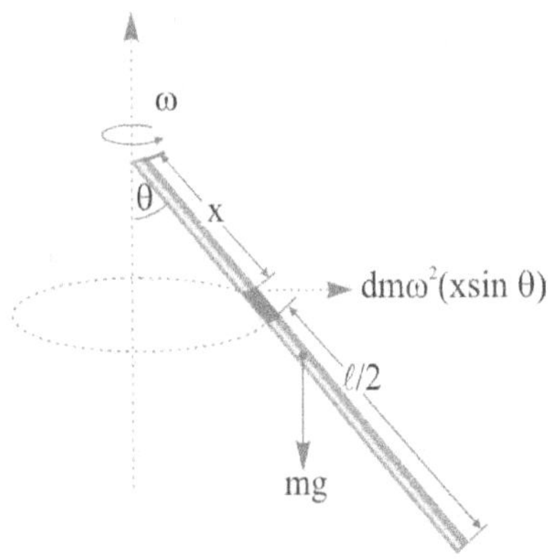

Figure. 6.47

Its moment of force about the hinge

$$d\tau = dF \times x \cos\theta$$

$$= (dm)\,\omega^2\,(x \sin\theta)\,(x \cos\theta)$$

$$= \left(\frac{m}{\ell} dx\right)\omega^2 x^2 \left(\frac{\sin 2\theta}{2}\right)$$

$$= \frac{m\omega^2}{2\ell} \sin 2\theta\; x^2\, dx \qquad ....(i)$$

For the moment of force of whole length of rod, integrating (i)

$$\tau = \frac{m\omega^2}{2\ell} \sin 2\theta \int_{0}^{\ell} x^2 dx$$

$$= \frac{m\omega^2 \ell^2}{6} \sin 2\theta. \qquad ....(ii)$$

In the rotating frame, apart from other forces the centrifugal force also act. For rotational equilibrium of the rod, we have $\sum \vec{\tau} = 0$.

Taking moment of all forces about hinge and putting their algebraic sum zero, we get

$$mg \frac{\ell}{2} \sin\theta = \frac{m\omega\ell^2}{6} \sin 2\theta$$

or

$$\cos\theta = \frac{3g}{2\omega^2 \ell}. \qquad \textbf{\textit{Ans.}}$$

MCQ Type 1   Exercise 6.1

LEVEL - I (ONLY ONE OPTION CORRECT)

Motion in Horizontal Circle

1. Which of the following statements is false for a particle moving in a circle with a constant angular speed ?

(a) the velocity vector is tangent to the circle

(b) the acceleration vector is tangent to the circle

(c) the acceleration vector points to the centre of the circle

(d) the velocity and acceleration vectors are perpendicular to each other

2. If the equation for the displacement of a particle moving on a circular path is given by $(\theta) = 2t^3 + 0.5$, where θ is in radian and t in second, then the angular velocity of the particle after 2 s from its start is:

(a) 8 rad/s   (b) 12 rad/s

(c) 24 rad/s   (d) 36 rad./s

3. The angular speed of seconds needle in a mechanical watch is

(a) $\dfrac{\pi}{30}$ rad/s   (b) 2π rad/s

(c) π rad/s   (d) $\dfrac{60}{\pi}$ rad/s

4. The length of second's hand in a watch is 1 cm. The change in velocity of its tip in 15 seconds is:

(a) zero   (b) $\dfrac{\pi}{30\sqrt{2}}$ cm/s

(c) $\dfrac{\pi}{30}$ cm/s   (d) $\dfrac{\pi\sqrt{2}}{30}$ cm/s

5. A particle is going in a spiral path as shown in figure, with constant speed.

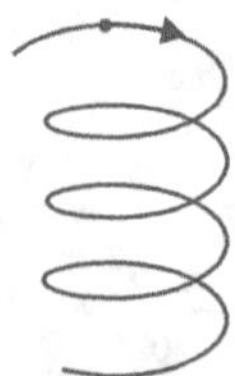

(a) The velocity of particle is constant

(b) The acceleration of particle is constant

(c) The magnitude of acceleration is constant

(d) The magnitude of acceleration is increasing continuously

6. A particle P is moving in a circle of radius 'a' with a uniform speed v. C is the centre of the circle and AB is a diameter. When passing through B the angular velocity of P about A and C are in the ratio:

(a) $1:1$ (b) $1:2$

(c) $2:1$ (d) $4:1$

7. A point mass m is suspended from a light thread of length l, fixed at O, is whirled in a horizontal circle at constant speed as shown. From your point of view, stationary with respect to the mass, the forces on the mass are

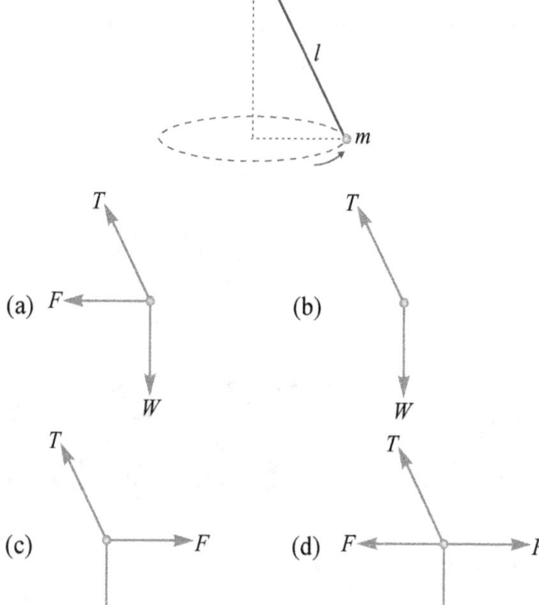

8. What is the value of linear velocity, if $\vec{\omega} = 3\hat{i} - 4\hat{j} + \hat{k}$ and $\vec{r} = 5\hat{i} - 6\hat{j} + 6\hat{k}$

(a) $6\hat{i} + 2\hat{j} - 3\hat{k}$ (b) $-18\hat{i} - 13\hat{j} + 2\hat{k}$

(c) $4\hat{i} - 13\hat{j} + 6\hat{k}$ (d) $6\hat{i} - 2\hat{j} + 8\hat{k}$

9. A particle moves along a circle of radius R with constant angular velocity ω. Its displacement magnitude in time t is :

(a) ωt (b) $2R \sin \omega t$

(c) $2R \cos \omega t$ (d) $2R \sin \dfrac{\omega t}{2}$

Answer	1	(b)	2	(c)	3	(a)	4	(d)	5	(c)
Key	6	(b)	7	(c)	8	(b)	9	(d)		

10. Two bodies are moving in concentric orbits of radii 2cm and 4 cm such that their time periods are the same. The ratio of their centripetal accelerations is :

(a) $\dfrac{1}{2}$

(b) $\dfrac{1}{8}$

(c) 2

(d) 4

11. A body is revolving with a constant speed along a circular path. If the direction of its velocity is reversed, keeping speed unchanged, then

(a) the centripetal force does not suffer any change in magnitude and direction both

(b) the centripetal force does not suffer any change in magnitude but its direction is reversed

(c) the centripetal force disappears

(d) centripetal force will be doubled

12. A particle of mass m rotates with a uniform angular speed ω. It is viewed from a frame rotating about the z-axis with a uniform angular velocity ω_0. The centrifugal force on the particle is:

(a) $m\omega^2 r$

(b) $m\omega_0^2 r$

(c) $m\left(\dfrac{\omega+\omega_0}{2}\right)^2 a$

(d) zero

13. For a particle in a non-uniform acceleration circular motion

(a) velocity is radial and acceleration is transverse only

(b) velocity is transverse and acceleration is radial only

(c) velocity is radial and acceleration has both radial and transverse components

(d) velocity is transverse and acceleration has both radial and transverse components

14. A particle moves in a circular path with decreasing speed. Choose the correct statement?

(a) angular momentum remains constant

(b) acceleration ($\vec{a}$) is towards the centre

(c) particle moves in a spiral path with decreasing radius

(d) the direction of angular momentum remains constant

15. A car is travelling with linear velocity v on a circular road of radius R. If its speed is decreasing at the rate a m/s^2, then the net acceleration will be

(a) $\dfrac{v^2}{R}+a$

(b) $\dfrac{v^2}{R}-a$

(c) $\sqrt{\left(\dfrac{v^2}{R}\right)^2+a^2}$

(d) $\sqrt{\left(\dfrac{v^2}{R}\right)^2-a^2}$

16. A particle of mass m is moving in a horizontal circle of radius R with uniform speed v. When it moves from one point to a diametrically opposite point, its:

(a) momentum does not change

(b) momentum changes by $2\,mv$

(c) kinetic energy changes by $\dfrac{1}{2}mv^2$

(d) kinetic energy changes by mv^2

17. A wheel is subjected to uniform angular acceleration about its axis. Initially its angular velocity is zero. In the first 2s, it rotates through an angle θ_1. In the next 2s, it rotates through an additional angle θ_2. The ratio of $\dfrac{\theta_2}{\theta_1}$ is :

(a) 1

(b) 2

(c) 3

(d) 5

18. An object moves at a constant speed along a circular path in a horizontal xy plane, with the centre at the origin. When the object is at $x=-2$m, its velocity is $-(4\text{m/s})\hat{\mathbf{j}}$. What is the object's acceleration when it is $y=2$m

(a) $-\left(8\text{m/s}^2\right)\hat{\mathbf{j}}$

(b) $-\left(8\text{m/s}^2\right)\hat{\mathbf{i}}$

(c) $-\left(4\text{m/s}^2\right)\hat{\mathbf{j}}$

(d) $\left(4\text{m/s}^2\right)\hat{\mathbf{i}}$

19. A rod of length 1 m rotates about the z-axis passing through the point O in the xy- plane with an angular velocity of $\omega = 10\,(\text{rad}/\text{s})+5\,(\text{rad}/\text{s}^2)t$, in the counter clockwise direction, and O is at rest the velocity and acceleration of point A, at $t=0$, are :

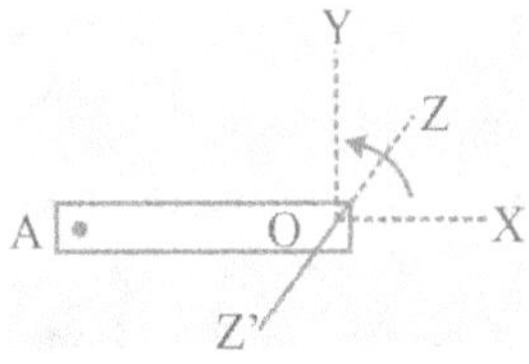

(a) $-10\,\hat{\mathbf{j}}$ m/s and $(5\,\hat{\mathbf{j}}-100\,\hat{\mathbf{i}})$ m/s^2

(b) $10\,\hat{\mathbf{j}}$ m/s and $(5\,\hat{\mathbf{j}}-100\,\hat{\mathbf{i}})$ m/s^2

(c) $-10\,\hat{\mathbf{k}}$ m/s and $(5\,\hat{\mathbf{k}}-100\,\hat{\mathbf{j}})$ m/s^2

(d) $-10\,\hat{\mathbf{j}}$ m/s and $(-5\,\hat{\mathbf{j}}+100\,\hat{\mathbf{i}})$ m/s^2

20. A mass is supported on a frictionless horizontal surface. It is attached to a string and rotates about a fixed centre at an angular velocity ω_0. If the length of the string and angular velocity are double, the tension in the string which was initially T_0 is now

(a) T_0

(b) $\dfrac{T_0}{2}$

(c) $4\,T_0$

(d) $8\,T_0$

Answer	10	(a)	11	(a)	12	(b)	13	(d)	14	(d)	15	(c)
Key	16	(b)	17	(c)	18	(a)	19	(d)	20	(d)		

21. A stone of mass of 16 kg is attached to a string 144 m long and is whirled in a horizontal circle. The maximum tension the string can with stands is 16 newton. The maximum velocity of revolution that can be given to the stone without breaking it, will be

    (a) 200 m/s   (b) 16 m/s
    (c) 14 m/s   (d) 12 m/s

22. If a cyclist moving with a speed of 4.9 m/s on a level road take a sharp circular turn of radius 4 m, then coefficient of friction between the cycle tyres and road is

    (a) 0.41   (b) 0.51
    (c) 0.61   (d) 0.71

23. A vehicle is moving with a velocity v on a curved road of width b and radius of curvature R. For counteracting the centrifugal force on the vehicle, the difference in elevation required in between the outer and inner edge of the road is

    (a) $\dfrac{v^2 b}{Rg}$ (b) $\dfrac{vb}{Rg}$

    (c) $\dfrac{vb^2}{Rg}$ (d) $\dfrac{vb}{R^2 g}$

24. One end of a string of length l is connected to a particle of mass m and the other to a small peg on a smooth horizontal table. If the particle moves in a circle with speed v, the net force on the particle (directed towards the centre) is

    (a) T (b) $T - \dfrac{mv^2}{l}$

    (c) $T + \dfrac{mv^2}{l}$ (d) zero

25. A particle describes a horizontal circle in a conical funnel whose inner surface is smooth with speed of 0.5 m/s. What is the height of the plane of circle from vertex of the funnel

    (a) 0.25 cm   (b) 2 cm
    (c) 4 cm   (d) 2.5 cm

26. A motor cyclist moving with a velocity of 72 km/h on a flat road takes a turn on the road at a point where the radius of curvature of the road is 20 m. The acceleration due to gravity is 10 m/sec^2. In order to avoid skidding, he must not bend with respect to the vertical plane by an angle greater than

    (a) $\theta = \tan^{-1} 6$ (b) $\theta = \tan^{-1} 2$
    (c) $\theta = \tan^{-1} 25.92$ (d) $\theta = \tan^{-1} 4$

27. A cyclist riding the bicycle at a speed of $14\sqrt{3}\ \text{ms}^{-1}$ takes a turn around a circular road of radius $20\sqrt{3}$ m without skidding. Given $g = 9.8\ \text{ms}^{-2}$, what is his inclination to the vertical?

    (a) 30°   (b) 90°
    (c) 45°   (d) 60°

Motion in Vertical Circle

28. A particle is fixed to one end of a massless rod of length l and rotated in a vertical circle about its other end. The minimum speed of the particle at its highest point must be

    (a) $\sqrt{gl}$ (b) $\sqrt{1.5gl}$
    (c) $\sqrt{2gl}$ (d) zero

29. A sphere is suspended by thread of length l. What minimum horizontal velocity has to be imparted to the ball for it to reach the height of suspension?

    (a) $\sqrt{(gl)}$ (b) $\sqrt{(2gl)}$
    (c) $2\,gl$ (d) gl

30. A simple pendulum of length l is oscillating with amplitude θ. At some instant it makes angle θ with the vertical, its speed of the bob is v. The acceleration of bob will be

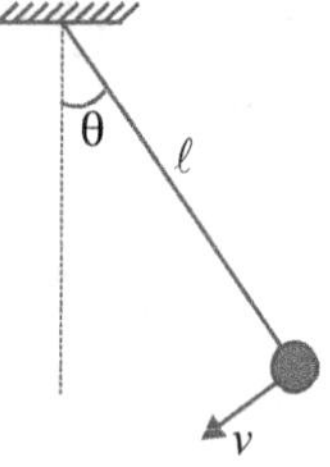

    (a) $g \sin \theta$ (b) $g \tan \theta$

    (c) $\sqrt{(g\sin\theta)^2 + \left(\dfrac{v^2}{l}\right)^2}$ (d) $\dfrac{v^2}{l}$

31. The string of a pendulum of length l is displaced through 90° from the vertical and released Then the minimum strength of the string in order to withstand the tension as the pendulum passes through the mean position is:

    (a) mg (b) $3\,mg$
    (c) $5\,mg$ (d) $6\,mg$

32. A simple pendulum is oscillating without damping. When the displacement of the bob is less than maximum its acceleration vector a is correctly shown in

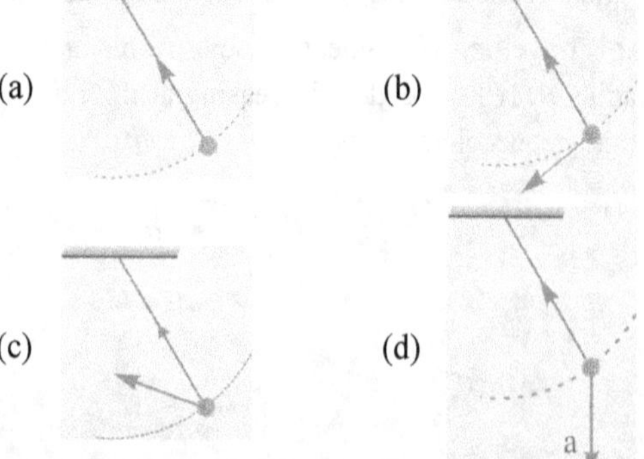

    (a)   (b)

    (c)   (d)

Answer	21	(d)	22	(c)	23	(a)	24	(a)	25	(d)	26	(b)
Key	27	(d)	28	(d)	29	(b)	30	(c)	31	(b)	32	(c)

33. A particle is moving in a vertical circle. The tensions in the string when passing through two positions at angles $30°$ and $60°$ from vertical (lowest position) are T_1 and T_2 respectively.

(a) $T_1 = T_2$

(b) $T_2 > T_1$

(c) $T_1 > T_2$

(d) tension in the string always remains the same

34. A car is moving on a curved road with constant speed. If N_1 and N_2 are the reactions at A and B then:

(a) $N_1 < N_2$

(b) $N_1 > N_2$

(c) $N_1 = N_2$

(d) none

35. A can filled with water is revolved in a vertical circle of radius 4 m and the water just does not fall down. The time period of revolution will be

(a) 1 s (b) 10 s

(c) 8 s (d) 4 s

36. A 2 kg stone at the end of a string 1 m long is whirled in a vertical circle at a constant speed. The speed of the stone is 4 m/s. The tension in the string will be 52 N, when the stone is

(a) at the top of the circle

(b) at the bottom of the circle

(c) halfway down

(d) none of the above

Answer Key	33	(c)	34	(a)	35	(d)	36	(b)

Motion in Horizontal Circle

1. A particle is moving along a circular path in the xy plane (see figure). When it crosses the x-axis, it has an acceleration along the path of 1.5 m/s^2, and is moving with a speed of 10 m/s in the negative y-direction. The total acceleration of the particle is :

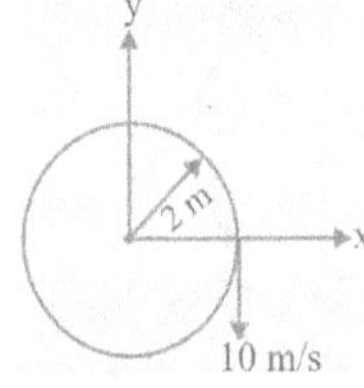

(a) $50\,\hat{i} - 1.5\,\hat{j}$ m/s^2

(b) $-50\,\hat{i} - 1.5\,\hat{j}$ m/s^2

(c) $10\,\hat{i} - 1.5\,\hat{j}$ m/s^2

(d) $1.5\,\hat{i} - 50\,\hat{j}$ m/s^2

2. A tube of length L is filled completely with an incompressible liquid of mass M and closed at both the ends. The tube is then rotated in a horizontal plane about one of its ends with a uniform angular velocity ω. The force exerted by the liquid at the other end is :

(a) $\dfrac{ML\omega^2}{2}$

(b) $ML\omega^2$

(c) $\dfrac{ML\omega^2}{4}$

(d) $\dfrac{ML^2\omega^2}{2}$

3. Keeping the banking angle same to increase the maximum speed with which a vehicle can travel on a curved road, by 10% the radius of curvature of the road has to be changed from 20 m to

(a) 16 m (b) 18 m

(c) 24.25 m (d) 30.5 m

4. A ball is held at rest in position A in figure by two light cords. The horizontal cord is cut and the ball starts swinging as a pendulum. The ratio of the tension in the supporting cord in position B, to that in position A is

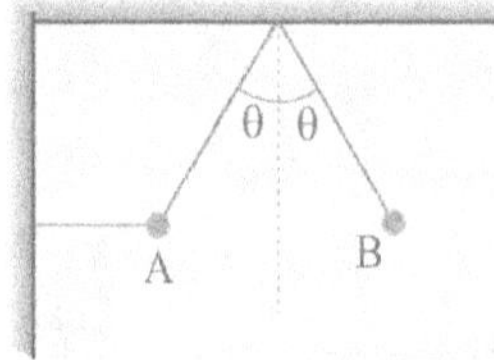

(a) $\sin^2\theta$

(b) $\cos^2\theta$

(c) $\tan^2\theta$

(d) $1 : 1$

5. When the angular velocity of a uniformly rotating body is increased thrice, the resultant force applied to it increases by 60 N. If mass of body = 3 kg, the initial and final accelerations are

(a) 2.5 m/s^2, 7.5 m/s^2

(b) 7.5 m/s^2, 22.5 m/s^2

(c) 5 m/s^2, 45 m/s^2

(d) 2.5 m/s^2, 22.5 m/s^2

6. Two identical particles are attached at the ends of a light string which passes through a hole at the centre of a table. One of the particles is made to move in a circle on the table with angular velocity ω_1 and the other is made to move in a horizontal circle as a contact pendulum with angular velocity ω_2. If ℓ_1 and ℓ_2 are the length of the string over and under the table, then in order that particle under the table neither moves down nor moves up the ratio $\dfrac{\ell_1}{\ell_2}$ is:

(a) $\dfrac{\omega_1}{\omega_2}$

(b) $\dfrac{\omega_2}{\omega_1}$

(c) $\dfrac{\omega_1^2}{\omega_2^2}$

(d) $\dfrac{\omega_2^2}{\omega_1^2}$

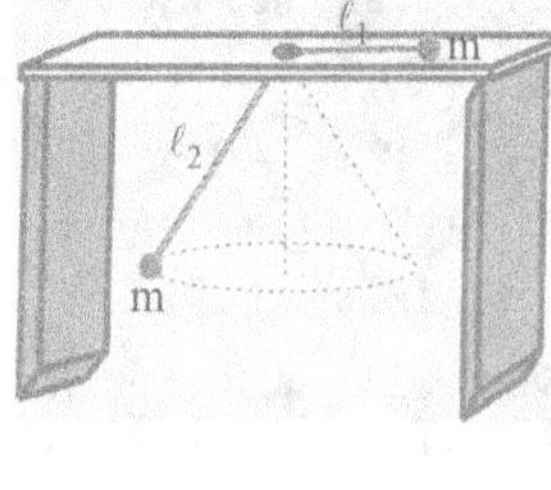

7. A car is moving in a circular horizontal track of radius 10 m with a constant speed of 10 m/s. A plumb bob is suspended from the roof of the car by a light rigid rod of length 1 m. The angle made by the rod with track is

(a) zero
(b) 30°

(c) 45°
(d) 60°

Motion in Vertical Circle

8. Figure shows a small mass connected to a string, which is attached to a vertical post. If the ball is released when the string is horizontal as shown, the magnitude of the total acceleration of the mass as a function of the angle q is:

[KVPY–2011]

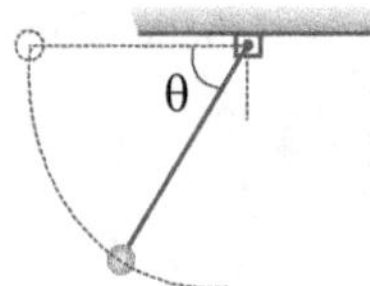

(a) $g \sin \theta$
(b) $g \cos \theta$

(c) $g\sqrt{3\cos^2\theta + 1}$
(d) $g\sqrt{3\sin^2\theta + 1}$

9. A particle moves in a circle with a uniform speed when it goes from a point A to a diametrically opposite point B, the momentum of particle changes by $\vec{F_A} - \vec{F_B} = (8\text{N})\,\hat{j}$, where $\hat{i}$ and $\hat{j}$ are unit vectors. Then the angular velocity of the particle is :

(a) 2 rad/s
(b) 4 rad/s

(c) $\dfrac{4}{\pi}$
(d) 4π rad/s

10. A block follow the path as shown in the figure from height h. If radius of circular path is r, then relation that holds good to complete full circle is:

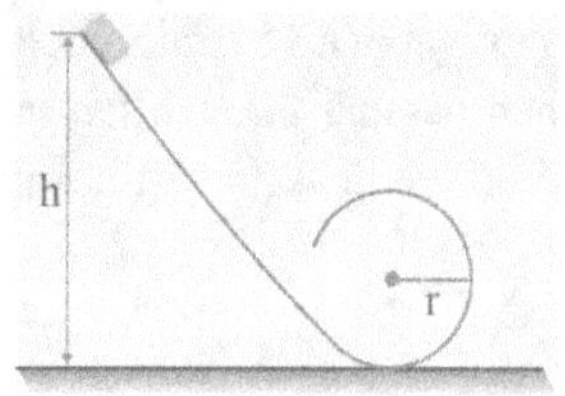

(a) $h < \dfrac{5r}{2}$
(b) $h > \dfrac{5r}{2}$

(c) $h = \dfrac{5r}{2}$
(d) $h \geq \dfrac{5r}{2}$

11. In the system shown, the mass $m = 2$ kg oscillates in a circular are of amplitude 60°. The minimum value of coefficient of friction between mass 8 kg and surface of table to avoid shipping is :

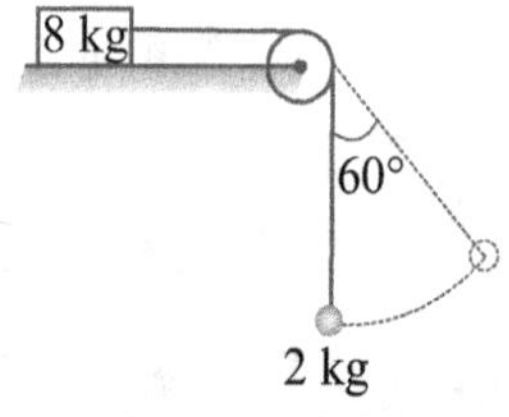

(a) 0.25
(b) 0.50
(c) 0.40
(d) 0.60

12. A body is tied up by a string of length ℓ and rotated in vertical circle at minimum speed. When it reaches at highest point, string breaks and body moves on a parabolic path in presence of gravity according to figure, in the plane of point A. The value of horizontal range AC is :

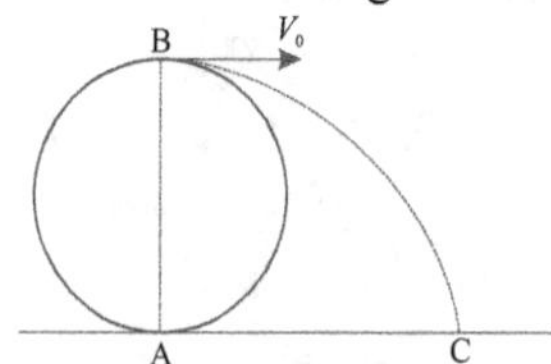

(a) $AC = \ell$
(b) $AC = 2\ell$

(c) $AC = \sqrt{2}\,\ell$
(d) $AC = 2\sqrt{2}\,\ell$

13. A thin but rigid semicircular wire frame of radius r is hinged at O and can rotate in its own vertical plane. A smooth peg P starts from O and moves horizontally with constant speed v_0, lifting the frame upward as shown in figure.

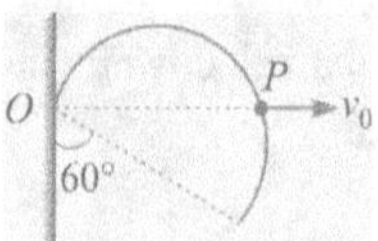

Find the angular velocity ω of the frame when its diameter makes an angle of 60° with the vertical :

(a) v_0 / r
(b) $v_0 / 2r$

(c) $2 v_0 / r$
(d) none

Answer	1	(b)	2	(a)	3	(c)	4	(b)	5	(d)	6	(d)	7	(c)
Key	8	(d)	9	(b)	10	(d)	11	(b)	12	(b)	13	(a)		

| Mechanics | **MCQ Type 2** | Exercise 6.2 |

MULTIPLE OPTIONS CORRECT

1. A ball tied to a string is swung in a vertical circle. The physical quantities those are not remain constant:
   (a) speed of ball
   (b) centripetal force
   (c) tension in string
   (d) earth's pull on ball

2. A body is moving with a constant speed v in circle of radius r.
   (a) its tangential acceleration is zero
   (b) its normal acceleration is zero
   (c) its normal acceleration is $\dfrac{v^2}{r}$
   (d) its total acceleration is $\dfrac{v^2}{r}$

3. Speed of a particle moving in a circle varies with time as, $v = 2t$. Then
   (a) angle between velocity vector and acceleration vector is increasing with time.
   (b) a_t is constant while a_r is increasing with time
   (c) a_t is decreasing but a_r is increasing
   (d) both (a) and (b) are wrong
   As a_r is increasing. Therefore θ will increase.

4. A car of mass m is moving on a horizontal circular path of radius r. At an instant its speed is v and is increasing at a rate a
   (a) the acceleration of the car is towards the centre of the path
   (b) the magnitude of the frictional force on the car is greater than $\dfrac{mv^2}{r}$
   (c) the friction coefficient between the ground and the car is not less than a/g
   (d) the friction coefficient between the ground and the car is $\mu = \tan^{-1}\left(\dfrac{v^2}{rg}\right)$

5. Particle A moves with 4 m/s along positive y-axis and particle B in a circle $x^2 + y^2 = 4$ (anticlockwise) with constant angular velocity $\omega = 2$ rad/s. At time $t = 0$ particle is at (2m, 0). Then
   (a) magnitude of relative velocity between them at time t is $(8 \sin t)$
   (b) magnitude of relative velocity between them is maximum at $t = \dfrac{\pi}{4}s$
   (c) magnitude of relative velocity between them is maximum at $t = \dfrac{\pi}{2}s$
   (d) magnitude of relative velocity between them at time t is $(8 \sin 2t)$

6. A body of mass 1 kg is attached to an inextensible string of length 1 m, is made to rotate in vertical circle about the free end. When body is at its highest position, the tension in the string is 10 N. Then
   (a) the tension in the string remains same for any position of the body
   (b) its velocity at highest position is $\sqrt{20}$ m/s
   (c) its velocity at its lowest position is $\sqrt{50}$ m/s
   (d) tension in the string at the lowest position of the body is 70 N

7. A simple pendulum of length L and mass (bob) m is oscillating in a vertical plane about a vertical line between angular limits $-\phi$ and $+\phi$. For displacement $\theta\{[\theta] < \phi\}$, the tension in the string and velocity of bob are T and v respectively. The following relations hold good under the above condition
   (a) $T \cos \theta = mg$
   (b) $T - mg \cos\theta = \dfrac{mv^2}{L}$
   (c) tangential acceleration $= g \sin \theta$
   (d) $T = mg \cos\theta$

8. A simple pendulum is vibrating with an angular amplitude of 90° as shown in figure, then

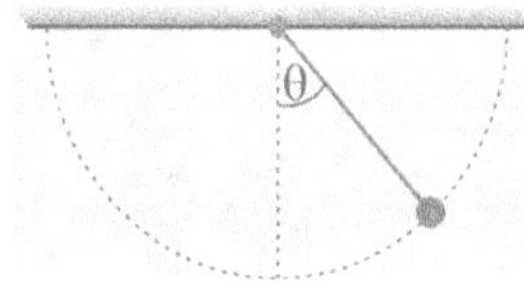

   (a) $\theta = 0$, acceleration directed downward
   (b) $\theta = 0$, acceleration directed upward
   (c) $\theta = 90°$ acceleration directed downward
   (d) $\theta = \cos^{-1}\left(\dfrac{1}{\sqrt{3}}\right)$, acceleration directed horizontal

9. A small sphere of mass m suspended by a thread is first taken aside so that the thread forms the right angle with the vertical and then released, then
   (a) total acceleration of sphere as a function of ε is $g\sqrt{1+3\cos^2\theta}$
   (b) thread tension as a function of e is $T = 3mg \cos \theta$
   (c) the angle θ between the thread and the vertical at the moment when the total acceleration vector of the sphere is directed horizontally is $\cos^{-1}1/\sqrt{3}$
   (d) the thread tension at the moment when the vertical component of the sphere's velocity is maximum will be mg

| Answer | 1 | (a, b, c) | 2 | (a, c, d) | 3 | (a, b) | 4 | (b, c) | 5 | (a, c) |
| Key | 6 | (b, d) | 7 | (b, c) | 8 | (b, c, d) | 9 | (a, b, c) |

10. A horizontal cylinder is fixed, its inner surface is smooth and its radius is R. A small block is initially at the lowest point. The minimum velocity that should be given to the block at the lowest point, so that it can cross the point P is u, then;

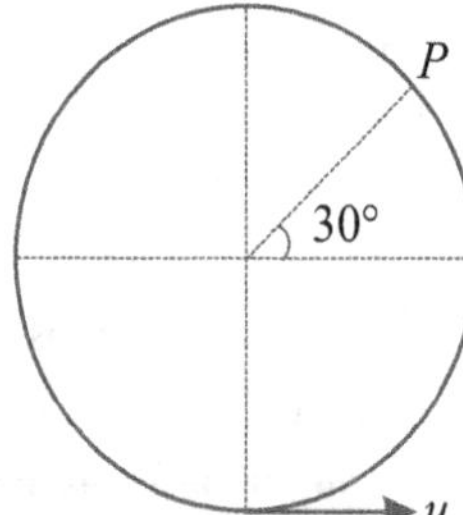

(a) if the block moves anti-clockwise, then $u = \sqrt{3.5gR}$

(b) if the block moves anti-clockwise, then $u = \sqrt{3gR}$

(c) if the block moves clockwise, then $u = \sqrt{3.5gR}$

(d) if the block moves clockwise, $u = \sqrt{5gR}$

11. A particle of mass m is moving in horizontal circle inside a smooth inverted fixed vertical cone above height h from apex. Angle of cone is θ then :

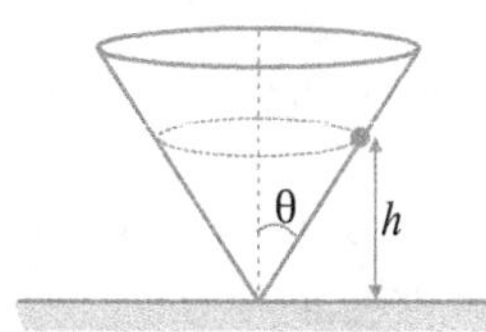

(a) Normal force on particle by surface of cone is $mg \cos \theta$

(b) Normal force on particle by surface of cone is $mg \operatorname{cosec} \theta$

(c) Time period of revolution of particle increase if θ increase keeping h constant.

(d) Time period of revolution increase if h increase keeping θ fixed

12. The coordinates of a particle moving in a plane are given by $x(t) = a \cos(pt)$ and $y(t) = b \sin(pt)$ where a, $b (< a)$ and p are positive constants of appropriate dimensions. Then

(a) the path of the particle is an ellipse

(b) the velocity and acceleration of the particle are normal to each other at $t = \pi / (2p)$

(c) the acceleration of the particle is always directed towards a focus

(d) the distance travelled by the particle in time interval $t = 0$ to $t = \pi / (2p)$ is a

13. A small ball is connected to a block by a light string of length ℓ. Both are initially on the ground. There is sufficient friction on the ground to prevent the block from slipping. The ball is projected vertically up with a velocity is, where $2g\ell < u^2 < 3g\ell$. The centre of mass of the block + ball system is C.

(a) C will move along a circle

(b) C will move along a parabola

(c) C will move along a straight line

(d) The horizontal component of the velocity of the ball will first increase and then decrease.

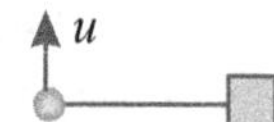

Answer Key							
10	(b, d)	11	(b, c, d)	12	(a, b)	13	(a, d)

Mechanics   **Reasoning Type Questions**   Exercise 1.3

Read the two statements carefully to mark the correct option out of the options given below:

(a) **Statement - 1** is true, **Statement - 2** is true; **Statement - 2** is correct explanation for **Statement - 1**.

(b) **Statement -1** is true, **Statement - 2** is true; **Statement - 2** is not correct explanation for **Statement - 1**.

(c) **Statement - 1** is true, **Statement - 2** is false.

(d) **Statement - 1** is false, **Statement - 2** is true

1. **Statement - 1**

Force required to move a body uniformly along straight line is zero.

Statement - 2

The force required to move a body uniformly along a circle is zero.

2. **Statement - 1**

A cyclist always bends inwards while negotiating a curve.

Statement - 2

By bending, cyclist lowers his center of gravity.

3. **Statement - 1**

Cream gets separated out of milk when it is churned, it is due to centrifugal force only.

Statement - 2

Centrifugal and gravitational forces play significant role to separate cream from milk.

4. **Statement - 1**

As the frictional force increases, the safe velocity limit for taking a turn on an unbanked road also increases.

Statement - 2

Banking of roads will increase the value of limiting velocity.

5. Statement - 1

The acceleration of a particle in uniform circular motion is constant in magnitude.

Statement - 2

The particle experiences centripetal force in uniform circular motion.

6. Statement - 1

If a body moving in a circular path has constant speed, then there is no force acting on it.

Statement - 2

The direction of the velocity vector of a body moving in a circular path is changing:

Answer	1	(c)	2	(c)	3	(d)
Key	4	(b)	5	(b)	6	(d)

Mechanics — **Passage & Matrix** — **Exercise 6.4**

PASSAGES

Passage for (Questions. 1 to 3)

The bob of mass 1 kg of a pendulum of length 1 m at rest is given a sharp hit to impart a horizontal velocity 10 m/s. ($g = 10$ m/s^2)

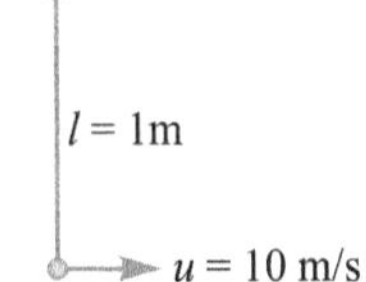

1. The tension in the string when, it is horizontal

  (a) 20 N   (b) 40 N

  (c) 60 N   (d) 80 N

2. The tension in the string, when the bob is its highest position

  (a) 20 N   (b) 30 N

  (c) 40 N   (d) 50 N

3. The tension in the string, when string makes 120° from the vertical is

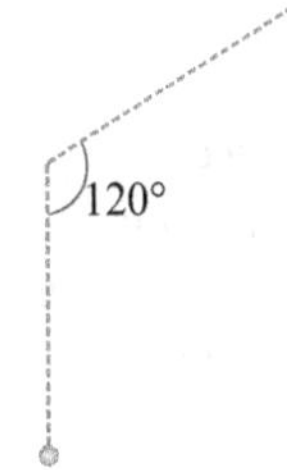

  (a) 40 N   (b) 55 N

  (c) 65 N   (d) 75 N

Passage for (Questions 4-6)

A pendulum bob can swing along a circular path on a smooth inclined plane, as shown in figure, where $m = 1.2$ kg, $l = 0.75$ m, $\theta = 37°$. At the lowest point of the circle the tension in the string is $T = 110$ N. Determine :

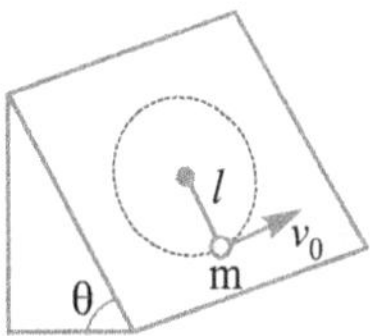

4. The speed of the bob at the lowest point is

  (a) 4.04 m/s   (b) 8.02 m/s

  (c) 10.20 m/s   (d) 12.02 m/s

5. The speed of the bob at the height point on the circle is

  (a) 6.83 m/s   (b) 10.20 m/s

  (c) 12.02 m/s   (d) zero

6. The tension in the string when bob is at the highest point is

  (a) 40.80 N   (b) 60. 50 N

  (c) 64.32 N   (d) 67.56 N

MATRIX MATCHING

7. A particle moves in a circle of radius 1m at a speed of, $v = 2t$, where v is in m/s and t in second. Then match the columns :

Column - I	**Column - II**
A. radial acceleration of the particle at $t = 1$s	(p) 1 m/s^2
B. tangential acceleration of the particle at $t = 1$ s	(q) 2 m/s^2
C. tangential acceleration of the particle at $t = 2$ s	(r) 3 m/s^2
D. total acceleration at $t = 1$ s	(s) 4 m/s^2
	(t) $2\sqrt{5}$ m/s^2

8. A small block of mass 1 kg is connected to an inextinsible string of length 1 m and made to rotate in a vertical circle about the free end of the string. The tension at the highest point of the block is 10 N. Then match the two columns; ($g = 10$ m/s^2)

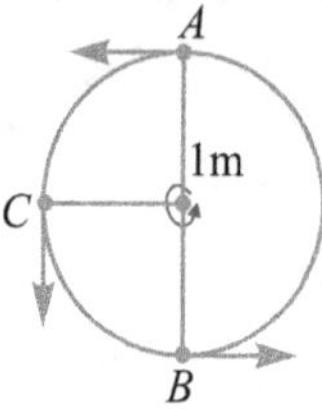

	Column - I			Column - II
A.	speed of block at A		(p)	$\sqrt{60}$ m/s
B.	speed of block at B		(q)	$\sqrt{20}$ m/s
C.	tension in string at B		(r)	40 N
D.	tension in string at C		(s)	70 N

9. A particle of 500 gm mass moves along a horizontal circle of radius 16 m such that normal acceleration of particle varies with time as $a_n = 9t^2$

	Column I			Column II
A.	Tangential force on particle at t = 1 second (in newton)		(p)	72
B.	Total force on particle at t = 1 second (in newton)		(q)	36
C.	Power delivered by total force at t = 1 sec (in watt)		(r)	7.5
D.	Average power developed by total force over first one second (in watt)		(s)	6

Answer	1	(d)	2	(d)	3	(c)	4	(b)	5	(a)	6	(d)
Key	7	A→s; B→q; C→q; D→t		8	A→q; B→p; C→s; D→r		9	A→s; B→r; C→p; D→q				

Mechanics   Best of JEE-(Main & Advanced)   Exercise 6.5

JEE- (Main)

1. A point P moves in circular-clockwise direction on a circular path as shown in the figure. The movement of P is such that it sweeps out a length $s = t^3 + 5$, where s is in metre and t is in second. The radius of the path is 20 m. The acceleration of P when $t = 2s$ is nearly   **[AIEEE -2010]**

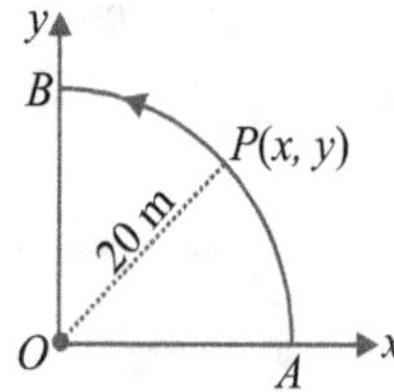

(a) 14 m/s^2 (b) 13 m/s^2

(c) 12 m/s^2 (d) 7.2 m/s^2

2. For a particle in uniform circular motion, the acceleration a at a point P (R, θ) on the circle of radius R is (here θ is measured from the x-axis)   **[AIEEE–2010]**

(a) $\dfrac{v^2}{R}\hat{i} + \dfrac{v^2}{R}\hat{j}$

(b) $-\dfrac{v^2}{R}\cos\theta\,\hat{i} + \dfrac{v^2}{R}\sin\theta\,\hat{j}$

(c) $-\dfrac{v^2}{R}\sin\theta\,\hat{i} + \dfrac{v^2}{R}\cos\theta\,\hat{j}$

(d) $-\dfrac{v^2}{R}\cos\theta\,\hat{i} - \dfrac{v^2}{R}\sin\theta\,\hat{j}$

3. A bob of mass m attached to an inextensible string of length ℓ is suspended from a vertical support. The bob rotates in a horizontal circle with an angular speed ω rad/s about the vertical. About the point of suspension: **[JEE-Main 2014]**
   (a) angular momentum is conserved.
   (b) angular momentum changes in magnitude but not in direction.
   (c) angular momentum changes in direction but not in magnitude.
   (d) angular momentum changes both in direction and magnitude.

JEE- (Advanced)

4. In insect crawls up a hemispherical surface very slowly. The coefficient of friction between the insect and the surface is $\dfrac{1}{3}$. If the line joining the centre of the hemispherical surface to the insect makes an angle α with the vertical, the maximum possible value of α is given by

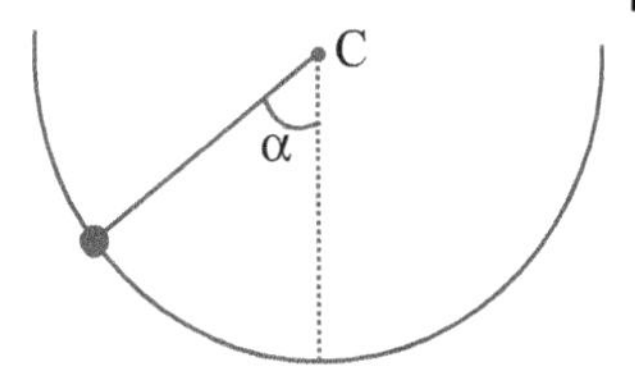

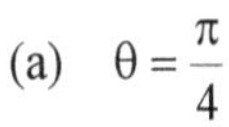

[IIT-JEE-2001]

(a) $\cot \alpha = 3$ (b) $\tan \alpha = 3$

(c) $\sec \alpha = 3$ (d) $\csc \alpha = 3$

5. A bob of mass M is suspended by a massless string of length L. The horizontal velocity v at position A is just sufficient to make it reach the point B. The angle θ at which the speed of the bob is half of that at A, satisfies   **[IIT-JEE - 2008]**

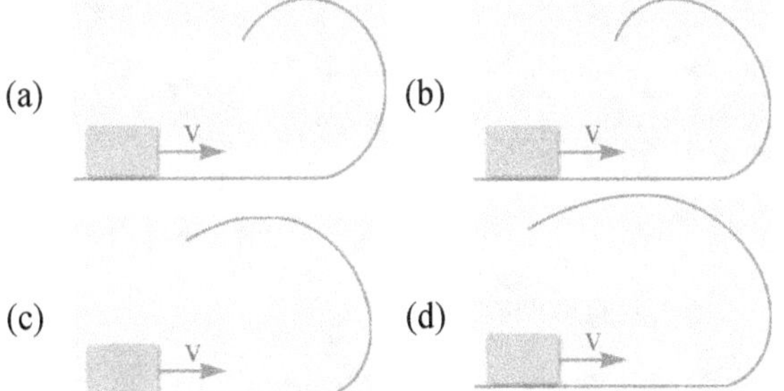

(a) $\theta = \dfrac{\pi}{4}$

(b) $\dfrac{\pi}{4} < \theta < \dfrac{\pi}{2}$

(c) $\dfrac{\pi}{2} < \theta < \dfrac{3\pi}{4}$

(d) $\dfrac{3\pi}{4} < \theta < \pi$

6. A small block is shot into each of the four tracks as shown below. Each of the track rises to the same height. The speed with which the block enters the track is the same in all cases. At the highest point of the track, the normal reaction is maximum in: **[IIT-JEE -2010]**

(a)   (b)

(c)   (d)

7. A ball of mass (m) 0.5 kg is attached to the end of a string having length (L) 0.5 m. The ball is rotated on a horizontal circular path about vertical axis. The maximum tension that the string can bear is 324 N. The maximum possible value of angular velocity of ball (in radian/s) is **[IIT-JEE 2011]**

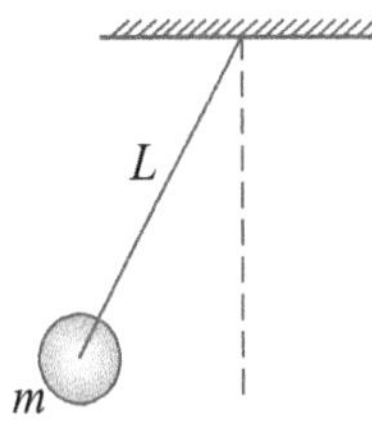

(a) 9   (b) 18

(c) 27   (d) 36

8. A wire, which passes through the hole in a small bead, is bent in the form of quarter of a circle. The wire is fixed vertically on ground as shown in the figure. The bead is released from near the top of the wire and it slides along the wire without friction. As the bead moves from A to B, the force it applies on the wire is   **[JEE Advance 2014]**

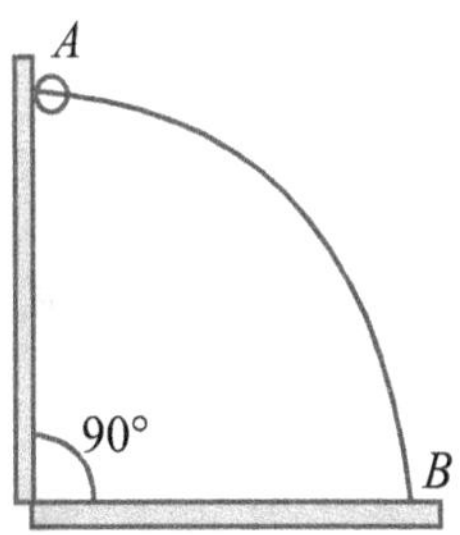

(a) always radially outwards

(b) always radially inwards

(c) radially outwards initially and radially inwards later

(d) radially inwards initially and radially outwards later

Answer	1	(a)	2	(d)	3	(c)	4	(a)
Key	5	(c)	6	(a)	7	(d)	8	(d)

Hints & Solutions

In Chapter Exercise -6.1

1. Earth revolve an angle 2π radian in 365 days.

$\therefore$ Angle revolve by earth in 2 days,

$$\theta = \frac{2\pi}{365} \times 2$$

$$= 0.0344 \ \text{rad} \qquad \textbf{Ans.}$$

2. Given $r = 50$ cm.

(i) Angular acceleration,

$$\alpha = \frac{\omega_2 - \omega_1}{\Delta t}$$

$$= \frac{2\pi(n_2 - n_1)}{\Delta t} = \frac{2\pi(400 - 100)}{5}$$

$$= \frac{\pi}{30} \ \text{rad}/s^2$$

(ii) Linear acceleration,

$$a = \alpha r$$

$$= \frac{\pi}{30} \times 50 = \frac{5\pi}{3} \ \text{cm}/s^2$$

3. Normal acceleration of the particle

$$a_c = \omega^2 r = 2^2 \times 0.4 = 1.6 \ \text{m/s}^2$$

Tangential acceleration of the particle,

$$a_t = \alpha r = 5 \times 0.4 = 2 \ \text{m/s}^2$$

Resultant acceleration,

$$a = \sqrt{a_c^2 + a_t^2}$$

$$= \sqrt{1.6^2 + 2^2} = 2.6 \ \text{m/s}^2 \qquad \textbf{Ans.}$$

$$\tan\theta = \frac{a_c}{a_t} = \frac{1.6}{2} = 0.8; \ \theta = 38°40' \qquad \textbf{Ans.}$$

4. If ℓ_1 and ℓ_2 are the lengths of the parts OB and AO respectively, then for same tension in both the threads we can write

$$T = m\omega^2\ell_1 \qquad ...(i)$$

and $$T = M\omega^2\ell_2 \qquad ...(ii)$$

$$\therefore \qquad \frac{\ell_1}{\ell_2} = \frac{M}{m}$$

or $$\frac{\ell_1}{\ell_2} = \frac{9}{3} = 3 \qquad ...(i)$$

Also $$\ell_1 + \ell_2 = 1 \qquad ...(ii)$$

From equations, we get

$$\ell_1 = 0.75 \ \text{m and} \ \ell_2 = 0.25 \ \text{m} \qquad \textbf{Ans.}$$

5. For circular motion of the particle

$$N\sin\alpha = \frac{mv^2}{r}$$

and $$N\cos\alpha = mg$$

$$\therefore \qquad \tan\alpha = \frac{v^2}{rg}$$

or $$v = \sqrt{(r\tan\alpha)g}$$

$$= \sqrt{hg} = \sqrt{0.098 \times 9.8} = 0.98 \ \text{m/s}$$

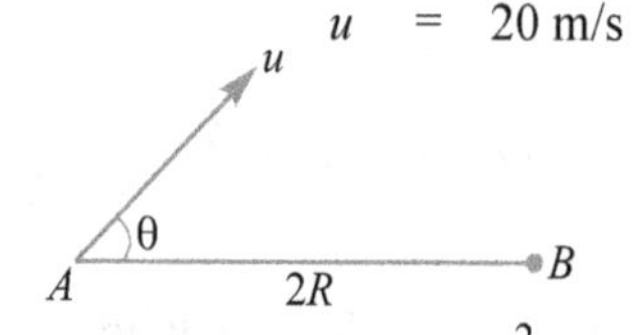

6. $$t = \pi R/v = 2u\sin\theta/g \qquad ...(i)$$

and $$(u\cos\theta)\,t = 2R \qquad ...(ii)$$

from (i) and (ii),

$$u = 20 \ \text{m/s}$$

7. Given, $$\phi = at^2.$$

Angular velocity, $$\omega = \frac{d\phi}{dt} = 2at; \ \alpha = \frac{d^2\phi}{dt^2} = 2a.$$

We know that $$v = \omega r$$

or $$v = (2at)r$$

$$\therefore \qquad r = \frac{v}{2at} = \frac{0.65}{2 \times 0.2 \times 2.5} = 0.65 \ \text{m}$$

Tangential acceleration $$a_t = \alpha r$$

$$= 2ar = 2 \times 0.20 \times 0.65$$

$$= 0.26 \ \text{m/s}^2$$

Normal acceleration $$a_c = \frac{v^2}{r}$$

$$= \frac{0.65^2}{0.65} = 0.65 \ \text{m/s}^2$$

Total acceleration $$a = \sqrt{a_t^2 + a_c^2} = 0.7 \ \text{m/s}^2$$

8. The mass of the element of width dx,

$$dm = \frac{m}{L}dx$$

By Newton's second law, we can write

$$(F + dF) - F = (dm)\omega^2 x$$

or $$dF = \left(\frac{m}{L}dx\right)\omega^2 x$$

or $$\int(dF) = \frac{m\omega^2}{L}\int_0^L x\,dx$$

$$F = \frac{m\omega^2 L}{2} \qquad \textbf{Ans.}$$

9. For the tangential motion of the particles, relative speed
$$u_r = v - v = 0$$
and
$$a_r = (a_\theta - 0) = a_\theta$$
The relative separation $s = \pi R$.
From second equation of motion,

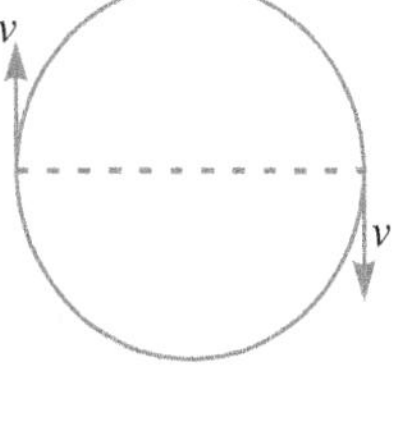

$$s = u_r t + \frac{1}{2} a_r t^2$$

$$\pi R = 0 + \frac{1}{2} a_\theta t^2$$

$$\therefore \quad t = \sqrt{\frac{2\pi R}{a_\theta}}$$

$$= \sqrt{\frac{2\pi R}{\left(\dfrac{72\ v^2}{25\ R\pi}\right)}} = \frac{5\pi R}{6v} \qquad \textbf{\textit{Ans.}}$$

10. For M to be stationary
$$T = Mg \qquad \text{...(i)}$$
For the circular motion of m, we have
$$T\sin\theta = m\omega^2 r = m\omega^2 \ell \sin\theta$$
or
$$T = m\omega^2 \ell \qquad \text{...(ii)}$$

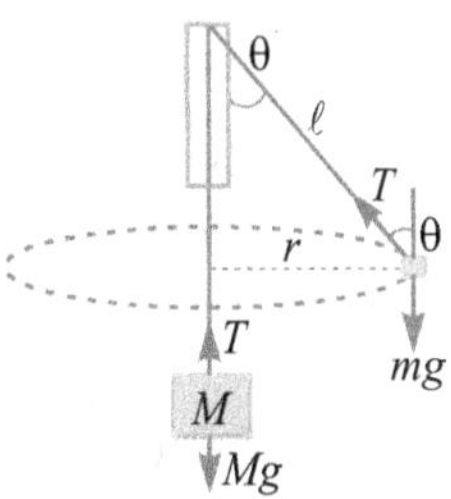

From equations (i) and (ii), we get
$$\omega = \sqrt{\frac{Mg}{m\ell}} \qquad \textbf{\textit{Ans.}}$$

11. To prevent overturning of the vehicle, we have
$$v \leq \sqrt{\frac{rga}{h}}$$

Here $\quad r = 50$ m, $a = \dfrac{1.7}{2} = 0.85$ m
and $h = 1$m.
$$\therefore \quad v = \sqrt{\frac{50 \times 9.8 \times 0.85}{1}} = 20.40 \text{ m/s}$$

In Chapter Exercise -6.2

1. For the first case, by conservation of mechanical energy, we have
$$\frac{1}{2}(2m)v_1^2 = (2m)g\ell$$
$$\therefore \quad v_1 = \sqrt{2g\ell}$$

In second case, if v_2 is the velocity given to mass at C, then velocity of mass at B will be $\dfrac{v_2}{2}$. Thus by conservation of mechanical energy, we have

$$\frac{1}{2}mv_2^2 + \frac{1}{2}m\left(\frac{v_2}{2}\right)^2 = mg\ell + mg\frac{\ell}{2}$$

$$\therefore \quad v_2 = \sqrt{\frac{12}{5}g\ell} \qquad \textbf{\textit{Ans.}}$$

2. The speed of the particle after falling vertical height h can be calculated as;
$$\frac{1}{2}mv^2 = \frac{1}{2}mv_0^2 + mgh$$
$$\therefore \quad v^2 = v_0^2 + 2gh \qquad \text{...(i)}$$
Geometrically, $\cos\theta = \dfrac{r-h}{r} \qquad \text{...(ii)}$
Now by Newton's second law, we have
$$mg\cos\theta - N = \frac{mv^2}{r} \qquad \text{...(iii)}$$

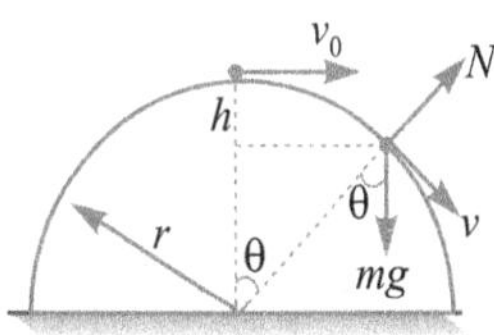

To leave the contact, $N = 0$
After solving above equations, we get
$$\cos\theta = \left[\frac{v_0^2}{3rg} + \frac{2}{3}\right] \qquad \textbf{\textit{Ans.}}$$

3. If v is the velocity of the object at A, then by conservation of mechanical energy, we have
$$\frac{1}{2}mv^2 + mg(R + R\cos\alpha) = mgH \qquad \text{...(i)}$$

The range $\qquad AB = 2R\sin\alpha$
$$= \frac{v^2 \sin 2\alpha}{g} \qquad \text{...(ii)}$$

After solving equations and substituting the given values, we get

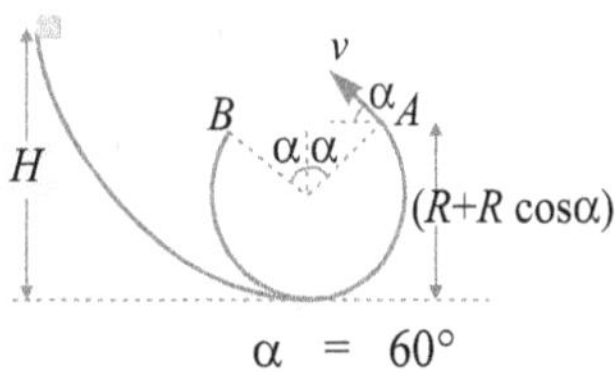

$$\alpha = 60°$$

1. (b) For a particle with constant speed, the acceleration vector tends towards centre of the path.

2. (c) $\quad \omega = \dfrac{d\theta}{dt} = \dfrac{d(2t^3 + 0.5)}{dt}$
$$= 3 \times 2t^2 = 6(2)^2 = 24\ rad/s$$

3. (a) $\quad \omega = \dfrac{\theta}{t} = \dfrac{2\pi}{60} = \dfrac{\pi}{30}$ rad/s.

4. (d) $\quad \Delta v = \sqrt{2}\,v = \sqrt{2}\,\omega r$
$$= \sqrt{2}\left(\frac{2\pi}{60}\right) \times 1 = \frac{\pi\sqrt{2}}{30}\ \text{cm/s}$$

5. (c) As its speed is constant and so its acceleration is also constant.

6. (b) From the geometry of the figure, the angle traverses about A and C are θ and 2θ respectively. So

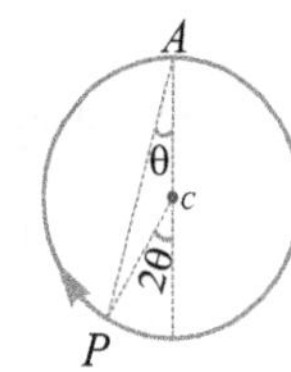

$$\omega_A = \frac{\theta}{t} \quad \text{and} \quad \omega_C = \frac{2\theta}{t} = 2\omega_A.$$

7. (c) In a frame attached to the mass, there are three forces on it, these are tension of string in the string and centrifugal force.

8. (b) $\vec{v} = \vec{\omega} \times \vec{r} = (3\hat{i} - 4\hat{j} + \hat{k}) \times (5\hat{i} - 6\hat{j} + 6\hat{k})$

$$= -18\hat{i} - 13\hat{j} + 2\hat{k}$$

9. (d) $PQ = \left| R\sin\dfrac{\omega t}{2} \right| \times 2$

$$= 2R\sin\dfrac{\omega t}{2}.$$

10. (a) As time periods are same and so

$$\frac{a_1}{a_2} = \frac{\omega^2 r_1}{\omega^2 r_2} = \frac{r_1}{r_2} = \frac{2}{4} = \frac{1}{2}.$$

11. (a) Centripetal force, $\dfrac{mv}{}$. So F_x remains as such, v is either positive or negative.

12. (b) The centrifugal force on the particle
= mass × acceleration of the frame

$$= m \times \omega_0^2 r$$

$$= m\omega_0^2 r$$

13. (d)

14. (d) For a particle moving with decreasing speed, it must have a torque along axis of rotation. Direction of momentum will not change.

15. (c) Centripetal acceleration, $a_n = \dfrac{v^2}{R}$

Total acceleration, $a = \sqrt{a_n^2 + a_t^2}$

$$= \sqrt{\left(\frac{v^2}{R}\right)^2 + a^2}$$

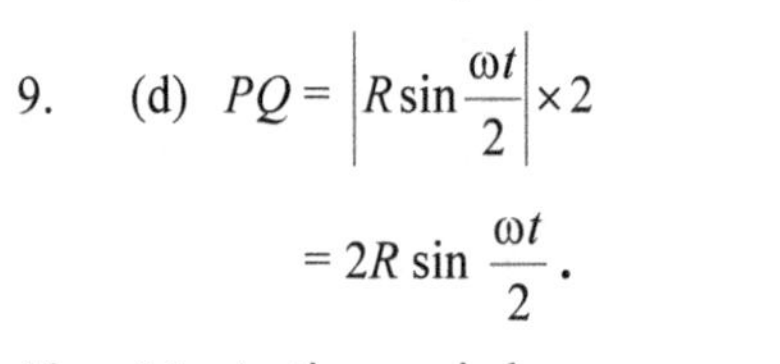

16. (b) $\Delta\vec{P} = \vec{P}_f - \vec{P}_i = -m\vec{v} - m\vec{v}$

$$\therefore \quad \Delta P = 2mv$$

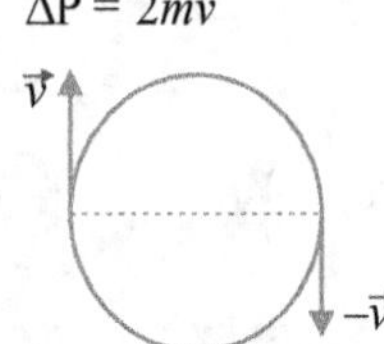

17. (c) $\theta_1 = \dfrac{1}{2}\alpha(2)^2,$

and $\theta_1 + \theta_2 = \dfrac{1}{2}\alpha(4)^2 = 4\theta_1,$

$$\therefore \quad \theta_2 = 3\theta_1$$

18. (a) $an = \dfrac{v^2}{r} = \dfrac{(4)^2}{2} = 8 \text{ m/s}^2,$

along negative z-axis.

19. (d) At $t = 0$, $\vec{\omega} = 10(-\hat{j}) = -10\hat{j}$ rad/s.

$$\alpha = \frac{d\omega}{dt} = \frac{d(10 + 5t)}{dt} = 5 \text{ rad/s}^2$$

$$\therefore a_t = \alpha r = 5 \times 1 = 5 \text{ m/s}^2$$

$$a_n = \omega^2 r = 10^2 \times 1 = 100 \text{ m/s}^2$$

$$\therefore \vec{a} = (-5\hat{j} + 100\hat{i}) \text{ m/s}^2$$

20. (d) $T_0 = m\omega^2 r,$

and $T = m(2\omega)^2 \times 2r = 8T_0.$

21. (d) $T = \dfrac{mv^2}{r}$

or $16 = \dfrac{16v^2}{144} \Rightarrow v = 12 \text{ m/s}.$

22. (c) $v = \sqrt{\mu rg},$

$$\therefore \quad \mu = \frac{v^2}{rg} = \frac{4.9^2}{4 \times 9.8} = 0.61$$

23. (a) $\tan\theta = \dfrac{h}{b} = \dfrac{v^2}{Rg},$

$$\therefore \quad h = \frac{v^2 b}{Rg}.$$

24. (a) It has the centripetal force, which is equal to the tension in the string (T).

25. (d) $N\sin\theta = \dfrac{mv^2}{r}$

and $N\cos\theta = mg$

$$\therefore \quad \tan\theta = \frac{v^2}{rg}$$

or $\dfrac{h}{r} = \dfrac{v^2}{rg}$

$$\therefore \quad h = \frac{v^2}{g} = \frac{0.5^2}{10} = 2.5 \text{ cm}$$

26. (b) $v = 72 \times \dfrac{5}{18} = 20 \text{ m/s}$

$$\tan\theta = \frac{v^2}{rg} = \frac{20^2}{20 \times 10} = 2$$

27. (d) $\tan\theta = \dfrac{v^2}{rg} = \dfrac{(14\sqrt{3})^2}{20\sqrt{3} \times 9.8} = \sqrt{3}$

or $\theta = 60°$

28. (d) As rod is a rigid body and so at the highest point, there can not be any slag in the rod even for compression in the rod. So at the point the minimum velocity can be zero.

29. (b) By conservation of mechanical energy, we can write

$$\frac{1}{2}mv^2 + 0 = mg(2\ell) + 0$$

or $v = \sqrt{2g\ell}$

30. (c) The centripetal acceleration at the instant,

$$a_n = \frac{v^2}{\ell}$$

Tangential acceleration

$$a_t - g\sin\theta$$

Total acceleration

$$a_t = \sqrt{a_n^2 + a_t^2} = \sqrt{\left(\frac{v^2}{\ell}\right)^2 + (g\sin\theta)^2}$$

31. (b)

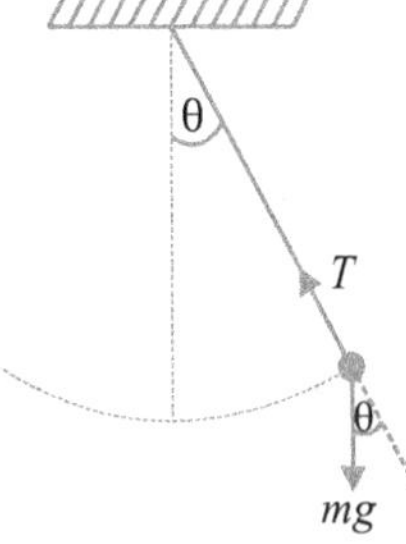

The velocity of bob at lowest position,

$$v = \sqrt{2g\ell}$$

At lowest position, $T - mg = mv^2/\ell$

or $T = mg + \dfrac{mv^2}{\ell}$

$$= mg + m \times \frac{2g\ell}{\ell} = 3\,mg$$

32. (c) At this stage, it has two accelerations, a_n and a_t, so its resultant will be like as shown in figure.

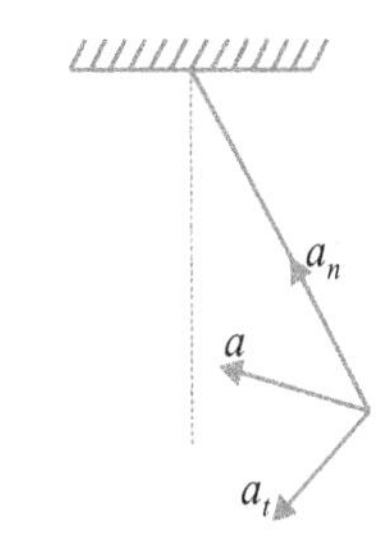

33. (c)

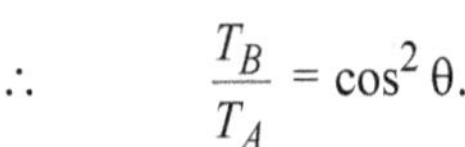

$$T = mg\cos\theta + \frac{mv^2}{R}$$

T will be greater when $\cos\theta$ is greater. $\cos\theta$ will be greater when θ is small.

34. (a)

$$mg - N = \frac{mv^2}{R}$$

or $$N = mg - \frac{mv^2}{R}$$

As $R_B > R_A$, and so $N_B > N_A$.

35. (d)

$$m\omega^2 r = mg$$

or $$\omega = \sqrt{\frac{g}{r}}$$

$$\therefore \qquad T = 2\pi\sqrt{\frac{r}{g}} = 2\pi\sqrt{\frac{4}{9.8}} = 4s$$

36. (b) At the bottom of the circle

$$T = mg + \frac{mv^2}{r}$$

$$= 2 \times 10 + \frac{2 \times 4^2}{1}$$

$$= 52 \text{ N.}$$

1. (b) $a_n = \dfrac{v^2}{r} = \dfrac{10^2}{2} = 50 \text{ m/s}^2$, along negative x-axis.

so $\vec{a} = -50\hat{i} - 1.5\hat{j} \text{ m/s}^2$

2. (a) Assume the total mass of the fluid at the centre of mass, which is at a distance of $L/2$ from the axis of rotation.

so $F = m\omega^2 r = m\omega^2 \dfrac{L}{2}.$

3. (c) $$\tan\theta = \frac{v^2}{rg} = \frac{v'^2}{r'g}$$

or $$\frac{v^2}{20g} = \frac{(1.1v)^2}{r'g}$$

$\therefore \qquad r' = 24.25 \text{ m.}$

4. (b) At position A,

$$TA\cos\theta = mg,$$

and at position B,

$$TB = mg\cos\theta$$

$$\therefore \quad \frac{T_B}{T_A} = \cos^2\theta.$$

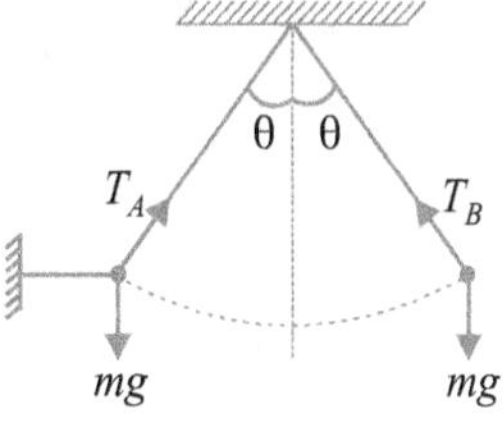

5. (d) Given, $F = m\omega^2 r$ ...(i)

and $F + 60 = m(3\omega)^2 r$

$$= 9\left(m\omega^2 r\right)$$ ...(ii)

From above equations, we get

$$F + 60 = 90\,F$$

or $\qquad F = 7.5$ N

Initial acceleration $= \omega^2 r$

$$= F/m$$

$$= \frac{7.5}{3} = 2.5 \text{ m/s}^2$$

Final acceleration $= (3\omega^2)r$

$$= 9 \times \omega^2 r$$

$$= 9 \times 2.5 = 22.5 \text{ m/s}^2$$

6.   (d)   For the particle on the table

$$T = m\omega_1^2 \ell_1$$

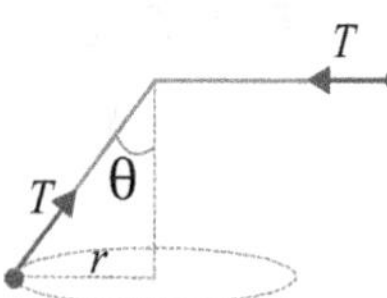

For the particle under the table

$$T \sin\theta = m\omega_2^2 r$$

$$= m\omega_2^2 \ell_2 \sin\theta$$

or $\qquad T = m\omega_2^2 \ell_2$

$\therefore \qquad m\omega_1^2 \ell_1 = m\omega_2^2 \ell_2$

or $\qquad \dfrac{\ell_1}{\ell_2} = \dfrac{\omega_2^2}{\omega_1^2}$.

7.   (c) $\tan\theta \simeq \dfrac{v^2}{rg} = \dfrac{10^2}{10 \times 10} = 1$

or

$$45°$$

8.   (d) $a_t = g \sin(90° - \theta) = g\cos\theta$

$$v = \sqrt{2gh} = \sqrt{2gl\sin\theta}$$

$\therefore \quad a_c = \dfrac{v^2}{l} = \dfrac{2gl\sin\theta}{l} = 2g\sin\theta$

$$a = \sqrt{a_c^2 + a_t^2} = g\sqrt{3\sin^2\theta + 1}\,.$$

9.   (b) $2mv = 2$ ...(i)

and $\quad 2\dfrac{mv^2}{r} = 8$ ...(ii)

From above equations, $\dfrac{v}{r} = 4$ rad/s

10.   (d)   At the bottom of the track, the speed needed

$$u = \sqrt{5gr}\,.$$

Thus $\quad mgh_{\min} = \dfrac{1}{2}mu^2$

$$= \dfrac{1}{2}m \times 5gr, \text{ or } h_{\min} = \dfrac{5r}{2}.$$

Thus to complete the circle $h \geq \dfrac{5r}{2}$,

11.   (b)   Velocity of the bob at mean position,

$$v = \sqrt{2g(\ell - \ell\cos 60°)}$$

Now $\quad T - 2g = \dfrac{mv^2}{\ell}$

and $\qquad T = \mu \times 8\,g$

After solving we get $\mu = 0.50$.

12.   (b) $2\ell = \dfrac{1}{2}gt^2$, $\therefore\ t = 2\sqrt{\dfrac{\ell}{g}}$

Now $AC = v_0 t = \sqrt{g\ell} \times 2\sqrt{\dfrac{\ell}{g}} = 2\ell.$

13.   (a) $\dfrac{x}{\sin 2\theta} = \dfrac{r}{\sin(90 - \theta)}$

$\Rightarrow \qquad x = 2r\sin\theta$

$\therefore \qquad \dfrac{dx}{dt} = 2r\cos\theta \times \dfrac{d\theta}{dt}$

$$\dfrac{d\theta}{dt} = \dfrac{dx/dt}{2r\cos\theta} = \dfrac{v_0}{2r\cos 60°} = \dfrac{v_0}{r}$$

1.   (a, b, c)

Because of gravitational force, speed of the ball continuously changes and so centripetal force and tension in the string.

2.   (a, c, d)

Body moving with constant speed,

$$a_t = 0, \text{ and } a_c = \dfrac{v^2}{r}$$

$\therefore \qquad a = \sqrt{a_c^2 + a_t^2} = \sqrt{\left(\dfrac{v^2}{r}\right)^2 + 0^2}$

$$= \dfrac{v^2}{r}.$$

3.   (a, b)

$$a_t = \dfrac{dv}{dt} = 2 = \text{constant}$$

$$a_r = \dfrac{v^2}{R}$$

As v increasing, therefore a_r is increasing.

$$\tan\theta = \dfrac{a_r}{a_t}$$

4.   (b, c) $F_t = ma$ and $F_c = \dfrac{mv^2}{r}$

$\therefore\ F = $ frictional force $= \sqrt{F_c^2 + F_t^2} > \dfrac{mv^2}{r}.$

Also $\mu = \tan\theta = \dfrac{F_t}{mg} = \dfrac{ma}{mg} = \dfrac{a}{g}$.

5. (a, c) $v_B = R\omega = 4\,\text{m/s}$

$\theta = \omega t = 2t$

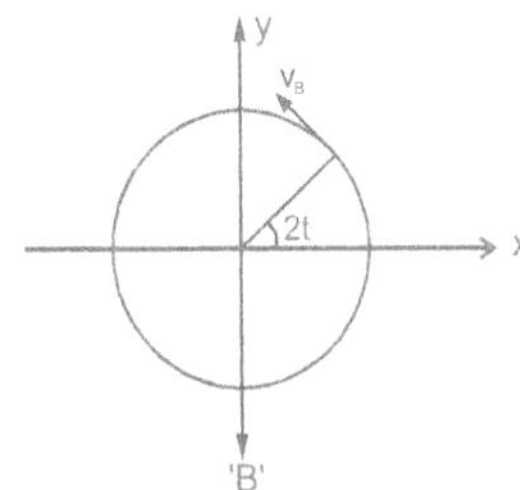

At time t : $\vec{v}_A = 4\hat{j}$

$\vec{v}_B = (-4\sin 2t\,\hat{i} + 4\cos 2t\,\hat{j})$

$\therefore \ \vec{v}_{AB} = (4\sin 2t)\hat{i} + 4(1-\cos 2t)\hat{j}$

$\therefore \ v_{AB} = 4\sqrt{1+1-2\cos 2t} = (8\sin t)$

v_{AB} is maximum at $t = \dfrac{\pi}{2}$

6. (b, d)

At the highest position, we have

$T_1 + mg = \dfrac{mv_1^2}{r}$

or $10 + 1 \times 10 = \dfrac{1 \times v_1^2}{1}$

$\therefore \qquad v_1 = \sqrt{20}\,m/s$.

At the lowest position,

$v_2^2 = v_1^2 + 2gh$

$= 20 + 2 \times 10 \times 2 = 60$

$\therefore \qquad T_2 = mg + \dfrac{mv_2^2}{r}$

$= 1 \times 10 + \dfrac{1 \times 60}{1} = 70\,\text{N}$

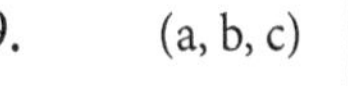

7. (b,c) For $0 < \phi, v \neq 0$

$T - mg\cos\theta = \dfrac{mv^2}{r}$

or $\qquad T = mg\cos\theta + \dfrac{mv^2}{L}$.

Also $\qquad a_t = g\sin\theta$.

8. (b, c, d) At $\theta = 90°$, $v = 0$, $\therefore\ a_n = \dfrac{v^2}{r} = 0$,

and $at = g\sin 90° = g$.

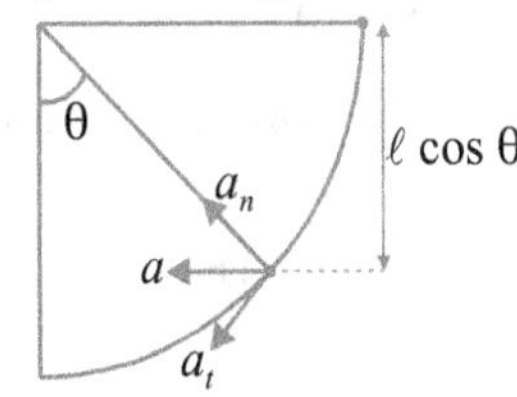

At any angular position θ, $h = \ell\cos\theta$

$\therefore \qquad v^2 = 2g\ell\cos\theta$

$a_c = \dfrac{v^2}{r} = \dfrac{2g\ell\cos\theta}{\ell} = 2g\cos\theta$

and $\qquad a_t = g\sin\theta$

Thus $\quad \tan\theta = \dfrac{a_c}{a_t}$

or $\qquad \dfrac{\sin\theta}{\cos\theta} = \dfrac{2g\cos\theta}{g\sin\theta}$

or $\qquad 2\cos^2\theta = \sin^2\theta$

$= 1 - \cos^2\theta$

$\therefore \qquad \cos\theta = \dfrac{1}{3}$.

9. (a, b, c)

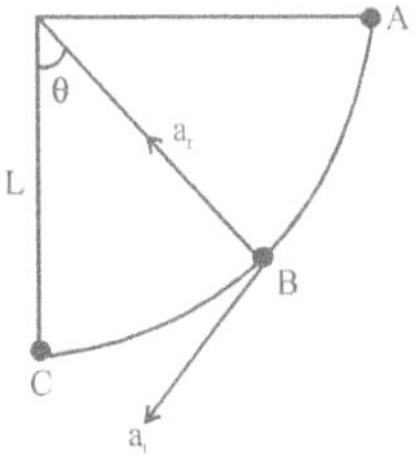

Between A and B, $\quad mgL\cos\theta = \dfrac{1}{2}mv_B^2$

$\therefore\ v_B^2 = 2gL\cos\theta$

Now, $a_r = \dfrac{v_B^2}{L} = 2g\cos\theta$

and $\quad a_t = g\sin\theta$

$\therefore\ a = \sqrt{a_t^2 + a_r^2} = g\sqrt{1 + 3\cos^2\theta}$

Now, at B : $T_B - mg\cos\theta = \dfrac{mv_B^2}{L}$

Put $v_B \Rightarrow T_B = 3mg\cos\theta$

When total acceleration vector directed horizontally

$\tan(90° - \theta) = \dfrac{a_t}{a_r} = \dfrac{g\sin\theta}{2g\cos\theta} = \dfrac{1}{2}\tan\theta$

On solving, $\quad \theta = \cos^{-1}\dfrac{1}{\sqrt{3}}$

10. (b, d) When block projected anticlockwise

$h = R + R\sin 30° = 3\,R/2$

If u is the velocity to reach the point P, then

$u = \sqrt{2gh} = \sqrt{2g \times \dfrac{3R}{2}} = \sqrt{3gR}$.

Therefore to cross point P, $u > \sqrt{3gR}$

11. (b, c, d)

12.   (a, b)

$$x = a \cos pt, \; \therefore \; \cos pt = \frac{x}{a}.$$

and $$y = b \sin pt, \; \therefore \; \sin pt = \frac{y}{b}$$

Now $$\frac{x^2}{a^2} + \frac{y^2}{b^2} = \cos^2 pt + \sin^2 pt = 1,$$

it represents an ellipse.

After calculation, we find $\vec{a}.\vec{v} = 0$.

13.   (a, d)

As the block does not move the ball moves along a circle. The centre of mass of the system lies somewhere on the string. Thus

$$\frac{1}{2}mv^2 + mg\ell \sin\theta = \frac{1}{2}mu^2$$

$$v_H = v \sin\theta$$

$$= \sin\theta \sqrt{u^2 - 2g\ell \sin\theta}$$

For max$^{\rm m}$ v_T, $\dfrac{dv_T}{d\theta} = 0$, which gives $\sin\theta = \dfrac{u^2}{3g\ell}$.

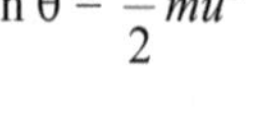
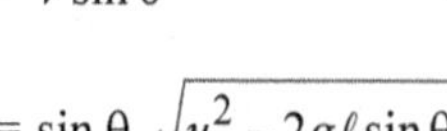

1.   (c)   Body moving along a straight line, will have zero acceleration, and so force needed, $F = 0$. But body moving along a circular path, will have centripetal acceleration, and so $F_n = \dfrac{mv^2}{r}$.

2.   (c)   By bending, he gets required centripetal force.

3.   (d)   Centrifugal and gravitational force both play the role in separating the cream.

4.   (b) $v = \sqrt{\mu rg}$, if μ increases, v also increases.

Also $\tan\theta = \dfrac{v^2}{rg}$

5.   (b)   Because of centre seeking, the direction of acceleration continuously changes.

6.   (d)   The direction of velocity vector changes and so it has centripetal acceleration.

1.   (d)

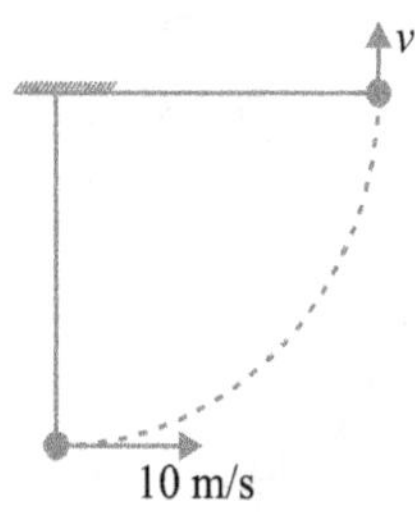

$$v^2 = 10^2 - 2g \times 1 = 80$$

Now, tension, $T = \dfrac{mv^2}{r}$

$$= \frac{1 \times 80}{1} = 80\,\text{N}.$$

2.   (d)   At the highest position

$$v^2 = 10^2 - 2g \times 2 = 60$$

$$T = \frac{mv^2}{r} - mg = \frac{1 \times 60}{1} - 1 \times 10 = 50 \text{ N}$$

3.   (c) $v^2 = 10^2 - 2g(1 + 1\sin 30°) = 70$

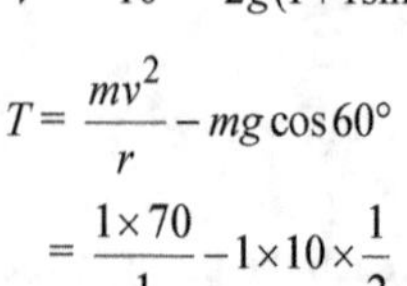
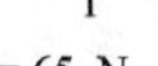

$$T = \frac{mv^2}{r} - mg\cos 60°$$

$$= \frac{1 \times 70}{1} - 1 \times 10 \times \frac{1}{2}$$

$$= 65 \text{ N}.$$

4.   (b)   If T_A is the tension in the string at lowest point, then

$$T_A - mg\sin\theta = \frac{mv_0^2}{l}$$

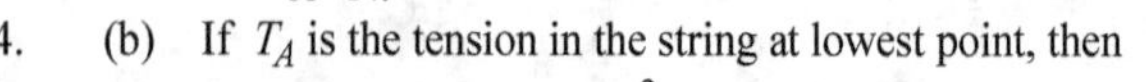

or $$v_0^2 = \frac{T_A l}{m} - gl\sin\theta$$

$$= \frac{(110)(0.75)}{(1.2)} - (9.8)(0.75)(\sin 37°)$$

$$= 64.34$$

or $$v_0 = 8.02 \text{ m/s}$$

5.   (a)   At the highest point,

$$T_B + mg\sin\theta = \frac{mv^2}{l}$$

From energy conservation between position A and position B,

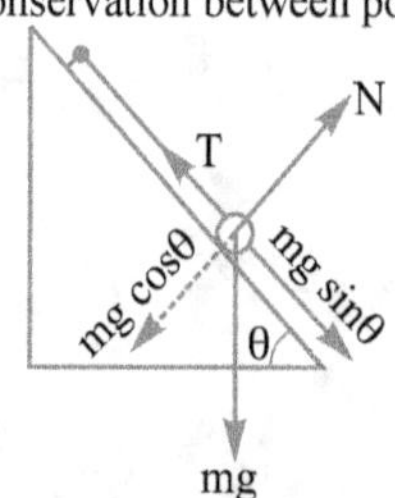

$$K_A + U_A = K_B + U_B$$

$$\frac{1}{2}mv_0^2 + 0 = \frac{1}{2}mv^2 + 2mgl\sin\theta$$

or $$v^2 = v_0^2 - 4gl\sin\theta$$

$$= (64.34) - 4 \times (9.8)(0.75)(\sin 37°)$$

$$= 46.7$$

or $$v = 6.83 \text{ m/s}$$

6. **(d)** From eqn. (2),

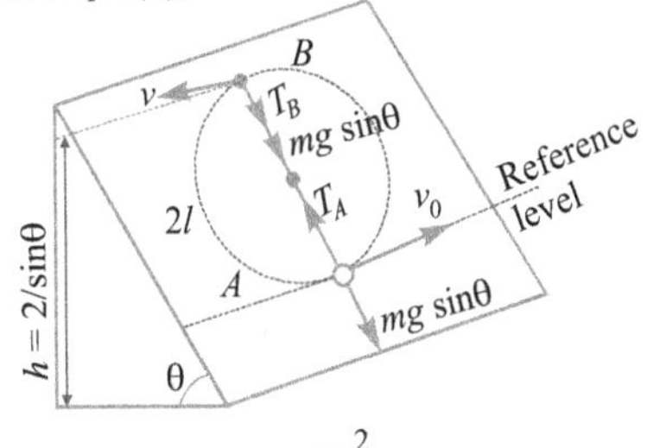

$$T_B = \frac{mv^2}{l} - mg\sin\theta$$

$$= \frac{1.2\times(6.83)^2}{0.75} - 1.2\times9.8\times\sin37°$$

$$= 67.56 \text{ N}$$

7. $A \to s ; B \to q ; C \to q ; D \to t$

At, $t = 1$s, $v = 2t = 2$ m/s.

$$\therefore \; a_n = \frac{v^2}{r} = \frac{2^2}{1} = 4 \text{ m/s}^2$$

$$a_t = \frac{dv}{dt} = \frac{d(2t)}{dt} = 2\text{m/s}^2$$

Now $a = \sqrt{a_n^2 + a_t^2} = \sqrt{4^2 + 2^2} = 2\sqrt{5}$ m/s^2

8. $A \to q ; B \to p ; C \to s ; D \to r$

At A; $\quad mg + T \quad = \dfrac{mv_A^2}{r}$

or $\quad 1\times10+10 \quad = \dfrac{1\times v_A^2}{1}$

$\therefore \quad\quad\quad v_A = \sqrt{20}$ m/s

Now $\quad v_c^2 \quad = \quad v_A^2 + 2g\times1$

$\quad\quad\quad = \quad 20 + 2\times10$

$\therefore \quad\quad v_c \quad = \quad \sqrt{40}$ m/s

$$T_c = \frac{mv_c^2}{r} = \frac{1\times40}{1} = 40 \text{ N}$$

At B;

$$v_B^2 = v_A^2 + 2g\times2$$

$$= 20 + 2\times10\times2$$

$\therefore \quad\quad v_B = \sqrt{60}$ m/s.

$$T_B = mg + \frac{mv_B^2}{r}$$

$$= 1\times10 + \frac{1\times60}{1} = 70 \text{ N}$$

9. $A \to s ; B \to r ; C \to p ; D \to q$

$$a_n = \frac{v^2}{16} = 9t^2 \Rightarrow v = 12t \quad \text{and} \quad \frac{dv}{dt} = 12$$

Tangential force $m.\dfrac{dv}{dt} = \dfrac{3}{2}\sqrt{16} = 6N$

Total force $= \sqrt{6^2 + \left(\dfrac{mv^2}{R}\right)^2} = \sqrt{6^2 + \left(\dfrac{9}{2}\right)^2} = 7.5\,N.$

Power $= F_T.v = 6 \times 3\sqrt{16} = 72$ watt.

Average power $= \dfrac{72}{2} = 36$ watt.

1. **(a)** $v = \dfrac{ds}{dt} = \dfrac{d}{dt}\left(t^3 + 5\right) = 3t^2$

At $t = 2s$, $v = 3(2)^2 = 12$ m/s

$$a_n = \frac{v^2}{R} = \frac{12^2}{20} = 7.2 \text{ m/s}^2$$

$$a_t = \frac{dv}{dt} = \frac{d\left(3t^2\right)}{dt} = 6t$$

$$= 6 \times 2 = 12 \text{ m/s}^2$$

$$\therefore \; a = \sqrt{a_n^2 + a_t^2} = \sqrt{(7.2)^2 + 12^2} = 14 \text{ m/s}^2$$

2. **(d)**

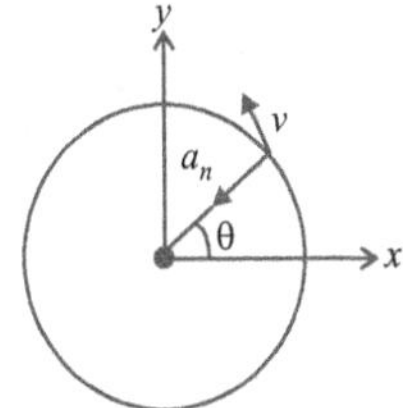

or $\vec{a}_n = -a_n\cos\theta\hat{i} - a_n\sin\theta\hat{j}$

$$= -\frac{v^2}{R}\cos\theta\hat{i} - \frac{v^2}{R}\sin\theta\hat{j}$$

3. **(c)** Torque working on the bob of mass m is, $\tau = mg \times \ell\sin\theta$. (Direction parallel to plane of rotation of particle)

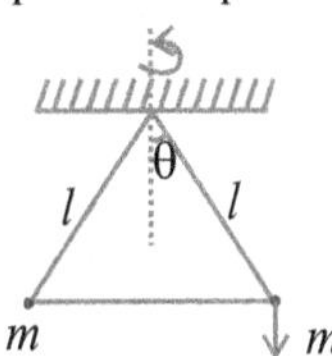

As τ is perpendicular to $\vec{L}$, direction of L changes but magnitude remains same.

4. **(a)**

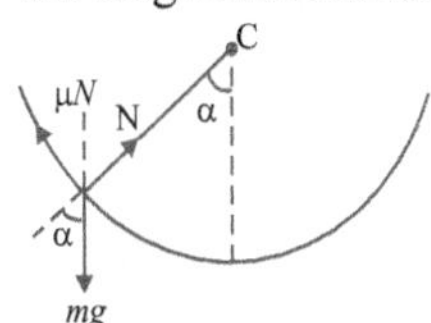

$N = mg\cos\alpha$

and $\mu N = mg\sin\alpha$

$\therefore \tan\alpha = \mu$

or $\alpha = \tan^{-1}(\mu) = \tan^{-1}\left(\dfrac{1}{3}\right) = \cot^{-1}3$

5. **(c)** If v is the required speed, then

$$0 = v^2 - 2g(2L),$$

$$\therefore \quad v = 2\sqrt{gL}\ .$$

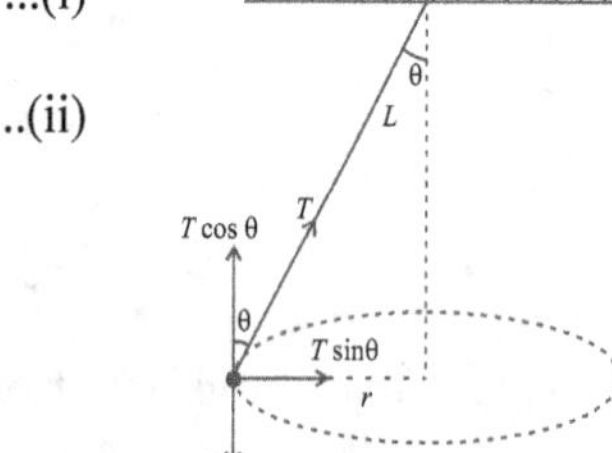

By conservation of mechanical energy, we have

$$\frac{1}{2}mv^2 = \frac{1}{2}m\left(\frac{v}{2}\right)^2 + mg(L - L\cos\theta)$$

$$\frac{1}{2}m[(2\sqrt{gL})^2] = \frac{1}{2}m(\sqrt{gL})^2 + mgL(1 - \cos\theta)$$

$$\therefore \quad \cos\theta = -\frac{1}{2} \text{ or } \theta = 120°$$

6. **(a)**
$$N + mg = \frac{mv^2}{R}$$

$$\therefore \quad N = \frac{mv^2}{R} - mg\ .$$

As R is least in (a), so N is greatest in this case.

7. **(d)** Here, the horizontal component of tension provides the necessary centripetal force.

$$\therefore\ T\sin\theta = mr\omega^2 \quad ...(i)$$

$$\text{Also } \sin\theta = \frac{r}{L} \quad ...(ii)$$

From (i) and (ii)

$$T \times \frac{r}{L} = mr\omega^2$$

$$\therefore\ \omega = \sqrt{\frac{T}{mL}} = \sqrt{\frac{324}{0.5 \times 0.5}} = \frac{18}{0.5} = 36\ \text{rad/s}$$

8. **(d)** 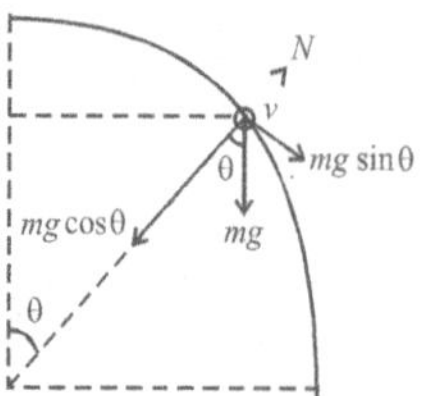

As the bead is moving in the circular path

$$\therefore\ mg\cos\theta - N = \frac{mv^2}{R}$$

$$\therefore\ N = mg\cos\theta - \frac{mv^2}{R} \quad ...(1)$$

By energy conservation, $\dfrac{1}{2}mv^2 = mg\left[R - R\cos\theta\right]$

$$\therefore\ \frac{v^2}{R} = 2g\left(1 - \cos\theta\right) \quad ..(2)$$

From (1) and (2)

$$N = mg\cos\theta - m\left[2g - 2g\cos\theta\right]$$

$$N = mg\cos\theta - 2mg + 2mg\cos\theta$$

$$N = 3mg\cos\theta - 2mg$$

$$\Rightarrow\quad N = mg\left(3\cos\theta - 2\right)$$

Clearly N is positive (acts radially outwards) when

$$\cos\theta > \frac{2}{3}$$

Similarly, N acts radially inwards if $\cos\theta < \dfrac{2}{3}$

www.ingramcontent.com/pod-product-compliance
Lightning Source LLC
Chambersburg PA
CBHW060119120726
48003CB00009B/2703